Ce

# OXFORD HISTORICAL MONOGRAPHS

*Editors*

BARBARA HARVEY       A.D. MACINTYRE

R.W. SOUTHERN       A.F. THOMPSON

H.R. TREVOR-ROPER

# CHESHIRE 1630-1660:
## COUNTY GOVERNMENT
## AND SOCIETY DURING
## THE ENGLISH REVOLUTION

BY

J.S. MORRILL

OXFORD UNIVERSITY PRESS
1974

*Oxford University Press, Ely House, London W. 1*

GLASGOW   NEW YORK   TORONTO   MELBOURNE   WELLINGTON
CAPE TOWN   IBADAN   NAIROBI   DAR ES SALAAM   LUSAKA   ADDIS ABABA
DELHI   BOMBAY   CALCUTTA   MADRAS   KARACHI   LAHORE   DACCA
KUALA LUMPUR   SINGAPORE   HONG KONG   TOKYO

ISBN 0 19 821855 9

©OXFORD UNIVERSITY PRESS 1974

TYPESETTING BY CAMPBELL GRAPHICS LTD.,
NEWCASTLE UPON TYNE
PRINTED IN GREAT BRITAIN
BY
WILLIAM CLOWES & SONS, LIMITED
LONDON, BECCLES, AND COLCHESTER

TO FRANCES

# PREFACE

I first started to think about seventeenth-century Cheshire in the spring and summer of 1964 when, with the help of my then history master, Mr. R.N. Dore, I took advantage of the months between the Oxford Scholarship examinations and my entry into university to engage in a local history project. This work was developed during my undergraduate days into a paper on 'The Allegiance of the Cheshire Gentry During the Great Civil War', which I submitted as part of my Honours School examinations and for the University's Arnold Historical Essay Prize. It proved a useful springboard for work for a doctoral dissertation submitted in 1971. This book is a revised version of that thesis. The first chapter has been completely rewritten, and I have made extensive modifications to chapters 3, 5, and 8. The remaining chapters are little changed. The aim throughout has been to improve the narrative at the expense of the narrowly analytical. Certain technical discussions of the sources, originally included to persuade examiners that I had adequately mistrusted the source material, have been omitted. Those who remain sceptical of my findings can follow up footnote directions to the relevant pages of the thesis, (see particularly chapter 3, section 5).

During the prolonged period of preparation, I contracted innumerable debts of gratitude. The following are only those whose assistance has been outstandingly important. The staffs of the Cheshire Record Office, Chester City Record Office, and John Rylands Library have all been unfailingly helpful and courteous despite my demands on their time and expertise. My old college friend, Angus Fowler, for a while archivist in the Cheshire Record Office, saved this book from some of the more crass confusions which appeared in the thesis, particularly about the Courts at Chester. I would also like to record my gratitude to fellow research students with whom I have had many profitable conversations, especially Dr. Blair Worden, now Fellow of Selwyn College, Cambridge, whose comments on my ideas opened up several important lines of thought.

My friend Peter Ruhemann arranged for the military accounts discussed in chapter 3 to be analysed by computer, saving me weeks of effort. I regret that the results were not as dramatic as I had anticipated, and that the theories which had led me to accept his offer proved untenable. Latterly he has performed with great care the arduous and unrewarding job of proof-reading the final typescript.

My development as a historian owes most to three people. Mr. R.N. Dore first introduced me to local history and unhesitatingly laid before me all the benefits of his many years' work in the field. He has also provided detailed comments on my thesis which have allowed me to correct several factual errors. Mr. J.P. Cooper's stimulating teaching was the highlight of my undergraduate days, and he has remained a constant source of illumination and encouragement since. Mr. D.H. Pennington supervised the thesis and has guided its transformation into this book. He has retained a basic enthusiasm throughout, while proving an implacable foe to woolly thought and clumsy expression. The inadequacies of this work are a measure of my failure to respond to their efforts.

But my overriding debt is to my wife. Without her patience, encouragement and assistance it would have been abandoned or torn up many times. I dedicate it to her, with love.

*Trinity College, Oxford*
July 1972

# CONTENTS

# ABBREVIATIONS

## 1. Repositories

| | |
|---|---|
| B.M. | British Museum |
| Bodl. Lib. | Bodleian Library, Oxford |
| C.R.O. | Cheshire Record Office |
| Chester City R.O. | Chester City Record Office |
| C.C.L. | Chester City Library |
| J.Ry.L. | John Rylands Library |
| P.R.O. | Public Record Office |

## 2. Calendars

| | |
|---|---|
| C.C.A.M. | *Calendar of the Committee for the Advance of Money* |
| C.C.C.D. | *Calendar of the Committee for Compounding with Delinquents* |
| C.S.P.D. | *Calendar of State Papers Domestic* |
| H.M.C. | Historical Manuscripts Commission |

## 3. Periodicals

| | |
|---|---|
| B.J.Ry.L. | *Bulletin of the John Rylands Library* |
| E.H.R. | *English Historical Review* |
| Ec.H.R. | *Economic History Review* |
| H.A.P. | *Historical Association Pamphlets* |
| J.C.A.S. | *Journal of the Chester and North Wales Archaeological Society* |
| T.H.S.L.C. | *Transactions of the Historic Society of Lancashire and Cheshire* |
| T.L.C.A.S. | *Transactions of Lancashire and Cheshire Antiquarian Society* |
| T.Salop A.S. | *Transactions of the Shropshire Archaeological Society* |

# NOTES

Throughout this book quotations are as in the original, except that I have banished the thorn and extended the standard abbreviated forms. I have also adapted some extreme punctuation to modern usage.

Dates are old style with the year regarded as beginning on 1 January.

# CHESHIRE ON THE EVE OF THE LONG PARLIAMENT

I

In 1450 the abbots, priors, clergy, barons, knights, squires, and commonalty of the County Palatine of Chester petitioned the King not to force them to pay the fifteenths and tenths voted by his Parliament at Leicester. Their defence was that 'the seide comite is and hath ben a comite palatyne als well afore the conquest of England as sithens distincte & separate from you coron of England', that no laws or taxes could be imposed without the consent of the *parliamentum* of the county meeting in Chester Castle, and that all royal justice must come through the Palatine Courts which had complete competence to hear all Crown and Common pleas. Henry VI responded by granting their wishes and categorically confirming all their liberties, freedoms, and franchises. It was the climax of the county's evolution as a distinct administrative unit within the kingdom.[1]

Between 1536 and 1543 this independence was seriously challenged, as Henry VIII set out to integrate the county into his national administrative machine. The local *parliamentum* was abolished and with it all financial exemptions; the shrievalty and sergeants of the peace were remodelled and a regular Commission of the Peace established; a new diocese was established at Chester and the right to send representatives to the House of Commons granted both to the county and the city of Chester.[2] But three centuries of separate development[3] were to leave their mark on the county

[1](Ed.) H.D. Harrod, 'A Defence of the Liberties of Chester, 1450', *Archaeologia,* 57 (1900), 75–6, 78.

[2]See J. Beck, *Tudor Cheshire,* Chester, 1969, pp.2–6.

[3]William I had created the Earldom of Chester for his nephew Hugh Lupus. It remained with his descendants until the failure of the male line in the early thirteenth century. After briefly passing through the female line to the childless Joannes Scoticus, it reverted to the Crown in 1236 and remained a distinct and personal possession of successive kings henceforth.

community, and even on county institutions, notably the Palatine Courts of Exchequer and Great Sessions.

The Exchequer was coeval with the County Palatine. It began as a court of revenue but later developed an exclusive jurisdiction in equity (and thus acted as a court of Chancery for the county). It was presided over by a Chamberlain (normally a high dignitary[1] who acted through a Vice-Chamberlain) assisted by a Baron of the Exchequer—acting like a Master in Chancery—and by a Seal Keeper.

Pleas of the Crown and at Common law within the Palatinate were heard at the Court of Great Sessions, extended in 1542 to include the North Wales circuit.[2] It became familiarly but wrongly known as the Assizes; its Chief Justice and puisne judge acted in every way like Assize Judges.

These courts were to remain in existence until 1830. Their continuation both helped to preserve the distinctiveness of the Palatine and sheltered the inhabitants from the costs and tribulations of endless lawsuits in London (and thus from contact with the outside world).[3] The only court not duplicated in the county was Star Chamber. The Cheshire gentry's determination to retain these special courts, and their fight to protect the county's independence, can be seen in their struggle at the end of the century to prevent the Council in the Marches from encroaching on the jurisdiction of the Exchequer Court.[4]

This tradition of independence was not simply based on institutional separatism. When Daniel King wrote in 1656,

---

[1] From 1559 onwards the office was usually held by the Earls of Derby, although Robert Dudley and Sir Thomas Egerton both held it for periods under Elizabeth.

[2] 34—5 Henry VIII, c. 26

[3] The Court of Great Sessions is discussed briefly below, in chapter 6; The immensely rich, untapped records of both courts from the thirteenth to the nineteenth century are in the P.R.O. (Ashridge depository). For a fuller account of these courts see *The Rights and Jurisdiction of the County Palatine of Chester...* (original, dated 1617, in C.R.O., DDX/2; partly reissued in an edition by J.C. Dewhurst, Chester, 1943). Also, J. Faulkner, *The Practice of the Court of Session for the County of Chester, Together With the Practice of the Court of the Exchequer at Chester*, Chester, 1822.

[4] C.R.O., DDX/2 *Rights and Jurisdiction...* pp.2, 13, 25—30.

'there is no county in England more famous for a long continued succession of Antient Gentry, then this of Cheshire',[1] he was simply echoing the view expressed by John Leland, William Smith, and William Webb, who had perambulated and described the county in the 1540s, 1580s, and 1620s. At least five families, each with collateral lines, could trace their county descent back to Domesday.[2] Of 106 families whose pedigrees have been studied,[3] seventy-one could trace their ancestry back within the county to the thirteenth century or earlier, and all but sixteen were fully established before the Reformation.[4]

In the 1540s John Leland drew up a list of what he termed the thirty-five 'chiefest gentlemen' in Cheshire.[5] On the eve of the Civil War, twenty-five of these families were still represented on the Commission of the Peace; of the remainder, two were prosperous Catholics and thereby excluded, five had died out, and only three had declined in status.[6] The active quorum in the years 1637—42 consisted of twenty-five families from Leland's list, three cadet lines sprung from these families, and seven rising gentlemen. But five of these were pre-Tudor Cheshire gentry families. Only the Cottons of Combermere and the Brookes of Norton were newcomers to the county, buyers of monastic land in the decades after the Reformation.[7] Cheshire would appear to

---

[1] D. King (ed.) *The Vale Royal of England,* London, 1656, which contains the latter two accounts.

[2] i.e. the Masseys, the Venables, the Mainwarings, the Davenports, the Leghs.

[3] I am grateful to Mr. R.N. Dore for these figures. They are based on genealogies in G. Ormerod, *History of Cheshire,* 3 vols. (revised edition, G. Helsby), 1882, and have been used critically in the light of other evidence.

[4] Detailed totals are, 11th century—5: 12th century—16: 13th century—50: 14th century—10: 15th century—4: 16th century—10: 17th century—11. The list contains all those families who served on the Commission of the Peace between 1603 and 1640, and many others.

[5] D. King, op. cit., p.56

[6] The Leycesters of Toft, the Pooles of Poole, and the Bulkeleys of Cheadle.

[7] Similarly a comparison of the earliest Commission of the Peace for Cheshire, issued in July 1539 (P.R.O., C66/687), with that one hundred years later, shows that almost two-thirds of the families in the former were still represented in the 1630s.

have had one of the most stable ruling élites of any county in England.[1]

The predominance and strength of this group of ancient county families is further underlined by the extent of inter-marriage. A further study of genealogies for the period 1590–1642 shows that almost two-thirds of all marriages contracted by members of Cheshire gentry families were with gentry of the same county. A further 12 per cent were between Cheshire gentry and families living in adjacent counties, particularly in south Lancashire; many of these families held lands in Cheshire (e.g. the Sneyds of Keele, Staffordshire, and the Powells of Horsley, Flintshire). Many of the remaining marriages were those involving leading recusant families who tended to have to look further for suitable partners. For example most of the Savage family marriages in this period were with other recusant families in the midlands and south. Marriages contracted by heads of families and their heirs show an even higher preponderance of local ties—over three-quarters married the daughters of Cheshire landowners.[2]

Socially and administratively, then, Cheshire presents a picture of relative self-sufficiency. As elsewhere, Cheshire men referred to the county, not to the kingdom, as their 'country', and this primary allegiance is of fundamental importance in the understanding of the early modern period. But it is not the whole of the story; there was nothing

---

[1] See the examples given by Professor Everitt for Kent, Suffolk, Leicestershire, and Northamptonshire in the four works by him cited in the bibliography. See also J.P. Ferris, 'The Gentry of Dorset on the Eve of the Civil War', *Genealogists' Magazine*, 15, No.3 (1965) and B.G. Blackwood, 'The Cavalier and Roundhead Gentry of Lancashire', *T.L.C.A.S.*, 77, (1967). In general Leicestershire and Lancashire appear to have been most like Cheshire; Dorset and Northamptonshire least like it.

[2] Based on my own calculations from a group of ninety-two genealogies, very similar to the group used by Mr. Dore. Full figures for (i) marriages between Cheshire families (ii) marriages between Cheshire families and those in neigh-bouring counties, (iii) all others, are: a) for all marriages: (i)242 (65%), (ii)44 (12%), (iii)85 (23%); b) heads and heirs only: (i)105 (75%), (ii)10 (7%), (iii)25 (18%).

All figures include remarriages by a Cheshire-born partner.

unitary in the geography of Cheshire[1] for example. The Cheshire plain extends across the Mersey into south Lancashire, while the tongue of moorland flicking up to the north-east of the county runs naturally into the Pennine regions and Derbyshire. There is no natural boundary to the south where the best dairying pastures run into Shropshire and north Staffordshire.

There were thus varied agrarian interests within the county; indeed, nine distinct regions have been identified.[2] Macclesfield hundred with its steep moorlands differed from the flat sandstone plains of the Wirral, skirted by coastal marsh and dune just as much as it did from the well-irrigated plains of the Dee, Mersey, Weaver, Dane, and Bollin. Although dairying was the predominant form of agriculture, and John Speed and Daniel Defoe would agree later in the century that Cheshire cheese was the best in the world, there was in fact much diversification, with ample arable farming to make the county self-sufficient in average or good years. What gave unity to the county's farming was not the presence of cows but the absence of sheep.[3] Although a large exporter of cheese, and 'progressive' in that almost the whole county had been peacefully enclosed by 1600,[4] there is little sign that Cheshire was conspicuously wealthy; few below the élite gentry were building elaborately in the sixteenth and early seventeenth centuries; and even they were not building the characteristic timber-framed houses until after 1600.

There was greater coherence about the pattern of settlement. The unitary nature of the ancient earldom led to the late spread of small, composite manors of a less closely settled type than in southern and eastern England. Manors were not closely integrated with townships; yet, as a recent

1 On this see (ed.) J. Thirsk, *The Agrarian History of England and Wales*, vol. IV, *1500—1640* Oxford, 1967, particularly pp.80—4; D. Sylvester, 'Rural Settlement in Cheshire', *T.H.S.L.C.*, 101 (1949); G.E. Russell, 'Four Centuries of Cheshire Farming Systems', *T.H.S.L.C.*, 106 (1954); D. Sylvester, 'The Manor and the Cheshire Landscape', *T.L.C.A.S.*, 70 (1960).

2 Sylvester, 'Rural Settlement. . .', pp.3—4
3 D. King, *The Vale Royal.* . . p.18.
4 Fussell, art. cit., pp.57—61.

map of the seats of the Tudor gentry has made clear, most Tudor manors were held singly,[1] and there was an increasing number of manors where the land had passed into the hands of a group of gentlemen-freeholders. A more striking contrast with southern England is the size of the parish; there were very few composite township-parishes in Cheshire: seventy parishes to 500 townships in the mid-seventeenth century. Budworth and Prestbury were at one time the second- and third-largest parishes in the country, comprising thirty-five and thirty-two townships respectively.[2]

The county was well served with waterways and stood on the main roads to Ireland and the north; it was on these that most of the eleven market towns stood.[3] Several were no larger than ordinary villages[4] and although several elected mayors and aldermen (Stockport, Congleton, Macclesfield, Chester), their autonomy (except for Chester)[5] was strictly limited and they were treated administratively as integral parts of the county. Thus, despite the existence of aldermen at Stockport in 1634, the Privy Council added Edward Warren to the county's Commission of the Peace after being told of the 'want of a settled Justice in the town'.[6] Only Congleton fought to establish a measure of independence, recruiting the services in the 1630s of a young lawyer, John Bradshaw, who thus made a quiet beginning to a spectacular career which was to culminate in his becoming titular head of state, 1649–51. Nantwich, the second town in the county, posed no such problems; it was dominated by the gentry, at least ten having houses in the town.

---

[1] (Eds.) D. Sylvester and G. Nulty, *A Historical Atlas of Cheshire*, Chester, 1958, p.31.

[2] D. Sylvester, 'Parish and Township in Cheshire and North East Wales', *J.C.A.S.*, 54 (1967), 27. The average number of townships in the midlands and southern England was nowhere greater than 1·75 per parish.

[3] There were also fairs at Over, Budworth, Brereton, and Hatton.

[4] e.g. Altrincham, Malpas, Sandbach, Tarvin.

[5] By an anomaly, there was also a mayor at Over who had inherited his position from the now defunct liberty of the 'city' of Edisbury within the forest of Delamere (D. King, *Vale Royal . . .*, p.248).

[6] P.R.O., SP 16, vol. 281, f. 68.

Chester, however, was a special case. Designated a county in its own right by the Charter of 1507, and with 4,500 or possibly 5,000 inhabitants on the eve of the Civil War, it was economically as well as administratively independent. A wide range of industries was carried on within its walls, though the predominant one—accounting for perhaps 25 per cent of its labour force—was the leather industry which depended for its prosperity largely on the import of skins from Ireland. Indeed, about three-quarters of all Chester's external trade was with Ireland, making the city's ties there much closer than those of the county, about twenty of whose gentry held Irish lands. Despite the silting up of the Dee, the volume of trade had not declined, but this was partly the result of the remarkably zealous defence of the city's economic privileges by the assembly, which in turn was the result of the city's success in maintaining its strict administrative independence. By the Charter of 1507, the city was governed by a large assembly of about eighty (a self-perpetuating oligarchy of aldermen, sheriffs—peers, and common councilmen) who rigorously controlled appointments to all civic offices (the Crown even failed to get its nominees accepted as Recorders). The network of city courts (Portmote and Pentice for civil jurisdiction, Crownmote and Quarter Sessions for Crown pleas) had wider powers than most borough courts in England (e.g. the Crownmote was at one time uniquely granted the power to hear treasons). Not content with this position, the city was constantly seeking to extend its independence further, as in the 1560s and 1570s when the assembly tried to reduce the jurisdiction of the Palatine Courts within the confines of the city.[1]

Despite its seeming invulnerability, the assembly did find itself during the early seventeenth century in dispute with the county over many issues; above all there was the question of Gloverstone, an enclave within the city not included in the Charter. Attempts were constantly made by the assembly to extend their jurisdiction over Gloverstone. Its existence posed several real threats; for example, unlicensed trading

[1] *Rights and Jurisdictions. . ., passim.*

there threatened the interests of city tradesmen. The levying of Ship Money brought this and several other disputes with the county to a head.[1] Since prominent gentlemen had interests in the city (e.g. Sir Thomas Aston was an importer of French wines), the county was also drawn into the bitter feuds between factions within the assembly.[2]

But, Chester apart, the administrative pattern was reasonably straightforward; the only other complicating factor was the development of the hundred as an administrative subdivision of the county, which can be most clearly seen in the less dominant role of Quarter Sessions in Cheshire than in other parts of the country. Most complaints, petitions, and presentments were sifted and then handed on to Justices in the particular locality to be investigated and dealt with. Only matters requiring a general ruling for the whole county were invariably settled at the Sessions. Long before the Book of Orders in 1630 directed that there should be monthly meetings of the Justices in each division of every county, there were semi-formalized hundredal meetings in Chesire. In fact they can be found as early as the 1590s. At these meetings, the mass of the Commission's administrative duties were performed: bridge and highway repairs were organized; the poor rate fixed for each township and parish officials nominated or confirmed; some ale-houses licensed and others suppressed. The reality of the hundred as an administrative unit is clearly seen in an order of 1616 which required all bridges to be repaired solely at the expense of the hundreds within which they stood. Similarly in matters of taxation, the proportion of each hundred was fixed by tradition, and disputes about the rate between villages or individuals within each hundred determined at monthly meetings.

[1] Many of these can be followed in B.M. Harleian MS. 2093, ff. 90–179.

[2] The above is largely based on my own work. But I am indebted to Dr. A.M. Johnson for allowing me to check my own conclusions against those in his thesis (otherwise closed to readers) 'Some Aspects of the Political, Constitutional, Social and Economic History of the City of Chester 1550–1662', Univ. of Oxford D.Phil. thesis, 1970. See also his article, 'Politics in Chester during the Civil Wars and Interregnum', in P. Clark and P. Slack (eds.), *Crisis and Order in English Towns 1500–1700*, London, 1972, pp.204–36.

Although Quarter Sessions remained the focal point in local government, the fact that Sessions were held at five different market towns within the county rather than simply in the Great Hall of Chester Castle is suggestive. Between 1608 and 1643 a fairly stable pattern developed; Epiphany Sessions were held at Chester; Easter Sessions at Knutsford; Midsummer Sessions at Nantwich; and Michaelmas Sessions either at Northwich or Middlewich. This does not mean that business from one part of the county was held over until a Sessions close by; all judicial business was dealt with immediately. Some routine business might tend to be heard at a convenient place (e.g. general rules for the house of correction were normally discussed at Nantwich), but specific problems might be settled at any Sessions. The average attendance by Justices at a Quarter Sessions in the early seventeenth century was eight out of an effective Bench of about forty,[1] but attendance was consistently higher at Chester and Nantwich than at the other Sessions towns. Some Justices only appeared at the Sessions nearest their homes (e.g. Sir Richard Wilbraham attended most Sessions at Chester and Nantwich between 1625 and 1638 but hardly any others; George Cotton only appeared at Nantwich, William Glegg, Henry Birkenhead, and Sir Henry Bunbury only appeared at Chester), but some attended in a more random pattern. The surprising thing is that there was no hard core of 'professional' Justices who turned up Sessions after Sessions. Only three men, Sir George Booth, Sir William Brereton, and Henry Mainwaring, were present on average more than twice a year after their appointment to the Bench.[2]

The role of the Assize Judges on their circuits in urging on the J.P.s in their administrative duties is an important one. Yet during the pre-Civil War period relations between the

[1] It varies slightly from time to time. The phrase 'effective Bench' is meant to exclude the largely honorary appointments of Court dignitaries and judicial officials.
[2] All the foregoing is based on the splendid series of Order Books and Sessions Files in Cheshire Record Office for the years 1625–60. For a full study, see below, chapter 6.

Cheshire Justices and the permanent Judges of the Palatine Court of Great Sessions were distinctly uneasy. In 1616—17 the Judges issued a long series of administrative instruments which set out to structure the Justices' approach to a wide range of issues, including several aspects of the poor law, the supervision of ale-houses, the upkeep of bridges, and the oversight of recusants.[1] Since the implementation of these orders was left entirely to the Justices, they appear not to have protested, but it is significant that the court made no further effort to lay down general rules until after the Civil War. What really upset the Justices was any attempt by the Judges to supersede their competence in specific cases. The most dramatic incident followed an attempt by the Judges in 1625 to lay aside an order made at Quarter Sessions for the repair of Warrington Bridge and replace it by a fresh order for the levy of a much greater amount from the whole county. The Justices protested violently, ordered the constables to ignore the Judges' ruling, and undertook to pay the fines imposed on any official for neglect of the order.[2] Later squabbles were less dramatic, but this is largely because, as the court's records reveal, the Judges after 1625 consistently referred all contentious petitions and presentments either to Quarter Sessions or to the Justices nearest the scene.[3]

The importance of the work of the Justices in their own areas reduced the independence and importance of the head constables, two of whom were appointed in each of the seven hundreds. Their principal task was that of supervising the constables in the assessment and collection of money whether in the form of taxation or local rates; they were thus in charge of issuing warrants to the constables for the collection of parliamentary or arbitrary taxation (e.g. subsidies or forced loans), and in the 1630s were responsible for Ship Money assessments under the authority of the

[1] P.R.O. Chester 21, vol. 3, ff. 367—72.

[2] C.R.O., Quarter Sessions File 1625, no.2, f. 81. A copy of this order in the Grosvenor MSS. at Eaton Hall (catalogued as 'Eaton 29') contains the signatures of sixteen Justices, all prominent gentry.

[3] The Sessions (Assize) Rolls, complete from the thirteenth century, are in the P.R.O., series Chester 24.

sheriffs. A similar task was that of levying rates in their hundreds for bridge repairs, and they had annual responsibility for the collection of the general county rate used to pay the pensions of maimed soldiers, the maintenance of the house of correction, and the subsistence of poor prisoners in Chester Castle. But they had no broader administrative initiative or responsibility. It is symbolic of the importance of the hundred as a unit that each adopted separate procedures for changing their head constables; Nantwich elected fresh ones annually at a monthly meeting, while Macclesfield retained theirs for years on end: Richard Wiche was head constable there from 1629 to 1640, with only two partners (James Ridgeway 1629–34, William Barrett 1634–9) during that time. Some hundreds did not elect their own head constables but presented a list at Quarter Sessions from which the Justices selected the most suitable.[1]

It has already been noted that in Cheshire township and parish were distinct in identity. The size of most parishes made it necessary for petty constables to be appointed for each township, not each parish, while other officials (overseers of the poor, surveyors of the highway, churchwardens) were appointed, as laid down by statute, for whole parishes. In some parishes, however, the statutory number was increased and responsibility for individual villages divided.[2]

The position of constable usually passed from house to house in a village on a rota, although if good cause could be shown to the Justices, those liable could pay an approved person to act for them. Other officers were nominated by the parish and approved by the Justices at hundredal meetings. All these officials served just for one year.

The head constables were one important link between village and county government; the Justices at their private sessions and monthly meetings were another. But there was a

[1] This is based on the lists of head constables and other general information in the Quarter Sessions Order Books in C.R.O.
[2] e.g. Prestbury; see C.R.O., Quarter Sessions Order Book 6a, ff. 435, 466, 485, 499.

third, the Grand Jury of Presentment. At every Quarter Sessions at least three juries were empannelled. One was a 'Jury for Prisoners' which heard the evidence and determined the guilt of all those indicted of criminal offences. The second jury was composed of the fourteen head constables who made presentments (i.e. a formal representation to the court of anything they believed to require the Justices' attention).

The third jury was the Inquest or Grand Jury which had a double function. On the first day of the Sessions they read through all the bills of accusation made against prisoners on remand or bail to the Sessions and decided whether there was a case to be answered. If so, the accused was formally indicted before the trial jury; if not, he was discharged. Their more important function came on the second and third day of the Sessions when they made a presentment far more comprehensive than that of the head constables.[1] In a typical year, 1629, the Grand Juries presented sixteen highways in need of repair, five unpassable bridges, several unlicensed alehouses, a corrupt official, some families who had taken in homeless strangers, two village feuds which required official action, and several offences against the game laws. At other times they presented Catholic recusants and reported on illegal enclosures and refusals to pay tithes, the playing of unlawful games, and the activities of unlicensed grain dealers. They could also be called upon to join the Justices in petitioning Parliament or the Crown as the authoritative voice of the county.[2] Their independence and 'political' significance was to increase in the years after the Civil War, but they were always an important feature of local government.[3]

Grand Juries normally consisted of fifteen men, although juries of thirteen or seventeen were occasionally used. They

---

[1] The presentments for every Sessions are written up in the Quarter Sessions Records in C.R.O. I have used the volumes covering 1618–72.

[2] e.g. B.M. Add. MS. 36913 (Aston MS.), f. 60, where the J.P.s, Grand Jury, and ministers begged the King not to leave England for Ireland in the spring of 1642.

[3] See below, pp.231–2.

were selected from a panel of twenty-four drawn up by the sheriff. Probably to avoid calling too many people from the far end of the county, they were always weighted in favour of the hundreds nearest the Sessions town. Thus Knutsford Grand Juries were always drawn predominantly from Macclesfield, Bucklow, and Northwich hundreds, Chester Grand Juries from Broxton, Edisbury, and Wirral. Nantwich, the most central of all the Sessions towns, drew its juries from the whole county, though a majority usually came from Nantwich hundred. Sheriffs were always seeking to find new freeholders to serve as Grand Jurymen, but they also sought to balance them with experienced men. Altogether 398 men served during the years 1625–42. Of these a third served only once and over half three times or less, but fifty served ten or more times—the most experienced being Humphrey Page of Yardshawe from the far north-east of the county, who was on thirty-three jury panels during these years. Some only sat at their 'local' Sessions (e.g. Robert Auger who was on the panel for fifteen of the seventeen years 1625–42 at Chester, or Lawrence Cotton, thirteen times at Nantwich). Others were regularly on juries at all five Sessions towns (e.g. Humphrey Page and Richard Whittingham of Over, who served at least four times at each of the Sessions towns).

Thus at any given Sessions, the majority would have served before, and although there might be four or five newcomers from the hundreds neighbouring the Sessions, there were always two or three widely experienced representatives of the further hundreds to redress the balance. The presentments themselves reflect this bias: they were weighted, but not unduly, around the hundreds nearest to the town where Sessions were being held.[1] The administrative machinery of Cheshire at all levels thus reflected the balance between the local and the county interest; neither predominated.

---

[1] Jury lists are bound into every Sessions File. At Assizes there were two Grand Juries (the second replacing the Jury of head constables). They were drawn from the same group of 400 as the Sessions juries, with a permanent weighting in favour of the western hundreds.

Discussion of the Grand Jurymen brings out another point. All 400 are styled 'gentleman' in the official records. So are a majority of the head constables.[1] Yet only five of these families were included in the Heralds' visitations. This raises an important question of definition. Professor Everitt has recently argued that

the problem of defining the 'gentry' in their lowest ranks is considerable, and more so in some counties than others. In Kent I have included all those who are known to have been armigerous, and a number who, while their right to arms is now difficult to prove, were widely reckoned as gentry at the time and usually intermarried with other armigerous families.[2]

It is clear, however, that this criteria are largely subjective. He specifically excludes some who styled *themselves* gentlemen but whom he considers did so without any right. Using his definition there would be about 400 gentlemen in Cheshire in the 1630s. Yet there were also the Grand Jurymen and head constables, all called 'gentleman' in official sources, but many of whom were no more than modest freeholders. Thus, to take an extreme case, seventeen gentlemen-freeholders from the village of Mobberley served as head constables or Grand Jurymen in the years 1625—42. This would indicate that Cheshire was one of those counties like Kent or Devon where the style of life of the minor gentleman and the yeoman was difficult to distinguish. But the problem is that contemporaries did not flinch from making these difficult distinctions.

Of course it is obvious that their way of life had nothing in common with that of great *rentier* landlords like Lord Cholmondeley or Sir Richard Wilbraham, each with upwards of 30,000 acres. But one is faced with the fact that there is no simple dividing line, and every possible gradation. It is clear that the Heralds were unreliable, but to use their visitations as the base, coupled with a little judicious extension, is not really helpful, at least not for Cheshire. Mr. J.P. Cooper, in a perceptive discussion of this problem, has pointed out how areas differed from one another—noting, for example,

[1] A majority of head constables had already served as Grand Jurymen.
[2] A.M. Everitt, *Change in the Provinces 1603—60*, Leicester, 1969, p.56.

that in Lancashire all but nine of the 660 men in the free-holders' book of 1600 were styled gentlemen.[1] Clearly in some counties—such as Northamptonshire—there was a sharp distinction between gentry and yeomen.[2] But one is left wondering whether, if Professor Everitt or Dr. Cliffe had a source for their counties like the Cheshire Grand Jury lists, they would feel so confident about holding so firmly to armigerous status, or discounting 'those who styled themselves gentry without due authority'.[3] It is most important to adopt criteria that make sense of the sources, however inconvenient for the modern historian.

Economic denominators for gentility are of no avail; I have styled as 'gentleman' anyone so called at the time.[4] But there is a distinction to be drawn, not in economic terms, nor in style of life (in the sense of outward show, style of building, etc.), but in terms of social relationships. There is a real difference between those gentlemen whose social intercourse —dinner parties, bowling matches, travelling companions— involved them with a county-wide network of families, and those whose social lives were largely bounded by their neighbours: the county and the parochial gentry. I shall return to this theme later,[5] but broadly there was a group of gentry who socialized with their 'cousins', while others—of almost equal estates—were always to be found with their neighbours. This does not preclude intermarriage between the two groups, but it marks a real distinction since there was a recognizable group of county families who intermarried to a remarkable degree, and there was a resultant split within the armigerous gentry. By the use of this approach, a group of

[1] J.P. Cooper, 'The Social Distribution of Lands and Men in England 1436–1700', *Ec.H.R.*, 2nd ser., 20 (1967), particularly 429–30.

[2] Everitt, op. cit. pp.37–8.

[3] Ibid., p.56; J.T. Cliffe, *The Yorkshire Gentry*, London, 1969, particularly pp.3–6.

[4] Fortunately there are virtually no cases where I have had to rely on self-attribution. One interesting point about these minor gentlemen is that they were frequently known as 'yeomen' during their father's lifetime and only became styled as 'gentlemen' on their deaths.

[5] See below, pp.233–4. The key source is the diary of Thomas Mainwaring of Baddiley and Peover, J.Ry.L. Mainwaring MS., Book 20a.

about sixty-five to seventy families can be distinguished from the rest. A study of forty genealogies reveals that of the marriages contracted by members of these families during the period 1590–1642, 48 per cent were with other families from the Cheshire élite. A further 28 per cent were with élite gentry families from other counties. Thus the Wilbrahams of Woodhey had marriage connections with the Savages, Dones, Grosvenors, Delves, Davenports, and Venables from amongst the Cheshire elite; the remaining marriage connections were with the heiress of the Solicitor General in Ireland, with Sir Humphrey Briggs, and with the lesser Cheshire family of Hurleston of Picton. It was from this group of almost seventy families that all the quorum of the Commission of the Peace, the deputy lieutenants, and (almost all) the sheriffs were drawn in the decades before 1642.

I have pointed out above how the pattern of attendance by each Justice at Quarter Sessions varied. But it should be noted that one whole group of Justices played no part in county government in the 1630s. Apart from Sir William Brereton, the most regular attenders in the 1630s were Sir George Booth (a J.P. for almost fifty years and *custos rotulorum* since 1614) Henry Mainwaring of Kermincham, Thomas Stanley of Alderley, Richard Brereton of Ashley, and Sir Richard Wilbraham of Woodhey. These were to form a single political group in 1640–2.[1] Opposed to that group in those years was another headed by Earl Rivers, Viscount Cholmondeley, Viscount Kilmorrey, Lord Brereton, Sir Edward Fytton, and Sir Thomas Aston. None of this latter group attended a single Sessions between 1630 and 1640. Nor were they active out of Sessions. The average number of documents signed by each of the six leaders of the 'active' group which can be found in the Quarter Sessions Files during the decade was 149; for the inactive group, nineteen.[2]

---

[1] See below, pp.32–4, 38–9, 45–56, 58–60.

[2] Attendant Justices are listed in C.R.O., Quarter Sessions Orders Books 6a(1618–40) and 9a(1640–50), *passim.* Many documents in the Files contain the signatures of individual Justices, and reflect their work out of Sessions; they are principally recognizances and examinations.

In 1603 there were no resident peers in Cheshire; by 1630 there were the four named above amongst the inactive justices.[1] It seems probable that their abstention from local government was the result of disagreements about precedence in the county between them and the older baronets, Booth, Wilbraham, and Delves. What made the situation worse was that there was no natural aristocratic overlord in Cheshire. The Lord Lieutenancy was held by the Earl of Derby, after 1629 in conjunction with his son Lord Strange, but although they held lands in Cheshire, and a town house in Chester, their interests were essentially confined to Lancashire and the Isle of Man, and they intervened little in Cheshire affairs.[2] Furthermore, the gentry kept clear of the scramble for places in the courts of the early Stuarts, although about twelve families held posts in the Irish administration, the most important being that of Sir Philip Mainwaring, who was Strafford's secretary.

William Smith, during his tour of Cheshire in the 1580s, recorded that the county was

In religion very zealous, howbeit somewhat addicted to Superstition, which cometh through want of preaching. For the harvest is plenty, but the Reapers are few. It is a thing to be lamented, and redresse to be wished; for in some places they have not a Sermon in a whole year.[3]

The problem was not just that of huge parishes and inadequate stipends (though even the Bishop claimed to be the poorest in the realm).[4] It was also the size and administrative hazards of the diocese, erected in 1541 and comprising all Lancashire and Cheshire together with parts of Cumberland, Yorkshire, and Flintshire.

During Elizabeth's reign the major problem for successive bishops was Catholicism. Over a quarter of all known recusants in the country were said to live in the diocese in

[1] The Earl of Bridgewater stayed occasionally on his Cheshire estates, but more normally in London or Northamptonshire.

[2] F.J. Leslie, 'James, 7th Earl of Derby', *T.L.C.H.S.*, 5 (1889). See also Canon Raines's introduction to vol.3 of 'The Stanley Papers', *Chetham Society*, O. S. 66–7 (1865).

[3] D. King, op. cit., p.19.

[4] R.C. Richardson, *Puritanism in North West England*, Manchester, 1972, p.1.

1568, during the slack administration of Bishop Downham.[1] Yet it was only in the 1580s that the authorities began to work effectively against recusancy, and, according to Mr. Wark, the campaign reached its height in the early 1590s.[2] But Catholicism was far stronger in Lancashire than in Cheshire, where it was concentrated in two parishes, Bunbury and Malpas,[3] though it retained several adherents amongst the gentry of the Wirral. This pattern was largely unchanged by 1640: 313 recusants were presented during a major anti-Catholic drive in 1640,[4] the majority from around Beeston (Bunbury parish) and Halton (Runcorn parish), homes of two branches of the ultra-Catholic Savage family, and from the Wirral. But compared with 1583, when twenty-four leading families were tainted with recusancy,[5] by 1640 only three families from amongst the élite remained outside the Church of England—the Savages, the Masseys, and the Stanleys of Hooton.

It is significant that the anti-Catholic drive should have gathered momentum in the 1580s. This is precisely the period during which, supported by the Privy Council, Bishop Chadderton (a former champion of Leicester's) was forming an alliance with puritanically inclined preachers and ministers in the diocese. In 1584, for example, a system of preaching exercises was set up at fourteen towns throughout the diocese (this is at the time of Whitgift's vigorous articles against Puritan preachers in Canterbury province)[6] and many of those already noted for their nonconformity in vestments and ceremonies were closely and explicitly linked with these exercises. Later, four Queen's Preachers were appointed in the diocese, several of them open Puritans.

[1] See J. Beck, op. cit., p.89.

[2] K.R. Wark, 'Elizabethan Recusancy in Cheshire', *Chetham Society*, 3rd ser., vol. 19, 1971.

[3] Mr. G. Chesters has suggested that this was partly the responsibility of two 'old priests' still working in these parishes in the 1570s (Wark, op. cit. p.133).

[4] C.R.O., Quarter Sessions Presentments, Book 8a, ff. 7–20.

[5] P.R.O., SP 15, vol. 27, f. 29; quoted and analysed in Wark, op. cit., pp.179–82.

[6] G.W. Prothero, *Statutes and Constitutional Documents 1558–1625*, Oxford, 4th edn., 1913, pp.211–12.

Despite haphazard and lukewarm attempts to enforce conformity, the Bishops of Chester were not particularly concerned to extirpate Puritanism; rather they saw it as an ally against Catholicism. It thus grew throughout the county, particularly in the central and eastern hundreds; the collegiate church at Manchester was one powerhouse, the activities of traders and merchants along the main roads and in the market towns may have been another.[1]

The result was that by the 1610s there was a distinctive lay Puritan movement in the diocese as well as strong clerical roots. Lectureships had been established in several Cheshire towns, the exercises were flourishing and spasmodic and partial attacks on ceremonial deviation were the only real signs of official disapproval. There had been a few spectacular converts amongst the Cheshire gentry,[2] but those accused of nonconformist practices were invariably below gentle status.[3]

Then in the years 1616—19 Bishop Moreton adopted a much tougher line, exemplified by his enforcement of the Book of Sports. Although there was some relaxation in the early years of the episcopate of John Bridgeman, there was a full-scale campaign from 1633 onwards, in which a reluctant Bridgeman was prodded into action by Archbishop Neale of York, who supplemented the diocesan's efforts by metropolitan visitations and the Northern High Commission.[4] Several ministers were silenced, and at least four took refuge from Cheshire abroad.[5] Persecution was redoubled after members of Chester corporation entertained and feasted William Prynne on his way to imprisonment at Caernarvon in 1637 for libelling the bishops.[6]

[1] For the foregoing paragraphs, see Richardson, op. cit., *passim.*

[2] e.g. John Bruen (see Richardson, op. cit., *passim,* particularly pp.122—4, and W. Hinde, *A Faithfull Remonstrance of the Holy Life and Happy Death of John Bruen,* London, 1641).

[3] Richardson, op. cit., *passim.*

[4] Ibid.; also (ed.) W. Urwick, *Historical Sketches of Nonconformity in Cheshire,* Manchester, 1864, *passim.*

[5] Thomas Paget, Samuel Eaton, Julines Herring, George Moxon (Urwick, op. cit., *passim).*

[6] For the Laud—Bridgeman correspondence following this incident, see *Cheshire Sheaf,* 1st ser., vol. 3, *passim.*

The effect of this persecution was to polarize attitudes, creating a radical anti-episcopal movement where none had existed before. It was essentially a popular movement enjoying the support of a few ministers and gentlemen, and calling for radical reform in liturgy and church government.[1]

At this stage, the majority of the gentry and clergy continued to support episcopacy and the established church, while looking for the reform of abuses and greater latitude over ceremonies and vestments. Samuel Clark recalled that several gentry and clergy 'took a journey unto London in 1640 ... in order to procure liberty, that men unconformable to ceremonies might not be thrown out'.[2] Samuel Torshell, a minister linked with the leading J.P.s, later said that in 1640 he still upheld the authority of bishops, and came to change his mind only in 1642—3.[3] John Ley was a close friend and correspondent of the moderate Archbishop Ussher in 1640, though he was later to be a leading Presbyterian and President of Syon College.[4] The great majority of the leading gentry were to oppose the root-and-branch petitions in Cheshire in 1641.[5] It seems that they were sympathetic to a preaching ministry and to a relaxation in Prayer Book rubrics, but not to change in fundamentals. They resented the change in policy by the bishops in the 1630s which looked innovatory and appeared to have created the radical movement which was to cause social unrest in 1640—2.[6]

They also resented Bridgeman's attempts to encroach on lay control of advowsons in the county: the Bishop's attempts to impose his own candidate on Nantwich were firmly resisted, for example.[7] Bridgeman's personal moder-

---

[1] For discussion of, and further references to, this and the following, see below, pp.45—56 and 263—76. Dr. Richardson fails to consider this whole question.
[2] Urwick, op. cit., p.166.
[3] See below, p.271.
[4] Urwick, op. cit., pp.399—400.
[5] See below, pp.45—56.
[6] See below pp.51—2.
[7] Richardson, op. cit., p.139.

ation[1] deflected much criticism from his office on to the Court in London which was held to be responsible for these changes in policy. For example, Sir Richard Grosvenor—a future Royalist and supporter of episcopacy, but an enemy of the 'Court' described Arminianism in 1629 as 'a plotting, undermining and dangerous sect'.[2]

Thomas Paget caught the ecclesiastical mood of 1640 well when he lamented that Cheshire, 'the chief shire, not long agone reputed and deservedly esteemed for the profession and power of religion', had now become fragmented into extreme factions—one 'a degenerate plant of a strange vine of the Lord' (Arminianism), the other which 'did not seek for Presbytery, but seemed rather to affect a popular government'.[3] In the middle stood the county establishment, appalled at the strange and dangerous social movement created by the wilful and novel policies of a remote central government.

## II

In general, the Cheshire gentry appear to have been reasonably well informed about events outside the county, and to have felt distaste for what they knew of the royal Court in the early decades of the seventeenth century. William Davenport of Bramhall, for example, kept a commonplace book throughout the period 1609—50 which throws interesting light on the political consciousness of a small provincial squire. He entered reports (in a highly disapproving tone) of many of the great Court scandals, such as the Essex divorce and the Overbury murder, but from the early 1620s he became increasingly preoccupied with the political disputes of the day, copying out, for example,

[1] For example, Bridgeman turned a blind eye to Puritans wherever he could do so without getting into trouble. At times he even advised Puritan ministers like John Angier to find new parishes farther from Chester 'for I study to do you a kindness but cannot as long as you are thus near me'. (Quoted in Urwick, op. cit., p.67).
[2] Cited in W. Notestein and F. Relf, *The Commons Debates of 1629*, Minneapolis, 1921, p.68. This also includes Grosvenor's Journal of the debates in this Parliament (pp.172—244).
[3] Quoted in Urwick, op. cit., p.xvi.

Abbot's eloquent and outspoken attack in the Council on the
projected marriage alliance with Spain (1623), the opposition
attack on Buckingham in 1628, and a highly critical account
of the Duke's Île de Rhe expedition, ('that most unfortunate
journey'). He also noted innovations in local government
such as the distraint of knighthood proceedings in 1631
(which he termed 'the strange commission'). His scrapbook
of anti-government sentiment continues up to Pym's address
to the Short Parliament, and then ceases. He records
Strafford's speech from the scaffold and thenceforth drifted
into an alliance with the Cheshire Royalists.[1]

Another minor squire who kept abreast of events was
William Moreton of Moreton. From about 1631 onwards he
received a series of letters from his son Philip, who lived on
the verge of the Court as a private secretary or tutor in
various great families. For example, he was at one point an
escort to the future Earl of Denbigh on a tour of Italy (where
Moreton remained as Charles I's resident in Turin). His letters
are full of Court intrigue, quoting the odds on the candidates
for high offices. He also gave elaborate reports on developments abroad in English diplomacy or the course of the war
in Germany.[2] Similarly, John Bradshaw, just back from the
Michaelmas law term of 1632 in London, wrote to the young
squire of Lyme (Peter Legh) giving an account of the effects
of the battle of Lutzen on events in Europe, which was at
once sophisticated in approach and demanding in the level of
knowledge it expected in the reader. Bradshaw also
commented on Sir John Eliot's failing health as he lay
immured in the Tower, and discussed the recent proclamation exiling the gentry from London.[3]

Provincial distrust for the ways of the central government
in the 1620s and 1630s is well demonstrated by Sir Richard
Grosvenor in a speech he made to the freeholders during the
1624 elections; Grosvenor, after all, was later to become an

[1] Chester City R.O., CR63/2/19, Davenport of Bramhall MSS., *passim.*
[2] B.M. Add. MS. 33936, *passim.*
[3] J.Ry.L. Legh of Lyme MSS., Box 64, unfoliated.

active Royalist. He began by calling for great care in the choice of suitable members; those elected must be

every way apted and fitted thereto, such as are quicke of Capacitie, nimble of apprehention, ripe in Judgmt, sound & untaynted in their Religion, faythfull and trustie, those that are conversant in the affaires of the countrey & who throughlie understand the nature of this Countie Palatine, and such whose courage uppon all occasions dare comaund their tongues without feare to utter their Countreyes iust complaints & grievences.

He then discussed the dangers facing the state, in particular the creeping toleration of recusants, the continued power of monopolists and a foreign policy of 'dependencie uppon forraine princes dangerous to any state'. Parliament, a body having 'an absolute Jurisdiccon and an unlimited power to dispose of the lives, lims, states, goods, honours and liberties of the subject, yea and of their Religion too . . .', was itself seen as threatened by 'some busie headed workinge Politicians attendinge opportunities and wicked advantages to bring in bondage both Church and Commonwealth'. His sombre appeal ended with an image which adumbrated the concept of the Crown 'seduced by evil counsellers' of 1642, when he said that though 'the fountaine itselfe bee pure cleare and uncontaminate', yet 'many of the streames issuinge from the fountaine [are] corrupt'. [1]

If the Cheshire gentry as a whole had few contacts with, and less respect for, the Caroline Court, neither did they have much contact with the organized 'Country' opposition.[2] Only one Cheshire landowner was at all closely linked to this mainstream of opposition: Sir William Brereton of Handforth, later to be the dominant personality in Cheshire politics, and already in the 1630s the most energetic county J.P.

Born in 1604 into the cadet branch of an ancient Cheshire family, Brereton had to endure a lengthy royal wardship

[1] This 3,000-word speech is in the Grosvenor MSS. at Eaton Hall, Cheshire, which are not available for inspection. I am most grateful to the staff of Cheshire Record Office for arranging for this and other Grosvenor MSS. there to be xeroxed. At the end of his speech, Grosvenor nominated two gentlemen who had been endorsed by 'these worthy gent. who sit about me'. They were duly elected.

[2] For a recent study, see P. Zagorin, *Court and Country*, London, 1969.

before coming into his estates in 1627. His 3,000 acres made him a substantial but not leading county landowner. Educated at Brasenose College, Oxford, and Gray's Inn, he soon demonstrated a keen ambition to advance himself. He married the daughter of Sir George Booth and was later elected, at the age of twenty-four, to Charles I's third Parliament, where he made a name for himself as a zealous opponent of the royal prerogative.[1] Despite this, he negotiated with Buckingham for a baronetcy, and was granted it in return for an undertaking to maintain thirty footmen in Ireland for the ensuing three years.[2]

At the same time he launched forth on a series of financial adventures, buying extensive lands on the Charles River in New England and coming into close touch with the Massachusetts Bay Company (the clearest evidence of his contacts with the 'Country' leaders: he does not appear to have been associated with the more important Providence Island scheme).

In 1631 he built a duck decoy on Saltney Marshes (near Chester), a business venture borrowed from the Dutch and from Norfolk, which brought him into legal confrontations with many outraged gentry whose sport he was wrecking. It is clear that he was generally regarded as an improving land-lord.[3]

The Journal of Brereton's visits to the Netherlands, Scotland, and Ireland—a splendid mixture of business memoranda and anecdote—reveals a lively and open mind at this early stage of his career. While in the Netherlands he visited churches of every denomination, being particularly attracted by the Lutheran church and dismayed at the lack of zeal and devotion he found in the Jewish synagogue. He was relieved to find that the Lutherans omitted the sign of the

[1] J. W. Stoye, *English Travellers Abroad 1604–67*, London, 1952, p.243.
[2] The main sources for his early life are his Journal (printed by the *Chetham Society*, O. S. 1(1842) and an early letter book now in Chester City R.O., CR63/2/702. These and other scraps have been profitably studied by R.N. Dore, 'The Early Life of Sir William Brereton', *T.L.C.A.S.*, 63 (1953), 1–26.
[3] For his adventures in New England and with the duck decoy, see R.N. Dore, art. cit., pp.4–8, 20–3; see also Chester City R.O., CR63/2/702, Brereton letter book, pp.1–116, for the decoy litigation.

cross in baptism and the ring in marriage and he approved of the pulpit in the central aisle.[1] But he was just as impressed with the church in Scotland, remarking at length on the system of church discipline.[2] A sound root-and-branch man, it might be thought; yet on his way to Scotland he called in to see Bishop Moreton with whom he discussed the practice of bowing to the altar,[3] and in Ireland he was deeply impressed by Archbishop Ussher whom he described as 'a most holy and heavenly man, and as pregnant-witted as any I have heard.'[4] He commended the Dutch policy of complete toleration.[5]

Brereton's curiosity was just as avid in temporal matters. He attended judicial proceedings both in the Netherlands and Scotland, and made a detailed study of poor relief in the former. He paid out large sums for exotic drinks, and went out of his way to examine 'a curious waterwork' in the house of one of the Amsterdam burghers.[6] Business interests were served by the first-hand study of Dutch duck decoys, and by unsuccessful bids for Irish land. He returned from Holland laden with souvenirs, paintings, gilt door-knobs, and tulips.[7]

None of this suggests the committed radical of the 1640s. His sympathies clearly lay with those demanding a less rigid church, but he was quite prepared to dedicate himself to local government and to channel his energies into a wide range of financial ventures. Although he was heavily rated for distraint of knighthood, and was in conflict with the city of Chester over the assessment of his interests there for Ship Money, he was not one of those named as having opposed the legality of either. He may have had contacts amongst the opposition, but in 1640 he still had to declare his hand.

---

[1] 'The Journal of Sir William Brereton', *Chetham Society*, O. S. 1(1842), pp.60–1, 63–4.
[2] Ibid., pp.106–10
[3] Ibid., pp.81–2
[4] Ibid., pp.139–40, 143.
[5] Ibid., p.70.
[6] Ibid., p.56
[7] Ibid., pp.34, 59

### III

Despite their general antipathy towards the governments of the 1620s and 1630s, the Cheshire gentry were remarkably restrained in expressing their opposition. The policy of 'Thorough' was widely implemented locally.

Although one would never realize it from Professor Zagorin's unsympathetic and inadequate account of the 'Court',[1] there was a coherent philosophy underlying the policies of the early 1630s: to take the financial expedients, whatever their spurious legalism, out of the context of the drive to streamline church and local government would be misleading. Laudian church politics were profoundly resented and misunderstood, but, as Dr. Hill has repeatedly shown, they were a genuine attempt to cope with the malaise of the church through tackling both its financial and its spiritual weaknesses.[2]

Similarly in local government, the personal rule was a geniune attempt at paternalistic and effective government rather than a scramble after solvency. The Book of Orders of 1630 sought to put the administrative work of the Justices on a more efficient footing, and for some months the Cheshire Quarter Sessions Files reflect the Privy Council pressure and show a real effort to implement the government's programme. But in the long run, the achievement was not impressive.[3]

Far more successful was Charles I's effort to improve the militia. As a result of prolonged Privy Council pressure, the Cheshire trained bands were purged of those 'decaied by age & impotencie', brought up to strength (except for the horse), rearmed and regularly trained (the deputy lieutenants paying for the retention of the training sergeants, sent for a limited period by the Council, out of their own pockets).[4]

[1] Zagorin, op. cit., pp.40—73

[2] See particularly, C. Hill, *The Economic Problems of the Church*, Oxford, 1956; also H.R. Trevor—Roper, *Archbishop Laud*, 2nd edn., London, 1962; and W. Lamont, *Godly Rule*, London, 1969, chapter 3.

[3] For a fuller examination of administration in the 1630s, see below, chapter 6.

[4] Chester City R.O., CR63/2/6, Militia Orders 1625—42 (compiled by Thomas Legh of Adlington). The frankness of the correspondence with other deputy lieutenants in comparison with that sent to the Privy Council is notable. There is a

Even the negative aspects of the Personal Rule, the financial expediency of Weston and Juxon, created little positive opposition before 1639. As the deputy lieutenants recorded, not altogether without justice, at the time of the second Bishops' War, (1640), 'we fynd [the gentry] very willinge and reddie to serve his Majestie in this present expedicon, as may very well appeare by theire forwardnesse upon former occasions as in the payment of lones, knighthuddes, ship moneyes &c . . .'[1]

In October 1625 the deputy lieutenants had told the Earl of Derby that the gentry 'distaste the motion' of the forced loan,[2] but they later told the Privy Council that they 'found ready obedience in the county to lend to the king'.[3] The accounts show that £2,178.13s4d. was collected in a short time, and the Earl of Derby claimed that the only resistance had come from 'the bould and impudent speeches used by many Romish Catholiques', which provided the occasion for a search for arms in the houses of all known Papists.[4] However, one Cheshire man, Sir Randle Crewe, Chief Justice of the King's Bench, refused to uphold the legality of the loan and was sacked.[5]

About 180 gentlemen were charged distraint of knighthood. The majority paid £10, but others made compositions of up to £70. Again there was little outcry, though we have already noted that William Davenport thought it a 'strange commission'. It would appear that great care was taken to assess the fines equitably, and there are only about fourteen gentlemen whose omission seems surprising.[6]

---

fuller account of these points in my thesis, (Univ. of Oxford D.Phil. thesis, 1971), pp.23–6. Cf. the militia book of Sir Hugh Cholmondeley 1595–1600, which reveals a much less healthy position (C.R.O., accession 1729).

[1] Chester City R.O., CR63/2/6, f. 79.
[2] *C.S.P.D.* 1625–6, p.129.
[3] Ibid., p.256.
[4] Chester City R.O., CR63/2/6, f. 12.
[5] R.N. Dore, *The Civil Wars in Cheshire*, Chester, 1966, p.4.
[6] The list of compounders is in a miscellany published in the *Lancashire and Cheshire Record Society*, 12 (1885), 199–210. One of the few whose compositions seems to have been at an excessive rate was Sir William Brereton (£35). This is in contrast to the Forced Loans which fell on 171 gentlemen, but which more leading families appear to have escaped.

Ship Money aroused much stronger feelings, however. This
was partly because it took on the appearance of a regular tax
and partly because more was demanded from it than from
the other expedients. But most of all, it was a tax which fell
on the whole community. With the probable exception of
fifteenths and tenths, few people below the substantial freeholder level ever paid taxation to the central government. But
for Ship Money assessments, successive sheriffs employed the
mise roll, that is the roll usually employed for levying money
for the poor, for bridge repairs, and for similar local
purposes. None-the-less, resistance only became marked in
the last two years.

In 1636, the Privy Council congratulated Sir Thomas
Aston on the speed with which he had got in the money.[1]
His successor as sheriff, Sir Thomas Delves, reported
difficulty in gaining the co-operation of the constables, and
was plagued by wrangling between neighbours about the
distribution of the levy, but by October 1637, several months
late, all the money was in[2] Similarly in 1637—8, Thomas
Cholmondeley collected the first £2,600 fairly quickly, but
the remaining £150 proved much more difficult, particularly
following the judgment in Hampden's case.[3]

Throughout these years various assessment disputes had
led to conflict between city and county authorities. The
initial problem was the city's claim that residents should not
be assessed by the county on income from lands outside the
city, but the most heated disputes surrounded the position of
Gloverstone, the problem of the Cathedral Close, and the
question of Sir Thomas Aston's profits within the city from
his farm of French wine imports.[4]

[1] *C.S.P.D.* 1635, p.595.
[2] *C.S.P.D.* 1636—7, pp.464, 493; *C.S.P.D.* 1637, p.475.
[3] *C.S.P.D.* 1637—8, pp.265, 300, 451; for a detailed account of Cholmondeley's
work, see his letter book, J.Ry.L. Eng. MS. 1091.
[4] For these disputes, see *C.S.P.D.* 1635—8, *passim;* B.M. Harleian MS. 2093, ff.
90—173; 2173, ff. 19—40. There is a full description of these disputes in the
thesis of A.M. Johnson (loc. cit., pp.120—39). Miss E. Marcotte of Yale University
is currently engaged on a thesis on Ship Money, with particular reference to
Cheshire and Northamptonshire.

By the time Philip Mainwaring took up office, the Privy Council had more or less decided these questions. But resistance within the county was now growing, though Mainwaring claimed that opposition was principally based on the belief that Cheshire was overrated in comparison with other counties. None-the-less, by April 1639 only £700 had been raised and Mainwaring had to threaten to distrain and imprison defaulters to achieve even this meagre sum.[1]

Sir Thomas Powell, Mainwaring's successor, was even less fortunate. He was confronted by more than the previous passive resistance, and the collectors were threatened by outraged freeholders like George Vernon of Whatcroft, who 'drew out his knife and threatened the constable to whett it in his gutts', while at Kinderton the tenants of Peter Venables gathered together and pursued the collectors with pitchforks.[2] By now opposition was general throughout the county; as Powell recorded in a personal letter, 'neither the trained bands nor the power of the county will assist mee in attaching delinquents in this service. They are all in generall possest with such dislyke thereunto'. And he added significantly, 'the great ones will trample us underfoot & his Majesties business also'.[3] On the other hand, with one possible exception, there is no evidence that the Justices advocated or practised violence themselves. They appear to have striven hard to lower the temperature of proceedings, and when Powell arrested George Edgley, head constable of Nantwich hundred, for his 'neglect and wilful contempt', the Justices at Quarter Sessions ordered his release and threatened to imprison Powell if he proceeded arbitrarily.[4]

In October 1640 the Justices decided to draw up a petition to Parliament stating the county's grievances. To do this, they appointed two commissioners in each hundred to hear the complaints of all parties, in particular about Ship Money and coat and conduct money: those appointed included the

1 *C.S.P.D.* 1639, p.8.
2 P.R.O., SP 16, vol. 466, f. 58.
3 ibid.
4 P.R.O., SP 16, vol. 459, f. 21; C.R.O., Quarter Sessions File 1641, no.4, f. 10.

future leaders of both the Royalist and Parliamentarian parties in the county. For example the Bucklow commissioners were Earl Rivers and Sir Thomas Aston, later arch-Royalists.[1]

Some months earlier, the gentry had also shown similar misgivings about Charles's demand for men for the second Bishops' War. Although the deputy lieutenants were willing to send men, they were not prepared to send the highly trained militia and the carefully acquired stock of expensive equipment which they had so zealously collected. Although Charles specifically asked that they 'take especiall care that there be a very good choyce made of the men of the trained bands', the deputy lieutenants ordered that 'non of the trayned bands be impressed, but if anie be, others to be chosen in their place'.[2]

A group of leading gentry met together to draw up a petition to Charles asking him not to reiterate his orders, and stressing their fears for security if the militia was taken from the county. The petition was drawn up by Sir Richard Wilbraham and circulated by him amongst the gentry of south and west Cheshire before being sent to Sir George Booth to be canvassed in north and east Cheshire. Booth was advised: 'This only causion in the signeing of it, Sir Richard desires that there be left a convenient place for the noble men of the countrey to write their names.'[3]

There is thus every sign that on the eve of the Long Parliament the gentry were united in their resentment of the government. They were prepared to submit to unpleasant and unusual burdens themselves not without grumbling and protest, but without taking a definite stand. But when the Crown's policies provoked undue rustlings of popular discontent—as its ecclesiastical and financial ones did, and as conscription for the Bishops' Wars threatened to do[4]—they stood in united but moderate opposition to the Crown.

[1] *C.S.P.D.* 1640—1, pp.146—7; C.R.O., Q.S. Order Book 9a, f. 13.

[2] Chester City R.O., CR63/2/6, ff. 63, 68, 74, 97.

[3] Ibid., f. 69. The significance of the last remark will become apparent in the course of the next chapter.

[4] Ibid., f. 96.

## 2

## THE EVOLUTION OF PARTIES, 1640–1643

### I

When Sir Richard Grosvenor shepherded the gentry nominees into the county seats in 1624,[1] he had managed the last peaceful election before the Civil Wars. In 1625 Sir Robert (later Lord) Cholmondeley and Sir Anthony St. John were elected after 'much contention'; the following year Sir Richard Grosvenor was soon accepted for first place, but the other seat was strongly contested. Young William Brereton of Handforth drew lots with Peter Daniell of Tabley and lost, but Daniell then had to contend with a fierce campaign from John Mynshull of Mynshull. All in all, Thomas Stanley of Alderley noted in a memorandum, the election caused 'a very great stirre, such as was never in Cheshire before'.[2]

Contention for the following Parliament was sharp but short-lived, for the factions among the gentry soon came to an arrangement and Grosvenor and Brereton were returned. Not everybody gained, however, for the many thousands who had come to Chester, 'repayring home so soone the citty buchers lost much, for they provided much meat thinking their stay would have byne longer, but it was a just punishment for they raysed flesh at so high a rate at the last chusing of the knights for the parlament.'[3]

A considerable amount of tension was always likely in Cheshire, since the county was grossly under-represented. The only seats apart from those of the county itself were the two for the city of Chester. One of these seems (certainly after 1603) to have gone automatically to the Recorder, and the second was sometimes given to the Earl of Derby's nominee. In 1628 two county gentlemen, Sir Randle Mainwaring and Sir Thomas Smyth (who were both also

[1] Eaton Hall, Grosvenor MSS., item 25. See above, pp.21–2.
[2] Printed in the *Journal of the Chester and North Wales Archaeological Society*, N. S. 24(1921–2).
[3] B.M. Harleian MS. 2125, f. 59.

aldermen), did contest the seat (most unfairly, according to Randle Holme who claimed, 'many were threatened unles the gave their voyses to Sr Ran & Sr Tho the should lose their houses, the 2 kts wrought so wth all the countrey gentlemen who had any tenants in Chester to give them ther voyces'). But they failed miserably, polling less than half the votes gained by the Recorder Edward Whitby and city lawyer John Ratcliffe.[1]

There are no signs in any of these contests that the candidates stood for distinct programmes. And so it was in the vigorous campaigning for the Short Parliament in the spring of 1640. We are fortunate to possess several letters from John Werden,[2] a small Cheshire gentleman, to Sir Thomas Smyth (who was away in the West Country, but was standing for election from the city of Chester); Werden's letters discuss the campaigns in both the city and the county.

In the county there were two distinct parties, that of the barons or lords (the leaders being named as Lords Cholmondeley and Kilmorey) and that of the baronets, or 'popular patriots' (headed by Sir George Booth and Sir Richard Wilbraham). Werden told Smyth, 'for aught I see, the matter grows very high and the contestation like to be the greatest that ever we heard of in our country'.[3] The name 'popular patriots' suggests that Booth and Wilbraham stood on a more directly anti-Court platform, but Werden was insistent that personal animosities lay behind the campaign.

I am sory in my heart to see the preparationes of discord, and I sit downe in sylence to see what God will doe in the ambytion of theise men that all raysed in their owne profit where there was a bare pretence of a public good and now rent the bowells of it to advance theire owne interests and popularitye.[4]

Perhaps the term 'patriot' became attached to Booth and Wilbraham following their sponsorship of the petition in 1639 which sought to safeguard local interests against royal

[1] The votes cast were Whitby—631, Ratcliffe—570, the knights—300 each. There are complete lists of Cheshire and Chester M.P.s, 1603—60, in the *Cheshire Sheaf,* 1st ser. vol. 2, items 1460, 1537, 1565, 1588, 1604, 1632, 1650.
[2] In the Calendar the signature is incorrectly transcribed as Thomas Moreton.
[3] *C.S.P.D.* 1639—40, p.564.
[4] P.R.O., SP 16, vol. 449, f. 14.

demands during the first Bishops' War.[1] Yet it is clear that the 'Barons' were expected to sign that petition, and later in 1640 both groups were involved in attacking Ship Money.[2]

The candidates who received the endorsement of the 'Barons', were Sir William Brereton and Sir Thomas Aston— soon to be leaders of the forces of Parliament and the Crown respectively. Brereton's radicalism, as I have suggested above, was still latent, but his likely attitudes in Parliament must have been known to the Lords. Furthermore, he was related to Sir George Booth, having married his daughter Susannah; she had died in 1637, but there is no evidence that the later ill feeling between Booth and himself had yet arisen. Booth had in fact earlier been a sleeping partner in the duck-decoy venture, which had, however, been opposed by Wilbraham.

As a candidate, Brereton had solid advantages. His experience at Westminster would count in his favour in such troubled times, and his popularity amongst the Puritan free-holders was well known and increasing.[3] If the barons were primarily interested in asserting their prominence in county politics, they must have found the joint sponsorship of a leading Puritan and of the leading champion of episcopacy in the county attractive. The vote was expected to be a close one, and Brereton's popularity might just have swayed the balance. The candidates endorsed by Booth and Wilbraham were referred to as 'the esquires', and they may well have been John Booth[4] and Thomas Wilbraham, their sons; this could explain why they did not sponsor Brereton. If so, all four candidates were among those gentlemen who were appointed to investigate the county grievances later in the year.

1 See above, p.30.
2 See above, pp.29–30.
3 P.R.O., SP 16, vol. 449, f. 14.
4 Another possibility is young George Booth (grandson of Sir George by his elder son William who had died in 1631). Sir George never got on well with his younger son John. On the other hand George was only seventeen in 1640, but we know that Sir George tried to get him elected at a by-election to the Lancashire borough of Newton in spring, 1642. (J.Ry.L. Legh of Lyme MSS., Box 53, unfoliated).

Again we are brought back to the conclusion that there is no evidence that the gentry were divided in their determination to put an end to those measures of Charles's government that had created local unrest. But they saw this as the ideal moment for a trial of strength between those who claimed pre-eminence for themselves in the community. The newly created barons could claim that their titles had elevated them to social supremacy. The baronets could reply that they had long been the leading magistrates—Sir George Booth had been *custos* for over twenty years, for example. Werden may well give the conclusive comment when he speaks of the lords as having 'so bitter a distaste of the neglect given them by our two great patriots'.[1]

In the event, however, the baronets stepped down, possibly through the intervention of Lord Strange, son of the Earl of Derby and joint Lord Lieutenant of the county. We are told that he 'declared for the barons part, tho' very temperately'.[2]

Brereton's radicalism emerged to the full in the course of the Short Parliament and this may well have alarmed the lords. In any case there was a significant change when the elections to the Long Parliament came to be held. There is no evidence that the baronets tried to elect their protégés, but the campaign once again raised 'much contention'. This was because a third candidate stood along with Aston and Brereton: this was Peter Venables of Kinderton. Since he was a son-in-law of Lord Cholmondeley and appears always to have been closely associated with him, he was probably meant as the barons' official candidate in place of Brereton, who was forced to run independently. Not unsuccessfully, however, for he won first place from Venables, and Aston was surprisingly left out.[3]

Brereton's support among the Puritans has already been referred to, and it is important to point to the vociferous Puritan campaign waged from pulpit and inn parlour. Many

---

[1] *C.S.P.D.* 1639–40, p.564.
[2] Ibid., p.580.
[3] B.M. Harleian MS. 2125, f. 133.

preachers who had stretched their consciences in previous years to prevent themselves from being ejected from their livings now stopped reading the Book of Common Prayer.[1] Others who lacked the courage to abandon it altogether still took the opportunity to adapt it, like the curate of Wybunbury who 'would not reade the absolucon nor the letany . . . and in the Creede (wch is most observable) when he should have said "I believe in the holy ghost, the holy catholic church" he read *"I believe there is a catholic church"* '.[2] There was nothing particularly new in this, though it seems to have become fairly widespread all at once in the last months of 1640 and the early months of 1641.

More worrying were those who preached vehemently against the Prayer Book, like John Jones who said that reading it was 'as badd or worse than the mumbling of the masse upon beades, that the Book of Common Prayer doth stinck in the nostrills of God; that the reading of Common Prayer hath bine the meanes of sending many soules unto hell'.[3] Sermons went far beyond attacks on the Prayer Book, however; one letter in April 1641 reported that,

The greatest newes wee have is that all our country churches are full of exercises for thanksgivings (this is the word of art) but the tenor of all these sermons are against the Bishops and their government. Last week there was one at Little Budworth, this week there was one at Barrow and Thornton, the next weeke at Tarvin etc. The New England Mr. Eaton and Mr. Holford preached at Barrow this weeke, but Eaton was modest in comparison of Holford, whoe railed most damnably against all church government as it is established.[4]

There were other wandering preachers, too. Thus two 'zealots' preached at Neston in the early months of 1641, John Werden adding to his description that they were 'of noe quality but that one of them was a son of Mr. Brereton, unckle to Sir W:B:'.[5]

---

1 e.g. West Kirby, B.M. Add. MS. 36913, f. 131, Tarporley, C.R.O., Q.S.O.B. 9a, f. 87.

2 B.M. Add. MS. 36914, ff. 214–15.

3 B.M. Add. MS. 36913, f. 136.

4 P.R.O., SP 16, vol. 483, f. 20.

5 B.M. Add. MS. 36914, f. 210.

The pulpit was also used for the furtherance of Puritan petitioning; where the minister himself did not lead the movement, lay Puritans did. 'Mr. Gerrard got very many all the tyme of divine service to subscribe some peticion at Frodsham & then lead them into church when the sermon began.'[1]

One of the features of this Puritan enthusiasm which caused most concern was the removal and destruction of painted windows and images from the churches. The Mayor of Chester reported that all the churches had been cleared, except the Cathedral where negotiations with the sub-dean were in hand. Leading Puritan Calvin Bruen made a special tour of the city churches in order to make an accurate report to the Mayor.[2] But elsewhere the refusal of the churchwardens or minister to co-operate led to violence. The House of Lords was told in April 1641 that disturbances in the churches of Cheshire were fairly common,[3] and in some parishes there is clear evidence of the breaking of windows or the pulling down of altar rails. Both these took place at Neston; of the windows it was said that Sir William Brereton's 'lady'

did send to the mynister or parson of the church to take down some painted ancyent imagery wch was in the glasse windowes. But the man beinge sober said he knew none that took offense at them. Neither woulde the churchwardens as he conceyved give any way unto it. But as he said, she came presently & brought a man wth her whoe wth a staffe most zealously broake all the wyndows . . . [4]

As a result of this kind of activity, a majority of the gentry came to be very distrustful of the nature and aims of the Puritan party in the county, and the support it was receiving from Brereton. They were also disturbed by the real threat to

[1] Ibid.
[2] C.R.O., Cowper MS. DCC/14/68.
[3] *Lords Journal,* vol. 4, p.225.
[4] B.M. Add. MS. 36914, f. 215. The 'lady' was probably Cicely Mytton, Brereton's second wife. The date of their marriage is unknown, but references to Brereton's absence from the House of Commons in February 1641 may well apply to his remarriage. The handwriting of the manuscript is wretched, and the setting could be Weston in Staffordshire, where Cicely lived. But the context of the passage clearly suggests a Cheshire location.

their position which they saw in the sermons of men like Samuel Eaton—referred to above as moderate in comparison to others. 'Certain positions' which he preached at St. John's Church, Chester, in January 1641 give some indication of his views: he was a strict Congregationalist, holding that 'the supreame power in church matters next under Christ is in the church, meaning (as he clearly explained himself) perticular congregacons for hee denyed all nationall, provinciall and dyocesan churches'. The office and government of bishops 'are heterogeneall to the world and anti-christian'; the Book of Common Prayer 'unsavoury and loathsome unto God'; and the minister of each congregation 'must be chosen by the people (otherwise) their entrance is not legall'.[1] Under such circumstances it is not surprising that Aston argued in his petition in favour of episcopacy that the removal of bishops must 'necessarily produce an extermination of nobility, gentry and order'.[2]

Fears of the effects of radical changes in church government must be seen in the context of a very real fear of the breakdown of order. There were frequent rumours of Catholic uprisings, the Justices themselves ordering the most thorough presentment of recusants for decades and calling for constant watch and ward in every township and the arrest of 'all such knowne Papists, strangers, and other persons wch ryde and travell in the nightime',[3] while on the Lancashire border a letter-writer reported 'that it is suspected the Papists are about to rise by commission; I myselfe heard a drum beate by a Papisticall captain'.[4] Linked with this was the fear of the Irish. The first rebels in Ireland in 1641 claimed to have a commission from Charles I, and in Lancashire and Shropshire fears of an imminent landing were extremely widespread; little direct evidence of extensive panic in Cheshire has survived, but it almost certainly did exist.[5]

[1] Bodl. Lib. Tanner MS. 65, f. 214.
[2] The petition has survived in numerous collections. Probably the most accessible is in the B.M. Thomason Tracts 669, f 4 (8).
[3] *Chetham Society*, N. S. 39 (1886), 75.
[4] *Chetham Society*, O. S. 50 (1859), 279.
[5] There are hints of fears in Cheshire in B.M. Thomason Tracts, E 148 (12), and *Lords Journal*, vol. 4, p.531.

These fears were mostly without substance. But there were other things that genuinely increased the concern created in the gentry by the religious disturbances. They were acutely aware of the dangers of having to keep together large numbers of armed troops: in May 1640 the deputy lieutenants asked the Earl of Derby that

The whole 500 men [intended for Charles's second campaign against the Scots] may not be drawn togeather in one bodie, nor have the armes of the countrey there to be trayned & exercysed, lest they fall to be mutenous & disordered wch we may have cause to feare, from a late experience we had of those 100 men wch we lately sent out of this countie, wch did growe to mutenie in the cittie of Chester.[1]

Indeed the city felt so uneasy about the state of affairs that at the beginning of October 1640, even before the Long Parliament had assembled, the city leaders decided to improve the defences 'in these warlike and dangerous times'.[2] As we shall see, the movement of troops through the county on the way to Ireland in the early months of 1642 had important effects on the political developments at that time.

On top of this, there was a general decline in public order. We have already seen that Sheriff Powell's attempts to raise Ship Money had been met by considerable violence from some tenant farmers. The Justices also took a stand, threatening to proceed against him at law, but it should be noted that their action followed after the violence. Furthermore, Thomas Stanley of Alderley was the only J.P. ever to advocate violence, threatening to shoot anyone who came to distrain his goods.[3]

This new resistance to taxation continued even after the ending of Ship Money collection. At the time of the collection of parliamentary taxation in 1641, a newsletter out of Cheshire reported that 'our popular patriots and grandees are at stand & move slowly in the subsydies, not being able to finde any collectors who will enter into bonds'.[4] (Note that the writer spoke of 'popular patriots' and

[1] Chester City R.O. CR63/2/6, Militia Correspondence, f. 96.
[2] Chester City R.O., Assembly File Calendar, item 205.
[3] *C.S.P.D.* 1640, p.444.
[4] B.M. Add. MS. 36914, f. 206.

'grandees', suggesting two distinct groups. There were twenty-six commissioners in all, who can be neatly divided into the two groups which opposed one another in the 1640 elections and the 1641 petitions.)[1] If we summarize in the terms and tone of the period,

wee do humbly pray that some such present course be taken as in yor wisdomes shalbe thought fitt to suppresse the future dispersinge of such dangerous discontent amongst the comon people, Wee haveinge great cause to feare that of all the distempers that at this present threaten the welfare of the state there is none more worthy the mature and grand consideracon of this honble assembly then to stopp the torrent of such spiritts before thee swell beyound the bond of Government . . .[2]

Divided over social pre-eminence in the county and by clashes of personality and troubled by threats to orderly government posed by religious extremists and a general mood of disaffection, how fully aware of the nature of the conflicts between King and Parliament were the Cheshire gentry, living 200 miles and three days' hard riding from the centre of events?

It is clear that they did not lack information and that many of them were kept well informed. In the previous chapter we saw how news from the Court and abroad was sent to several Cheshire squires in the 1620s and 1630s. For the period 1640–2 there is not a single family collection with any surviving correspondence that does not reveal some evidence of real awareness of what was happening in London. Thus the Aston papers contain a copy of the King's warrant and instructions to Strafford and Conway for the better ordering of the King's business in the North (October 1640) and an account of the negotiations at Ripon in the same month. From April 1641 comes the King's 'answere to certaine demands of both Houses of Parliament delivered to the Banquetting House'.[3] The Woodnoth Papers contain a copy of Charles's warrant for the arrest of the five members,[4]

---

[1] J.Ry.L. English MS. 1091, f. 41. The list contains sixteen members of the Booth–Wilbraham group and eight members of the Cholmondeley group.
[2] C.R.O. Cowper MS. DCC/14/88, undated gentry petition.
[3] B.M. Add. MS. 36913, ff. 46, 49–52, 86.
[4] B.M. Add. MS. 6032, f. 2.

while William Davenport's memorandum book contains notes on important speeches in the early days of the Long Parliament, the Scots army petition, and a copy of Strafford's speech from the scaffold.[1] These were all the result of the filtering through to the county of official propaganda, and each side became more active in presenting its case once the King had retired from London. Most of the important statements made by each side seem to have been widely read in the county. It was after reading some of these that a large group of the gentry, in a petition to Lord Strange, wrote that 'it appears by [sic] his Maty & both Houses of Parliament doe intend one and the same thinge, and doe declare to the world theire ends are the same'.[2]

The Cheshire gentry were not dependent on official propaganda, however. Fellow countrymen who for one reason or another were in London or else-where sent back reports to friends in the county. As early as December 1639 Thomas Cotton of Combermere was being told by a friend in Antwerp that there were rumours there that

as for the Parlament, some are as confident as others diffident that wee shall have one after Easter. And say one come, if it consist not of choyce men (that have God's glory & their K. or countries good for their chiefest scope) and be directed & blessed of God, things may prove rather worser than better. Our eye therefore must be up to God not down upon a Parlament.

This sense of foreboding was confirmed once Parliament was called. As a Lancashire gentleman, Peter Egerton, observed, too many members like Sir John Trevor were too bound up with their own interests and personal suits.[3]

A letter from Sir Francis Gamull, Long Parliament member for the city of Chester, to Sir Richard Grosvenor in May 1641 throws particularly interesting light on the times. He began with lengthy comments on the news he had heard from Cheshire (of the deaths of friends, on the progress of a

---

1 Chester City R. O., CR63/2/19, Bramhall MSS., ff. 81—4.
2 Bodl. Lib. Ashmole MS. 830, f. 282. See below, pp.60—2.
3 Chester City R. O., CR/72, Cotton of Combermere Papers (Box marked 'Letters C17th and C18th). The first letter also gives news of events in France, the Netherlands, and Germany.

dispute over fishing rights, and about a lawsuit over his Chester water mills), and then turned to national affairs and discussed the rumours of a plot against the Commons. After an aside criticizing the private morals of Cheshire M.P. Peter Venables (adding 'in delivering my scould from my hart farr bee itt from me to sett difference betwene man & wife'), he returned to state affairs, discussing the bill to remove the bishops' votes in the Lords, the bill to end High Commission and Star Chamber, the Commons' attack on the customs farmers, and the raising of money to pay off the Scots. He concluded with a paragraph about the fate of Cheshire petitions for and against episcopacy. Gamull was a Royalist hothead during the war, but his account of all this was quite dispassionate, the only time that his own feelings showed at all being when he gloomily wrote 'maney are more zealous against Bishops. I spare not to say they will destroy that order'.[1]

The Legh of Lyme papers contain two letters from 1642 which are equally detailed and equally moderate. Peter Legh, member for Newton in Lancashire (soon to be killed in a duel) described the attempt on the five members, the retreat of the Court, and the swift action taken by Parliament to deal with the new dangers. Although he expounded the proposed 'Heads of the grievances', the only real statement of his own opinion came when he wrote: 'the Kinge and wee are not so well united together as I could wish, but wee receved daylie gratious expressions of his mind and good intentions towards us wich makes us hope to see better times then now'.[2] A letter from Elias Ashmore to Francis Legh on 26 June 1642 perhaps deserves to be quoted at length.

The baron[3] ... is now joyfull to perceive some dawneing of a cleere understanding betwixt the King & Parliamt for yesterday the house fell into debate about the Kings answer to the 19 Proposicons made by

1 B.M. Harleian MS. 2081, f. 93.
2 J.Ry.L. Legh of Lyme MSS., Filing Box 53, unfoliated.
3 Peter Venables, Cheshire M.P., was always known as the 17th Baron of Kinderton. The origins of this title are obscure, though it is clear that it was simply an honorary title used in the county and was not based on any actual royal grant.

both houses (wch is amongst other bookes that he comanded me to inclose). In wch debate it appeared that there were many agt the other side, much afected to accomodacon & moderacon being infinitely troubled, that such things wch were propounded (& wch is by all confest to have byne heretofore sometymes denyed as well as yielded unto) should by the overpressing of them & standing too much upon them, be the occasion of any civill warr & therefore were thought fitter to be declyned. To those things wch the king is pleased to give noe answer too, a comitie is appointed to take consideracon of them & to back them wth as good arguments & presidents as may be produced but altogethr to declyne their former way of demanding them; when this vote had passed (in wch was included many othr thinges tending to accomodacon) Mr. Pym, Mr. Hollis, Mr. Stroude, Mr. Hampden & divers othr of that side went out of the house in a discontent before the speaker could reassume his chaire . . .[1]

Moderation, accommodation. These were to be the hall-marks of the bulk of the Cheshire gentry throughout these years. The only man busy stirring up enthusiasm for the King was Sir Thomas Aston who wrote to William Moreton in May 1641 with a wordy attack on Brereton's behaviour in Parliament. Since he was not connected to Moreton (he began his letter 'Though I have not had the good fortune to bee earlier knowne to you')[2] there is a distinct possibility that this is just one of many letters which Aston wrote to influential gentlemen to gain support for the Crown at a difficult time. But the political behaviour of the Cheshire M.P.s other than Brereton in Parliament represented the essential moderation of the views of the majority once the immediate problems which had united them in opposition in 1640 had been solved.

Peter Venables, returned behind Brereton to the Long Parliament, was one of the few associates of the barons' party in Cheshire who had been at all active in the 1630s, not so much by attendance at Sessions but by the amount of work he got through in his own hundred, Northwich.[3] In parlia-

---

1 J.Ry.L. Legh of Lyme MSS., Filing Box 53, unfoliated.
2 B.M. Add. MS. 33936, f. 232.
3 He attended eleven Sessions in the years 1635—40, but in the same period (according to a count of the documents signed by him in the files) he was the third most active Justice out of Sessions.

ment he played an inconspicuous role, serving on few committees and none of any real importance—the nearest being his appointment in August 1641 to a committee for the disarming of recusants.[1] Like all his fellow Cheshire M.P.s, his name is absent from the list of those who opposed the Attainder of Strafford,[2] and again like the other three, he was amongst those who signed the Protestation on 4 May 1641, the day of its appearance.[3] His attitude to the later great divisive votes such as the Grand Remonstrance is unknown, but he was not one of those who withdrew with the King on 10 January 1642. On 5 April 1642 he was amongst those named to ensure that the troops intended for Ireland were speedily transported there[4] and there is evidence that he was still attending the House in May.[5] He was not amongst those named Commissioners of Array by the King on 20 June, but he was back in Cheshire and in attendance by the time of the King's visit in September.

A similar course of action was adopted by Sir Thomas Smyth, the Chester member whose family was a classic example of the merchant turned landowner. He was a third-generation country gentleman and was fully accepted socially by the leading Cheshire squires, but he still retained important commercial interests and an aldermanic seat in the city of Chester. He sat on at least six Parliamentary Committees in the period up to June 1642, including two committees on religion (to deal with idolatry and superstition[6] and the profanation of the Sabbath).[7] In May 1642 he was appointed to the important 'Committee to consider the defence of the kingdom'.[8] In June his name was joined with Brereton's with responsibility to see that the Militia Ordinance was effectively obeyed in Cheshire,[9] and

[1] *Commons Journal*, vol. 2, p.267.
[2] Rushworth, *Historical Collections*, vol. 5, pp.248–9.
[3] *Commons Journal*, vol. 2, pp.132–3.
[4] B.M. Add. MS. 11333, f. 134.
[5] Ibid., f. 130.
[6] *Commons Journal*, vol. 2, p.84.
[7] Ibid., p.165.
[8] Ibid., p.589.
[9] Ibid., p.615.

Peter Venables's name is conspicuously missing; at the same time he voluntarily lent £100 for the service in Ireland.[1] Clearly his defection followed soon afterwards for he did not return to London with Brereton in September. In January 1644 he was amongst those who signed the letter from the Royalist Parliament at Oxford to the Earl of Essex.[2]

The other city M.P., Sir Francis Gamull, was a leading Chester merchant and monopolist. Though he had acquired estates in the county he was still essentially a city rather than county figure. As such he spent most of his time at Westminster fighting the city's causes (and trying to preserve his own monopolies). He sat on no committees; it is difficult to tell when he withdrew, but it must have been earlier than the other two since the King appointed him to be Commissioner of Array for the city of Chester on 27 June 1642.[3] On the other hand the moderation of his letter to Grosvenor of May 1641[4] might be taken as evidence that he was one of those seriously alienated from Parliament at the time of the Grand Remonstrance.

By contrast with these three, Sir William Brereton sat on over twenty Parliamentary Committees in the period up to June 1642. Several of these were unimportant: more significant were the committees on the bill for annual Parliaments, for the security of the true religion, and for the abolition of the Council in the Marches and several Committees on Irish affairs. When the subscription list for Ireland was opened in March 1642, Brereton was one of the first to invest, and his stake of £1,000 was one of the largest.[5]

Aston was at pains to point out Brereton's religious radicalism to county moderates; he even accused him of malpractice to achieve his end. His letter to Moreton tells the following tale: 'Sir Wm was Fayne to slip away a friend or

---

[1] Ibid., p.618.
[2] Rushworth, *Historical Collections,* vol. 6, p.573.
[3] Chester City R.O., Cowper MSS. vol. 2, f. 4.
[4] See pp.40—1.
[5] Rushworth, *Historical Collections,* vol. 5, pp.564—5.

tow when they went to vote it[1] then got the committee cald & there wanted one of the number to vote it, wch perceaved, some were soe playne to tell him he deservd to bee put out of the House.'[2] It was at this time also that the stories about Brereton's wife's behaviour at Neston church were being spread abroad.[3] As a result there seems to have been a marked reaction against him amongst the gentry. Thus John Werden speaks of having met 'one that loved Sir Wm Brereton well, but yet, as I doe, loves decency, order and good discipline better'.[4]

At a time when the gentry were worried about disobedience and unrest among the lower orders, Brereton's influence with the Puritans in the villages could take on sinister implications. Thus the following incident was reported as a dangerous as well as an amusing example of his influence:

On Sunday last one to whom I had given a copy of the king's letter did reade it at Tarvyn amongst divers precisians [Puritans] and very unhappily said it was directed to Sir William Brereton. They broke into a sudden blessinge both of God & the king wch they had noe sooner done but he shewed them it was directed to the Lords whereat these credulous men changed cheere and said they would not beleve but what it was counterfeit.[5]

Brereton was in an isolated position; the cultured, conscientious, popular gentleman of 1640 was now seen as a danger to the peace and security of the county. The bulk of the gentry were moderate in their views, looking for the compromise between King and Parliament that would allow the nation to settle back into peace and security.

Despite this, Brereton was able to exploit divisions within the county élite which emerged during a prolonged campaign of petitions and pamphlets concerning ecclesiastical reform. The protagonist was Sir Thomas Aston,[6] whose campaign to

---

[1] i.e. the petition sponsored by Sir Thomas Aston in favour of episcopacy.

[2] B.M. Add. MS. 33936, f. 232.

[3] See p.36.

[4] B.M. Add. MS. 36914, f. 215.

[5] Ibid., f. 211.

[6] Sir Thomas was probably the poorest of the Cheshire baronets, but was an improving landlord who had done much to raise the prestige of a local family which had never previously been prominent, even at a county level. He had served

save episcopacy was openly opposed by the Cheshire Puritans and hesitantly and partially rejected by men like Sir George Booth and Sir Richard Wilbraham.

The opening shot was fired when Aston presented a petition to Parliament in March 1641 purporting to represent the views of over 6,000 noblemen, gentry, clergy, and free-holders of Cheshire. It set the tone for the whole of Aston's campaign, a restrained defence of episcopacy combined with a vicious attack on the subversive nature of Puritanism.[1] The Puritan reply which was printed soon afterwards was probably composed in London and never seen in the county,[2] though it claimed 12,000 Cheshire signatures. At this point Aston committed a serious error: he produced a second petition and presented it to Parliament in the name of the county of Cheshire, but without sending it down there to be circulated amongst the gentry. Forty-eight leading gentlemen responded with an 'Attestation' in which they rebuked Sir Thomas for his temerity, but also specifically dissociated themselves from the Puritan petition.[3] The situation was complicated yet further when forty-three leading gentry wrote an open letter to Aston in which they told him that 'wee have not onlie thought fitt with these few subscribers ... to testify yor greate care and diligence for your countrey and our approbation thereof, but to pray you not to be discouraged herein but still to presse as there shall be an opportunity'.[4]

The situation is immediately clarified if we examine the separate groups of signatures on this letter and on the Attestation. The list of Aston's supporters is headed by Lords

---

as an officer in the Thirty Years War and held a minor office in the Royal Household, as a Privy Chamberman. (See 'The Journal of John Aston, 1639', printed in 'North Country Diaries', *Surtees Society*, 118(1910). John Aston was Sir Thomas's brother).

[1] For an exposition of his views, see below, pp.49—51.
[2] See below, p.51.
[3] The original petition is in *C.S.P.D.* 1640—1, p.528; the Puritan reply is ibid., p.529. Aston's second petition is in the Aston MSS., B.M. Add. MS. 36913, f. 62; the Attestation ibid., ff. 63—4.
[4] B.M. Add. MS. 36914, ff. 222—3. ff. 224—5 is another letter of support.

Cholmondeley and Kilmorrey (the 'Barons'), Sir Edward Fytton, and Thomas Brereton of Malpas, while his leading opponents turn out to be Sir George Booth, Sir Richard Wilbraham, and Sir Thomas Delves (the 'Baronets'). The divisions appear to be the same as those that had existed at the time of the elections to the Short Parliament, and the central issue once again is the struggle for local pre-eminence.

This point is clearly established by the manoeuvrings in the county that followed Aston's original decision to petition Parliament on behalf of episcopacy. A rough draft of the petition had been drawn up by him, in consultation with Lord Cholmondeley, Lord Kilmorrey, Thomas Brereton, and Thomas Cotton of Combermere, and had been circulated amongst their friends and tenants. But since it was felt that 'wheere publique interest was, all private respects would be set apart', it was decided to approach Sir Richard Wilbraham to see whether his party would support the petition. Wilbraham, however, was 'pleased to take many exceptions to what had bin with the assistance of very good advice rough drawne'. None-the-less, he agreed to call a meeting of his friends to discuss the matter further, and 'Lord Cholmondeley sent a gentlemen along ... purposely to signify that it pleased him to send to those gentlemen'. It was hoped that this might lead to a joint meeting of both groups, but 'truly a generall meeting then had as many obstacles in it as before the meeting'. After a final vain attempt to get Sir George Booth to endorse it, the petition was sent off to London and received a mixed response from the Houses.[1]

The situation was now altered by developments in London, for this was the time of Strafford's Attainder and execution, which marked the first significant shift of opinion in favour of the King. William Davenport, who had for thirty years carefully noted down every available piece of Court scandal and Country propaganda in his commonplace book, now copied down Strafford's speech from the scaffold and henceforth showed more interest in statements issued by the

[1] B.M. Add. MS. 36913, ff. 65–6. This is a letter from Aston to one of Wilbraham's supporters, justifying the proceedings of the 'Barons' ' party.

King then in those of the Parliament.[1] It was later alleged
that the first delinquency of Lord Rivers was to denounce
the execution of Strafford,[2] and Aston himself went to visit
the Earl in the Tower shortly before his death, though
ostensibly about a debt.[3] Shortly afterwards we learn that
Aston had been approached by the Court and had agreed to
draw up a fresh petition on behalf of the bishops, which was
to be sent down to Cheshire with a royal letter of commend-
ation. Aston entrusted John Werden with the task of
organizing this campaign in the county itself,[4] and he was
soon writing back to Sir Thomas and describing the response
of the county leaders to this fresh development. The Judges
at Chester had declared the petition 'a prop to theire
ffidelityes & orthodox professions of the religion established', but the covering letter met with far greater
enthusiasm:

I have noe abylityes to expres the ioy of the most honourable Earle [of
Derby] to whom I delivered his Majesties Grace and from him I have
transmytted it to the other Lords, of whom I am able to say
(pertyculary for my Lord Cholmeley) he hath a Jubilee of ioy.

Once again, after he had gained a favourable response from
all those who had signed the earlier petition, Werden turned
his attention to the Booth–Wilbraham group. But Sir
Richard could hardly be expected to change his mind about a
set of proposals which had always troubled him and which
were now being advanced in so partisan a fashion. Werden
had said that his endorsement would 'prove a reconcyler and
gayn myriad more hands'. But Wilbraham's refusal meant
that this petition, like the former one, had to be sent up to
London without the clear mandate of the whole county
establishment.[5]

[1] Chester City R.O., CR63/2/19, f. 86.
[2] C.R.O., Cholmondeley MSS., DCH/X/15/4.
[3] *Commons Journal*, vol. 4, p.176.
[4] B.M. Add. MS. 36914, f. 216.
[5] This account is based on B.M. Add. MS. 36914, ff. 214–16, 220. The petition
could be either that printed in B.M. Thomason Tracts 669, f. 4 (8), or the
undated petition in B.M. Add. MS. 36913, f. 55.

From this time on, Aston and his large body of supporters developed their link with the Court of Charles I. In the summer of 1642 all the leading figures in this group were appointed Commissioners of Array, and Aston himself was employed by Charles as a personal emissary to Parliament.[1] Meanwhile, in November 1641, Aston produced a two-hundred-page tract *A Remonstrance Against Presbytery*,[2] which was answered by the Cheshire Puritans,[3] and the early months of 1642 saw a fresh exchange between the two sides, this time over the compulsory use of the Book of Common Prayer.[4]

There is a remarkable consistency in Aston's position throughout his writings. His defence of episcopacy as an institution is studiedly moderate. He rejected Arminian views and Laudian innovations. He freely cited Calvin, Bucer, Melancthon, and other reformers in his discussion of the nature of the church.

To us the suppressing of Poperie, the increase of able pastors, the removing of innovations will be equally acceptable as to other subjects; only we conceived our modest submissions to the judgment of that great counsell [i.e. Parliament] to regulate the rigour of ecclesiastical courts to suit with the temper of our lawes and the nature of free men, would to so grave a Senate administer as much matter as serious consideration, implie as much need of Reformation as a large invective full of bitter reviling which might more convicte us of want of charitie than the Bishops of moderation.[5]

This comes from his fullest treatment of the problem in the *Remonstrance Against Presbytery*. But the same views were expressed in the original petition where the need for some reforms was admitted and where arguments for the divine institution of bishops were adduced from the Bible and the history of Christianity.[6] But just as important for him was the need for a hierarchical structure in church and state, which he saw as being undermined by Presbyterianism.

---

[1] B.M. Add. MS. 36913, f. 92.
[2] I have used the copy in Chester City Library.
[3] B.M. Thomason Tracts E 178 (4).
[4] Ibid. 669, f. 4 (74); ibid. E 148 (12); B.M. Add. MS. 36913, f. 136.
[5] *Remonstrance Against Presbytery*, Preface.
[6] *C.S.P.D.*, 1640–1, p.528.

He fully drew out the social implications of Puritanism: in his self-justification, written after the Puritan rejoinder to his initial petition, he attacked those who proselytized their views amongst 'all the vulgar people & many others whoe cannot well imagin soe bold a presumption . . . to father such a bastard upon the county'.[1] In the Remonstrance he treated the theme at length.

Let us then ere wee imbrace the thoughts of such a totall subversion of the Fabrick of a Church and State examine whether such Reformers aime at our liberty or their owne advancement . . . is it not really to pull downe 26 bishops or set up 9324 potentiall Popes?[2]

His fears of the dangers inherent in Presbyterianism extend far beyond that of ecclesiastical jurisdiction:

freedome of their consciences and persons is not enough, but they must have their purses and estates free too . . . Nay they go higher, even to the denyall of the right to proprietie in our estates. They would pay no fines, do no boons no; duties to their landlords or at best bring them within the arbitrarie jurisdiction of the Presbyter who must be chancelour betwixt Lord and Tenant.[3]

His vision of the social consequences of root-and-branch reform was brilliantly caught in the following passage:

I consider the Nobilitie and Gentrie of this Isle (this nurserie of honour) situate as the Low Countries in a flat, under the banks and bounds of the Lawes, secured from the inundations of that Ocean, the Vulgar, which by the breach of those bounds would quickly over-whelme us, and deface all distinctions of degrees or persons: and cannot but with admiration observe that Sampson like in their full strength (but as blind with inconsiderate zeale, as he by treacherie) any such should lay hold on those pillars of our state that prop up the regulated fabrick of this glorious monarchy, and by cracking them, wilfully burie themselves and us in the rubbish of chaos, wch they so pull upon their owne heads seeking to turne our freedome into fetters by can-celling our ancient lawes (the Charters of true liberty) and exposing us eternall apprentices to the arbitrarie jurisdiction of a new corporation of apron elders, mechanick artisans; as if they had forgotten the old Rule, *Haec natura multitudinis humiliter servit, aut superbe dominatur.*[4]

Such an outburst was not irrational. Aston was perfectly aware of the views of men like Samuel Eaton,[5] and of the contents of Puritan petitions from the county. As he

---

[1] B.M. Add. MS. 36913, f. 62.   [2] *Remonstrance Against Presbytery*, section A5.
[3] Ibid., section A8.       [4] Ibid., section A13.        [5] Ibid., section A9.

correctly pointed out, Cheshire Puritans based their case on 'the manifold unsupportable burdens wherewith our consciences and estates have been long oppressed', in particular 'the usurping prelates, their lawlesse dependent officers and their irregular manner of worshipping God prescribed unto and cruelly imposed upon us by them'. He also noted their complaints against lay impropriations and the ruination of men's estates in lawsuits 'unnecessarily detained in civil courts'.[1]

Finally, he laid stress on the imminent breakdown in public order, already taking place in the face of Parliament's vacillation. This point was underlined by his supporters when they wrote to him about

divers outrages ... [including] pullinge downe the rayles in one of the most publike churches ... at the noone daie wch have caused muche effusion of blood; besides the practises of other innovators ... to the greate griefe and discouragement of his Majesties moderate and well affected subjects.[2]

It is unclear precisely what those opponents of Aston who signed the Attestation stood for. They went out of their way to dissociate themselves from the radicals, calling the Puritan petition for the abolition of episcopacy 'a late printed libell in answeare to [Aston's] former petition which wee disclayme as ever approved or seene in this county till the presse made it common'. They gratuitously mentioned that Aston's original petition 'found the good approbation of the House of Lords.[3] We have seen that Wilbraham took exception to part of that petition,[4] but Aston was convinced that the Attesters' dissent was only about details. He noted that 'most of the subscribers of this Attestation did desire the

---

[1] From the petition in the Epistle Dedicatorie to the *Remonstrance*.
[2] B.M. Add. MS. 36914, ff. 224—5.
[3] B.M. Add. MS. 36913, ff. 63—4. Further doubts are cast on the authenticity of the Puritan petition by the supposed number of signatures. There just were not eight Cheshire peers or 140 ministers as the petition claimed. In every case the number of signatories of each social group in Aston's petition had simply been doubled.
[4] See above, p.47.

contents of my petition, though perhaps in other words'.[1]

Thus we are forced back on the view that the divisions within the ruling group were essentially personal ones, concerned simply about precedence in county affairs. The hallmark of the Attestation is the claim that 'wee whoe in respect of our interests hold ourselves to be a considerable part of this shire, doe utterly dislike that any one man should take soe much power upon himselfe without publique trust & appoyntment to use the name of the county'. Certainly there is no evidence that *at this point* the Booth–Wilbraham party were interested in seeing the destruction or emasculation of the existing system of church government.[2]

The existence of separate lists of gentry supporters for the Aston-Cholmondeley and Booth–Wilbraham groups affords important evidence of the weakness of militant Puritanism amongst the Cheshire gentry. A comparison of these lists with a further list of all those involved in county affairs in the 1630s (appointments to the Commission of the Peace, as deputy lieutenants, etc.) reveals that only five families out of over seventy did not take part in the dispute: Brooke of Norton, Crewe of Utkinton, Duckenfield of Duckenfield, Hyde of Norbury, and Brereton of Handforth. Significantly these five were amongst the handful of gentry families who can be clearly shown to have been Puritans in the 1630s. Furthermore, together with the Bradshaws of Marple, Jonathan Bruen of Stapleford, and John Legh of Booths, they were to be the leaders of a militant faction within the Parliamentarian movement in Cheshire during the Civil War under the leadership of Sir William Brereton.[3]

What scraps of circumstantial evidence have survived also suggest that these men were the leaders of the campaign

---

[1] There is a second copy of the Attestation in the Aston Papers, B.M. Add. MS. 36913, ff. 67–81, covered with Aston's remarks. These dwell on the theme that the attack on him is unwise at a time when sectaries threaten the very bases of order.

[2] See below, pp.270–1.

[3] See below, chapter 4 *passim;* the other families with extensive estates not included in either list are all recusants—Savage of Clifton, Massey of Puddington, Stanley of Hooton.

against episcopacy. Authorship of one Puritan petition is ascribed specifically to Calvin Bruen, and John Werden clearly implied that the initiative had come from the city of Chester rather than the county.[1] As far as possible, both other gentry groups tried to make out that no one of any significance was involved.[2] But at one point Werden reported that the Puritans had found a loophole in Aston's case. They had discovered that agents of Lord Cholmondeley and Sir Henry Bunbury had 'signed all or most of the wholle of the inhabitants & tenants of Stanney's names without their pryvity to the petition'. This news had been communicated to Sir William Brereton in London and he had sent back an express to John Crewe of Utkinton which, according to Werden, was intended 'to helpe to speede those certificates wch must discredit our petition or they were at a foule losse'.[3]

We also know that at about this time Robert Duckenfield began to sponsor Samuel Eaton, the strident Congregationalist, and in the early months of 1643 installed him in a specially created chapel at Duckenfield. There thus seems little room to doubt that a strong radical group was forming at this time which was to become the nucleus of one faction during the ensuing wars.

Similarly, Aston's shift in the spring of 1641 into open friendship with the Court was to commit a much larger section of the Cheshire gentry to future Royalism. Already a stable interest in county affairs at the time of the 1640 elections, this group remained remarkably stable throughout the war years. Of the forty-three known supporters, there was to be only one significant desertion to Parliament in 1642, Henry Mainwaring of Kermincham.

The other main group—comprising those who had signed the Attestation, was eventually to divide against itself, sixteen of its leaders becoming Royalists, twenty-five Parliamentarians. But before they divided, they were to

[1] B.M. Add. MS. 36914, ff. 214–15.
[2] Ibid., ff. 205, 212.
[3] Ibid., ff. 210, 211.

spend eighteen months desperately seeking to prevent the
deepening of divisions within the county, trying to halt the
gradual breakdown of civil administration and public order,
and discountenancing all the evidence from London and
elsewhere of the drift into civil war. Two further signed
petitions in the winter of 1641—2 reveal that the strength of
this group was increasing rather than diminishing. The first
concerned the mutinous and violent behaviour of troops
passing through Cheshire bound for Ireland. The petitioners
wanted clearer general instructions and orders to be issued,
and the Cheshire Justices to have wider supervisory powers.[1]
On this occasion Brereton made it his duty to support the
'Baronets' in the House of Commons, and measures were
taken in hand in accordance with the petitioners' demands.

The second petition was a response to rumours that the
King intended to cross to Ireland to take charge of the
suppression of the rebellion there. Parliament assumed that
his plan was to make peace there and then cross to England
with a large field army to reassert his authority. Under the
circumstances    the    Cheshire    petition    was    remarkably
moderate: it gave three reasons why he should desist from
the venture, the first being that 'you expose us [to danger]
by the popish faction when yor Matie shall leave us naked,
we not being putt into a posture of defence to repell the rage
and attempts of the enemies to our religion'; the second that
it would 'deprive us at once of that poore remaynder of our
hope we have to reape further good by the indeavors of yor
Parliament; whereof we shall dispaire when yor presence shal
be wanting to perfecte ther proposalls and conclusions'. The
final reason was that he should heed the example of King
David who had been persuaded by the pleas of his people not
to lead his army against the rebels.[2]

[1] B.M. Add. MS. 11333, f. 130.
[2] The text of this petition is in B.M. Thomason Tracts E 148(12). The text I
have used here (which also contains the signatures of fifty-three gentlemen,
fifteen ministers, and an Inquest Jury of twenty-nine minor gentlemen) is in B.M.
Add. MS. 36913, f. 60.

The King's reply revealed that he was aware that those who had signed the petition were not linked with the interests of Parliament:

His Majestie observes very well, that this Petition is not like others which by an untimely zeal, have desired Him to return to His Parliament; you onely desiring Him there to reside, where with more conveniency and security He may consult with His great Councell, then by going into Ireland.

He also spoke of the 'former good expressions you made of your Loyalty and right-set affections to the good of the whole kingdom' and ordered them to petition Parliament 'to apply themselves to a right understanding of His Majesties wayes and intentions'.[1]

If we look at the signatures to these petitions, we find that all those who signed the Attestations were still there, but that there had been an erosion of support from amongst the lesser gentry in the Cholmondeley group, and about a dozen were (temporarily) supporting the stand taken by Booth and Wilbraham. None the less, not one of the leaders of the 'Court' group, Cholmondeley, Kilmorey, (Lord) Brereton, Aston, Fytton, was among the defectors.

That the Booth—Wilbraham group was distinct from those already committed to Parliament's reform programme is clear from the existence of another petition of this period. This was issued in the names of 'the esquires, gentlemen, ministers, freeholders and others' of the county (i.e. neither the barons nor the baronets); it began with a warm appreciation of Parliament's actions, and called for further measures along the same lines. In particular, episcopal and Dean and Chapter lands should be used to augment the pay of the clergy and a systematic attempt should be made to overhaul legal procedures and to reduce the fees charged by the courts.[2]

---

[1] B.M. Thomason Tracts 669, f. 5(18). The text of both the petitions and reply are contained in a single pamphlet in Chester City Library (Pamphlet Collection), item 71. This collection contains most of the pamphlets cited here as also in the Thomason Collection.
[2] B.M. Thomason Tracts E 148 (12).

In the months from June to October 1642 the positions of all these groups hardened. When the King was at York in June, Aston and Rivers went across from Cheshire, returning shortly afterwards with a Commission of Array containing seventeen names. All of these had supported Aston against the Attestation, though two of them had crossed over to support Booth and Wilbraham in their petitions earlier in 1642. Shortly afterwards there arrived a list of those whose houses were to be searched because they had executed Parliament's Militia Ordinance; those named hardly formed a distinguished group, and they included only two men who had ever openly supported any of the Booth—Wilbraham petitions; several of the remainder were later to be close associates of Brereton.[1] A majority of the leading gentry, including almost every active Justice of the 1630s, had been ignored by both King and Parliament.

One of the most valuable services that Professor Everitt has provided for the understanding of this period has been his development of the view that 'for [the county communities] bounded as they so often were by local horizons, a more urgent problem was the conflict between loyalty to the nation and loyalty to the county community. This division cut across the conventional divisions like a geological fault'.[2]

The effect of this was a marked reluctance of all but a minority of the gentry to become involved in the war. Dr. Manning devoted a substantial section of his unpublished thesis to a study of the attempts made by Royalists and Parliamentarians in various local communities to opt out of the general conflict by local neutrality agreements.[3] Professor Everitt has shown this mentality at work in Kent and Leicestershire, and demonstrated why it did not exist in

---

[1] Commissioners of Array, B.M. Add. MS. 36913, f. 122, Militia Commissioners, ibid., f. 103.
[2] A.M. Everitt 'The Local Community and the Great Rebellion', *H.A.P.* G 70 (1969), p.8. See also his 'Change in the Provinces 1603—60' *Leicester University Occasional Papers in Local History,* 2nd ser., no.1, 1969.
[3] B.S. Manning, 'Neutrals and Neutralism in the English Civil War', Univ. of Oxford D.Phil. thesis, 1957.

Suffolk.[1] But this kind of neutralism is quite different in character from that attempted by Sir Richard Wilbraham, Sir George Booth and their supporters in the summer of 1642: the armed intervention of the county against the forces of both King and Parliament. A similar movement certainly existed in Staffordshire,[2] and probably also elsewhere,[3] but nowhere does the evidence appear so clearly as in Cheshire.

As tension mounted throughout the country and the struggle for control of the militia built up, Lord Strange's attack on Manchester and the arrival of Sir William Brereton with significantly wide powers[4] precipitated the crisis in the county. In both the Aston Papers and the Portland Manuscripts a feeling of growing anarchy can be sensed, but the attempts of the middle group to prevent violence are first recorded in the war diary of Thomas Malbon. He relates how confrontations between trained bands, some obeying royal and others parliamentary warrants, took place at Stockport and Northwich in early August. In both cases he records that 'some gentlemen who desired peace' persuaded them to draw apart.[5] In 1654 John Bretland of Thorncliffe, in an appeal against sequestration, made the interesting claim that in the summer of 1642 he was sent by Sir George Booth to Adlington Hall, where Thomas Leigh was raising forces for the King, in an attempt to persuade Leigh either to disband or to use his troops to suppress forces raised by either side.[6]

The ideas behind these attempts at pacification are best expressed in two petitions of the period. One took the form of a letter to Lord Strange. It began with a detailed examin-

[1] A.M. Everitt, *The Community of Kent and the Great Rebellion,* Leicester, 1965, pp.95–110; also 'The Local Community and the Great Rebellion', pp.10–13; also 'Suffolk and the Great Rebellion', *Suffolk Record Society,* 3(1960), xli.

[2] D.H. Pennington, 'County and Country: Staffordshire in Civil War Politics', *N. Staffordshire Journal of Field Studies,* 6 (1966).

[3] e.g. R.W. Ketton-Kremer, *Norfolk in the Civil War,* London, 1969, pp.137–8, 150–1. The author tries to interpret material that appears to point to the existence of neutralism in terms of lukewarm Royalism.

[4] *Lords Journal,* vol. 5, p.134.

[5] Malbon, 'Memorials of the Civil War in Cheshire', *Lancashire and Cheshire Record Society,* 19(1889), 24. See also Chester City R.O., Cowper MS. 2, f. 6.

[6] P.R.O., SP 23, vol. 149, f. 143.

ation of the general political situation, an examination which was hopelessly inadequate. By quoting the printed statements put out by Court and Parliament, the writers concluded with the hope that 'some moderate persons may be imployed betweene his Majesty and the saide houses of parliamt for the state of the question and cleeringe of the points in difference betweene his Majesty and the said twoe houses of Parliamt'. In the meantime the petitioners called for a 'cessacon of Armes upon both sides'.[1] As an adjunct to this petition, and as a sign of their firmer grasp of the reality of local politics, they made seven suggestions to ensure that Cheshire remained at peace. The Commission of Array and the Militia Ordinance were to be suspended in the county and the militia was to be controlled by the Justices (since they were most experienced in dealing with breaches of the peace). They went on to assert their right to prevent any 'amunicon or forces wtsoever' from entering the county, their right to escort 'any caridge for the household either of K: or P:' and their right to use force against anyone who contrived damage to another's house or property. Finally, they suggested that there should be an amnesty for all 'delinquents of either party'. The key sentence is: 'The whole county shall rise against them which are enemies against the peace.'[2]

In the middle of August a petition was sent up to Parliament with 8,376 signatures, which have all survived.[3] It called for joint action by King and Parliament and condemned all those who sought to distinguish their powers. Loyalty consisted in cordial affection to the sovereign and Parliament, for they 'being like Hypocrates twinns, they must laugh and crye, live and dye together, & both of them are so rooted in our loyall harts that wee cannot disioynt them'. The conclusion summarized this attitude of pure neutralism, and suggests a fear of the breakdown of order which partly underlay it:

we . . . declare and professe ourselves enemys to all those (whoever they bee) that shall bee discovered to be agents in makinge our wounds

---

[1] Bodl. Lib. Ashmole MS. 830, f. 282.      [2] Ibid.      [3] B.M. Harleian MS 2107.

deeper by fosteringe & fomentinge the unfortunate mistakes and fearfull jealousies betwixt head and body, his Majestie and his Parliament: and wch . . . doe thretten the dissolucion of the Fabrick of this blessed Government.

The petition was signed on a parish-by-parish basis, but one folio contains the names of the leading sponsors. It begins 'Sir George Booth, Sir Richard Wilbraham, Sir Thomas Delves, Henry Delves, Philip Mainwaring, William Marbury . . .'[1] and it is a roll-call of the centre group; as the list develops, it is clear that this group was still basically undiminished from its original strength at the time of the Attestation and still contained over one-third who were soon to become Royalists[2] It is in fact interesting that this petition was drawn up on a parochial basis, with the minister writing up the names of those who could only make a mark; the Aston petition in favour of episcopacy was drawn up on a manorial basis.[3] It is thus possible that although a majority of the ministers were eventually to be ejected or sequestered as Royalists, they had lent little support to Aston's campaign to defend the bishops.

Although the centre party was still unbroken in the middle of August, it became increasingly difficult for it to hold its position. Despite its strong words, it never did make any serious attempt to gain control of the militia, and without means of backing up its aims its attempts at local conciliation became increasingly unrealistic. It would appear that the polarization of the centre occurred at the time of the King's visit to Cheshire at the end of September. He summoned the leaders of the neutrals before him, and carried five of them comfortably but involuntarily away in his train to Shrewsbury. The five included Sir Richard Wilbraham, Sir Thomas Delves, and Philip Mainwaring,[4] and the fact that they had answered his summons seems to indicate that they had not yet thrown in their lot with the Parliament. How-

[1] Ibid., f. 6.

[2] A similar attempt at neutrality appears to have been made in the city of Chester; see B.M. Thomason Tracts 669, f. 6(55).

[3] See B.M. Add. MS. 36914, ff. 210–11.

[4] Malbon, loc. cit., pp.25–6.

ever, this was the moment of Sir George Booth's defection to Parliament, since he refused to attend the King's summons. With many of their leaders gone, the centre collapsed. They even lost control of Quarter Sessions. From the beginning of 1641 the Barons, aware of the political role that Sessions could assume, began to attend with their supporters: but it was not until October 1642 that the moderates ceased to have a majority on the Bench. In the last two Sessions before the outbreak of civil war, the Royalists took charge. In January 1643 Sessions were held in the city of Chester, which was already a Royalist garrison, and only the King's supporters were summoned. Thomas Piggot, head constable of Macclesfield hundred, which already lay under the control of Parliamentarian troops, wrote: 'I am informed . . . that the Quarter Sessions is houlden tomorowe at Chester which is a thing unknowne on our syde, & the counterie, [sic] theare being noe notis as yeat given neither in church nor market.'[1]

It is impossible to say with any certainty what determined the choice of sides made by each member of the centre party, but the correspondence between them and Lord Strange in the last weeks before the polarization took place gives some indication of the local factors involved. For on 6 September the moderates met together, in what they termed an 'association at Knutsford', to study a reply to a letter they had sent to Lord Strange. In this letter they had complained that

the countrey is putt in feare not onely by severall meetings of the Commissioners of Array for this County amongst themselves but alsoe wth Comrs of other Countys adiacent, And that some of them have given out threatenings and desparate language, that they would plunder, batter downe, burne the houses and disarme the persons of all such as complie not wth them in their way, thoughe otherwise have taken the protestacon to be aideing to king and Parliament . . . all wch speeches and undertakeings, wee conceive to bee expressely contrary to his Matys frequent declaracons for the maintainance of the right and property of the subject.

They then pledged themselves to oppose all such violence 'with all our strength and force'.[2] Strange replied in a most

---

[1] C.R.O., Quarter Sessions File 1642, no.4, f. 27.
[2] B.M. Harleian MS. 2095, f. 254; see also 2135, f. 100.

conciliatory way, not denying the charges against the Commissioners, but saying: 'I assure you there is noe such direccon or consent of myne, But contrariwise I shall send unto them to beware thereof, wth this declaration, that if they doe contrarie to my owne request unto them, I will take part with others against them.'[1] This letter was addressed to Richard Brereton (of Ashley) and Hugh Wilbraham. Both had supported Sir George Booth and Sir Richard Wilbraham throughout the war of petitions; both were subsequently to be Royalists.

The central preoccupation of this exchange of letters was once again the threat to the ordered pattern of county life. There was no questioning of the Commissioners' legality, no reference to Parliament's condemnation of the Array; it was the departure from usual local procedures and the fear of violence that lay behind this appeal to Strange. His reply was probably quite genuine. It had taken him a long time to declare for the King, and, shortly after this exchange of correspondence, he was actively involved in promoting a neutrality pact between his Royalist friends and the Parliamentary party in Lancashire.[2] It is therefore quite likely that he too was troubled by the proceedings of the Commissioners of Array.

It is difficult to say to what extent the charges made against the Commissioners of Array were true. The most frequent and serious charges were that they had sacked the houses and arbitrarily arrested the persons of their opponents, and that their actions had provoked the common people into widespread rioting. As early as August Parliament was sending out a stream of statements attacking the behaviour of the Cheshire Commissioners, and these statements were either printed or ordered to be read from the pulpits. They were based on reports sent back by Sir William Brereton during his visit to the county in July and August.

[1] Ibid. 2095, f. 254; see also 2135, f. 89.
[2] See particularly, 'Farrington Papers', *Chetham Society*, O.S. 39(1856), 80–5, 'Lancashire Lieutenancy Papers, vol. ii,' ibid. 50(1859), 282–7, and 'Stanley Papers, part III', ibid. 66(1865), lxix.

He wrote at least three letters, to the Speaker, to Oliver Cromwell, and to Lancashire member Raphe Assheton.[1] In his letter to Cromwell he reported that at least four ministers had been imprisoned without trial for their refusal to 'publish such books, warrants and commands in their churches as they have sent unto them'. The Commissioners had also committed Thomas Bennet, constable of Willaston, to prison, and Brereton had applied for a writ of habeas corpus on his behalf. In an enclosure, Bennet revealed that he had simply failed to turn up in response to a warrant from the Commissioners of Array.[2] A few days after Parliament's condemnation of these actions, it issued a declaration to be read in every church and market-place warning the people 'lest they, being deceived by the specious pretences made by the said Lord Strange, should assist him with Men, Money, Munitions or any other Provision, and so make themselves guilty of the like treason'.[3] A further Parliamentary decree elaborated the charge of illegal imprisonment, and also asserted that the Commissioners had 'imposed great taxes upon the country, fining, imprisoning and disarming the inhabitants thereof, who would not submit to their illegal commands'.[4]

It was only by the pamphleteers that charges of looting were made.[5] But even there, no claim of absolute licence by the troops was asserted. Thus we are told by 'W.R.' that 'they took arms from Crew Hall for 20 men but did no other violence; Sir Thomas Delves left his house empty, and much arms on the hall table for them; They dealt more hardly at Mr. Vernons, taking many other things besides arms'.[6]

---

[1] H.M.C. *Portland MSS.* vol. 1, pp.44—6, 51—3.
[2] Parliament's response was a resolution declaring that anyone who obeyed or issued such a warrant was 'an enemy to the Commonwealth and disturber of the peace of the kingdom'. Rushworth, *Historical Collections*, vol. 5, pp.687—8. See also B.M. Thomason Tracts E 116(18).
[3] *Lords Journal*, vol. 5, p.358.
[4] *Commons Journal*, vol. 2, p.866.
[5] 'Tracts Relating to Cheshire During the Civil Wars', *Chetham Society*, 2nd ser., vol. 65, pp.63—4.
[6] Ibid., p.62.

Certainly the Commissioners of Array were instructed to search houses, but it was made perfectly clear that they were to be 'very careful to avoyed any spoyl of our subiects goods *in case there be noe resistance*'.[1] None the less they were impowered to 'take the aide and assistance (in case of opposicon) of such of our troopes as are in those partes'.[2]

Throughout his correspondence with the Cheshire Commissioners, Charles I seemed determined to restrain their zeal. In reply to a query from them in July, Endymion Porter on behalf of the King wrote that his Majesty 'thinkes much fitter that spetiall and severe prosecution bee made at the assizes against the persons you name than to send for them by a messenger hyther, which as it is not soe legall, soe it is not soe advantagious to his service'. He also instructed them 'where the gentry are soe well affected, the iustices of peace bind not over or comitt all those loose persons eather preachers or others against whom just exception can be taken'.

Thus, for example, 'incalcitrant' constables were not to be replaced until the Assizes and then by the Justices, not by the Commissioners of Array.[3] Even judged by their own reports, the Commissioners of Array clearly ignored some of the instructions of the Court. Thus at a meeting at Warrington they decided that 'such of the said freehold & trayned forces as shall refuse to come to the rendezvous & absent themselves shall bee . . . held as enemies to their Kinge & countrey'.[4]

On balance, then, it is quite possible that the behaviour of the Commissioners of Array was viewed with alarm by those moderates whose primary aim was to lower the temperature in the county. Misgivings might have been increased by side issues. Thus a primary objective of the Commissioners was to

[1] B.M. Add. MS. 36913, f. 103. (my italics).
[2] Ibid.
[3] See B.M. Add. MS. 11332, f. 122. For instructions in the following months which are just as cautionary, see B.M. Add. MS. 36913, ff. 98—9, B.M. Harleian MS 2173, f. 8.
[4] C.R.O., Cowper MS. DCC/47/42.

disarm those who did not openly support them, yet the Lancashire Catholics had successfully requested the King that 'we may be received into your most gracious Protection from violence, [and] have our arms which have been taken from us, redelivered in this time of actual war'.[1] The behaviour of the King's field army while he was in Cheshire was not encouraging. It was most unwise of him to allow the wilful destruction of Brereton's duck decoy, unpopular though it had been; this incident was viewed by the moderates as an unfortunate exercise of arbitrary power.[2] The Commissioners of Array were also accused of being unable to control their troops. After the gentlemen's mediation between the two sides near Northwich in August, it was reported that the Royalists behaved boisterously in the neighbouring villages while the Parliamentarians departed peacefully.[3] Early in 1643 Aston confessed that he had not always been able to prevent his troops from plundering.[4]

The atmosphere of tension bred fresh dangers and lawlessness. For example, a complaint to Quarter Sessions stated that a group of men 'pretending that they had a commission to search yor peticoner's house for armes did violently, riotiously, and forcibly breake downe a doore ... and rifled all his coffers, cupboard and roomes'.[5] There are several such incidents of thieves taking advantage of the times.

The Parliamentarians had not been standing idly by however.[6] Even before the King's visit, Brereton had been exercising some of the militia, volunteers had been raised in the north-east of the county, Brereton had made an

[1] Chester City R.O., Cowper MS. 2, f. 14.

[2] 'Civil War Tracts of Cheshire' (loc. cit.), p.74.

[3] Malbon, op. cit., pp.24–5.

[4] B.M. Harleian MS. 2128, f. 54. For the extreme sensitivity of the county about the dangers of unruliness amongst troops, see the following which refer to the passage of troops through the county to Ireland in the early months of 1642: B.M. Add. MS. 11333, ff. 130–4, C.R.O., Cowper MSS. DCC/47/24,26 and DCC/14/29, 56–7, and H.M.C. Portland MSS., vol. 1, pp.32–3.

[5] C.R.O. Quarter Sessions Order Book 9a, f. 86.

[6] The events of the last months of 1642 are covered by R.N. Dore, The Civil Wars in Cheshire, pp.14–15.

ignominious attempt to win over the support of the citizens of Chester (and had been thrown out),[1] and Nantwich had been garrisoned. But their behaviour was moderate in comparison with that of the Royalists. Partly this was the result of their lack of strength; they still possessed the support of only a handful of gentlemen. Though a commission had arrived for the arrest of the leading Royalists,[2] Brereton admitted that he was incapable of carrying it out.[3] The departure of the King transformed the situation; he took with him two regiments under Earl Rivers and Sir Edward Fytton, three troops of horse under Sir Thomas Aston, and a strong contingent of gentlemen and common soldiers for his lifeguard. All were to fight at Edge-hill,[4] but less than half were to return to the county. At the same time the gentry of the middle group took sides, and the majority joined Parliament.[5] They swiftly started to raise troops, and by the beginning of December the two sides were roughly equal in strength, the Royalists having secured themselves in Chester, by guile it was said,[6] and the Parliamentarians having retaken Nantwich, lost by a trick during the King's visit.[7]

It is clear that when the centre party broke up in the last months of 1642, it did so reluctantly, and in the main its members remained determined to contain the war (at least in Cheshire) while the field armies of King and Parliament decided the issues between them elsewhere. This was the reasoning behind the neutrality pact made between the two sides in the county in December which received the full support of men like Sir George Booth.[8] But when, in the last

---

[1] See particularly, B.M. Harleian MS. 2155, f. 108.
[2] B.M. Add. MS. 36913, f. 88.
[3] H.M.C. *Portland MSS.*, vol. 1, p.45.
[4] See P. Young, *Edgehill, 1642*, Kineton, 1968.
[5] e.g. one Pamphlet says that Sir Richard Wilbraham and Sir Thomas Delves 'declared themselves for the Ordinance of the Militia' at the time of the King's visit, ('Civil War Tracts of Cheshire', loc. cit., p.61).
[6] Ibid., p.89ff.
[7] B.M. Thomason Tracts E 119(5).
[8] See below, pp.67—9.

months of 1642, the vigorous action of the Royalists forced them to make a stand, many may have had strong reasons for believing that their best hopes of preventing an escalation of the war lay with the Parliamentarians. The Commission of Array was dominated by men of equal social and economic standing with themselves. Especially in view of the distrust between them and the Array, the leaders of the Booth group would find it easier to make their case heard if they assumed the leadership of a Parliamentarian party whose early champions were no match for them in birth or status. As we shall see, they were unable to assume this leadership, but such a failure was far from inevitable in these early days.

Nevertheless it was significant that about a third of the old moderate leadership became Royalists. Possibly the early successes of the King's party in neighbouring counties[1] made them confident that the area could be quickly subdued for the King and peace restored in the county that way. Clearly many smaller landlords were overawed by a neighbouring garrison into making an expedient declaration for the party concerned: Richard Brooke asserted that no one in the north of the county had declared for Parliament (except himself) until the end of 1642 because of Earl Rivers's garrison at Halton.[2] Many seem to have followed the example of Edmund Jodrell and given support to both sides, a course of action which did not prevent his being punished by each in turn.[3] Perhaps, in the last resort, the preaching of such ministers as Samuel Eaton proved too much for some moderates, who preferred the King's supporters, whatever their disadvantages, to working alongside such Congregationalists.

The pacification which was arranged at Bunbury on 23 December was thus entirely different in character from the neutrality bids which had been attempted the previous

---

[1] Only in Derbyshire had the Militia Ordinance been properly executed. In Lancashire, Staffordshire, Shropshire, and North Wales the Royalist party seemed firmly in control.

[2] C.R.O. Cholmondeley MS. DCH/X/15/14, f. 1.

[3] Malbon, op. cit., appendix 'C', pp.239–53.

summer. Whereas those had been the work of mediators separate in identity and distinct in allegiance from the two sides, the Bunbury treaty was the work of representatives of two armed parties. While the previous ones had spoken of the county as a beleaguered fortress prepared to fight anybody who tried to break the peace and the county's neutrality, this was a demilitarization. It called for the staggered disbandment of all forces, the destruction of all newly erected fortifications, the release of all prisoners, and the restoration of all goods and arms seized by either side.

The treaty was negotiated by two men on each side, Lord Kilmorrey and Orlando Bridgeman for the Royalists,[1] Henry Mainwaring and William Marbury for the Parliamentarians. William Marbury had been a member of the Booth-Wilbraham group from the first, but Henry Mainwaring had had a more varied career in 1640–2.[2] Kilmorrey had always been one of the leaders of the 'Barons' party, while Bridgeman—son of the Bishop of Chester—was a London-based lawyer who only arrived in the county in June 1642. However, behind the scenes, we can discern that it was Sir Richard Wilbraham and his distant relative Roger Wilbraham of Derfold who had been 'The Solicitors for peace, as heretofore they were'.[3] The author of the same pamphlet also tells us that

*Many gentlemen for the militia and all the souldiers at Nantwich* were exceedingly offended, thinking it an hard thing to make peace with them whom the Parliament had voted for high delinquents. But Mr. Marbury and Mr. Mainwaring, deputie-Lieutenants, who took upon them this matter, hearkened to the motion, and were desirous of an accomodation for these causes.[4]

---

[1] On the first day of the negotiations at Tarporley, the Royalists were represented by Lords Kilmorrey and Cholmondeley. This meeting led to an agreed ceasefire pending further negotiations at Bunbury, where Cholmondeley was replaced by Bridgeman.

[2] Mainwaring was one of only two supporters of Aston in 1641 to become a Parliamentarian; he was an early convert, for as early as July 1642 he was raising troops to help the Parliamentarian garrison at Manchester. He was subsequently dismissed for 'great disservices' to Parliament.

[3] The terms and a lengthy partisan discussion of them is to be found in 'The Unfaithfulness of the Cavaliers' in 'Civil War Tracts', loc. cit., pp.89–97.

[4] My italics.

The 'gentlemen for the militia' and the soldiers were the old
Parliamentarian group, the original hard-liners. The 'deputie-
lieutenants' were new appointments of the autumn of 1642
and represent the conversion of moderate but high-ranked
gentry. On the Parliamentarian side at any rate, it seems to
have been the work of that moderate group with whose
fortunes we have been much concerned. Both the pamphlet
cited above and Dr. Manning have stressed that purely
military considerations contributed greatly to the need for a
truce; the Parliamentarians were weak in cavalry and could
not expect to engage the Royalists in the field (at least until
Brereton arrived with reinforcements), while the Royalists
too were expecting fresh troops and were already desperately
short of money, thus experiencing difficulty in keeping their
troops together. It was even rumoured that they feared an
uprising from their tenants.[1]  But these considerations can be
exaggerated; this was not a truce but a thoroughly worked-
out scheme for dissolving the whole military system recently
created. And we are told by a Parliamentarian that the
pacification was 'laboured by the said Ld Killmorrey (and as
it was believed) really intented by him'.[2]

It didn't work. There was too much mutual suspicion;
though the numbers of troops were run down, fortifications
were not touched and both Brereton[3] and Aston were known
to be hurrying back to the county with fresh forces. The
King ratified the agreement, but by the time of Parliament's
bitter condemnation of it, it was probably already a dead
letter (7 January). Parliament's grounds for cancelling it are
interesting. They began by asserting somewhat unjustly that
the treaty was unequal and favoured the Royalists, then went
on to make more significant points against it, claiming that
none of the parties had any authority to enter into such an
agreement, that 'it was very derogatory to the power and
authority of Parliament that any private men should take

---

[1] See B.S. Manning, 'Neutrals and Neutralism...', pp.81—102. He fails to
observe the nature of the earlier attempts at neutrality.

[2] C.R.O., Cholmondeley MS. DCH/X/15/14, clause 13.

[3] Brereton had been in London since his expulsion from Chester in September.

upon them to suspend the execution of the Ordinance of Militia', and that 'it is very peiudiciall and dangerous to the whole kingdome that any county should withdraw themselves from the assistance of the rest to which they are bound by Law and by severall orders and declarations of Parliament'.[1]

The failure of Bunbury meant the temporary triumph of the Westminster viewpoint; the national interest conquered the community interests of the Cheshire leaders. But those who saw the dangers to the 'fabric of this blessed government' threatened by incomprehensible differences between King and Parliament were still in a position to make their views felt.

## II

So far we have been chiefly concerned with the one hundred or so gentry families who were actively involved in the petitioning before, and in organizing the preliminary stages of, the Civil War. But there were far more gentlemen in the county than this,[2] and it is necessary to say something about the nature of their allegiance during the war, and the underlying factors determining it. In a recent article[3] I have dealt with this question at length. Despite the treacherous nature of the source material, particularly the records of the Parliamentary committees for sequestration of and composition with Royalists,[4] a reasonably reliable estimate of the strength of the two sides provides us with a list of 185 and 176 Parliamentarians, but analysis of these figures has provided little evidence of the kind of underlying economic causes that historians would have hoped to see emerging. My own feeling is that estimates of income derived from most of

[1] The only copy I have seen is in Chester City Library, Pamphlet Collection, item 38.

[2] See above, pp.14–16.

[3] Since I have dealt with this question at length elsewhere, only a summary of my conclusions will be given here. See J.S. Morrill and R.N. Dore, 'The Allegiance of the Cheshire Gentry in the Great Civil War', *T.L.C.A.S.*, 77(1967).

[4] Some of these problems will emerge in the course of chapters 4 and 5.

the sources used by Dr. Cliffe[1] (particularly from sequestration records) are dangerously inadequate, as are figures for the extent of estates contained in Inquisitions *post mortem*. There is an insufficient number of surviving family estates' papers to make any sort of reliable estimate of the comparative wealth of the two sides. However, by a judicious combination of the evidence from all these sources and by a counting of manors,[2] it seems probable that the Royalists predominated in wealth; they owned two-thirds of the manors which can be allocated to one side or the other.[3] Furthermore, while the Royalists had the support of twenty heads of families whose rank was that of knight or above (including all four resident peers), the Parliamentarians could boast the support of only six knights and baronets;[4] the Royalists could also claim to have the support of two-thirds of the Bench of Justices, though, as we have seen, the Parliamentarians were supported by almost all the most active Justices. On the other hand, the Royalists seem to have had a much stronger hold on the minor gentry, those who were little better than freeholders, while the Parliamentarians were predominant among the middling gentry.

Mr. Dore's analysis of genealogical material reveals that an almost equal number of families on each side could trace their descent back to any given century (e.g. thirty-seven Royalists compared with thirty-four Parliamentarians can be traced back to at least the thirteenth century). But it is interesting that there were more Parliamentarian cadet branches of Royalist main lines than there were Royalist cadets of Parliamentarian families.[5] Both sides were equally represented among the handful of newcomers in the sixteenth and seventeenth centuries, and both contain the

[1] J.T. Cliffe, *The Yorkshire Gentry From the Reformation to the Eve of Civil War*, London, 1969, *passim.*

[2] J.P. Cooper, 'The Counting of Manors', *Ec. H. R.* 2nd ser., 8 (1955–6), shows conclusively the inadequacy of this as a form of determining economic strength. But it might still be useful for giving some indication of a landowner's influence.

[3] 43 per cent of all manors were Royalist, 20 per cent were Parliamentarian.

[4] This is not particularly meaningful since 180 gentry were fined distraint of knighthood, of whom just over half were subsequent Parliamentarians.

[5] I am grateful to Mr. R.N. Dore for providing me with these figures.

same number of families who supplemented their income from land by trade, the law, or by the 'industrial' exploitation of their estates (notably salt). There was a high incidence of Royalism, however, amongst those who can be shown to have been in financial troubles in the 1620s and 1630s.

In religion, most of the known Puritans were Parliamentarians and the handful of known Laudians were Royalists; the Roman Catholics, with the notable exception of the Savages, were remarkably inactive. But evidence of religious conviction is scarce, and some of the sources sometimes used by historians are not altogether convincing. A 'Puritan' will, for example, in some cases says more for the religion of the minister who wrote it down than for that of the man whose testament it was.

There was little difference in the education of the two sides, either in numbers or the universities or Inns of Court chosen, except that ten of the twelve Cheshire men at Brasenose College, Oxford, between 1603 and 1629 were subsequently Parliamentarians, eight extremely active, while the two future Royalists were only passive supporters of the King. There was also a considerable majority of Parliamentarians among those who attended Gray's Inn.

My lack of enthusiasm for these figures arises partly out of a series of methodological weaknesses which I believe to exist in these and similar figures for other counties. But it also arises from a refusal to accept that the Civil War can be meaningfully studied in terms of two coherent, static parties. Many who were active for the King in 1642 submitted quiescently once Parliament gained control of most of the county in 1643. There were also many who changed sides throughout the war. Henry Mainwaring and Henry Vernon, two active Parliamentarians in the first twelve months, were dismissed from all their posts in 1644 'for disservice to Parliament in many parts',[1] and were subsequently sequestered for delinquency. Two Royalist commanders betrayed Hawarden Castle to Sir William Brereton and took

[1] *Commons Journal*, vol. 3, p.484.

up commissions for Parliament. There are twenty or so other cases ranging from the top to the bottom of the gentry.

Another sign of the complex nature of allegiances in these years is provided by the existence of individuals who opted out of the conflict by giving aid to both sides, or who tried to avoid involvement altogether. The problems of the small landowner whose interests were purely local are exemplified by the case of Edmund Jodrell. In December 1642 he found on his desk simultaneously letters from his 'loving friends' the Parliamentarian leaders (who demanded £100 'otherwise that course wilbe used wch will not anyway tend to yor good') and from Thomas Legh who demanded—in a less coarse-grained fashion—that he attend a Royalist muster with horse and arms. He was subsequently imprisoned for failure to pay up to Parliament, obtained his release by settling their (inflated) demands, and subsequently paid everything demanded of him; alas, he also contributed to the Royalists and was subsequently sequestered for delinquency.[1] Others adopted the same policy with the same painful results.[2] Still, as Robert Elcocke pointed out, what choice did he have? Living midway between a Parliamentarian garrison at Nantwich and a Royalist one at Beeston, he contributed to both sides, 'a demeanour necessary for his preservation'.[3]

Fear of the consequences of non-co-operation, that pragmatic acceptance of *de facto* authority which men always plead to excuse political offences, featured largely in the delinquents' pleas to the Committee for Compounding. Thus Thomas Bromley of Hampton claimed that he 'could do no other, having garrisons all around' (and indeed he lived next to staunch Royalists Lord Cholmondeley and Sir Rowland Egerton).[4]

There were still honorific aspects in the relationship between gentlemen with tiny estates and the great land-owners, as with Stephen Bovile, gentleman, who called

1 Malbon, op. cit., appendix 'C', pp.139—52.
2 e.g. George Cotton, *C.C.C.D.*, p.898.
3 Ibid., p.1157.
4 *C.C.A.M.*, p.804.

himself a 'servant' of Lord Cholmondeley. At a lower level, many tenants were bound by their leases to provide armed men at their lord's demand.[1]

The temptation for the gentleman to stay put and to support whoever was predominant was very strong. Less than one-third of the supporters of each side actually took up a military or civilian position in the years 1643–5. Many more moved into a neighbouring garrison for protection, but the decision to leave home and property to the ravages of the enemy (or at least the weather), was a difficult one to make. Not all those who moved away did so out of sympathy for a particular cause: thus a certificate from the Parliamentarian county committee in April 1644 argued that William Leversage only went to live in a Royalist garrison at Kinderton because, being infirm, he was afraid for his life in view of the violence of the defeated Royalists fleeing after the battle of Middlewich, and that he had returned home as soon as Fairfax and Brereton had re-established Parliament's authority.[2] There are some grisly stories of the manhandling of ministers by soldiers of both sides in the highly partisan accounts of Walker and Calamy,[3] and there was a certain amount of wilful destruction, but, on the whole, the safety of those who did not turn their homes into garrisons was little threatened, and where it did occur it was usually due to undisciplined soldiers rather than vindictiveness by the officers and politicians.

In many ways, the war could be ignored. The resourceful inhabitants of Farndon, finding that at the height of the siege of Chester the ferry across the Dee had ceased to operate, petitioned Sir Richard Grosvenor in the beleagured city, asking his permission to use his property to land those travellers they intended to transport in a coracle across the river.[4] When the Royalist John Leche's father died at his

[1] B.M. Add. MS. 11332, f. 72.
[2] *C.C.A.M.*, p.337.
[3] (Ed.) A.G. Matthews, *Walker, Sufferings of the Clergy, (revised)*, London, 1948, and also *Calamy, Treatment of Ministers Ejected and Silenced, (revised)*, London, 1934.
[4] *Cheshire Sheaf*, 3rd ser., vol. 20, p.75 (from B.M. Harleian MS. 2084, f. 171).

home in Parliamentarian-controlled Carden in 1644, Henry Harper sent a letter of condolence from Chester. In it, he pointed out that 'touching his burial, surely the times will not suffer you to do that which we all desired, nor can more be expected than privately to inter him—I do not mean in the night—but in such a manner as the necessity of the times enforces'.[1]

The bulk of the gentry were reluctantly involved in the conflict. The fact that they appear on my list on one side or another is often accidental. It makes little sense to explain the Civil Wars in terms of unconscious economic motivation when both sides were riven by feuds and a majority had no deep-seated conviction behind their choice of sides.

In his diary the Royalist William Davenport of Bramhall angrily noted 'being at Widford with my cosen Davenport I had my mare forcibly taken from me by one Robert Norbury of Captain Standleyes troope and had by them some reproachfull wordes given me because I was unwilling to part with her . . .'; yet a fortnight later he noted: 'I had received a letter from (Parliamentarian) Captaine Standley containing many kind expressions of frendship and that what iniurie his men had done me in taking my mare from me was without his commission or knowledge with a promise to have her restored.' It is in this, the barely broken unity of the county community, that the nature of the conflict lies, not in dubious statistics and rigid categories.[2]

---

[1] Ibid., 3rd ser., vol. 46, p.23.
[2] Chester City R.O., CR63/2/19, Bramhall MSS., ff. 89—90.

# 3

# WAR, FINANCE, AND ADMINISTRATION, 1643–1646

## I

The course of the Civil War in Cheshire has been well served by local historians, particularly by Mr. R. N. Dore.[1] From their work, the pattern has been established of constantly successful local Parliamentarian forces frequently disrupted by the intervention of Royalist field armies from outside.

In the early months of 1643 both sides were fairly balanced in strength, with perhaps 2,000 to 2,500 men each. The Royalists had fortified at least a dozen manor houses, perhaps twenty, as well as the strongly defended city of Chester. Parliament was hurriedly garrisoning the other main market towns, Nantwich, Northwich, Knutsford, and Middlewich. In the early clashes neither side showed many signs of stamina or tactical awareness, but Brereton's natural strategic sense gave him two successes over Sir Thomas Aston. As a result, the Royalists adopted an excessively timid policy and abandoned the countryside to the Parliamentarians: except in the areas immediately around their garrisons and the hundreds of Broxton and Wirral, they allowed Brereton to spend the summer establishing control of

---

[1] R.N. Dore, *The Civil Wars in Cheshire,* Chester, 1966, gives an excellent recent account. For a longer survey which prints many original documents, see R. Morris, 'The Siege of Chester', *J.C.A.S.,* N.S. 25 (1923). For detailed treatment of some of the most important episodes, see the articles of Mr. Dore and Dr. J. Lowe referred to in the Bibliography. The essential sources apart from the obvious ones (State Papers etc.) are the Brereton Letter Books (B.M. Add. MSS. 11331–3 and Birmingham Reference Library 595611) and four contemporary accounts of the county at war. Two are Royalist ones, those of Randle Holme (B.M. Harleian MS. 2155, ff. 108–40) and of the sometime Governor of Chester, Lord Byron (Bodl. Lib. Rawlinson MS. B210). The others offer contrasted Parliamentarian views, one by Thomas Malbon of Nantwich (an associate of Sir William Brereton) 'Memorials of the Civil War in Cheshire', *Lancashire and Cheshire Record Society,* 19(1889), and the other by Nathaniel Lancaster, a Presbyterian minister, critical of some of Brereton's actions (printed in *Cheshire Sheaf,* 3rd ser., 38(1943), *passim*).

the villages. By the end of the year he had even been allowed to take his troops off to Staffordshire to help his allies there.[1]

From then onwards there was stalemate. The Royalists had lost the county—most of their garrisons were soon taken or surrendered—but Brereton could never create a sufficiently strong army within Cheshire to take Chester. He had to depend on outside help. Gradually he was able to build up support in the surrounding counties for an all-out siege of the city, but only captured it in January 1646 at his third attempt. More dramatic than this gradual drawing together of help from neighbouring counties was the direct intervention of major forces from the south. Rupert ravaged the county on three separate occasions, the King led an army there in person, and the army brought over from Ireland after the Cessation landed in Cheshire and almost turned the course of the war in the county by a desperate siege of Nantwich. Twice the county was the scene of battles of real significance, first in January 1644 when Fairfax crossed the Pennines and joined Brereton in crushing the Royalists from Ireland at the battle of Nantwich, and later in September 1645 when the King's last major army was defeated under the walls of Chester at the battle of Rowton Moor.

In May 1645 the county nearly witnessed the very climax of the war, when there was a possibility that Brereton, Cromwell, and a force of Scots under Lesley might meet the King's army during its northward sweep in the Naseby campaign.[2]

All this activity reveals the significance that Charles attached to the safety of Chester. As the main port for Ireland and as a bastion to North Wales—a crucial area for Royalist recruiting and finance—it had immense strategic

[1] See the above references, and also B.M. Add. MS. 36913, ff. 122—6.
[2] R.N. Dore, 'Sir William Brereton's Siege of Chester and the Campaign of Naseby', *T.L.C.A.S.*, 67 (1957). A full list of the forces which entered Cheshire during the war is given in a letter from the deputy lieutenants to Lenthall in Bodl. Lib. Tanner MSS., vol. 59, f. 232. Although written by Parliamentarians, it asserted that the Scots had done most damage to the county.

significance. When Rupert rested there after Marston Moor, it was even rumoured that he might make Chester his new headquarters. His visits were always disastrous for the city, however, since he invariably took away more men and supplies than he had brought with him.

As I have already implied, Parliament's success depended on far greater co-operation between its forces in the wider area of the north-west than the Royalists achieved. Furthermore, this occurred despite the fact that the latter had included Cheshire in an association of counties,[1] while Parliament left the county to fend for itself, with Brereton as commander-in-chief[2] (two attempts to associate Cheshire with other counties were ended by Parliament's creation of Denbigh's Midland Association).[3] Brereton's success was partly due to his disruption of Denbigh's power in Staffordshire and Shropshire, but it also depended on backing for his plans from the Committee of Both Kingdoms.[4] Above all, Brereton won the support of powerful groups in other counties by coming to their aid so willingly in 1643. By the time of the final siege of Chester, he could assemble an army of over 8,000 men from Cheshire, Staffordshire, Shropshire, Yorkshire, Lancashire, and North Wales; the total Cheshire contingent cannot have been much more than half.[5] He did experience some difficulty in getting the co-operation he needed, particularly from the Scots and

[1] B.M. Harleian MS. 2173, f. 8; 2135, ff. 62—3; B.M. Add. MS. 36913, f. 114.

[2] *Commons Journal*, vol. 3, p.19 (25 Mar. 1643).

[3] These proposals are in the *Lords Journal*, vol. 5, p.708 (10 Apr. 1643) and in a printed version of *'An Ordinance ... that Sir Thomas Myddleton knight be appointed to be Serjeant Major General'* of the combined forces of Cheshire, Shropshire, Lancashire, and North Wales (Chester City Library, Pamphlet Collection, item 76). For the North Midlands Association, see *Lords Journal*, vol. 6, p.92.

[4] See D.H. Pennington and I.A. Roots, *The Committee at Stafford 1643—45*, Manchester, 1957, pp.lxxiv—lxxxiii (also chapter 4 below).

[5] This is an estimate made from all the evidence in Brereton's letter books and elsewhere. See particularly the army lists in B.M. Add. MSS. 11331, f. 45 and 11333, f. 116, which estimates the troops present in December 1645 as 7,660, though not including Yorkshire or Shropshire horse. According to Brereton the Cheshire contingent in May 1645 was 4,140 foot and 790 horse. (B.M. Add. MS. 11331, f. 44.)

Yorkshire troops, but the support he could count on was far greater than the Royalists in Chester ever received from other county forces.[1]

Brereton also seems to have enjoyed one other enormous advantage—the support of the common people. He referred to it on several occasions. Once he even claimed that they 'judge our cause by the demeanour of our army', and since on the whole his troops were better disciplined and less rapacious 'wee then gained their harts'.[2]

Significantly, the Royalists admitted that they did not enjoy popular support. Lord Byron, Royalist commander at the battle of Nantwich, wrote that 'in this ill-affected countrey I could never get intelligence save by troops of horse', and another Royalist claimed that 'the common people of Cheshire are extremely poysoned by the industrie of seditious preachers'.[3] Clarendon summed up in his account of Lancashire and Cheshire,

the difference in the temper of the common people of both sides was so great, that they who inclined to the Parliament left nothing unperformed that might advance the cause, and were incredibly vigilant and industrious to cross and hinder whatsoever might promote the King's: whereas they who wished well to him, thought they had performed their duty in doeing so, and that they had done enough for him that they had done nothing against him.[4]

One particularly striking example of the behaviour of the common people is contained in a letter which William Davenport of Bramhall received from his tenants in September 1642 after he had asked for their assistance on the King's behalf. They replied:

Howsoever wee would not for the world harbour a disloyall thought against his Majestie, yett wee dare not lifte upp our handes against that honorable assembly of Parliament whom wee are confyddantly assured doe labour both for the happiness of his Maiestie and all his kingdom.

1 For the Scots e.g. P.R.O., SP 18, vol. 21, pp.160–1, for the Yorkshire troops, e.g. B.M. Add. MS. 11331, ff. 32, 40, 70, etc.
2 B.M. Add. MS. 11331, f. 25.
3 Cited in R.N. Dore, *The Civil Wars in Cheshire*, pp.18–19.
4 Edward Hyde, Earl of Clarendon, *History of the Great Rebellion*, ed. W.D. Macray, Oxford, 1887, book 6, sections 272–3.

Davenport recorded in his diary that

the verie next day (and it beinge the saboth day too) not stainge or belyke caringe much for me or my ans[wer] : they wth some others of my tenants enrowled their names and listed themselves wth Capt Hyde of Norburie to become souldiers for the Parliament under his command.[1]

If the tenants of many Royalists acted in such a fashion, it is not surprising that Parliament had raised by the spring of 1643 several regiments of foot and troops of horse recruited quite independently of the trained and freehold bands.

## II

Of the differing types of dominant figure who emerged in various counties during the war, two were particularly common. Men like Sir Thomas Barrington in Essex or Sir Nathaniel Barnardiston in Suffolk were representatives of families already among the county elite, whose capacity for hard work and unimpeachable connections brought them to the fore. But in some counties there emerged a man whose estates and birth did not make him automatically a leading figure. Such a man was Anthony Weldon in Kent; another was Sir William Brereton in Cheshire.[2] Although, as we have seen, he had been extremely active in the 1630s in all the pursuits of a gentleman, his prominence was based to a great extent on the fact that he was the only Cheshire member of Parliament who continued to sit in the Commons after July 1642. This gave him immense powers of patronage and influence which he was able to exploit and, to the shock of the local community, he was rapidly promoted by Parliamentary ordinance into a position whence he could dominate the organization of the war effort in the county.

From the beginning, orders from Westminster were addressed to 'Sir William Brereton . . . and the rest of the deputy lieutenants of that County',[3] while by the traditions

---

[1] Chester City R.O., CR63/2/19, Bramhall MSS., f. 88.

[2] In some counties no dominant personality emerged (e.g. Staffordshire, Shropshire, Lancashire).

[3] *Lords Journal*, vol. 5, p.134.

of the county, the old and venerated Sir George Booth should have been honoured by being thus personally addressed. The personal slight which the older and wealthier saw in such presumption by Brereton must be seen as one of the factors underlying the friction within the Parliamentarian party which became more marked as the war went on.[1]

The extent of his power grew out of two ordinances. The first, issued in March 1643, gave him supreme military command in the county.[2] This meant that not only was he able to co-ordinate local strategy and tactics, but also that he was granted sole right to make military appointments.[3] On his arrival in Cheshire in January 1643, he had written back to the Commons, complaining that there were five troops of horse in the county 'not subject to command'; he asked specifically to be given over-all command of these troops and the request was granted.[4] Among the captains who had raised troops by their own endeavours were young George Booth and Philip Mainwaring of Peover, both of whom were Brereton's social superiors.

Indeed in the last months of 1642 and the early months of 1643 many of the leading gentry of the old neutralist group raised troops for Parliament. As well as Booth and Mainwaring, these included William Marbury of Marbury, Henry Mainwaring of Kermincham, Ralph Arderne of Harden, and Edward Hyde of Norbury. Yet by the early months of 1645 only George Booth of this group still held a commission, and he was threatening to resign. Except for Henry Mainwaring (the most industrious military leader the Parliamentarians produced before Brereton's return to the county in February 1643) who was sacked for 'disservice to Parliament in many particulars',[5] these men's abdications of their military powers are not easy to explain. But the result

---

[1] See chapter 4, *passim.*
[2] *Commons Journal,* vol. 3, p.19 (March 1643).
[3] e.g. B.M. Harleian MS. 1970, f. 73.
[4] H.M.C. *Portland MSS.,* vol. 1, pp.95—6. For the names of the captains, ibid., p.94.
[5] *Commons Journal,* vol. 3, p.484. See also below, p.215.

was that by 1645 all the leading positions in Brereton's chain of command were held either by professional soldiers from outside the county, like Michael Jones or James Lowthian, or by lesser Cheshire gentlemen like Robert Venables, Henry Bradshaw, and Gilbert Gerard. The only substantial gentlemen to hold commissions under Brereton were Robert Duckenfield, Thomas Croxton, and John Legh (of Knutsford Booths). Significantly, none of them had been associated with the moderates in the period 1640–2; nor had they held any administrative post in local government during the 1630s. Brereton's army was controlled by men who owed their advancement to him alone.[1]

The second vital source of his power was an ordinance passed in March 1644[2] (replacing an earlier one of January 1643).[3] The earlier one vested full administrative powers in five or more deputy lieutenants. The later ordinance changed this by insisting that power was to be exercised by 'the sd Sir Wm Brereton together with the deputy lieutenants. . . or any two or more of them'. This meant that in various crucial decisions relating to the government of the county Brereton had an effective veto. Without his signature nothing could be achieved. Among the powers listed in the ordinance were the powers to establish committees for the sequestration of delinquents, for the advance of money, and for the examination of ministers and schoolmasters thought to be delinquent or otherwise unsuitable. Since he could always count on the support of at least two of the other deputy lieutenants he could effectively select committees to cover these vitally important fields which would support his objectives rather than those of men like Booth and Mainwaring. Indeed it is clear that he proceeded to use his powers in precisely that fashion. The most controversial of all his measures was to adopt a system of hundredal sequestration committees to which Booth and his supporters were bitterly opposed.[4]

[1] For lists of his officers, see B.M. Add. MSS. 11331, f. 45, and 11332, f. 3.
[2] *Lords Journal,* vol. 6, p.486.
[3] Ibid., vol. 5, pp.538–41.
[4] See chapter 5, section IV.

As a result of his full exploitation of these powers, he came to accumulate an enormous amount of personal initiative and responsibility. He was a secretive leader and no one could be sure just what he was doing. In 1651 Parliament asked the county to supply information on the amount of 'moneys, horse, armes, plate etc' voluntarily subscribed in the county during the war. Three former deputy lieutenants rather sourly replied that

some of us & divers of the Comrs of this County intermedled not wth such receipts, nor have wee seene any account of his as to such moneys or (hee beeinge nowaies chargeable to accompt but to the house whereof hee is a member) nor doe wee certenly know who his assignees were in this service.[1]

On top of these vast powers he was always being awarded fresh ones, such as the power to set an excise of a halfpenny a gallon on salt,[2] and he was busily accumulating positions on the more important committees of Staffordshire, Shropshire, Lancashire, Surrey, and Pembrokeshire.[3] He was not slow to exploit the potential placed before him by a House of Commons which was thankful for his loyalty.

### III

In most counties the last months of 1642 and the early months of 1643 saw the emergence of a county committee.[4] Frequently they evolved from informal meetings of the deputy lieutenants, and successive Parliamentary ordinances granted them complete control of the collection and distribution of loans and taxes (except the Excise) in their counties and, later, powers of sequestration and administration of Royalist lands; effective power then lay

[1] B.M. Harleian MS. 2128, f. 158.
[2] *Commons Journal*, vol. 3, p.331.
[3] These committees are listed by Mr. Pink in his notes on members of the Long Parliament in J.Ry.L. English MS. 307.
[4] The best study is that of Pennington and Roots, *The Committee at Stafford 1643–45*. But see also A.M. Everitt, 'Suffolk and the Great Rebellion', *Suffolk Record Society*, 1960. Both give good accounts of the development and power of the county committees and edited texts of original order books. Everitt's *The Community of Kent and the Great Rebellion* contains a good straightforward account.

with the men who could manipulate these bodies. But in Cheshire no such committee was created. There was a group of men who were variously called 'the committee at Nantwich', the 'Councell of Warr', or simply 'the committee'. But far and away the most frequent title they used about themselves and by which petitioners addressed them is simply 'the deputy lieutenants' or 'the deputy lieutenants and committee (or gentlemen) of Cheshire'; they are always called 'the deputy lieutenants' in Commons business.[1] An examination of several hundred documents signed by this group of men in the period 1643–6 suggests that they formed a committee which met spasmodically, usually at Nantwich. There is no Parliamentary ordinance establishing them, and several members were never appointed to any official position by Parliament.

Altogether there were twenty-three members of this committee. Of these sixteen were at one time or another appointed by Parliament as deputy lieutenants. One of these died during the war and two were removed for treachery. The number at any given time was thirteen. Those who formed the stable membership between the early months of 1644 and the middle of 1646 included six leaders of the moderate party from the period 1641–2 (Sir George Booth and his grandson George, Thomas Stanley, Philip Mainwaring, William Marbury, and Roger Wilbraham); these men were also the leaders of the group which consistently appears whenever there was opposition to Brereton. Then there were Brereton himself, with his two closest associates (Robert Duckenfield and John Legh) and three others who wavered in their support but who were broadly behind Brereton—Henry Brooke (sheriff 1644–7) Edward Hyde, and Thomas Croxton. The thirteenth of these deputy lieutenants was John Booth, younger son of Sir George, controversial governor of Warrington, and at loggerheads with everybody.[2]

[1] This statement is based on numerous letters and orders in the Brereton letter books, in P.R.O., SP 28/224 and 225, in the *Commons Journal*, and Chester City R.O., CR63/1, Earwaker MSS., Box 30, correspondence of Henry Brooke, 1643–6.

[2] See below, pp.118–19.

The remaining seven whose signatures appear during this period were never appointed deputy lieutenants by Parliament, and they never signed documents except in the presence of at least three of the deputy lieutenants. They seem to have acted as supernumeraries, helping the deputy lieutenants to get through their work but unable to take any initiative themselves. Their position may well have been similar to that of those peace-time Justices of the Peace who were not included in the quorum.

The supernumeraries were all moderates. Five had been members of the moderate party in 1641—2, and five were to be involved in the movement against Brereton's leadership in 1645—6;[1] all seven were involved in one or both. The assumption must be that they were co-opted by the moderates, but since Brereton and two of his supporters could meet any time to make the crucial decisions, these seven minor gentlemen were in no position to influence policy.[2]

We can discover something about the work of this committee from the fact that they most often chose to call themselves 'deputy lieutenants'. The prime function of such officials before the civil war had been control of the militia, and throughout the period 1643—6 the militia remained distinct from the other forces under Brereton's command. Surviving military accounts indicate that responsibility for payment of the two sections of the local Parliamentarian forces was divided,[3] the deputy lieutenants reserving to themselves control of the maintenance of the bands of the five eastern hundreds.[4]

---

[1] See B.M. Add. MS. 11331, ff. 67—8, Bodl. Lib. Tanner MSS., vol. 60, f. 221.

[2] The seven were Thomas Aldersey, Richard Egerton, William Raven, George Spurstowe, Thomas Walthall, John Wettenhall, and Richard Wright, all of whom possessed only modest estates, but who were distinctly of gentry stock in comparison with some of Brereton's nominees to the sequestration committees.

[3] See below, pp.103—5.

[4] For some time Wirral and Broxton hundreds were under Royalist control. When Brereton established his hold in this area, what militia were raised there was placed under the special committees at Tarvin, Hooton, and Puddington, which he nominated; see below, pp.87—8.

Even when Brereton was absent from the county, responsibility for the main field army was placed in other hands. When the Self-Denying Ordinance took effect and Brereton was recalled to Parliament, seemingly permanently, military control was handed over to two professionals in service in the county, Michael Jones and James Lowthian, but control of the financial aspects of the siege of Chester was vested in a new committee, consisting of the two George Booths, Henry Brooke, Thomas Croxton, Robert Duckenfield, and John Legh. The transference of responsibility to the deputy lieutenants as a body was not effected. This was clearly the result of action by Brereton's allies in London.[1]

More interesting still was the system that operated during Brereton's absence from February to June 1644. An analysis of warrants for payment received by the treasurer, James Croxton, during this period shows that the bulk of the responsibility for organizing the payment of the army fell upon five men, Thomas Croxton, William Massie, Robert Venables, John Bromhall, and William Marbury. All except the fifth were smallish Cheshire squires who owed their swift rise to senior military appointments to Brereton. The names of Booth, Mainwaring, Wilbraham, Stanley, are almost completely absent during this period.[2] It is odd that Duckenfield and Legh were not active, but the main point remains: responsibility for the distribution of pay to the army was in the hands of a group of army officers, presumably nominated by Brereton.

The main source of money for the army was the weekly pay, later to become the monthly assessments. In other

[1] B.M. Add. MS. 11331, ff. 44, 86, 97, 122, 131, particularly f. 122.

[2] P.R.O., SP 28/224 and 225 contain 754 warrants to James Croxton for payments from his funds during his period as treasurer; in the bundles they have become randomized. They consist of a dated order for the payment of a particular sum to a person or for a purpose specified, and also the signatures of those authorizing payment. Sometimes a particular source (e.g. the profits of sequestration) is specified from which payment was to be made. I am very grateful to Mr. P.M. Ruhemann for arranging for these warrants to be sorted and analysed by computer. The main results of his efforts will be seen in the next section.

counties the assessment and collection of this was normally a headache to be borne by members of the county committee: in Cheshire, responsibility fell on a special committee appointed by Parliament and separate in identity from the deputy lieutenancy. Between 1643 and 1645 this committee consisted of ten (later eleven) men,[1] including moderates like Sir George Booth, Thomas Stanley, William Marbury, and Philip Mainwaring; there were also Brereton and his supporters Duckenfield and Brook, the two deputy lieutenants sacked for disloyalty in 1644, Henry Mainwaring and Henry Vernon, and two men who otherwise never appeared as active Parliamentarians in the county during these years, John Crewe of Utkinton[2] and John Bradshaw, the last being a radical much too active as a legal representative on various open Parliamentary committees in London ever to appear in the county. Most other sources of revenue seem to have been controlled by Brereton or his nominees.[3]

The same group was appointed by the first Sequestration Ordinance of 1643 to seize and administer the estates of all those they considered to be Royalists,[4] but the important commission twelve months later, giving Brereton sweeping powers to appoint committees, agents, etc., spoke about the neglect shown by this first committee.[5] Within six weeks the Commons passed a resolution adding twelve new commissioners.[6] Apart from Philip Mainwaring, all were officers or civilians linked with Brereton. Within a few weeks, however, the whole scheme was scrapped and in its place committees were appointed in each hundred with full power

[1] C.H. Firth and R.S. Rait, *Acts and Ordinances of the Interregnum*, London, 1911, vol. 1, pp.90, 147, 228, 543, 642.

[2] John Crewe, son of the former Lord Chief Justice sacked by Charles I in 1627, had married the heiress to the very extensive Done estates and thus become one of the greatest landowners in the county. A moderate in 1641—2, he was only rarely active for Parliament between 1642 and 1660, though he was continually reappointed as a J.P. He was sheriff of the county in 1652.

[3] See below, section IV.

[4] Firth and Rait, op. cit., pp.106—17.

[5] *Lords Journal*, vol. 6, p.487.

[6] *Commons Journal*, vol. 3, p.484.

to execute the ordinances for sequestration.[1] All the officials on these committees were minor gentry, the only one of any real substance being Henry Bradshaw, who was chairman of the Macclesfield committee. The others all came from the same stratum as the pre-war head constables, indeed some of them, including Randle Palin, John Bradbourne, and Thomas Kirkes, had served in that office, while several had previously served as Grand Jurymen at Quarter Sessions. Others seem to have had some professional qualification, like William Bentley, described as 'medicus'.[2] Each hundred had between three and six commissioners, but the total number for the county was only twenty-two, since several men were appointed to sit for two or three hundreds. Thus Thomas Warburton sat in Bucklow, Edisbury, and Northwich hundreds, Thomas Robinson in Broxton, Edisbury, and Northwich, and Richard Johnson in Wirral and Northwich.[3] Beneath the committees were agents who administered their decisions and who were responsible for the collection of rents and the sale of personal estates etc. These men were usually freeholders, frequently yeomen, and only occasionally—like Philip Downes and William Leftwich in Northwich—gentlemen with experience as head constables or Grand Jurymen.[4]

Brereton also established committees of his allies amongst the gentry in certain garrison towns around Chester, mainly at Tarvin, Hooton, and Puddington,[5] and these took over responsibility for organizing the assessment and collection of

---

[1] There are many documents containing their names. Here are examples for each hundred: P.R.O., SP 23, vol. 129, f. 485, vol. 148, f. 101, vol. 246, f. 37, vol. 247, ff. 69, 73, 94, 108. For evidence that Brereton appointed them, see e.g. SP 20, vol. 3, f. 347.

[2] Evidence of previous administrative experience comes from lists of head constables in Quarter Sessions Order Books and lists of Grand Jurymen in Quarter Sessions Files for 1625–42 in Cheshire Record Office.

[3] e.g. the Northwich Committee consisted entirely of men who also sat in other hundreds; Macclesfield and Nantwich committee men sat nowhere else; the other four had mixed committees.

[4] For a good example of the way in which the separate layers worked, see Chester City R.O., CR63/2/19, Bramhall MSS., ff. 90–2.

[5] There is an isolated reference (B.M. Harleian MS. 2126, f. 18) to a committee at Weaverham, but this gives no indication as to its membership or nature.

all contributions and taxation in the surrounding area. Hooton and Puddington divided responsibility for Wirral hundred between them, while the Tarvin committee was responsible not only for Edisbury, but also for an ill-defined wider area: for example, it ordered money from Northwich to be paid to its messenger.[1] It was not until the fall of Chester that full sequestration powers were granted to the committees Brereton appointed in Wirral and Edisbury. He clearly preferred to leave powers of deciding who was to be sequestered in the hands of his close collaborators rather than with the less-important and less-experienced men employed specifically as sequestrators. Thus John Rutter of Kingsley 'was sequestered by the late committee at Tarvin when Chester was a garrison for the late Kinge' and responsibility for his estates was handed over to the Edisbury committee only after the fall of the city.[2] Whereas in other hundreds leasing of sequestered estates was left to the local committee, in Edisbury the Tarvin committee had the right to intervene and alter the leasing arrangements made. For example, the Edisbury committee in their accounts speak of the arrears 'that were returned. . . .the committee [at Tarvin] exceptting[3] of their ould rents insted of rackes in regard of trouble of the times and the poverty of the partyes'.[4] Similarly in Wirral the sequestrators explained that they received no rent for the demesne lands at Birkenhead because the Hooton committee gave permission for those who lived near Chester 'to bringe theire cattle into the sd demesne lands at Berkett [sic] aforesaid for the better secureing and preserving of theire said cattle from the said plunder of the aforesaid enemye'.[5]

---

[1] P.R.O., SP 28/224, f. 5, signed by three men, Jonathan Bruen, Robert Gregg, and John Hardware; all were officers in the army, all were men of ancient gentry families but modest estates, none had played any part in the moderate movement of 1641—2: typical Brereton men.
[2] P.R.O., SP 23, vol. 148, f. 105. See also B.M. Harleian MS. 2144, f. 38.
[3] Presumably for 'accepting'.
[4] B.M. Harleian MS. 2126, f. 64.
[5] Ibid. 2018, f. 37.

Brereton's powers were completed by his control of the appointment of other minor officials, those men who acted as liaison officers between the central and local government; he nominated men like Henry Cockson, the Cheshire solicitor for sequestrations, and Richard Worrall, who was put in charge of the receiving of money in London for the service in Cheshire.[1]

The pattern is fairly clear. By the early months of 1644 Brereton had steadily encroached upon those powers that in other counties were being practised by a county committee. When he went up to Parliament for a few weeks, he appointed a committee of his military appointees to ensure the flow of money to the army; upon his return he resumed the dominant position in the administration. Of the warrants for out-payments received by James Croxton, county treasurer between June 1644 and June 1645, 83 per cent were signed by Brereton alone, and over half the remainder by committees nominated by him.[2] When in June 1645 he finally surrendered his command in accordance with the Self-Denying Ordinance, he arranged for power to pass to a committee whose membership contained his most influential military supporters but only two of the civilian deputy lieutenants; after October 1645 when Brereton was restored to his command, even these two fell into the background. The old county families, who might have been expected to control the war-effort in Cheshire, only came to assume real authority after the fall of Chester, when Brereton turned his attention first to Staffordshire and then to his position in Parliament.

---

[1] P.R.O., SP 20, vol. 1, p.6, B.M. Add. MS. 11332, f. 4. Brereton had rescued Worrall from the clutches of the Commissioners of Array in 1642 and used him as a messenger to London (H.M.C. *Portland MSS.*, vol. 1, p.52) See also B.M. Add. MS. 11332, ff. 71, 124, *Lords Journal*, vol. 7, p.709.

[2] According to analysis of the warrants in P.R.O., SP 28/224 and 225, and despite the ordinance that county treasurers were only to make payments authorized by seven deputy lieutenants or county commissioners. Warrants signed by the deputy lieutenants usually had five or more signatures, never less than three.

## IV

We have drawn a very skeletal plan of the organization of the war-effort in Cheshire. The essential point that has emerged is that there failed to develop in the county the kind of strong committee dominated by old county families which existed in most other counties during the years 1643—6. Such a committee existed in an embryonic form, but it was never given an opportunity to develop naturally. Its growth was stunted, but it did come to possess one unusual and striking power.

The Committee for Taking the Accounts of the Kingdom set up subcommittees in each county to aid in its task of checking up on the financial activities of local commanders and committees. Sensibly, it ruled that no one who had sat on committees before was to sit as a subcommissioner of accounts. This frequently led to the necessity of employing very minor or quiescent Parliamentarians, and relations between these new officials and the major county figures were frequently embittered, even violent.[1]

In Cheshire something quite unlike this happened. Several of the deputy lieutenants sat upon and dominated the sub-committee of accounts. The Nantwich sequestrators called them 'many gent of wisdome & good meanes',[2] and in a subsequent letter clearly pointed out that 'the deputie lieftents & sherryf for this countie have by ordinance of Parliamt . . . power (as we conceive) to take our accompts wch they have donn ever scythens wee were ymployed in the servys for Sequestracons'.[3]

In fact there have survived several dozen documents from the years 1643—8 containing the signatures of men calling themselves subcommissioners of accounts, and a total of

---

[1] For an excellent treatment of this committee, see D.H. Pennington, 'The Accounts of the Kingdom', in F.J. Fisher (ed.) *Essays in the Economic and Social History of Tudor and Stuart England, in Honour of R.H. Tawney* Cambridge, 1961, Some of the most exciting conflicts can be traced in P.R.O., SP 28/208 and 256.
[2] B.M. Add. MS.5494 f. 84.
[3] Ibid., f. 85

twenty-one men seem to have acted at one time or another.[1] Of these, only five were deputy lieutenants, but four of them, Sir George Booth, Thomas Stanley, Philip Mainwaring, and Roger Wilbraham, were civilian opponents of Brereton; only one, Thomas Croxton, was a military man and a supporter of the commander-in-chief. Another commissioner was Thomas, son of Philip Mainwaring. The remaining fifteen were minor gentry, but they formed a very different group from those whom Brereton had employed. Altogether sixteen out of the twenty-one had belonged to the moderate party in 1641–2, while virtually none of Brereton's nominees on other committees had done so; fourteen of them openly opposed Brereton in the course of 1645. Only three, Henry Birkenhead, Robert Gregg, and William Bentley, appear to have been supporters of Brereton.

Since they were able to circumvent Brereton's committees and gain some limited control over county finances by browbeating collectors and other minor officials, the Moderates' power in the county was clearly not altogether destroyed.[2] But neither they nor Brereton made any attempt to carry out those duties that, as Justices of the Peace, they could still have accomplished. Clearly the military situation precluded the holding of Quarter Sessions, but the administrative powers of Justices out of Sessions were broad and the issue of a fresh Commission of the Peace by Parliament in May 1644[3] indicated that the Houses expected day-to-day civil administration to continue as far as possible.

In some matters this is hardly surprising: the strategic need to destroy important bridges[4] added to a general process of dilapidation, and nothing was done to keep them in repair.

---

[1] A complete list can be obtained by looking at the following: B.M. Add. MS. 5494, f. 87, B.M. Harleian MS. 2128, f. 73, P.R.O., SP 28/224, ff. 274, 305, 306, P.R.O., SP 28/257 (unfoliated letter from Gilbert Gerard to the Committee for Taking the Accounts, 27 Mar. 1647), SP 28/225 (unfoliated letter from Brereton to Scoutmaster Walker, 2 Dec. 1644). This committee is sometimes called 'the Committee at Mr. Waring's House' (see B.M. Harleian MS. 2126, f. 92).
[2] See below, pp.125–6.
[3] P.R.O., Index 4213, p.3.
[4] C.R.O., Q.S.O.B. 9a, f. 111.

Even before the fighting began, the head constables of Wirral were unable to collect money for the repair of Warrington Bridge because 'the whole cuntry wthin our severall divisions refuse payment, and returne answeare & say, itt is noe tyme nowe to repaire bridges'.[1] Highways too fell into disrepair and in 1646 the Justices spoke of 'a generall complaint this day made that by reason of the distractions of the times there hath byn greate neglect in amending the highwayes' and pointed out that in many parishes no supervisors or surveyors had been appointed'.[2] Though this meant that in many parts of the county roads became 'impassable and very dangerous for travellers', it was essentially a nuisance. For the aged and impotent, the breakdown in poor relief was far more serious. Again, the lack of Quarter Sessions to ensure that officials were being appointed seems to have led to a cessation of activity at parish level. In July 1646 the inhabitants of Astbury informed the Bench that no overseers or church-wardens had been appointed there for four years.[3] Of the handful of churchwardens' accounts books that have survived, most contain gaps covering the Civil War years.[4] In 1651 a large petition from Nantwich ascribed the deterioration in relief to the war years when 'the statute lawes were not at all put in execucion'.[5] Petitions to the Sessions after their resumption at the end of 1645 show how everyone suffered—old, maimed soldiers, impotent poor, orphans.[6] Nor was it simply that the traditional forms of parochial or county relief had never been collected; knowing that there were no courts to enforce old orders, fathers of bastards just ceased to meet the maintenance orders.[7] Although the first post-war Sessions set to work to organize

[1] C.R.O., Q.S.F. 1642 no.4, f.15.
[2] C.R.O., Q.S.O.B., 9a, ff.103, 139.
[3] C.R.O., Q.S.F. 1646, no. 2, f. 63.
[4] e.g. C.R.O., P/13/22/1 (Middlewich, no entries 1641–7) and P/39/7/1 (Marbury, no entries 1643–5).
[5] C.R.O., Q.S.F. 1651, no. 4, f. 81.
[6] e.g. Q.S.F. 1645, no. 3, f. 115.
[7] Ibid., f. 90.

relief for maimed Parliamentarian soldiers, it is clear that up to that time most had had to fend for themselves as best they could.[1]

The whole system of control of those engaged in the corn trade (badgers, maltsters, ale-house-keepers) and of the careful supervision of the erection of cottages for the poor on waste ground clearly collapsed during the war, and created problems which the Justices spent years sorting out.[2] It was only after the war that they were able to intervene in those matters where authority had collapsed with the demise of the ecclesiastical courts. It took them until 1648 to persuade the parishioners of Tarvin to repair their church; according to the churchwardens 'divers of the inhabitants there by reason of theise distracted times conceiving that the consistory cort beeing nowe out of use, theire is noe lawe to inforce them, doe refuse to pay theire leyes assessed on theire liveings for that purpose'.[3]

In April 1647 the Justices had to deal with 'lewde persons [who had] unlawfully entred into the House of Correction in Middlewch and made there abode & dwelling there'.[4] This house had been erected at great charge and effort in the 1630s and only opened in 1641. The fact that it took three orders over twelve months to oust the squatters reveals something of the extent of the breakdown in organization. But that the house had been empty at all shows more completely the failure of those men charged with carrying on the work of the Justices in the years 1643–6.

Occasionally it is possible to glimpse *ad hoc* procedures employed by the deputy lieutenants to help extreme cases: some almsmen at Woodhay were to be paid out of sequestered rents,[5] an unmarried mother was to receive relief from sequestrated revenue.[6] But even in these cases the lack of respect for the deputy lieutenants shows through. In May

[1] C.R.O., Q.S.O.B. 9a, f. 91.
[2] Ibid., f. 107
[3] Ibid., f. 155.
[4] Ibid., f. 133.
[5] B.M. Harleian MS. 2166, f. 35.
[6] C.R.O., Q.S.F. 1645, no.3, f. 94.

1644 the deputy lieutenants heard the claim for relief of a man, whose land had been traversed by a new military road. They ordered that he should receive compensation from sequestered rents, but the order was ignored until Brereton gave it his personal endorsement three months later.[1]

V

Financial administration both at national and local levels was in a muddle throughout the Civil Wars. No two counties appear to have developed alike, and the administrative fragmentation and the personal ascendancy of Sir William Brereton certainly resulted in a distinctive pattern emerging in Cheshire.

An initial difficulty was that Parliament, while relying to a great extent upon local forces, failed utterly to make financial provision for their upkeep. Ordinances relating to the major sources of revenue, Propositions, weekly pay, Excise, sequestrations[2]—all required the money thus raised to be sent up from the counties to central treasuries in London.[3] When these provisions were simply ignored by the county committees, there was little that Parliament could do, except come to some sort of compromise,[4] or accept the situation. Ultimately they turned to composition fines as a means of benefiting from Royalist wealth,[5] and later still introduced measures to sell off the estates of the church, the Crown, and some 780 recalcitrant gentry.[6]

[1] P.R.O., SP 28/225 (unfoliated petition of Richard Merchant, 24 May 1644).
[2] For a discussion of these, see below, pp.96–111.
[3] e.g. one of the Ordinances of Sequestration (that of May 1644) laid down that county treasurers who failed to send up money to London within forty days of receiving it were to be fined 2s. 6d. in the pound for every week's delay (Firth and Rait, op. cit., vol. 1, p.437).
[4] The Eastern Association, for example, were permitted to keep one-third of all money received from sequestrations. As a result of this agreement, some money was sent to London from this area. In general, as the accounts of Samuel Avery, treasurer of the Committee for Sequestrations, reveal, only those counties close to London ever sent money from Royalist lands to the central government.
[5] See below, pp.203–21.
[6] e.g. B. Tatham, 'The Sale of Episcopal Lands during the Civil Wars and Commonwealth', *E.H.R.* 23(1908); I.J. Thirsk, 'The Sales of Royalist Lands during the Interregnum', *Ec.H.R.*, 2nd ser., 5(1952–3).

But if the counties kept for themselves a very high proportion of the money that should have been sent up to the central government, they were also frequently under pressure to allocate funds to the committee of the association of which they were members. Although Cheshire was not part of an association, the presence of large numbers of troops from other counties for prolonged periods at the siege of Chester raised questions of a similar nature about the mutual responsibilities of the counties concerned.

There was even the question of the centralization of finance within each county. In some areas all the money passed through the hands of a county treasurer and all disbursements were made on the immediate authority of the county committee. This was the system required by Parliamentary ordinances, but again it was widely ignored. In Staffordshire, for example, the committee granted various garrison commanders and other officers powers to receive the weekly assessments or other sources of revenue from a specified group of villages, the money never reaching the treasurer's hands.[1] Not even the institution of subcommittees of accounts, to whom this practice was anathema, stemmed it.

All counties were thus disorganized to some extent. But Cheshire appears to present an extreme case. Not only did virtually no money leave the county for London, at least until the introduction of compositions (effectively from the spring of 1646),[2] but large sums were actually being sent down from the capital: about £37,000 had come into Cheshire by the middle of 1647.[3] Furthermore, in the three years following his appointment as county treasurer in June 1644, James Croxton received barely a third of the money raised in the county from sources for which he was officially responsible.[4]

The pattern was set from the beginning. In June 1642, as war approached, Parliament took its first tentative steps

[1] Pennington and Roots, op. cit., pp.xxxi–xxxiii.
[2] See below, pp.203–4.
[3] See below, p.106.
[4] See below, p.107.

towards raising money by asking for loans in the form of cash, plate, arms, and horses. These loans became known as the Propositions; they were to be repaid once the peace of the kingdom had been restored, 8 per cent interest being offered as an inducement to subscribers. Initially the M.P.s for each county were to nominate the receivers, but in January 1643 Parliament ordered that, with regard to Cheshire, the proceeds were to be 'employed in such manner as shall bee agreed, directed and appointed by the said Sir William Brereton . . . or in default or neglect, by 3 or more of the deputy lieutenants'.[1] This was shortly followed by a general ordinance by which contributions on the Propositions was made compulsory on all.[2] But its collection remained haphazard and disbursement was localized within each division of the county.[3] Brereton's control was specifically confirmed in the ordinance of March 1644,[4] but since most of the collectors were his close associates (e.g. Robert Duckenfield, Gilbert Gerard, Ralph Judson), the decentralized system had doubtless always suited him well enough, particularly as he was deeply distrustful of the first county treasurer, George Spurstowe.[5]

Since subscriptions were reduced to a trickle by the end of 1643, Brereton was granted fresh powers to assess forcibly all who had failed to subscribe hitherto. In this respect, he was the local agent of the Committee for the Advance of Money sitting at Haberdasher's Hall in London, created specifically to handle money from this source. Assessments were supposed to represent one-fifth of non-subscribers' income from land and one-twentieth of their movable goods. The committee's work in Cheshire was staggeringly unsuccessful even in comparison with other areas.[6]

Once it became clear that there was to be no immediate, clear-cut victory by either side, Parliament had had to create

---

[1] *Lords Journal*, vol. 5, p.539.
[2] See Pennington and Roots, op. cit., p.xxxiv.
[3] See below, pp.101–3.
[4] *Lords Journal*, vol. 6, p.486.
[5] See below, p.203.
[6] e.g. for Kent see Everitt, op. cit., pp.156–7. Also below, pp.102–3.

a more systematic instrument of finance. In February 1643 an ordinance for a weekly assessment was introduced,[1] initially for three months. It was then renewed, and was to remain the main form of Parliamentarian taxation until the Restoration (it soon became a monthly instead of a weekly tax). It was an attempt to tax all income and, unlike the older subsidies, it fell on a majority of the population, that is, on all those not receiving alms. Professor Everitt has suggested that it represented an income tax of 2s.6d. in the pound on Kent, and Mr. Johnson has suggested a rate of 2s. in the pound for Buckinghamshire.[2] Its only progenitor as a source of government revenue was Ship Money, and in Cheshire the same assessment rolls were used. Perhaps the most striking provision was that where land was let for a real or rack rent, the tax was to be paid by the landlord; where an old or unimproved rent was paid, coupled with high entry or other fines, the burden was to be shared between lord and tenant. There must have been some machinery in the county for handling complaints and disputes, but there is no evidence that the Committee for Monthly Assessments or any other body ever considered this matter.[3] At a local level the petty and head constables were made responsible for its assessment and collection,[4] but up to mid-1645 they were ordered to hand the proceeds over, not to James Croxton, but to a special receiver.[5]

From the outset Parliament was aware that some counties (particularly those under Royalist control) could only make limited contributions. The Houses therefore assessed some areas far more heavily than others. Thus the greatest burdens were imposed on the south and east of the country: Kent was assessed at £1,250 per week throughout 1643–4,

[1] Firth and Rait, op. cit., vol. 1, p.85.

[2] Everitt, op. cit., pp.159–60; A.M. Johnson, 'Buckinghamshire 1640–60', Univ. Coll. of Swansea, M.A. thesis, 1963, pp.117ff.

[3] There is a single reference in the Quarter Sessions Records (Q.S.F. 1645, no.3, ff. 93, 98) to four Justices ordering the tenants on rack rents in Mobberley to pay part of the burden hitherto borne solely by the freemen.

[4] e.g. see the accounts of John Page, head constable of Northwich hundred 1645–6, B.M. Harleian MS. 2128, ff. 129–37.

[5] Ibid., ff. 84–96. See below, pp.103–4.

Buckinghamshire at £430 per week.[1] Cheshire by contrast, was asked to find less than 1 per cent of the national total— just £175 per week.[2] Whereas in some areas the assessment represented easily the most important single item in county finances, (over 50 per cent in Kent and Buckinghamshire),[3] in Cheshire it constituted only 15 per cent of the total handled by county officials in the years 1643—7.[4] Furthermore, as we shall see, compared with Kent, where, according to Professor Everitt, 'the efficiency of the tax was remarkable', in Cheshire it was collected late and only with difficulty. There is evidence that, in this respect at least, Cheshire is the more typical.[5]

A completely separate set of accounts was made for the trained and freehold bands (the militia regiments). As I have already pointed out, these remained the personal responsibility of the deputy lieutenants, who up to the end of 1645 adopted a policy of ordering each parish or village to pay and maintain a fixed number of men in the bands. But during Brereton's absence in London, the bands became increasingly integrated into the army besieging Chester, and payment of them as a separate body became less realistic. As a result, the system was regularized so that assessments were paid to the head constables and passed on to James Croxton to form part of his general fund. Since the monthly assessment itself was also now handed over to him and retained for local purposes, the distinction between it and the £500 or so per month raised ostensibly for the militia became meaningless.[6]

[1] Everitt, op. cit., p.158; Johnson, op. cit., pp.117ff.

[2] Firth and Rait, op. cit., vol. 1, p.86.

[3] Everitt, op. cit., pp.158—9, 162; Johnson, op. cit., pp.117ff.

[4] See below, pp.105—6.

[5] Everitt, op. cit., p.159; Johnson, op. cit., pp.117ff., where it is claimed that only £31,000 out of £57,600 assessed in the years 1643—8 had been received by the end of 1649. See also C. Holmes, 'The Eastern Association 1642—6', Univ. of Cambridge Ph.D. thesis, 1969, pp.306ff., for a splendid analysis of the delays and problems of collection in Suffolk, Cambridgeshire, and East Hertfordshire.

[6] P.R.O., SP 28/128, Accounts Book of James Croxton ff. 7—13. C.R.O., Q.S.F. 1645, no.3 f. 93.

The only assessment that appears to have been made in the county for employment elsewhere was the sum of £2,219 collected between August 1646 and April 1647 for the relief of the army in Ireland. This constituted about 80 per cent of the sum assessed.[1]

In Kent sequestrations were a flop.[2] In Cheshire they were to form by far the most significant single form of revenue. First authorized by Parliamentary Ordinance in March 1643, redefined in August 1643 and again in May 1644,[3] sequestration machinery was only really effective in Cheshire from the middle of 1644, following Brereton's return from London and the establishment of sequestration committees in every hundred.[4] These committees were empowered to seize and sell the personal estates of all whom they considered delinquents (i.e. Royalists) or Papists, and to take possession of their lands; they were to collect rents from existing tenants and to let demesne lands for the best possible return. The proceeds were supposed to be forwarded to London within forty days; in fact only a small percentage even reached the county treasurer, at least three-quarters being disbursed at a hundredal or even manorial level. Unlike the other forms of revenue hitherto discussed, the local agent was not the village constable, but specially appointed collectors acting for a group of manors or freeholds.[5]

The last major source of taxation introduced by Parliament was the Excise, first levied by ordinance in July 1643. It proved the most unpopular of all taxes. It was to fall on a wide range of goods, particularly beverages (including home-made beer) but despite regular attempts to settle it in the county, the tax appears to have remained a dead letter in Cheshire until 1648. Following one attempt to impose it in August 1646, some of the Justices complained that 'the Excise is hitherto wholly obstructed and the people in a tumultuous manner have risen against the Commissioners'.[6]

[1] P.R.O., SP 28/128, Accounts Book of James Croxton ff. 1–4.
[2] Everitt, op. cit., p.160.
[3] Firth and Rait, op. cit., vol. 1, pp.106–17, 254–60, 437.
[4] See above, pp.86–8.
[5] For a fuller treatment of these themes, see below, pp.111–17.
[6] H.M.C. *Portland MSS.*, vol. 1, p.390.

The only money from this source was probably the excise on salt, whose collection was made Brereton's responsibility in the middle of 1643. Perhaps the fact that in December 1643 Parliament ordered that the receipts from the salt excise should be employed for the payment of the Cheshire forces made its collection easier.[1]

The situation is thus a complex one. Only about 2 per cent of the money raised in the county before the introduction of compositions[2] was sent out of the county. The rest was employed within Cheshire or to pay debts specifically incurred by the county authorities (e.g. for the acquisition of arms). Furthermore, barely a third of the money raised between June 1644 and July 1647 reached the county treasurer, James Croxton. His summary accounts book for this period shows that he received a total of £77,494,[3] though I have argued elsewhere that the total amount levied during the same period (exclusive of compositions) was nearer £200,000.[4] This is despite the fact that Brereton's commission appointing him county treasurer had specifically laid down that he be given sole responsibility for handling county funds.[5]

For the previous eighteen months Croxton (from a very minor gentry family) had been deputy to the first county treasurer, George Spurstowe, a Cheshire squire of modest estates but ancient lineage (and cousin of the prominent

---

[1] *Commons Journal*, vol. 3, p.331. There is a fragmentary record of the collection of the salt excise at Nantwich in late 1643 in the accounts book of James Croxton (before he became county treasurer), P.R.O., SP 28/152, book 3, ff. 1—2. In October 1644 Brereton ordered all the proceeds to be paid to the townsmen of Nantwich who 'have binne reddy in the absence of the trayned bands to watch for the safetie and deffence of the said towne . . . and have never receaved any pay for their service' (P.R.O., SP 28/225, unfoliated).

[2] From March 1645 onwards most Royalists who submitted themselves to Parliament and who paid a fine proportiate to the capital value of their property were allowed to repossess their estates. These composition fines had to be paid by the compounder into the treasury at Goldsmith's Hall. See below, pp.203—6.

[3] P.R.O., SP 28/128, Accounts Book of James Croxton.

[4] See my thesis, pp.127—40 for a detailed analysis of available source material and a defence of this figure.

[5] P.R.O., SP 28/225, one of two unfoliated orders of 22 June 1644. For the deputy lieutenants' assent to his appointment, *C.S.P.D.* 1644, p.387.

Presbyterian minister of the same name). Brereton disliked
him and suspected him of disloyalty; he was later sequestered
as a delinquent, and though the papers relating to the charges
against him have not survived it is known that his personal
estate was sold and his rents confiscated.[1] Spurstowe was
closely linked to the Booth-Wilbraham group in 1641—2 and
was later one of Booth's allies in the attempt to destroy
Brereton's power in the county.[2]

The nature of Spurstowe's commission is unclear, and it is
unlikely that much money passed through his hands since, as
we shall see, money, plate, etc. advanced on the Propositions,
weekly assessments, and the maintenance of the militia all
remained decentralized within the county, and the
Sequestration Ordinance had hardly been implemented
during 1643. In fact, there are only four surviving warrants
belonging to the period of his treasurership up to the middle
of February 1644, though there are 130 from his last four
months in office.[3] However, this extreme variation may
simply result from the destruction or disappearance of the
relevant records.

This situation raises several awkward questions. Why did
the system remain so untidy, and how far did the leading
gentry on the deputy lieutenancy and other committees have
control over finances? The evidence is fragmentary, and even
an examination of each set of records in turn will only
provide a tentative answer.

The first money came in on the Propositions, and only
scattered records of its collection have survived. There were
local treasurers in each area, though strangely not all were
appointed to deal with a whole hundred. Thus, although
Robert Duckenfield was responsible for the whole of
Macclesfield hundred (and received £625 by the end of
1642)[4], Gilbert Gerard was receiver for an area based on

[1] *C.C.C.D.*, pp.1728—9; B.M. Harleian MS. 2144, f. 18.
[2] See below, p.157; also B.M. Add. MSS. 36913, ff. 60—67—81; 11331, ff. 67, 165.
[3] P.R.O., SP 28/224 and 225. Between them they authorized the disbursement of £1,654.
[4] P.R.O., SP 28/196.

Great Budworth and comprising a compact body of parishes in Bucklow, Edisbury, and Northwich hundreds. Between February 1643 and August 1646 he received £1,732.[1] By the end of 1643 Ralph Judson had received £2,878 from an area comprising parts of Nantwich and Broxton.[2] None of these men had been involved with the moderates in 1642, and all were to be amongst Brereton's closest allies in the struggle for power within the Parliamentarian movement in the county in 1644–6. These receiverships were in the gift of the county M.P.s, and it is difficult not to see the appointments as an early and deliberate attempt to bypass the traditional financial machinery of petty and head constables controlled by the Justices which would have given control over money to the 'middle group' gentry, newly recruited to the Parliamentarian cause late in 1642.[3]

From these fragmentary records, and the evidence of constables' accounts[4] it seems probable that something in excess of £30,000 was raised on the Propositions. By comparison, the attempt by the Committee for the Advance of Money to enforce the payment of the fifth and twentieth parts[5] from those who had not contributed

---

[1] P.R.O., SP 28/208, Accounts Book of Gilbert Gerard.

[2] P.R.O., SP 28/208, Accounts Book of Ralph Judson.

[3] A document drawn up by the Restoration lieutenancy, containing the names of all who acted in local government against the Crown in 1642–60, has survived in the Commonwealth Exchequer Papers, P.R.O., SP 28/225, unfoliated. The Northwich hundred list specifically names nine men as having acted as receivers on the Propositions; six of them can be closely identified with Brereton (Gerard, Thomas Croxton, John Legh, James Croxton, William Eaton, and Thomas Rathbone): one, Henry Mainwaring, was his opponent. The other two, William Peartree and Nathaniel Lancaster, were Presbyterian ministers; Lancaster was later to be an opponent (see below, pp.165–6), but in the early days of the war his radical religious ideas might have made him obnoxious to the moderates (see above, p.35). For more about the Restoration list, see Dore and Morrill, art. cit., *passim*.

[4] This estimate may be conservative. The complete records for the villages of Dutton, Frodsham, Hollingworth, Kingsley, Lawton, Over, Mere, and Nether Whitley show that these eight between them contributed almost £700 on the Propositions. If they were typical of the whole county, over £50,000 would have been raised. (B.M. Harleian MSS. 1943, ff. 2–8; 1999, ff. 75–92; 2126, ff. 3–39, 101; 2128, ff. 4–15, 41–6, 60–2, 149–52).

[5] See above, pp.95–6.

voluntarily was a dismal failure. Initial assessments would have produced over £40,000 for the committee in London, but many assessments were hopelessly optimistic. Thomas Leigh of High Legh, for example, was assessed at £2,000, but this had to be later reduced to £220; there were similar adjustments to other original assessments (e.g. that of Sir Thomas Smyth). Some assessments were confirmed after further investigation, but the revised totals brought down expected income to between £16,000 and £20,000. Yet only a little over £2,500 was collected, much of this in the late 1640s. Only 10 per cent of those adjudged liable to pay had been discharged by 1648.[1] This is consistent with the national pattern described by Mrs. Green in her introduction to the Calendar of the Committee's records, where she estimated that only £260,000 out of £1,700,000 had been paid by the beginning of July 1644.[2] Despite the increasing reliance by this committee on the machinery of the Committee for Sequestrations, apathy in Cheshire towards assessments, the proceeds of which could not readily be converted to the county's use, may have hindered the committee's work. Once again the comparison with Kent is illuminating. Professor Everitt found that far more was raised by the assessments than on the Propositions themselves, though he also shows that there, as in Cheshire, original assessments were much too high.[3]

The early history of weekly assessments is wrapped in mystery. The village records do not reveal the burden of the tax, and the earliest surviving record is the accounts book of John Wettenhall, appointed receiver from the head constables of five[4] of the seven hundreds between March and December 1645. During that time the amount that should have been raised was £4,700: in fact his receipts were £2,336. The other

---

[1] Based on all the cases given in the *C.C.A.M.* This does not give the full picture, however, since Mrs. Green did not calendar every case, though she claims that those omitted are the smallest and least well-documented cases.

[2] Preface to the *C.C.A.M.*, vol. 1.

[3] Everitt, op. cit., pp.155—7.

[4] Macclesfield, Nantwich, Northwich, Bucklow, Edisbury.

two hundreds, Broxton and Wirral, were those where
Brereton had established special committees (at Hooton,
Puddington, and Tarvin),[1] and it seems reasonable to suppose
that responsibility for the collection of assessments there lay
with these committees. Wettenhall's accounts reveal that he
disbursed the bulk of the money for the payment of troops
and services and the repayment of loans, only £619 being
passed on to James Croxton. This fits in well with entries in
the county treasurer's accounts book.[2]

From August 1645 Croxton began to act as receiver of the
monthly assessments. Between that date and the completion
of his accounts in July 1647, he received £15,500 from this
source: this was out of £21,000 which ought to have been
collected. Figures for individual hundreds suggest that in
those areas most firmly under Parliamentarian control,
receipts were high (over 90 per cent in Macclesfield hundred,
over 80 per cent in Nantwich hundred). By contrast, in those
areas where the Royalists had been strong, the yield was very
low (less than 40 per cent in Broxton and Wirral hundreds).
Croxton said that the rest was 'remaining in the said
hundreds'[3] Since in his separate accounts for the special
assessments for Ireland the pattern was very similar (over 80
per cent in Macclesfield, Bucklow, and Nantwich, barely 40
per cent in Wirral and Broxton) and since in these accounts
he speaks of the remainder specifically as 'arrears', it seems
probable that he was referring to unpaid assessments rather
than to money retained by local treasurers.[4] Further
evidence is afforded by the accounts of John Page, head
constable of Northwich hundred 1645—6, who stated that he
had only managed to get in £444 out of the £552 from that
part of the hundred for which he was responsible. This
percentage (78) is close to the figure for Northwich hundred
as a whole in Croxton's accounts.[5]

---

[1] See above, pp.87—8.
[2] Wettenhall's accounts are in B.M. Harleian MS. 2128, ff. 84—96; the relevant
entries in Croxton's accounts are in P.R.O., SP 28/128, ff. 8—10.
[3] Ibid.
[4] Ibid., ff. 1—4.
[5] B.M. Harleian MS. 2128, ff. 129—37.

The centralization of assessments at the end of 1645 is further shown by the records of payments for the trained and freehold bands. Until the summer of 1645 each village was directly responsible for levying and maintaining its own quota in the militia, but from September 1645, Croxton began to act as treasurer for these payments also. The merger of militia regiments into the general forces at the siege of Chester probably made this an administrative convenience. It is also clear, however, that both these changes could be connected with Brereton's recall to London following the New Model Ordinance; both occurred before rumours of his imminent reappointment to his old command reached the county. Previously Brereton had taken primary responsibility for the payment of his field army, the deputy lieutenants for the militia. This general reorganization may have seemed not only an administrative convenience, but also a means of reducing the residual powers of Brereton's old subordinates.

Revenue from sequestrations remained largely decentralized. Croxton received a total of £17,000 from this source between 1644 and 1647, but this is only a fraction of the total sum raised from Royalists' estates. Job Murcot, the solicitor for sequestrations in Cheshire from 1643—9, estimated that the amount raised during those years totalled £106,000, of which perhaps £90,000 would have come in during the years 1644—7, the period corresponding to Croxton's accounts.[1] This estimate is probably reliable.[2] We possess accounts books of the hundredal treasurers for most of the county, which show that in most cases only half the money sent in to them by the collectors was sent on to Croxton.[3] A careful estimate averaged out year by year and

---

[1] *C.C.C.D.*, p.3209. Sequestrations were hardly effective before 1644; the majority had compounded by the end of 1647 and had had their estates restored. (See below pp.203—6).

[2] See my thesis, pp.132—5.

[3] The exception is Bucklow, whose treasurer Thomas Warburton sent only 18 per cent of his receipts to Croxton. But there special circumstances prevailed: see my thesis, p.133. The surviving accounts are in B.M. Harleian MSS. 2128, ff. 18—19; 2130, ff. 52—106, 213—91; 2136, ff. 51—2, 63—79; 2137, ff. 23—49, 127—141, 198—208; 2144, ff. 37—64; P.R.O., SP 28/208 (Warburton's accounts).

hundred by hundred to cover all the gaps in the records suggests a total of about £40,000 received at hundredal level. But the local collectors within each division only sent off between one-third and one-half of the rents collected by them. Not only did these agents disburse the statutory one-fifth allowed to the wives and families of some delinquents—it was thought unjust that they should suffer unduly for the political follies of their husbands and fathers—but they sent large sums directly to local garrison commanders and other officers, as well as making payments to ministers and for several other purposes.[1] There seems little reason to doubt that the total revenue passing through their hands was well in excess of £80,000.

The largest single item in Croxton's receipts was the sum of over £30,000 received in the form of cash grants from Parliament. Despite the failure of the county to meet its obligations to hand over the revenue from sequestrations and monthly assessments to Parliament, the central government on several occasions reacted to financial and military crises in Cheshire by sending down money. Altogether £37,000 was voted for the county (separate grants of £5,000 in March and June 1644 and in December 1645, £10,000 in September 1645, and £12,000 in September 1646). Almost £30,500 reached Croxton (82 per cent).[2]

Detailed records of two of these grants (the £10,000 of September 1645 and the £5,000 of December 1645) have survived.[3] They show that Brereton appointed the agents to receive these grants in London and to bring them down to the county. These men took the opportunity to pay off the county's outstanding debts in London (mostly for ammunition) and on the way down to Cheshire met other demands (e.g. one of them, John Bradshaw, took the opportunity to pay his brother part of his arrears); the residue was then handed to Croxton.

---

[1] See also below, pp.123–5. The collectors' accounts are in B.M. Harleian MSS. 1999, 2018, 2126, 2128, 2130, 2136, 2166, *passim*.
[2] P.R.O., SP 28/128, ff. 12–13.
[3] P.R.O., SP 28/152, Books 8 and 9.

The treasurer's receipts are completed by miscellaneous payments of £3,888. These include such items as the profits from the sale of cheese and cattle seized in other counties, but most of it, over £3,000, took the form of undischarged loans.

As a result, his book records total receipts during his period as treasurer as £77,494.[1] But my own estimate of the total sum raised and employed in the county on Parliamentary ordinances between 1642 and the summer of 1647 is £250,000.[2]

This appears a surprisingly low figure. Professor Everitt has calculated that £400,000 was raised in assessments alone from Kent during the years 1643–8.[3] But it must be remembered that Cheshire was one of the smaller counties, that it remained the scene of constant military activity until the early months of 1646, and that it was not a naturally wealthy county. None-the-less, tax burdens were many times heavier than ever before. And this was not the full cost. Surviving constables' accounts afford a far more vivid impression of the effect of the war at a village level. From them it becomes clear that the incidental costs of war, in free quarter, plunder, and destruction, were at least as great as those from taxation.

Both sides resorted to free quarter throughout the war. Officially the constables of each village were to keep a record so that each inhabitant could be subsequently recompensed when the soldiers' arrears were made up and the relevant sums deducted from their pay. In practice he was only ever repaid in a case of acute individual hardship.[4] Several detailed village records have survived, the clearest being that

[1] The exact figures from his book, P.R.O., SP 28/128, are i) from Parliamentary grants £30,473; ii) from weekly and monthly assessments £15,468; iii) from assessments for the trained and freehold bands £10,654; iv) from sequestrations, £17,021; v) from other sources £3,888.

[2] For justification, see my thesis, chapter 3, section V. Details: i) on the Propositions, £40,000; ii) assessments, £30,000; iii) for freehold and trained bands, £25,000; iv) from sequestrations, £90,000; v) from Parliamentary grants, £37,000; vi) Miscellaneous (including undischarged loans, Excise), £25,000.

[3] Everitt, op. cit., p.158.

[4] See below, p.122.

for the township of Over.[1] Although undated, internal
evidence suggests that the account was drawn up in the
summer of 1646. There is no mention of assessments, since
this is essentially a claim for the repayment of debts incurred
by Parliament in Proposition money, free quarter, and
plunder seized by its forces. Over £160 had been contributed
on the Propositions, £250 spent in quarter, and £400 lost in
plunder and destruction. The sufferings of each inhabitant is
separately recorded, and the account makes clear that only
the freeholders and tenants were involved, the only
substantial men in the town being Royalists whose estates
were under sequestration.[2] At the other end of the scale were
the townships of Hollingworth on the Derbyshire border and
remote from the fighting and Nether Whitley, a quiet
Bucklow village away from the main highways. Yet even here
the cost was enormous. In Hollingworth, where the figures
are not totalled and might be incomplete, the town laid out
£266 up to August 1645, over half of it in quarter and
depredations.[3] In Nether Whitley, the comparative figure was
£372 (this is only to the end of 1644).[4] In Lymm, a village
on the main road to Warrington, the total cost for the years
1642—5 was £1,164.[5]

The same picture emerges from all the records. As much
again was spent in coping with the movement of
Parliamentarian troops as on taxation of all kinds. If the eight
examples cited above were typical, it would indicate that as
well as £100,000 raised in direct taxation and on the
Propositions in the county by the summer of 1646 (a figure
perfectly compatible with that derived from the accounts
committee material above), over £120,000 would have been
expended on quarter and about £90,000 seized or destroyed

---

[1] B.M. Harleian MS. 2126, ff. 3—39.
[2] Despite its special status in its election of a mayor, Over was no larger than
other villages (see its assessment on the mise roll).
[3] B.M. Harleian MS. 2128, ff. 4—15.
[4] Ibid., ff. 39—45.
[5] Ibid., ff. 46—50. See also Dutton, ibid., ff. 149—52, Church Lawton, B.M.
Harleian MS. 1943, ff. 2—8, and Frodsham, B.M. Harleian MS. 1999, ff. 75—92.

in goods.[1] These figures are based on the accounts of villages none of which was close to the main battle zones at Chester and Nantwich (those closest, Frodsham and Over, were also those where the incidental costs were highest), and do not include figures from the market towns like Middlewich, Northwich, Knutsford, and Tarvin which housed permanent Parliamentarian garrisons. The total cost may well be sub- stantially higher than the estimates given above. Further- more, we have no figures on which to make an estimate of the sums paid to Royalist troops either garrisoned in the county or passing through it. Rupert's army had both a local and general reputation for rapacity.[2]

The terrible effects of the demands made even by 'friendly' forces on the march on the livelihoods of the population at large are difficult to document. Fifty-one horses were taken by passing troopers in Lymm alone,[3] and in Wirral the sequestration committee spoke about 'the greate wante and scarcitie of cattle'.[4] In a predominently pastoral community, the seizure of large numbers of animals must have had serious long-term effects on the rural economy. A typical case might well have been that of Robert Whittingham of Over, who recorded that there had been 'taken by Maior Manwaring's & Maior Croxton's soldiers Twelve cowes & three heffers & one calfe & a cheare wch the calfe was tyed wth'. It cannot have been easy for a small freeholder like Whittingham to make up losses valued at £40.[5]

Soldiers were not just interested in cash and food. Widow Ryder recorded losses of shoes, stockings, and oats to Sir Thomas Fairfax's men as they passed through Dutton,[6] while the Scots troops not only took some pewter from Thomas

---

[1] With the addition of these sums to the money raised during that period in sequestrations and compositions, the total cost to the county would thus have been well in excess of £400,000.

[2] e.g. B.M. Add. MS. 11331, f. 54, Bodl.Lib. Tanner MSS. vol. 59, f. 232.

[3] B.M. Harleian MS. 2128, ff. 46–50.

[4] B.M. Harleian MS. 2018, f. 37.

[5] Ibid., 2126, f. 19.

[6] Ibid., 2128, f. 150

Shawe's house at Church Lawton, but also removed a bible—
only one of several seized in that village alone.[1]

Many of these cases concerned theft by individual soldiers,
but there is little evidence that they were carried out with
violence; certainly the word 'looting' is never used. Not until
the summer of 1646 is there any sign of a civilian backlash
against the behaviour of the troops.[2] Certainly there is no
evidence of a Clubman movement in Cheshire at any stage.[3]
As a result of civilian acquiescence, the soldiers do not appear
to have done much physical damage. In Hollingworth, for
example, the only complaints were about the breaking of
Charles Shufflebotham's windows, and of the destruction of
a crop of peas by troops carelessly wandering through the
fields. Otherwise, indignation centred round an incident
when John Beech had his hat snatched off his head.[4]

When a regiment or company was desperate for provisions,
the officers would frequently intervene and requisition goods
to avoid more serious trouble. It is clear that they had no
authority to do this, but there is also no doubt that it
effectively prevented trouble. For example, Captain Shipley
commandeered 50 measures of oats for his men in the
summer of 1646.[5] Elsewhere food, clothing, and drink were
taken over and above normal quarter in exchange for a
promise of future repayment.[6] The strangest example is that
of Captain Rathbone's company who, finding themselves
semi-permanently quartered at Burton, commandeered a field
to their own use and sowed their own wheat.[7]

At the beginning of 1647 Peter Warburton, a young lawyer
newly appointed assistant Justice to John Bradshaw at
Chester, reported to the Committee of Accounts in London
on the state of finances in Cheshire. His impression was very

[1] Ibid., 1943, f. 69.
[2] See below, pp.194—203.
[3] See below, p.190, n. 2, for a brief bibliography of the Clubman movement.
[4] B.M. Harleian MS.1943, ff. 48, 68. For the more violent atmosphere in other
counties, see my article, 'Mutinies and Discontent in English Provinical Armies'
*Past and Present*, 56 (1972), 64—5.
[5] B.M. Harleian MS. 1999, f. 70.
[6] Ibid., 2128, f. 14; see also 2126, ff. 6, 101; 1943, f. 13.
[7] Ibid., 1999, f. 71.

similar to the one that I have tried to give in this section.

These are to let you understand that I fynd our gent in Cheshyir that are of the Comittee of accounts very willing to act, but that they fynd they are more likely to putt the state in debt by the large demands of the Captains then anyway to ease it, by laying a surcharge upon them, partly because they have not in these troublous tymes had such store of mony to pay there souldiers with by the hands of setled treasorers, but soelye have paid them part by there hands, part by sequestrators, much and very much by taxes & levies upon the Country & also in regard that free quarter hath beene so usually & generally taken uppon the country that the busynes seemes endles to ascertaine, it being past and spent, though they warned the country generally to bring in notes what free quarter hath beene taken, yet they rather sitt downe wth ease for the most part having beene so long deteyned from there country occasions then put themselves to such charge & attendance in looking for it, especially since they have no present mony and could give nothing in [    ] but either good wordes or a piece of paper.[1]


## VI

The most complex and involved of all Parliament's attempts to raise money was the administration of the sequestered estates of delinquents and Papists. Professor Everitt thought that in Kent sequestration was inefficient; 'The mountains laboured and brought forth a fiscal mouse.'[2] In Cheshire, though administration of the estates was inevitably patchy, it is difficult to reach any such categorical conclusion. The general impression is one of conscientiousness marred by a lack of precision and over-all control.

There are, for each hundred, comprehensive inventories of goods from the homes of most of those sequestered. Particularly careful checks seem to have been made to ascertain whether any of the goods listed and valued belonged to other men. However, we possess little evidence of the manner of disposing of these personal estates except for some thirty cases in Macclesfield hundred.[3] After estimates of their value had been made, most of them were

[1] P.R.O., SP 28/259, unfoliated letter of 27 Feb. 1647.
[2] Everitt, *Community of Kent. . .,* p.160.
[3] B.M. Harleian MS. 1999, ff. 162–97.

bought back either by the delinquents themselves or by friends acting on their behalf. Thus Edward Barlowe of Poynton personally recovered his possessions on payment of £70.[1] Others sought to evade payment by concealing their goods or selling them while the question of their delinquency was still being examined and before the valuers arrived[2]. Early compounders were entitled to the immediate restoration of their personal estate without payment, a situation which angered the local committees[3]. The following account of the committee's proceedings in the case of John Bretland summarizes their problems and persistence:

The said John Bretland beinge a notorious delinquente, the committee caused his personall estate to be inventoryed and valued . . to the value of 556li 16s 08d (other partes of his estate to a greate value beinge conveaed away into darbishire wher he hath some lands) the agents in purshute of an order from the committee for the fetchinge away and makinge sale of the said goods and havinge seized some of his cattell to make sale therof were rescued by 13 men and wimen at one tyme . . . [When they succeeded in taking away some cattle, at the third attempt], Mrs. Bretland wth other freinds of hers made propositions to by the said estate . . the committy then takinge into consideration, the gret charge, troble and danger ther agents had beene put unto conserninge the same estate, as alsoe the charge and trouble the were like to undergoe in the removall of the rest of the estate before the could conveniently make sale of the same, did then make sale of all the whole estate soe inventoried . . to the said freinds of Mrs Bretland for the some of 420li . . well knowinge it was for the best advantage of the commonwealth rather soe to doe then to make salle of them by parsells consideringe the trouble, danger and expences insedente therunto . . .[4]

The much more numerous records dealing with the administration of sequestered real estate confirm that the hundredal committees were broadly sympathetic towards the interests of the deprived landowners. In a few extreme cases, admittedly usually after the delinquent had started the process of negotiating the size of the fine to be paid as the price of regaining his estates,[5] the committee even allowed him to nominate some of his own friends to whom the demesne might be leased; Robert Tatton of Wythenshawe was one who benefited from this concession[6]. Far more

[1] Ibid., f. 182.    [2] Ibid., f. 179.    [3] Ibid., f. 194.
[4] Ibid., f. 178.    [5] See below, pp.115–16.    [6] B.M. Harleian MS. 2130, ff. 230–1.

frequent are records that money was spent on maintaining the demesne or repairing the manor house. Thus most of the profits from Wythenshawe Mill were reinvested to keep it in good repair.[1] Entries like the following, 'paid for repaireing the out-buildinge at Kinderton & for glaseinge the hall winders ... 3li'[2] are far more common than complaints about disregard. One of the comparatively few charges of official slackness concerned Cholmondeley House, where the tenants installed by the sequestrators were said to have 'convert[ed] it into a hogsty and render[ed] it unusefull and unfit for a place of residence for a person of such quality' (as Lord Cholmondeley).[3] But measures were rapidly adopted to rectify this situation, and this is indicative of the high level of probity amongst sequestration officials.

Equally significant was their failure to produce a level of profit from the estates to match that being made before the Civil War. In 1647 the Wirral commissioners thoughtfully drew up a list of delinquents giving the annual value of the estates (in rents and in profits from the demesne) in 1640–1 and the profit which they were able to make in 1645–6. The former totalled £4,277 per annum, the latter £2,276, that is barely half the pre-war value.[4] There are no comparable figures for other hundreds, but it is clear that the committees throughout the county were struggling to increase the rentals. It seems that there was no great decline in the rents paid by sitting tenants: they simply paid the same sum they had previously paid to their landlords to the agents of the sequestrators. On the other hand there are few entries in all the detailed accounts for the various hundreds that suggest that much effort was made to collect or raise money from the various incidents of tenure, such as fines for the renewal of leases.

A greater problem, however, was the leasing of the extensive demesnes, since it was impossible for the sequestrators to farm them directly themselves. A detailed

[1] B.M. Harleian MS. 2126, ff. 106–11.   [2] Ibid., 1999, f. 93.
[3] C.C.C.D., p.1479.   [4] Ibid., p.60.

examination of some of the most complete accounts from individual sequestrated estates reveals that the lands were only leased out on a year-to-year basis and that after being let at a very low level in 1644 and 1645, there was a tendency for the rents to rise in 1646 and 1647. This was simply a tendency; there were variations even within the same estates. Thus in a typical case, that of Lord Kilmorey's estates in Bucklow Hundred, some land was let for the same rent in all four years, in one area (the Dutton demesne let to Richard Janion) the rent was actually lowered by 20 per cent in 1646, but in most of the lands the trend was towards increased rents, in some cases by 100 per cent: the complete rental rose by 30 per cent to £597. Even where the whole demesne was let as a single block of land, the same pattern emerges. Thus Earl River's Bucklow estates were let as a whole for £200 in 1645, £305 in 1646, and £310 in 1647. Variations from estate to estate and the inadequacy of many of the records make any general estimate of the over-all pattern uncertain, but the movement towards improved profits is clear.[1]

The Bucklow sequestrators, like their colleagues in Wirral, drew attention to their failure to raise a revenue comparable with that of the same estates in the years before the war. Although they gave no figures, they did offer an explanation. They pointed out that although they had been ordered to value every man's estates

as they were worth before the warrs, for so every delinquent was to compound for them ... for the settinge of delinquents' estates the Ordinance doth not appoynte that they shalbe sett accordinge as they be valued, but for so much as anyone would give for them, for upon such an appoyntmt the estates might have lyen wholly waste and nothinge at all made of them.[2]

The war itself not only added to the uncertainty and thereby lowered the price men were willing to pay, but also at times directly destroyed the profits. Richard Button, accounting for the Tatton estates, noted that

---

[1] The above examples are from B.M. Harleian MS. 2137, ff. 127–41. Other good examples are P.R.O., SP 28/208 (Thomas Warburton's accounts) ff. 1–26, or B.M. Harleian MS. 2126, ff. 91–7.

[2] B.M. Harleian MS. 2128, ff. 127–8.

by reason of those 2 yeares wch were sor destracted and flyinge before the Army of Prince Rupert, Mrs. Tatton put in a man to looke to the ground & soe till after the fight at Yorke much of the proffits of the demesne were lost by the meanes of troupers & others wch brought goods & cattell into the ground.[1]

Yet more losses were incurred through the fears of the leaders that those areas where Royalism had flourished were only partially subdued. Whenever the threat of relief for Chester was great, the tenants of former Royalists were given preferential treatment in order to keep them loyal. Thus one collector noted in his accounts: 'the sd tenents & divers other hereafter set downe were (by order made by the comittee at Hooton) to paie hut halfe theire rents because the Garrisons & forces in Wirrall were not able to secure them from the enimie.'[2]

The deputy lieutenants were also involved in ensuring that the tenants were given relief to reduce the risk that they might be tempted to join the Royalists. Thus in January 1646 they ruled that the level of taxation was so high that in some sequestered townships a rebate of 25 per cent was to be made of all 'laies' against their rent 'not onelie thenceforward but alsoe for twoe yeares last past before the date of the said order'.[3] At Lymm, where the deputy lieutenants thought the sequestrators' demands had been too high, they intervened and ordered a partial repayment 'beinge remitted in regarde it did arise from poore people'.[4]

As I have said, it seems clear that most land continued to be leased to the same families as had held it before the war.[5] The problem lay in leasing out the demesne. In exceptional circumstances friends of the delinquent were granted the lease.[6] Sometimes the Committee for Sequestrations at Westminster would order the local committee to lease land to

[1] Ibid., 2126, ff. 131.
[2] Ibid., f. 160. For a similar order see B.M. Harleian MS. 2018, f. 37.
[3] Ibid., 2130, f. 232.
[4] Ibid., 2128, f. 48.
[5] See, for example, B.M. Harleian MS. 2174, ff. 4—80, a series of surveys and valuations which demonstrate the extent to which many tenants still paid their rents in kind and labour services.
[6] See above, p.112.

a Parliamentary officer at preferential rates to offset arrears in salary, as in the case of Robert Duckenfield.[1] Rather more frequent was the practice for the sequestrators in one hundred to lease land to their fellows or their relatives from other hundreds. Thus the Wirral sequestrators leased part of widow Chauntrell's lands to Thomas Coventry of Noctorum, one of the sequestrators in Broxton.[2] But the most frequent solution seems to have been to lease the demesnes either in small portions to individuals who were already amongst the more substantial tenants, or as a whole to a consortium of local tenants and freeholders who joined together to raise the advance necessary to get possession of the lands.[3] For example, while the hall and mill of Peter Venables's demesne at Marston were let in 1645—7 to William Millington, a minor local gentleman who possessed lands of his own in the neighbouring township of Millington and already rented some lands in Marston, the demesne itself was let to a group of tenants headed by a local yeoman, John Heath.[4]

It has always been widely assumed, and for some areas of the country successfully demonstrated, that the sequestrators were either extremely inefficient, or where efficient, very harsh in their dealings with Royalists' estates, allowing the woods and amenities to be exploited and ruined. This brief survey of Cheshire has suggested quite the contrary; that the sequestrators were thorough in their attempts to raise money from delinquents' estates, but also that they took their position of trust seriously, aware of the wider considerations of not abusing their power, and seeking always to be equitable in their dealings with all concerned, the rights of tenants and of the original owners. The Lancashire commissioners wrote in July 1645 that 'the Ordinance of Sequestration is fully executed when the people are well-affected, but in Colonel Rigby's division, most of the people were sequestrable but few sequestered because the condition

---

[1] P.R.O., SP 20, vol. 1, f. 366.
[2] B.M. Harleian MS. 2018, f. 47.
[3] Ibid., 2137, ff. 127—41, or P.R.O., SP 28/208, accounts of Thomas Warburton.
[4] B.M. Harleian MS. 2137, ff. 128, 136, 140.

of the county would not admit it in safety'.[1] Such a degree of caution was probably unusual. But certainly in Cheshire those responsible for the administration of Royalists' estates were concerned not to alienate tenants or owners more than was absolutely necessary.

## VII

Patterns of official expenditure during the Civil War in Cheshire are even more difficult to discover than those of revenue. Nothing on the scale or with the penetration of Dr. Holmes's analysis of expenditure in the counties of the Eastern Association can be attempted here.[2] Thus, although we possess James Croxton's summary accounts book, we have seen that he only handled a small percentage of the county revenue. A great deal of work can produce some estimates of expenditure in general categories by the treasurers at hundredal level and by local sequestration agents, but many entries are unclear and ambiguous. The massive reliance on free quarter and the unsanctioned levying of provisions make the accounts of army officers difficult to interpret. I shall here aim to do little more than attempt to elucidate the general administrative pattern.

At the heart of the matter lay increasingly diffuse patterns of military organization. Initially Brereton's forces comprised the militia of five of the seven hundreds[3] and several volunteer regiments of horse and foot raised by several leading gentlemen. But increasingly the militia came to be treated as a force apart, being used predominantly to garrison market towns and manor houses in central Cheshire, while Brereton developed a flexible field army comprised of the original volunteer regiments supplemented and expanded by levies from the countryside (enlisted by landlords or

---

[1] *C.C.A.M.*, p.47.
[2] C. Holmes, 'The Eastern Association 1643–6', Univ. of Cambridge Ph.D. thesis 1969, *passim.* This excellent thesis is at its best in its unravelling of Civil War finance.
[3] The militia of Broxton and Wirral seem to have been under Royalist control until early 1644.

sequestration committees); there was also a growing contingent of forces from other counties. This army was employed both in Cheshire and other counties and its payment was kept distinct from that of the militia, which Brereton saw as the financial responsibility of the deputy lieutenants. The money in Croxton's hands, and in particular that coming into the county from London, was reserved for his field army.[1] But this pattern could not be strictly followed; militia regiments were brought up to the siege of Chester, particularly in 1645, and enlisted companies were used for garrisons in Broxton and Wirral. The need for a separate establishment to maintain these garrisons may well have been the major administrative reason for the creation of the special committees at Tarvin, Hooton, and Puddington in 1644.[2] Numerous warrants have survived showing how these committees allocated taxes directly for the upkeep of garrisons in the area under their control.[3] In the eastern hundreds, standing orders were issued to the sequestrators to pay fixed sums to particular garrisons or companies—£9 a week from Bucklow and Edisbury to the garrison at Halton Castle, for example, or all the profits of the estate of the sequestered Lawrence Wynington of Armitage to Major Mainwaring's troop.[4]

The most complex of these standing arrangements, and one which created considerable trouble, was that allocating all the money raised in the twenty-nine townships in the upper division of Bucklow hundred to John Booth's garrison in Warrington—across the Mersey in Lancashire.[5] He was granted this concession 'by an order from the Counsell of Warr at Namptwich' some time towards the end of 1643. The accounts of Thomas Warburton, treasurer of Bucklow sequestration committee, show that up to the end of April

[1] e.g. B.M. Add. MS. 11332, ff. 119, 128. See below, pp.120—1.
[2] See above, pp.87—8.
[3] P.R.O., SP 28/224 and 225, passim, P.R.O., SP 28/208 (accounts of Gilbert Gerard), p.31.
[4] P.R.O., SP 28/225, unfoliated warrants of 25 Mar. and 23 Apr. 1644.
[5] All the following is based on unfoliated material in P.R.O., SP 28/225, except where otherwise specified.

1644 he paid £328.18s.2d. to John Booth, almost exactly half the total raised from sequestrations in the whole hundred during the same period.[1] Payments then ceased abruptly. For on 2 March 1644 Sir Thomas Fairfax, nominally commander-in-chief while Brereton was in London, had ordered that all sequestration money must be paid directly to the county treasurer. Booth entered a vociferous protest at Nantwich, but in May Brereton arranged for Parliament to confirm Fairfax's order.[2] Booth continued to remonstrate and made every effort to get hold of money from the area. Several orders from Nantwich in the summer and autumn of 1644 attempted to restrain him, but this proved impossible. At one point two collectors, John Lawrenson and John Bruch, were imprisoned at Warrington for a space of twelve weeks for handing over their money to Warburton rather than to Booth.[3] The situation reached crisis point in the spring of 1645 when Booth was further prohibited from recruiting in Bucklow. At the same time, the committee at Nantwich decided that two fresh regiments should be raised for the field army at Chester, and fixed a proportion for Bucklow. Booth was determined to prevent this, and armed clashes resulted between his troops and those of Brereton's recruiting officers. One group of recruits was forcibly disbanded.[4] Only the arrival of the King and Prince Maurice on the borders of Cheshire forced the two factions to sink their differences.[5]

It is easy to see both sides of the argument. John Booth, younger son of Sir George Booth, was a Cheshire gentleman who had raised his regiment in Cheshire. Warrington was a Booth manor, but on the 'wrong' side of the Mersey. By ending his special position in Bucklow hundred, Brereton was cutting him off from his only source of supply, since the

---

[1] Warburton's accounts are in P.R.O., SP 28/208.
[2] *Commons Journal,* vol. 3, p.484.
[3] B.M. Harleian MS. 2137, ff. 56, 62.
[4] B.M. Add. MS. 11331, f. 43.
[5] For other incidents and for the resolution of the crisis, see B.M. Add. MS. 11331, *passim,* particularly ff. 10–11, 14–15, 42, 69, (postscript to Brereton's letter of 8 May 1645), 78–9, 134–5, and H.M.C. *Portland MSS.,* vol. 1, p.239.

Lancashire committee disclaimed responsibility for him. Yet, as far as Brereton was concerned, Warrington was palpably a Lancashire responsibility, and he could claim that Cheshire's resources were already inadequate for his other commitments.

The pressure on resources and the lack of reserve funds to meet crises led to an increasing tendency for all county officials to supplement standing orders by individual orders to particular officers. There are hundreds of warrants surviving addressed by Brereton or the deputy lieutenants to the sequestration agents or treasurers; for example, to pay a specified sum, or in kind, for a new saddle, to the impoverished widow of a soldier killed in action, or to a minister for his services as a peripatetic preacher. This system was particularly employed in relation to the disposal of delinquents' goods. A record was supposed to be kept so that the concession could be deducted against pay. Thus there has survived a list of 'the goods Sr William Brereton had for his owne use out of Sr Richard Grosvenor's goods'.[1] Robert Venables bought £30 worth of books and other items from the sequestrators and was then granted an order that these could be credited against £30 worth of arrears.[2] Others were given a credit note in advance: William Massie, for example, was to be allowed 'three feather bedds well furnished and some chayres and stooles or other household goods'.[3]

The resulting chaos in accounts can be imagined. Sequestrators were supposed to inventory the goods of all Royalists before disposing of them, but one committee reported that because of the need to make speedy payments and to forestall mutinies, they had been 'forced to bring very much goodes into the Comon Hall . . . and there they were intermingled and sold together'.[4]

[1] P.R.O., SP 28/224, ff. 341—2.
[2] Ibid., f. 232.
[3] P.R.O., SP 28/208, blue packet tied with pink ribbon, unfoliated order of 25 June 1646.
[4] Ibid., unfoliated and undated. See also B.M. Harleian MS. 2137, ff. 104, 201 (from Lord Kilmorey's estates and for Captain Richard Brooke).

It is only against this background of muddle that general remarks about patterns of expenditure can be understood. And here again, only the accounts of the county treasurer afford a clear picture.

James Croxton's accounts are overwhelmingly concerned with the payment of troops. His summary disbursements for the period up to June 1647 total £77,494.2s5d.[1] Of this £66,045.2s.9d. (86 per cent) was paid out to army officers as pay for themselves and their men. This sum in turn can be divided into three almost equal portions; the first being paid to the main Cheshire regiments serving within and outside Cheshire under Brereton; the second to the trained and freehold bands who remained in the county and were responsible for most of the garrisons, including Nantwich, although many of them were brought up to the siege at the end of 1645; the third (over £20,000) was paid to troops from other counties who came to the siege.[2] On top of all this, a further £4,500 was spent on other directly military expenditure, such as arms and ammunition, and in payments to auxiliary personnel like surgeons or scouts. £2,000 was spent on the repayment of loans, £750 on the pay of officials (clerks, collectors, Croxton himself), and £400 paid to travelling ministers as their remuneration.[3]

It was these particular categories, where the figures look suspiciously low, which were supplemented by the money laid out by Brereton's agents in London who collected the sums voted to the county by Parliament. The bulk of the money not given to Croxton from the grants in 1645 was used to buy arms and ammunition in London.[4] Furthermore Brereton kept a personal account book of his own expenses. He received money from various sources, notably from London out of the money granted for Cheshire in 1644. He

---

[1] P.R.O., SP 28/128, James Croxton's accounts, ff. 15—21.

[2] For a fuller discussion of this case, see below, pp.168—71.

[3] With so many ministers having their livings sequestered, and with no time or powers to settle new ones immediately, the administration in Cheshire was prepared to pay preachers willing to move week by week to different parishes. They received periodic payments for their services from the treasurer or from the sequestrators.

[4] P.R.O., SP 28/152, books 8 and 9.

used it as a constant source of petty cash, to pay messengers, intelligencers, scouts, and other such agents, but also in times of real crisis, to help Croxton to pay off mutineers, to clothe soldiers whose garments were threadbare, or to help to rush through emergency supplies of ammunition.[1]

Croxton's surviving warrants[2] help to explain the payments of over £4,000 to various civilians which complete the entries in his account book. Most of them are concerned with the payment—usually retrospectively—of civilians for delivering provisions to the army, for free quarter, or for the restitution of goods taken or destroyed by troops. The remainder concerned payments for services: for the hire of carts and the payment of civilian messengers, or for the pay of labourers hired to supplement the work of soldiers on constructing or repairing defence works. There were even some payments towards the repair of churches and bridges, and a few pensions for those maimed or widowed by the war. The sums involved were small compared with the total cost to the county of these items, but it is clear that some attempt was being made to alleviate the worst sufferings of the common people.

In almost every case these repayments were made on the orders of the deputy lieutenants. Admittedly most of them were made in 1646—7 after the end of the war, but some effort had always been made. Thus in May 1644 it was ordered that Richard Merchant of Nantwich was to be paid £4 immediately and £8 per annum henceforth in compensation for the necessary destruction of his house to allow defence works to be constructed. It was made clear that compensation was not automatic but was granted in this case because 'the peticoner's condicon & necessity [are] worthy of a due consideracon'.[3] In this and many similar cases, the deputy lieutenants showed a preoccupation with civilian sufferings. The problem was simple: there was just not enough money to go round.

[1] Brereton's accounts are in P.R.O., SP 28/152, book 7. The total expenditure was about £7,200.
[2] P.R.O., SP 28/224 and 225.
[3] P.R.O., SP 28/225, unfoliated.

Brereton seems to have made his absolute priority the payment of the army to prevent serious mutinies and a breakdown of the war effort. The deputy lieutenants feared the consequences of a policy that neglected altogether the sufferings and consequent unrest in the countryside, and preferred to alleviate the more extreme misfortunes of the villagers. There is no evidence that the deputy lieutenants received less money during Brereton's absence in London. The records suggest that money continued to flow steadily. Yet the most serious unrest in the army during the whole period 1643–6 occurred at two moments when Brereton was absent, October 1645 and July 1646.[1] It seems quite possible that this was because the deputy lieutenants, during these periods when they had greater control of finance, were allocating funds more broadly and that consequently the army were running up greater arrears than when Brereton was directing all available money to them. Only once did Brereton direct an order for the payment of compensation for civilian losses, to Mrs. Elizabeth Spencer because of excessive losses incurred by her in quartering troops, and then he added the rider 'this to bee done so soon as conveniently and not before'.[2] It typifies his attitude.

The comparative lack of references in Croxton's accounts to provisions for the army is only partially explained by the heavy reliance on free quarter.[3] For the records of the sequestration treasurers show that more than half the money received by them and not forwarded to Croxton[4] was used to buy provisions (particularly grain and cheese) for particular regiments or garrisons. In fact many tenants paid their rents in kind, and these goods could be immediately despatched to a body of troops.[5]

The remainder of the money passing through their hands

[1] See below, pp.171–3, 195–9.
[2] P.R.O., SP 28/224 f. 59.
[3] See above, p.107–111.
[4] See above, p.105–6.
[5] See also B.M. Harleian MS. 2174, ff. 4–80 for a series of surveys and valuations drawn up in Macclesfield hundred in 1643, showing the continued importance of labour services and payments in kind as integral parts of the village economy.

was employed for civilian purposes. The largest item, constituting over 6 per cent of the total, was their own pay and that of their agents. A further 3 per cent of the total was paid out to itinerant ministers,[1] and a similar amount was handed over to the head constables to make good expenses incurred by them or others in administration; slightly less was expended on running repairs to buildings in their charge on sequestered demesnes. The remainder forms a large miscellaneous category—including such items as the £85 for new army uniforms paid to a Manchester clothier,[2] the £1 paid towards 'the charge of a petition in the country's behalf', and sums that were paid out for the repair of churches.[3] One growing category was the payment of small sums to soldiers to help village and hundredal officials collect arrears of tax or rent. For example, 29s. was paid to 'corporall dudley & others of Maior Zankey troope to helpe the collectors to strayne upon the unruly'.[4]

A similar pattern is clear in the accounts of the collectors within each hundred.[5] Under half of the money collected was sent on to the hundredal treasurers; a further 18 per cent took the form of supplies or money for garrisons or other forces, 11 per cent was kept by the agents for their expenses and pay, 5 per cent was sent to head constables, 5 per cent used to pay civilians for such jobs as the repair of fortifications, and 5 per cent paid out to ministers. The remainder constitutes a miscellany, although it contained several sums ploughed back into the repair and maintenance of sequestered property. This does not take into account, either at manorial or hundredal level, the considerable sums handed over to wives and dependents of delinquents. In many cases they were entitled to up to one-fifth of the revenue of their husbands' estates, and in many cases it was claimed and received. But since claimants had explicitly to accept Parliamentary authority, many were reluctant to claim. In some cases the deputy lieutenants can be observed exerting pressure on the agents to maintain these payments.[6]

[1] See below, p.167.    [2] B.M. Harleian MS. 2130, f. 91.    [3] Ibid., 2144, ff. 75–6.
[4] B.M. Harleian MS. 2136, f. 68.  [5] See above, p.  [6] e.g. B.M. Harleian MS. 2136, f. 39.

This raises the whole question of the authority of these officials to disburse the money passing through their hands. Clearly there was no statutory provision, since all the money should have found its way to London. Given the extremely poor relations between the hundredal committees and the deputy lieutenants over a wide range of administrative and financial matters,[1] it seems implausible to look for co-operation between these bodies over the disbursement of money at the hundredal level. The only clear statement of responsibility is to be found at the head of Thomas Warburton's accounts as treasurer to the Bucklow sequestration committee, where he speaks of 'Ordrs from the then deputy Lieutenants of the County of Chester, Comittees & Comrs appoynted accordinge to ordinance of Parliamt or some of them'.[2] It must be that these 'committees and commissioners' were the sequestration commissioners themselves. The ensuing detailed accounts of his disbursements give no indication of the authority in each case, except for a few payments on the orders of the Parliamentary Committee of Appeals.[3] Significantly, in 1649, when the hundredal committees were dismantled, Warburton began to record most payments as being authorized by the deputy lieutenants.[4] This might be taken as negative evidence that they had not previously intervened. In Edisbury and Wirral, on the other hand, we know that in 1644–6 control of expenditure lay largely with Brereton's special committees at Tarvin, Hooton, and Puddington.[5]

This is of importance for the argument to be advanced in the next chapters, that the committees appointed by Brereton—including the sequestration committees—joined with him in a struggle for control of the county against the deputy lieutenants. If the latter did fail to exercise control

[1] See below, pp.168–171.
[2] P.R.O., SP 28/208, accounts of Thomas Warburton 1643–8, f. 27.
[3] Ibid., f. 33.
[4] P.R.O., SP 28/208, accounts of Thomas Warburton, 1649, f. 4.
[5] e.g. B.M. Harleian MS. 2018, ff. 48–53. The exception was the payment of fifths to dependents. Here the deputy lieutenants were the driving force (e.g. B.M. Harleian MS 2136, ff. 38–43).

over the disbursement of the substantial sequestration
revenues, it would further indicate their subjection to
Brereton in the years 1643—6.

On the other hand, there is no doubt that the deputy
lieutenants were able to influence the pattern of expenditure
through the hands of the local sequestration agents. Thus in
September 1643 they ordered a Northwich agent, William
Leftwich, to pay £20 to Philip Mainwaring,[1] and in January
1646 they ordered the agents in parts of Macclesfield
hundred to arrange a rebate for the tenants of Warford manor
who had been overcharged in the past.[2] But the hundredal
committees also assumed powers to order the agents to make
disbursements. Thus Marc Jolicoeur, a Nantwich agent,
recorded[3] that he had 'Payd to Henry Hayes by order from
the sequestrators for monies hee had layed out for the
mayntenance of the Almsmen wich are maintened out of Sr
Tho Wilbrhms estaett. . . 5li 10 0'. and William Leftwich
recorded that the Northwich sequestrators had consented to
his paying £5 to some Lancashire soldiers to induce them to
remain one night longer at Northwich 'for preservacon
thereof fro the enemy'.[4] It is impossible to determine from
the available scraps of evidence which of these authorities
was primarily responsible for authorizing their disbursements.

It would be wrong to conclude this impressionistic survey
without pointing out the inadequacy of the sums raised to
meet all the county's commitments. In a letter to the Speaker
in December 1645, Brereton and the deputy lieutenants
together estimated that the cost of the siege of Chester
simply during the previous sixteen weeks had been over
£70,000, a figure which did not include the cost of
ammunition.[5] A petition to Parliament in April 1646
estimated that arrears to the troops totalled £80,000.[6] The
accounts of individual commanders bear out the problem

[1] B.M. Harleian MS. 1999, f. 313.
[2] Ibid., 2130, f. 234.
[3] Ibid., 2166, f. 31.
[4] B.M. Harleian MS 1999, f. 314.
[5] B.M. Add. MS. 11333, f. 116.
[6] Birmingham Reference Library 595611, p.59.

graphically. Robert Duckenfield reckoned in his accounts that the total sum due to himself and his officers and men up to the middle of 1647 was £5,900; his total receipts were £5,443, his arrears £4,056.

These figures reflect the position after eighteen months of peace in the county, when the deputy lieutenants had had considerable time to catch up on arrears.[1] More dramatic are the figures for John Bromhall's regiment: between the end of 1643 and September 1645, they had received only £909 out of the £6,880 to which they claimed to be entitled,[2] a mere 13 per cent of their due. The accounts of other commanders reveal the same pattern. Robert Venables had received only £561 out of £2,113 owing to his men by 1647.[3] Since all these claims were checked and certified by the accounts sub-committee there is no reason to assume that they were greatly exaggerated. The hardships and frustrations of the soldiery led to two major mutinies in the summers of 1646 and 1647, despite a compromise settlement made after the first.[4] But the soldiers were not the only sufferers from the shortage of money. No one escaped lightly.

Many civilian officials remained unpaid for their services. Those able to deduct their pay from cash in hand were fortunate,[5] but most of the others fell heavily into arrears. Thus it was decided in July 1645 that since Richard Golborne 'hath long livved as a clark to the committee of warr . . . and hath no cirtayne allowance for his payne and expenses' he was henceforth to receive 20s. a year.[6] Similarly, in December 1645 Brereton ordered Henry Cockson to be paid £31 since he 'hath beene imployed in the service of this countye ever since the beginning of these trobles and hath little or noe satisfaction'.[7] Such orders could be multiplied many times, but some men had to wait

[1] P.R.O., SP 28/128.
[2] B.M. Harleian MS. 2128, ff. 20–33.
[3] Ibid., 1999, ff. 62–3.
[4] See below, chapter 5, section III.
[5] e.g. the Bucklow sequestrators, P.R.O., SP 28/208, ff. 34–5.
[6] Ibid., 28/224, f. 14.
[7] Ibid., 28/225, unfoliated.

far longer for the satisfaction of their arrears: Thomas Warburton was awarded four years' arrears as late as November 1649.[1]

Parliamentary administration in Cheshire during the Civil War was, therefore, fragmented and in many ways haphazard. Indeed there are clear signs, which we shall examine in detail in the following chapter, that this was not simply a reaction to the demands of war and the necessity of relying on decentralized county government to meet immediate military demands for provision and quarter, but rather more the result of a profound disunity within the Parliamentarian leadership.

Yet it is clear that this internal dissension never led to the more moderate elements deserting Parliament for the Crown. A brief examination of Royalist administration will help to suggest why this was so. For the Royalist party in the county proved by their behaviour that they could offer no viable alternative to the discontented Parliamentarians: their actions were more arbitrary, and their divisions more damaging and self-destructive. The Parliamentary leaders, whatever their problems, never failed to be effective.

## VIII

At the end of 1642 the prospects of the Royalists in Cheshire looked in many ways better than those of the Parliamentarians. Plans were on foot to ensure that the county was integrated with the neighbouring areas already thoroughly in Royalist hands; the city of Chester was by far the strongest and most readily defensible town in the region and had been secured; it was generally felt that the Earl of Derby's decision to fight for the Crown would ensure the loyalty of Lancashire and Cheshire since he was 'believed to have a greater influence upon those two counties, and a more absolute command over the people in them, than any subject in England had in any other quarter of the kingdom'.[2] In fact, serious divisions within the Royalist leadership and massive strategic blunders negated these advantages.

[1] Ibid., 28/224, ff. 300, 301.
[2] Clarendon, *History of the Great Rebellion*, vol. 6, section 269.

According to a royal letter of October 1642,[1] Cheshire, Shropshire, Denbigh, and Flintshire were associated together 'for the mutuall security of one & another', and the reality of this association in the King's mind is shown by his continued references to it throughout 1643 and 1644.[2] If these counties had made a really serious effort to work together, then Cheshire might have been saved. But throughout the early months of 1643 very little mutual assistance was forthcoming. To some extent each county was preoccupied with its own problems, but although the Shropshire Royalists were in a far stronger position than Cheshire's Parliamentarians in the summer of 1643, they allowed Brereton to go with the bulk of his forces to the aid of Staffordshire.

While all too ready to take forces from the county for his main armies, the King was also far too willing to impose an outsider as commander of the area. Nicholas Byron, Abraham Shipman, William Legge, and John Byron were made Governor of Chester in turn; none was popular.[3] Even more serious, each was given different or just vague powers,[4] and the conflicts between them, the Commissioners of Array, and the city authorities were prolonged and bitter. On the one occasion on which the King did contemplate appointing a local man as governor, he made the worst possible choice, Sir Francis Gamull, a man supremely unpopular with the gentry and common people in Chester.[5] In fact it is difficult to see how the King could have imposed a firm control on the government of the city. Every governor was opposed but the divisions were not simply those of local forces against imposed Royalist commanders. There was antagonism between the city leaders, the leading gentlemen (the Commissioners of Array), and that group of lawyers and courtiers who had seized control of the city in August 1642, headed by the Bishop and his son Orlando Bridgeman.

---

[1] B.M. Harleian MS. 2173, f. 8.

[2] e.g. B.M. Add. MS. 36913, f. 114, B.M. Harleian MS. 2135, ff. 62–3.

[3] See below, pp.131–8.

[4] See Byron's complaints about the restrictions placed on his power in his account of the siege, Bodl. Lib. Rawlinson MS. B210.

[5] For the plan to appoint him, see B.M. Harleian MS. 2135, f. 52; for the hostile reaction in Chester, see B.M. Add. MS. 18981, f. 53.

Thus in April 1644, the city authorities wrote to some of their members in Oxford complaining that 'The nobility & gentry & clergie . . . utterly refuse to continue their weekely contributions towrds the maintenance of the garrison though the same was assented unto & ordered by the Lo: Byron'.[1] The charge that Royalist squires who had taken refuge in Chester were not pulling their financial weight can also be found in the surviving lists of the citizens' grievances.[2] On the other hand, the gentry were no more happy than the commanders when Charles gave way to the city over the demand that no citizen was to be made to fight outside the city but was to be allowed to stay within the boundaries to aid the defence.[3]

In general, the city leaders were the most narrow-minded element in the complex of Royalist leadership, insisting on the utmost priority of the defence of the city. The Commissioners of Array, representing the landlords and county magnates, sought a more realistic policy of attempting to break out of the confines of the city to establish a wider base for finance and recruiting, though they were no doubt largely preoccupied with saving their estates from sequestration and plunder. None-the-less, their bitter protest to Charles I about the way the war had been controlled seems an exaggerated but still basically correct diagnosis of the strategic errors made by the leadership in the early months of the war. The policy of concentrating all their strength at Chester and letting Brereton occupy the rest of the county was blamed upon city leaders in a list of twenty charges. Typical of these charges is the following.

When . . . newes of Brereton comeing downe [arrived] Mr Bridgeman did not . . . seize upon Nantwich or some other considerable place of strength or situation in the heart of the country to prevent the enemy but out of his owne timerousnesse pretending danger of the citty where none was . . . retreated.[4]

---

[1] B.M. Harleian MS. 2135, ff. 9—10.
[2] Ibid., ff. 40—3.
[3] Ibid., ff. 11—12, 35.
[4] B.M. Add. MS. 36913, ff. 122—6, part 3, item 7.

Equally, when Brereton's siege operations at the end of 1645 really put the pressure on the inhabitants, it was the city leaders rather than the professional officers or the gentry who decided that the time for surrender had come. The mayor at the time of the surrender was Charles Walley, who was called 'the principal means of the surrender of the city'.[1]

Though relations between commanders and gentry leaders were little better (Byron complained about 'that cursed Commission of Array').[2] resentment was at its greatest between city and governors. Sir Nicholas Byron begged Rupert that 'it will not be thought fit I should be left at Chester under the comande of the major & his Regement of Cytizens'.[3] The Archbishop of York told Ormonde that 'they do not love their present Governor [Legge]'[4] and Rupert was said to have upset even those 'who were most vehement in their cause who now repine and murmur',[5] during his rest in Chester following Marston Moor. The bitterest conflict of all came over the decision of the governor, Sir Abraham Shipman, to set fire to the Handbridge suburb 'lest his enemy should have come & sheltered there'.[6] This was expressly denounced in a public statement by the mayor, aldermen, 'and military commanders' who 'will not fail with their lives to defend the suburb from any violence'. Shipman was personally attacked for his stated intention.[7] Six months later Handbridge was 'levelled' in a peremptory order from Rupert,[8] which suggests that the city had succeeded in their initial obstruction of Shipman's order.

---

[1] *C.C.C.D.*, p.1176. Also B.M. Add. MS. 11333, f. 120. Walley was originally elected mayor in 1644 against his own wishes and after a heated campaign (B.M. Harleian MS. 2125, f. 147). According to Brereton, he was an opponent of the Excise then proposed for the city and was 'a more moderate man than his chief opponent, Sir Francis Gamull' (H.M.C. JP4, *Letter Book of Sir Samuel Luke*, p.360).

[2] *C.S.P.D.* 1644–5, pp.435–6.

[3] B.M. Add. MS. 18981, f. 2.

[4] T. Carte, *Original Letters*, London, 1739, vol. 1, p.67.

[5] R. Morris, *Siege of Chester*, p.64.

[6] B.M. Harleian MS. 2125, f. 67.

[7] Chester City R.O., ML/2/293.

[8] B.M. Harleian MS. 2135, f. 108.

To complete the sorry picture, the feuds at Royalist head-quarters were reflected amongst the commanders in the area. Legge, described as one of Rupert's creatures, and Lord Capel, the nominal commander-in-chief of the north midlands, were personal enemies,[1] and there was considerable ill feeling also between Legge and Lord Byron.[2]

The feuds and disharmony reflected and contributed towards Royalist inability to mobilize the resources of the county adequately. I have already suggested that the common people may have felt generally more sympathetic to the Parliament. By their strategic errors, however, the Royalist leaders compounded this disadvantage and abandoned all hope of creating an effective base for men and money in the county. It is clear that it was indecision that led to their failure to gain control of the militia. Brereton informed Ralph Assheton that the Royalists, finding he had pre-empted them in summoning the militia to Ranmore in August 1642, resorted to the expedient of calling out the *posse comitatus,* the medieval force commanded by the sheriff, untrained even by the standards of the militia.[3] Aston himself had a more sophisticated excuse: he explained that when the militia were summoned to Northwich by the Commissioners of Array,

The Lord Generall came to the asembly and (according to Mr Bridgeman's principle to fetch in the adverse party by treaty) applied himselfe solely to some of their freinds not at all considerable in respect of their power, wholly neglecting the Commissioners, in so much that the trayned soldiers who had soe oft soe affectionately followed the commissioners, seeing themselves under another command, and a visible disrepect given them, they most part went away in the night and disbanded.[4]

Whatever the reason, with the possible exception of Wirral and Broxton hundreds, the Royalists failed to gain the support of the trained bands. As a result, they had to rely on

[1] T. Carte, 'Original Letters', vol. 1, p.67.
[2] C.S.P.D. 1644—5, pp.137—8, Meldrum—Committee of Both Kingdoms, 20 November 1644.
[3] H.M.C. Portland MSS. vol. 1, pp.51—2.
[4] B.M. Add. MS. 36913, f. 123.

the forces raised by their leading supporters amongst their tenants; this is how Lord Savage first garrisoned Halton Castle for example.[1] Since the King took two regiments of foot and three troops and horse away with him to fight in the south, Royalist strength was seriously weakened from the beginning.

The concentration of their strength in Chester, and Aston's defeat at the battle of Middlewich in April 1643 left most of the countryside in their enemy's hands.

Once Parliament had set up a system of tax-collection in the parishes and hundreds, it had an immense advantage. Whenever a Royalist field army passed through the county, Brereton divided his men amongst the garrison towns and waited for them to depart. Though they tended to act as a plague of locusts, stripping the county of all the cash and provisions they could find, these Royalist armies never succeeded in establishing any kind of administrative machinery in, or even attempted to take systematic contribution from, the countryside.

Royalists themselves were fully aware of the disadvantage this situation put them in. When Rupert, during the preliminary phases of the Naseby campaign, came to the borders of Cheshire to relieve the besieged in Chester, a group of gentlemen petitioned him to settle for a while in the eastern hundreds, and pointed out that only then could they collect the 'considerable sume of money formerly imposed upon the countrey but not leviable without an armie that is master of the field'.[2] One of the reasons the Commissioners of Array gave in 1644 for Royalist collapse in Cheshire was that the gentry were ordered into Chester for protection,

soe as the people haveing noe heads to repaire to, but seeing themselves deserted by their landlords, must needs submitt to the first power that setled amongst them: which caused them to submitt to Sr William Brereton finding noe protection against him.[3]

[1] C.R.O., Cholmondeley MS. DCH/X/15/14.
[2] Chester City R.O., CR63/1, Earwaker MSS., Box 35, undated, headed, 'The Humble Petition of his most Excellent Majesty's Loyal Subjects of the County Palatine of Cheshire'.
[3] B.M. Add. MS. 36913, f. 123.

An oversimplification, no doubt, particularly in view of the
evidence that the tenants may well have been predominantly
pro-Parliament, but the summoning in of Royalist landlords
to Chester so early in the war must have affected recruitment
and certainly affected revenue: hence the central paradox.
Chester was the strongest garrison in the north-west and was
held for the King, but without control of a far wider area for
provision and taxation, the garrison was never strong enough
to dominate the surrounding area in the sense of having a
capacity to initiate offensives.

Far more even than the Parliamentarians, the Royalists
were faced by a high level of unrest amongst the civilian
population at the outrages committed by the soldiery, while
the troops' mutinies over the failure of the administrators to
provide pay and provisions were far more marked in Chester
than amongst Brereton's troops.[1] The citizens drew up lists
of their grievances against the soldiers. They claimed that the
troops were constantly molesting citizens or fighting amongst
themselves, that they demanded better quarter than the
citizens were able to provide, that they seized animals and
supplies without regard to the need to keep up stocks for the
future, that they interfered with trading in the market, that
they commandeered horses and carts without proper
authority, and that they 'never goe to serve god or to any
church'.[2] In this respect, the troops from Ireland, whatever
the hopes that they might restore a military balance, proved
supremely unpopular. Their arrogance and violence was such,
the city leaders claimed, that 'the poorer sort are unable &
readie to leave their homes & give up all, because they can
noe longer undergoe the burden the Irish strangers have
beene'.[3]

These complaints all dated from the period before
Brereton was strong enough to undertake a rigorous siege of

[1] e.g. Chester City R.O., ML/2/290, for a proclamation dealing with mutiny
amongst and plundering by the troops, or B.M. Harleian MS. 2135, ff. 9–10, for
the complete breakdown of order in the city after the battle of Nantwich.

[2] B.M. Harleian MS. 2135, ff. 40–3, 54–8. These give a reasonable cross-section
of the immense range of complaints.

[3] Ibid., f. 9.

Chester. Once he did so, discipline seems to have improved, but ill feeling between citizen and soldier remained.

The Royalists' attempts to raise money followed closely those adopted by Parliament. Initially they relied upon voluntary contributions, and attempts to gather money in this manner were continued until at least November 1643,[1] and the city plate was periodically raided to deal with emergencies.[2]  But the bulk of the money was raised by a weekly assessment which continued in operation right up to the time of the surrender. It seems to have been in operation by February 1643,[3] but it never operated smoothly. The Commissioners of Array were upset because the city garrison was awarded the receipts from Broxton and Wirral (as they claimed, by false information being sent to the King), for by that time Broxton and Wirral were the only hundreds where Royalist warrants were obeyed. This meant that the Commissioners had no cash with which to raise fresh forces to contest Brereton's control of the countryside.[4] Later there were problems about the distribution of the assessment between the citizens and the gentry who had crowded into the city for protection; the ensuing row was only temporarily patched up by the decision to divide the burden on a 60:40 basis.[5] More than once there was a breakdown of payments and a general refusal to contribute; the second time this happened the soldiers were ordered to move in to collect arrears.[6]

From mid-1644 onwards, the Royalists also resorted to an Excise.[7] This proved to be even more unpopular in the city than Parliament's Excise in the countryside, presumably because so many citizens, already threatened by the stop in Chester's trade to and from the rest of the kingdom, and

---

[1] Chester City R.O., Assembly Book Calendar (1624–85) p.1.
[2] e.g. ibid., pp.5, 8.
[3] Ibid., p.3.
[4] B.M. Add. MS. 36913, f.124.
[5] Chester City R.O., Assembly Book Calendar (1624–85), p.7.
[6] Ibid., f. 10 (October 1645). The earlier incident is reported in B.M. Harleian MS. 2135, ff. 9–10.
[7] Ibid. 2135, f. 29.

particularly Ireland, were dependent on trade for their livelihood. Charles Walley was elected mayor as an opponent of the Excise, but it was still put into operation. It is clear from the city records that resistance to the tax remained strong. For example, in October 1644 the keeper of the Common Hall reported that 'of late all or most of the merchandize brought to the city had been taken to private houses and there secretly sold, instead of first being taken to the Common Hall to be pitched'.[1]

According to an order printed in the *Lords Journal* in March 1643, the Commissioners of Array in Cheshire were granted powers by the King 'to seize and sell all the Goods, and to sequester and lease out the Estates of all such Persons as have or shall appear in Rebellion, or, having withdrawn themselves, shall be any ways aiding and assisting to the Rebels in any place whatsoever'.[2] There is no other evidence to prove the existence of such a commission, and nothing seems to have been done about it; perhaps the collapse of Royalist power in the county in the following months so dampened the Commissioners' spirits that they did not begin even in those areas still under their control.[3] In any case, in November 1643 similar powers of sequestration were granted to the mayor and aldermen of Chester for the city and countryside within five miles, and Digby, on behalf of Charles, pointedly mentioned that Chester was specially chosen for the privilege of being granted such powers.[4] On 1 January 1644 Charles sent a lengthy order to the mayor and named aldermen, laying down in detail the manner after which they were to exercise their powers; although generally similar to that of the Parliamentary Sequestration Ordinance, it contained other and commendable features. All the lands

[1] Chester City R.O., Assembly Book Calendar (1624—85), p.8.

[2] *Lords Journal,* vol. 5, p.669.

[3] Some personal estates were seized, but there is no evidence that any attempt was made to lease out the lands, or even to deprive the delinquent of his profits, except through stiff assessments.

[4] B.M. Harleian MS. 2135, ff. 2—3, 4. The significance of the commission was realized by the younger Randle Holme in his chronicle of the mayors of Chester, where he made it the leading event of 1643—4: ibid. 2125, f. 135.

seized were to be let, if possible to the existing tenants, after 'severall perticulers indented tripartite' had been made; goods were only to be sold after being 'valued and appraised at the best rates', and again after the inventories had been indented. A striking act of leniency was to leave one-half the value of all possessions with the delinquent.[1]

The effect of the ordinance was nullified by the failure to administer it properly. According to a complaint at the end of 1644, income from confiscated estates produced only £300 where the pre-war income had been £3,000.[2] But there was also great bitterness aroused over the allocation of the money raised. Charles's order under letters patent had granted the money for the supply of the garrison, which the mayor and aldermen interpreted to mean the city militia, though they reluctantly handed over £40 to Rupert's foot while they were part of the garrison.[3] The Commissioners of Array showed their bitterness in the course of their general protest against the leadership in Chester,[4] while a letter from four of the aldermen complained that confusion reigned over the allocation of the profits. For example, the Commissioners of Array had seized most of the personal estates, the King had made special provision for some of the rents, and others were 'taken fro us by Mr Russell, whoe under pretence of his Comission as Comissary to the Armie hath entered upon the same'. Sir Nicholas Byron had laid claims to yet more of the rents, 'and the same remaine in suspence till his Majesties pleasure be furthr knowen. . .'.[5] Internal dissension once more marred a good scheme.

The distrust, the misunderstandings, and the pettiness of proceedings within Chester were well known to the Parliamentarians. Brereton carefully noted, for example, the divisive effect of the Excise.[6] In view of the extreme tensions that built up between Brereton and the deputy lieutenants,

1 Ibid. 2002, ff. 68–70.
2 Ibid. 2135, f. 40.
3 Chester City R.O., Assembly Book Calendar (1624–85) p.9.
4 B.M. Add. MS. 36913, ff. 122–6.
5 B.M. Harleian MS. 2135, ff. 9–10.
6 Quoted in R. Morris, op. cit., p.63.

this is highly relevant, since it would act as a powerful deterrent against any of them swinging over to the Royalist cause. The deputy lieutenants' suspicions about some of Brereton's activities, their fear of his departure from traditional procedures, and their fear that the common soldiers might get out of hand, were precisely concerned with those features of the Civil War that moderate Royalists were condemning in their own leaders.

The divisions within the King's party produced other results. They led to a lack of nerve, a paralysis of all sense of initiative. The city of Chester was defended bravely enough, but there was no boldness in the leadership to strike out at their opponents. Unless the walls were assaulted, those within remained withdrawn and preoccupied with their own problems. As Brereton told Luke, 'it is great wonder to us that the enemy suffered us to fortify Tarvin within 4 miles of Chester and lie so long in Wirral, and many times to go to their very walls and not to give us one alarm fitting to take notice of. . .'. [1]

Brereton exploited the divisions in the city. As Lord Byron pointed out in his account of the siege, he wearied the town with 'industry and patience. . . (wherein certainly few excel him)' and then 'caused divers papers to be shot into the Town, containing many specious arguments to move the Citizens to mutiny and rebellion'. In the end Brereton's tactics succeeded, and a conspiracy of the common people and the city leaders forced Byron to treat out of fear for his own life;[2] his own conclusion, 'I found by sad experience what it was to be in a garrison of Burgers whose experience is tied more to their Mayor than their Governor', is a telling epitaph on the Royalist movement in Cheshire.

[1] H.M.C. JP4, *Letter Book of Sir Samuel Luke*, pp.359–60.
[2] Bodl. Lib. Rawlinson MS. B210, f. 64.

## 4
## SIR WILLIAM BRERETON'S WAR POLICY
## AND ITS OPPONENTS, 1643—1646

So far we have made no attempt to analyse the nature of the conflicts that caused the Parliamentarian movement to be so seriously divided against itself. In this chapter I shall look at this problem in some detail and try to compare the pattern in Cheshire with the one that has emerged in other local studies. The general pattern appears to be one in which radical minorities sought, frequently successfully, to displace ruling cliques of moderates who were determined to prevent the fabric of local society from disintegrating under the pressures of all-out war. A model for Cheshire might seem to have existed in Kent where, according to Professor Everitt, 'increasingly those ... who thought in terms of county politics were being forced from the core by those who, for various reasons, now looked to the state and thought nationally.'[1]

Certainly the events of 1640—2 had suggested that many of the leading gentry families on Parliament's side still thought in essentially insular terms, while over a wide range of issues Brereton was already displaying a more radical bent. The same kind of model is also suggested by what we know of Brereton's activities outside Cheshire during the war. Mr. Pennington and Professor Roots have shown how Brereton became involved in the military and political affairs of Staffordshire and was a leading figure there in the struggle to end the Earl of Denbigh's power and influence over the Parliamentarian forces raised in the county,[2] while Professor Underdown has suggested that Brereton was deeply committed to a plan by the Independent leaders at Westminster to influence the outcome of by-elections

---

[1] A.M. Everitt, *The Community of Kent...*, p.151.
[2] Pennington and Roots, *The Committee at Stafford...*, pp.lxxiv—lxxxiii.

throughout the north and west midlands in 1645 and 1646.[1]

In fact the pattern in Cheshire was not so straightforward. The issues dividing the Parliamentarians were diffracted through the personalities and tensions of the local community, and Brereton's relations with the deputy lieutenants make an illuminating contrast with his intervention in the affairs of other counties.

In Staffordshire, conflict existed within the Parliamentarian movement long before Brereton interested himself in that county. It began with the appointment in the summer of 1643 of the Earl of Denbigh as overlord of the associated counties of Shropshire, Staffordshire, Warwickshire, and Worcestershire. The son of a Royalist, the young Earl was constantly suspected of seeking a negotiated settlement with the King on terms generally felt to be dishonourable; he was also a dilatory and unimaginative soldier. His main power and influence lay in the two southerly shires of his association, and before long there grew up in Staffordshire, and even more in Shropshire, groups on the county committees opposed to his policies and influence. Towards the end of 1643 two captains of Staffordshire regiments, backed up by members of the Staffordshire committee, refused to follow Denbigh's orders to march into Shropshire, saying that they received their commissions directly from the Earl of Essex and were not subject to Denbigh's authority. They also claimed that they intended to co-operate with Philip Skippon, who had been driven south by Newcastle's Royalist advance. This would indicate that they were thinking in broader strategic terms, preferring to send aid to the north-east where the situation was grave, rather than to Shropshire where the situation was less serious, at least until the arrival of the Royalist army from Ireland. Their link with Skippon, himself a consistent radical in the terms of the war years, shows that Brereton was not the only alternative leader for the more aggressive Parliamentarians. Although he had brought his troops to the aid of the county

[1] D. Underdown, 'Party Management in the Recruiter Elections, 1645–8', *E.H.R.* 83(1968), 252–3.

in 1643 and was a member of the county committee, Brereton did not become the real champion of the Staffordshire war party until after he had seized control of Eccleshall Castle and had been appointed chairman of the Commons Committee to examine the condition and safety of Lancashire, Cheshire, Staffordshire, and Shropshire (a committee which ignored the geography of the Midlands Association).[1] But from then on he was constantly involved in the conflict within Staffordshire and, when another crisis did arise at the end of 1644, he was heavily committed to, and involved in, its resolution.

This crisis began when Denbigh's supporters made a sustained campaign to undermine the radicals. At Quarter Sessions a Grand Jury was induced to make a veiled attack on the policies pursued by Brereton and his supporters.[2] It is clear that this attack was followed by a petition to Parliament, and Brereton reacted swiftly by circulating a petition of his own and enlisting the support of his sympathizers at Westminster. While the Commons hesitated, the Committee of Both Kingdoms, suspicious of the activities of several of Denbigh's key supporters, arranged for Brereton to seize control of Stafford, arrest several leading moderates, and send them up to London. Denbigh counter-attacked in the House of Lords with a strong speech against the radicals, and made some headway,[3] but the issue became swallowed up in the much larger furore over the Self-Denying Ordinance, and Denbigh, temporarily at least, was swept aside.

[1] Most of the material about these problems, including a careful assessment of the Eccleshall affair, is cited in Pennington and Roots, op. cit., pp.lxxiv–lxxxiii. But they do not cite the invaluable documents Bodl. Lib. Tanner MSS. vol. 62, ff. 364, 381–2, 402–8, 420–1, 453–5, which substantiate and clarify the conflict in the final months of 1643.

[2] Once again this is based on arguments and documents given in Pennington and Roots. Particularly important are the Grand Jury petition and the Committee's answer (appendix VII, pp.342–4), and Brereton's reaction (appendix VIII, pp.345–7). To judge from this latter, the petition which was sent up to Parliament was a revised and more openly hostile form of the Grand Jury Presentment printed in the Quarter Sessions Order Book.

[3] *Lords Journal*, vol. 7, pp.123–4, 280. The first gives a list of eleven charges made by Denbigh against six named members of the county committee. The second is Henry Stone's reply to the charges, and led to an order that he be arrested for contempt.

Brereton's involvement in Staffordshire, therefore, reveals not only that he was an opponent of Denbigh and the 'peace party' line in the north midlands, but also that he was actively engaged in and committed to the struggles over the conduct of the war then being waged at Westminster. But personal interests can also be seen, particularly in Brereton's tenacity in getting control of Eccleshall and the revenues from the western division of Pirehill hundred. This episcopal seat was a worthy substitute for his own Staffordshire house at Weston, which lay in Royalist lands. Furthermore, Eccleshall, lying to the west of Stafford, was particularly well situated to aid his extending his influence in the county.

Yet there seems little reason to suppose that Brereton's behaviour was dominated by the thought of personal gain. As we shall see later, he tended to be heavy-handed in dealing with those who sought to obstruct him, and made no concessions to other men's scruples in pursuing his determination to destroy the King's power. Like Cromwell, however, he sought to advance himself simply to further that end, and not from vainglory or consideration of personal profit. If at Eccleshall and later as steward of Macclesfield Forest, it might seem that he was thinking of his own pocket,[1] it was a pocket which he had unhesitatingly emptied for the Parliament's service, and it was not until years after the war that generous awards restored and improved on his pre-war wealth.[2] It is far too cynical to think that he poured out so much in order to stake a claim to the pickings of victory. His bluntness with his opponents does not make any less credible his protestations of his own inadequacy, or his preparedness to accept the authority of temporary visiting generals.[3] Though he was occasionally accused of claiming credit for himself where it was not due, there is no evidence that he ever did so, and his generous

[1] See below, p.277.
[2] For his personal accounts see P.R.O., SP 28/152, item 7.
[3] e.g. B.M. Add. MS. 11331, f. 4, for a touching disclaimer of his own importance. For his generous apology to Leslie for having misrepresented his intentions in failing to come to the aid of Cheshire in April 1645, see ibid., ff. 46–7.

tributes to his superiors and subordinates also suggest otherwise.[1] He did not intervene in the affairs of other counties out of a desire for vainglory: it is clear, for example, that he found the purge of his Stafford opponents a painful duty.[2]

This general estimate of Brereton's intentions is confirmed by the evidence we possess of his intervention in the government of other counties.

In Shropshire, as in Staffordshire, a party grew up within the committee which opposed the policies of Denbigh, and a crisis arose in the middle of 1644 when Denbigh appointed Thomas Mytton, A Shropshire gentleman, to be Governor of Oswestry with powers independent of those of the committee.[3] Personal feeling was already running high after one of the Committee members had been kicked in Denbigh's presence by some of his officers without rebuke.[4] Denbigh pledged his support for Mytton: 'I will not trouble you with the injuries that are offered to you and myselfe by the Committee of Wem. I am sure you have deserved more of the Parliament than the rest of the Committee.'[5]

In September Sir John Meldrum complained to the Committee of Both Kingdoms about the refusal of the Wem commissioners to supply Mytton. It was at this point that we

[1] Sir John Meldrum suspected that Brereton had claimed more credit for the victory at Montgomery than he was entitled to, but the Committee of Both Kingdoms replied that 'Sr Wm Brereton in his letter has attributed to you your due honour'. *C.S.P.D.* 1644–5, pp.5–6, 24.

[2] *C.S.P.D.* 1644–5, pp.242–3. His essential moderation also comes out in a letter to Major Hawkesworth in December 1645 (B.M. Add. MS. 11333, f. 71) 'touching the busines betwixt him and Col Colemer', in which he begged Hawkesworth 'not too much to insist upon that wch you may apprehend to be your right', but to refer himself to the decision of the Staffordshire committee, where he promised to use his influence. He was not interested to use the situation to overthrow Colemer, one of the last Staffordshire commanders who had remained loyal to Denbigh.

[3] Many of the more important documents are printed in full in an otherwise inadequate article by the Revd. J.E. Auden, 'My Case with the Committee of Salop', *Transactions of the Shropshire Archaeological Society*, 48(1936). Also his 'Lieutenant Reinking in Salop', *ibid.* 47(1933).

[4] J.E. Auden, 'My Case. . .', p.51.

[5] Ibid. p.51. The committee at Wem was the county committee.

hear that the committee were going behind Mytton's back.
'in procuring hands in the garrison [at Oswestry], without
the privity of the colonel, to elect Sir William Brereton
general over Shropshire. Many soldiers were seduced, but wee
have endeavoured to rectify all'. Very shortly afterwards a
second letter to Denbigh reported that the officers of
Denbigh's Wem regiment 'are reduced [to extremities] by the
destructive courses adopted by the committee of Wem to the
end that they may overthrow us by pollicy, it not being in
their power to disband us'.[1]

The situation seemed to be developing in the same
direction as that in Staffordshire. Fortunately Mytton turned
out to be an excellent soldier and co-operated closely with
Brereton and Myddleton, both at Chester and in some
exciting raids into Wales[2] (in 1645 he replaced Myddleton as
commander in North Wales). There is no evidence that
Denbigh was able to exert any influence over him or that
from this time on Denbigh ever exercised any authority in
Shropshire whatsoever. Brereton, on the other hand, forged
the closest links there, since he was able to remain on
excellent terms with Mytton while continuing to develop and
deepen his alliance with the county committee. His letter
books are full of their warm and co-operative
correspondence. In April 1646 for example, he wrote
informally asking them to support his nominee in the
forthcoming recruiter elections in the Shropshire boroughs.
He added that thereby 'you may doe mee a great courtesie,
soe you may do yourselves and your countrey much right
and I (who have neglected noe opportunity to doe you
service) shall thereby apprehend myselfe further engaged'.[3]

As a result of Denbigh's withdrawal from his
responsibilities, relations between the committee and Mytton
settled down, although there was some residual suspicion and

[1] Both letters in H.M.C. *4th Report,* p.271.
[2] For a good example of their co-operation, see how, at a crucial stage of the
first siege of Chester, Brereton lent troops to Mytton to surprise Shrewsbury
(cited in R.N. Dore *Civil Wars in Cheshire,* p.43).
[3] Birmingham Reference Library 595611, pp.211—12.

distrust. In February 1646 there was a serious row about the supposed failure of the Wem committee to pay the troops at Oswestry, but the affair was ended by some marvellously tactful diplomacy by the Committee of Both Kingdoms, though not without a few arrests and some blooded noses.[1]

Although he never intervened directly in the affairs of Derbyshire, Brereton was concerned to watch the developments there. Power in Derbyshire lay in the hands of Sir John Gell, one of the less attractive of the Parliamentarian leaders. Of indeterminate politics and religion (Lucy Hutchinson said of him 'no man knows for what reason he chose that side'), he was elsewhere called 'a man vindictive and dishonest'.[2] He co-operated closely with Brereton in Staffordshire during the summer of 1643. He seems to have been a dominant figure in the arrest of Denbigh's supporters at Stafford,[3] and at least until the end of 1645 he was a most diligent Parliamentarian commander. Yet he seems to have wanted to spare the defeated Royalists the full rigours of sequestration and composition. This was clearly demonstrated by his underhand activities at Tutbury in April 1646; while Brereton's official negotiators were striking a stern bargain for the surrender of the castle, Gell was secretly negotiating an altogether more lenient settlement—which Brereton called 'the strangest and most dishonorable articles that I have seen'.[4] Gell also used his troops to secure the election of his brother as recruiter M.P. for Derby. Thomas Gell proved to be one of the most conservative members of the Commons and was secluded at Pride's Purge.[5]

Brereton was no doubt needled by Gell's insistence that he was too busy in Nottinghamshire to come to the siege of Chester, and he responded by keeping a watch on Gell's

[1] See J.E. Auden, 'My Case. . .' The documents he cites are from Bodl. Lib. Tanner MSS., vol. 60, ff. 444, 461, 463. The five letters from the Committee of Both Kingdoms are in P.R.O., SP 21, vol. 22, pp.239–43.

[2] Cited in Underdown, art. cit., p.244.

[3] Cited in Pennington and Roots, op. cit., p.lxxx.

[4] Birmingham Reference Library 595611, p.12. See also pp.23, 37, 38, 39, 48.

[5] Underdown, art. cit., p.244, and D. Brunton and D.H. Pennington, *Members of the Long Parliament*, London, 1954, p.232.

activities. In a letter to Sir Henry Vane in November 1645, Brereton reported that 'it hath been as I have often heard Sir John Gell's main endeavor to ruine' Major Sanders, commander of a regiment of Derbyshire horse, 'consisting of soe many faithfull, godly, valliant and substantiall men'. Brereton asked Vane to use his influence to prevent Gell from having Sanders dismissed by the committee of Derby on trumped-up charges.[1]

Oddly, the county where Brereton intervened least was Lancashire, the county with the strongest historical connections with Cheshire. The main reason for this seems to have been that far more stable military–civilian relations existed there. No striking military figure emerged in the county, the only two who enjoyed any independence of command being Sir John Meldrum and Colonel John Moore.[2] They and the other military commanders sat on the county committee, which appears to have organized itself well to deal with an initially strong Royalist position, a position which benefited from the leadership of the Earl of Derby, and the remarkable talent for defence shown by Derby's French wife, the Comtesse de la Tremouille. Furthermore, the policies adopted by the Lancashire committee were, throughout the war, hallmarked by moderation. That Lancashire got closer to establishing Classical Presbyterianism than anywhere else is well known;[3] less widely appreciated is that the Lancashire committee were particularly generous in their treatment of defeated Royalists,[4] and that many of the most active members of the committee had also been leading figures in the attempts within the county in 1642 to reach a

---

[1] B.M. Add. MS. 11332, f. 58.
[2] Both were moderates. For Meldrum, a Scots professional, see below p. Moore employed the Cheshire Presbyterian Adam Martindale (see pp.356ff.) as a chaplain. His wartime career can be judged from his published papers, *Lancashire and Cheshire Record Society*, 67(1913).
[3] For the fullest account see W.A. Shaw, *A History of the English Church During the Civil Wars and under the Commonwealth;* London, 1900, vol. 2, pp.23–5, 393–9.
[4] *C.C.A.M.*, p.47.

position of neutrality.[1] Of the fourteen Lancashire M.P.s elected in 1640, or as recruiter M.P.s, 1645–7 eleven ceased to sit after Pride's Purge and one of the others was temporarily disabled from January 1644 to June 1646.[2]

The predominance of the moderates in Lancashire was such that whenever Brereton needed to make tactful overtures for help from the Lancashire committee, he wrote not to them directly but to the deputy lieutenants in Cheshire to persuade them to write on his behalf; whatever the mutual distrust between him and Booth, Sir George never let him down over this.[3] On one occasion Brereton had to ask Parliament to order the Lancastrians not to seize arms and ammunition intended for him.[4] The Lancashire committee seem to have had personal suspicions about Brereton and once, when he tried to speed up aid from them, they reacted sharply.[5] Although one of Brereton's leading contacts at Westminster was the Lancashire M.P. William Ashurst, there does not appear to have been any sizeable radical group on the committee. The only row occurred in May 1645, when Colonel Thomas Birch wavered in his support for Parliament because of the extent of Parliamentary taxation, claiming that 'the said order [for monthly assessment] was illegall and the Earle of Strafford lost his life for such a like act and that yor proceedings therein were arbitrary'.[6]

The main conclusion to be drawn from this brief survey of Brereton's intervention in the affairs of other counties, therefore, is that he was not primarily interested to extend his own influence, but would intervene only where there existed divisions and feuds in order to advance the position of those who sought a more flexible and decisive strategy, and

[1] For these attempts and the men involved, see B.S. Manning 'Neutrals and Neutralism in the English Civil War', Univ. of Oxford D.Phil thesis, 1957, pp.66–81.
[2] Brunton and Pennington, op. cit., p.201.
[3] See for example B.M. Add. MS. 11333, ff. 13, 44.
[4] Ibid., f. 40.
[5] *Commons Journal*, vol. 3, p.484 (May 1644).
[6] P.R.O., SP 16, vol. 507, f. 115.

that he was prepared to use his influence at Westminster to advance his colleagues in other counties.

We do not have space here to elaborate the scope and soundness of Brereton's own strategic ideas; these have been amply demonstrated by the articles of Mr. R.N. Dore.[1] But it should be stressed that in many ways Brereton's ideas made him a kindred spirit to Cromwell, though without the latter's remarkable imaginative flair. Indeed, in his brilliant reconstruction of the Naseby campaign, Mr. Dore has brought to light two hitherto unpublished letters of Cromwell which show that both he and Brereton had reached the same conclusions about the desirability of seeking to crush the King's last major army in Cheshire by joining together the forces of Leslie, Brereton, and the New Model detachments of Cromwell and Browne (who actually came as far north as Coventry).[2] Both were opposed to the conservative strategy of the Committee of Both Kingdoms who feared decisive action and looked for a far-flung net to contain the King's progress while avoiding a pitched battle.

In general Brereton's leadership was characterized by immense energy, an ability to think in terms of a broad area of action, and a certain boldness of purpose that only rarely erred on the right side of caution: thus when the King was moving into Cheshire in May 1645, Brereton kept up his sieges of Chester and Hawarden until the last possible moment, and then made a masterly retreat.

There were those who thought he was not bold enough. Thus Sir Thomas Myddleton, who had been on excellent terms with him in 1643, was antagonized by his failure to make the reconquest of North Wales a top priority. Myddleton had a case: North Wales was crucial to the Royalists' requirements in provisions, money, and recruits,[3]

---

[1] i.e. those listed in the Bibliography. Particularly important are 'Sir William Brereton's Siege of Chester and the Campaign of Naseby', *T.L.C.A.S.* 67(1957), and 'Sir Thomas Myddleton's Attempted Conquest of Powys', *Montgomeryshire Collections,* 57(1962).

[2] See the first article cited above.

[3] Rupert raised a fresh force for himself in North Wales after his defeat at Marston Moor.

and, after the middle of 1644, Chester itself had to depend on supplies from Denbighshire and Flint. It could be claimed that the conquest of Wales was easier than the capture of Chester, and that the latter would be much facilitated by the former. Yet Brereton was charged as commander-in-chief of Cheshire to put the capture of the city first and he believed that by abandoning the siege for the conquest of North Wales he would not greatly improve the chances of taking Chester, for the counties of Denbigh and Flint had few suitable garrison towns and the overrunning of those counties would not have led to control of the countryside while Chester stood. Indeed, he was proved right by events following the battle of Montgomery, when Myddleton made headway in Montgomeryshire but not in Denbighshire. Brereton also had to consider the real dangers of an invasion of Irish Catholics via Chester.[1] He never refused aid to Wales in times of crisis—for example, he drew out Cheshire forces to aid Meldrum and Myddleton in the defeat of Byron at Montgomery. Indeed the Cheshire foot were said to have been chiefly responsible for the victory.[2] But he was unprepared to make the complete change of strategy involved in committing a significant proportion of his forces to enable Myddleton to carry out his invasion of Powys. The problem was the best use of limited resources, and Brereton was not less sound and full-blooded in his strategy for his refusal to change his priorities.[3]

The outcome was that relations between the two men deteriorated rapidly. There is a quite noticeable cooling off in the tone of their letters to one another in the early months of 1645. Having accepted that Brereton was not going to devote himself to the conquest of Wales until after the fall of Chester, Myddleton still pressed a hopelessly ambitious plan on him. Through his kinsman William Myddleton, he argued

[1] e.g. B.M. Add. MS. 11331, ff. 15–16 for an account of the shipwreck of Lord Glamorgan, a Catholic on a mission from Charles I to the Confederacy.

[2] B.M. Thomason Collection E10 (4). Printed in J.R. Phillips, *Memorials of The Civil Wars in Wales and the Marches*, London, 1874, vol. 2, pp.201–9.

[3] For a general discussion of Brereton's response to the problem of North Wales, see R.N. Dore, 'Sir Thomas Myddleton's Attempted Conquest of Powys. .', which takes a view broadly similar to the above.

at Brereton's councils of war in May 1645 that the siege should not be abandoned 'unless an enemy appear' (at that moment the King was 20 miles away). This overlooked the fact that half Brereton's army was across the Dee with no way of rejoining the main body if the King got any closer.[1] Frustrated by the resistance of the city, Myddleton roundly condemned Brereton for failing to press the siege vigorously enough, charges without foundation which brought swift, angry reactions from Brereton and Michael Jones.[2]

Although Myddleton was an energetic and active Parliamentarian, he did not share any of the other attributes of the more aggressive Parliamentarian leaders. He was the type of Anglican who would have preferred to see episcopacy retained, but was prepared to see it go if that was essential in order to cleanse the church; he opposed independency and toleration in religion. He was a moderate in his treatment of the defeated Royalists and made no attempts until 1647 to sequester their estates even in the area under his control. Member of Parliament for Denbighshire, he was secluded at Pride's Purge, and was one of the leading figures in the rising of 1659, when, unlike Booth, he openly proclaimed Charles II.[3] This probably means that there was more to his disagreement with Brereton than simply the divergence of their military priorities. Most significantly, Denbigh wrote that 'Sir Thomas Myddleton hath great interest in the Cheshire gentlemen',[4] yet this interest cannot have been created by their agreeing with Myddleton over the need for Cheshire troops in Wales, though they were not altogether set against the idea. It seems more likely that they wanted Myddleton as an ally in the wider aspects of their opposition to Brereton's policies.

[1] B.M. Add. MS. 11331, ff. 113—14, 130.
[2] Ibid., ff. 36—7, 38: the charges were made by one of Myddleton's officers, Col. John Jones. Myddleton himself was suspected by Brereton, but cleared by William Ashurst in a letter to Brereton (ibid., f. 43).
[3] The best impression can be gained from A.H. Dodd, 'Studies in Stuart Wales', Cardiff, 1953, passim, and from R.N. Dore, 'Sir Thomas Myddleton's. . .'; G.R. Thomas, 'Sir Thomas Myddleton, 1588—1666,' Univ. Coll. of Bangor M.A. thesis, 1966, which I have seen only recently, differs from the above view of Myddleton in no important respect.
[4] See R.N. Dore, art. cit., p.97.

This brief survey of Brereton's relations with other counties and other commanders reveals something of the complexity of the pattern of communal thought and action even in neighbouring counties; Brereton was seriously at odds with Denbigh, Myddleton, and Gell, yet the differences between their own views were as marked as their differences from Brereton. In Staffordshire and Shropshire Brereton was able to ally himself with radical elements on the county committees; in Lancashire and Cheshire the committees were predominantly moderate. There are clear indications of local versions of the polarities that had occurred in Parliament itself: Brereton's conflict with Denbigh is analogous to that between Cromwell and Manchester, or between Essex and Waller; Denbigh, Myddleton, and Gell were all Presbyterians (of the more Erastian kind) while Brereton inclined towards the Independents. If there was anything in common in the issues in the various counties, however, it is more a matter of mentality than of programme; Brereton sought out and encouraged those who put the broadest possible prosecution of the war above all other considerations.

We have seen that personal antipathies and selfish interests played a part, but not a highly significant one, in these matters. Pennington and Roots wisely point out how we cannot separate out 'the mixture of personal and public interests on each side,'[1] and in Cheshire and elsewhere the two co-existed. It seems probable that Brereton's successful request in February 1643 that he might be placed in command of those troops of horse independently raised and captained by several leading gentlemen, including young George Booth and Mainwaring of Peover, antagonized them from the beginning.[2] Brereton was not a leading gentleman in terms of wealth, estates, or prestige, and the very fact that he had been so noisy and active an opponent of the Crown in 1640–2 would not endear him to those who took up arms so late and so reluctantly. Disagreements between Brereton and the deputy lieutenants were common knowledge to Royalists

[1] Pennington and Roots op. cit., p.lxxvii.
[2] H.M.C. *Portland MSS.*, vol. 1, pp.95–6.

and Parliamentarians alike by the middle of 1644. Sir John Meldrum, the Lancashire commander, referred in his letters not only to a personal dislike of Brereton but to those elements in Brereton's character that caused most trouble, particularly his 'immodesty', i.e. high-handedness.[1]

None the less, personal animosities worked within the context of a far more fundamental disagreement between Brereton and the leading gentry. Between May 1645 and April 1646 the gentry made five specific attempts, in petitions and appeals to Parliament, to break Brereton's power in Cheshire. In only one of them is there explicit evidence of personal antipathy: at the end of September 1645, hearing that Brereton's reappointment was being considered by the Commons, and that his supporters had sent up a petition calling for his return,[2] they rushed off a hasty appeal for a continuation of their own leadership. In it they complained that when Brereton had left for London, the soldiers were in a mutinous condition and the county exhausted. They claimed that they had put matters right and now had the siege more completely in hand, yet,

we are informed there are some factious petitions presented to you, bearing the character of the whole county, but indeed being the act but of a few . . intimating a necessity of Sir William Brereton's return and so insinuating an odium and scandal upon us and our actions.

They called for a confirmation of their powers.[3] The Commons reacted by noting that 'notwithstanding anything in the letter; nothing doth reflect upon Sir William Brereton or is to his prejudice'.[4] In their letters to and from Brereton, there is usually a certain coolness, but only occasionally a hint of suspicion or protest.[5] But Brereton's own reaction to the first of the petitions of the deputy lieutenants (May 1645) shows his personal distaste for them. He told Sir William Ashurst,

though the sheriffe Coll Brookes and Coll Duckenfield signed this yet upon further deliberacon they have repented and I have given order for

1 *C.S.P.D.* 1644–5, pp.5–6.
2 *Commons Journal,* vol. 4, p.284.
3 H.M.C. *Portland MSS.,* vol. 1, p.279.
4 Ibid., also *Commons Journal,* vol. 4, p.302.
5 e.g. B.M. Add. MS. 11332, ff. 119–20.

their names to be rased out, the rest are such who have either sleighted the Parlt service or are discontent that others are imployed and not themselves and I beleeve you will not find one of these subscribed thereunto (except the sheriffe and Coll Duckenfield who have recanted) who ever served the Parliamt dilligently.[1]

The other signatories (thirty-two in all) contain all the pre-war Justices on Parliament's side and their friends and clients. That Duckenfield, Brereton's closest associate, should even temporarily sign is surprising. Yet Brereton's secretive and completely personal control of finance at times exasperated even his closest colleagues. Just before this petition was drawn up, Duckenfield had complained to Sir Samuel Luke, himself a close correspondent of Brereton's, that Brereton allowed his own troops double pay while arrears to the rest of his army soared.[2] But this disagreement was short-lived, and Duckenfield's complaint probably unjust. Certainly relations between the two men were generally very close.[3]

Mutual suspicions amplified and developed the nature of wider conflicts, then, but the central areas of tension would themselves have produced considerable unrest. Personal factors must be borne in mind, but not allowed to obscure the very real differences in policy and approach that did exist.

Our analysis of the role of the leading gentry in the period 1640–2 might lead us to imagine that they would favour a very limited and localistic strategy in comparison with Brereton's. But this is too crude a view and is not supported by the documents.

Very occasionally they complained about his use of Cheshire troops outside the county, as when they begged the Committee of Both Kingdoms 'that the small forces belonging to this countie may by yor order be confined to the defence thereof dureing the potencie of our intestine enemyes and the invascion of others'.[4] In his record of the

[1] B.M. Add. MS. 11331 f88 (also ibid., f. 61)
[2] H.M.C. JP4, *Letter Book of Sir Samuel Luke*, p.505.
[3] e.g. B.M. Add. MS. 11332, f. 26.
[4] B.M. Add. MS. 11331, f. 147; they repeated their request in a moderate letter to Brereton, ibid., f. 165.

siege of Chester, the Presbyterian minister Nathaniel Lancaster, who consistently played down Brereton's role and exalted that of the deputy lieutenants, wrote that

upon the approach of Prince Maurice with a farre less force we quit that side of the river [i.e. the Welsh side] and upon Prince Rupert's advance towards him with accession of force, we quit both the Leaguers [Chester and Hawarden], and having strengthened the garrisons drew to the further side of Cheshire, remotest from danger. This proved fatal to the countrey for the enemy at Holte burnt Farne [Farndon], Chester [garrison] burnt Christleton. . . [etc].[1]

On the other hand, these complaints were exceptional. There is no evidence that the leading gentry had opposed any of Brereton's frequent excursions into Staffordshire, Shropshire, or Wales in 1643—4, and, once Chester had fallen, they seem to have been prepared to send pay to Cheshire forces in Staffordshire despite the enormous arrears owing for past services.[2] Indeed the Cheshire troops themselves never showed any of the reluctance shown by troops in other counties to cross the border to fight elsewhere. Cheshire troops were reluctant to follow their commander only when they were fighting at one end of the county and 'foreign' troops were billeted on their homes and reported to be plundering their own families. Colonel Duckenfield's soldiers deserted *en masse* twice over this.[3]

The deputy lieutenants showed far more reluctance to pay for the troops of other counties serving in Cheshire, and this was one of the themes that recurred in the various documents drawn up by them in the course of 1645 in their attempts to ensure that Brereton's command was not exempted from the conditions of the Self-Denying Ordinance, and later to forestall his reinstatement as commander-in-chief.

These grievances are contained in a total of five petitions (three of which include lists of signatories) which were drawn up between May 1645 and April 1646. The first was the product of a meeting of the leading civilian deputy

---

[1] *Cheshire Sheaf,* 3rd ser., vol. 48, *passim.*
[2] e.g. Birmingham Reference Library 595611, p.198.
[3] March 1644, (B.M. Add. MS. 18979, f. 147); and May 1645 (ibid. 11331, f. 70). See below, p.193—4.

lieutenants at Knutsford on 3 May 1645.[1]  A modified form of this petition was sent up to London a week later with an impressive array of thirty-two signatures (and a promise of 'divers others').[2]  Both these petitions were inspired by the need to ensure that Brereton's command was discontinued once the Self-Denying Ordinance took effect, and also by the desire to make his departure the occasion for a complete reconstruction of the county administration. At the end of July, hampered by the system that Brereton had arranged to replace him, the deputy lieutenants issued a remonstrance which approached the main problem in a more direct way.[3] In September, troubled by rumours that Brereton was about to be reappointed to his old command, they petitioned London and made a more personal attack on him.[4] Finally, in April 1646, they made one last attempt to get their own views heard.[5]

The very first petition is in many ways the most interesting. At first sight, there is no direct sign that it was aimed at anyone in particular. It was moderate and seemingly constructive in tone, yet it was the most comprehensive of all the attacks on the administrative edifice erected by Brereton. Both on that account and because it reveals something about the deputy lieutenants' own ideas about how the war should be managed, it warrants being reproduced here in full.

To the Right Honoble the Lords and Comons of the Comittee for the Safety of Both Kingdomes.

The humble Petition of the Gent: of the County Pallatine of Chester in the behalfe of themselves and of the whole County. Humbly sheweth

That wee yor Petitioners and inhabitants of the said county (entred into the Nationall Covenant) in pursuance thereof have bin and are still ready to prostrate our lives and the remainder of our fortunes at the King and Parliaments service as hath bin and dayly is manifested by our frequent and sharpe encounters wth the enemyes both in this and in the adjacent countyes, our advanceing of moneyes in all manner of ways, even above the extent of our abilityes, our almost continuelly free

---

[1] B.M. Add. MS. 11331, ff. 54—5.

[2] Ibid., ff. 67—8.

[3] Bod. Lib. Tanner MSS., vol. 60, ff. 220—1.

[4] H.M.C. *Portland MSS.*, vol. 1, p.279.

[5] Birmingham Reference Library 595611, pp.57—9 (some parts elaborated on pp.59—61).

Quartereing and payeing of straungers wch wee are alwayes enforced to relaive amongst us: for our assistance and defence both against the Potencey and force of our instestane [sic] enemyes (being very many and of virulent and active speritts) and also agt the frequent invasion of straingers, wch this Place a frontier Country our inroade is most obnoxious unto, as wee by sad experience have found by the Irish Rebbles and out of other places of England and Wales wch have bin and dayly are threatned to be powered in upon us. All wch considered wth the great losses wee have sustained by the enemyes horse Plundreing the Country this last yeare togeather wth the Constant insupportable charge imposed upon us for the Maintenance of our owne and other garrisones and forces, of our freinds wch wee are Constrained to invite agt the Rage and Power of the enemy in such numbers that wee are scarce able to determin whether the intollerable burden thereof or the Power of the enemy will be more destructive unto our Exhausted fortunes and Estates, All wch preseures and distraccons will be much augmented through the defect of an able souldr and comandr in cheefe and all this makes us confident to affirme to your honrs that there is not any County within the power of the state more Justly the obiect of your compassion and regard nor over wch all the misseryes and distracon attendeing these dangerous tymes are more impendent.

These few particulars are a breefe representacon of our distresses and the others in the Paper annexed as the epitome of our earnest desires, wee humbly beseech may be taken into consideracon being some meanes (as wee conceive amongst many others) to rescue this countie from destrucon and Ruine. And yor petitioners will ever Pray. Propositions humbly presented to the Comittee of both Kingdomes from the County Pallatine of Cheshire.

1. That since Sr W Brereton is called from us by Ordinance wee may (if it is thought convenient) have Sr John Meldrum or such other comandr in cheefe for our millitary affaires as the Lo:Lt: of this County and the maior part of our Deputie Lts may approve.

2. That a convenient number of shipes may attend to intercept the Irish Rebbells passage hither to infest these coasts.

3. That a considerable number of land forces to Joyne wth such of our owne County may be appointed to these parts to attend the Irish rebbles Landeing and in the meanetyme for the more certain & speedie reduceing of Chester and North Wales & other places in the enemyes possession: and that there may be moneyes and provisions advanced out of other counties and places for their pay and substinance since wee are not able to mainetaine our owne.

4. That the Comittee appointed by the first Ordinance of Parliament for Sequestracons & such other Gent of quallity as your honours shall thinke fitt, who have responsable estates, and not others unlesse deputed by them and such as they themselves will answer for may execute the said Ordinance.

5. That the deputy lts. or any three of them or more may have power to Compound wth Mallignants and Delinquents that shall submitt themselves (except such as you shall except) rendereing an answere and accot thereof to the Publique upon oath.

6. That some course may be taken for a supply of our defect in Parliamt, having neither kt. nor burgesse to appeare for us there.

7. That untill suply be made for the forenamed defeccons, the honourable house and the Comittees thereof will be pleased to passe noe particular Ordinance Order or vote upon private informacons concerneing this Countie without knowledg of the Comittees opinions for this Countie how they conceive it will tend to the good or hurt of the Publique service in this Countie.

8. That a settled Comittee for the melitia may be speedily appointed and those only of the Cheefe Gent of the County whose interests will make them more vigilant and industrious then others and their counselles more secret, and that unto these may be added Lt Coll Jones and Maior Louthane, two souldrs of eminency and desert.

Brereton added this marginal note to his transcription of the document: 'Att Knuttsford 3 May 1645: There was a meeteing of Chesh: gentlemen. Att wch Time this Petition & the Propositions anexed were subscribed by Sr Geo. Boothe Col. Geo. Boothe, Thomas Standley, Philip Mainwareing, Edw Hyde, Roger Wilbraham, George Spurstowe.'

Taken together, the eight specific requests form the basis of a comprehensive assault on Brereton's policies which the preamble serves to underline. Each request must be seen, however, in its local perspective.

The first assumes that Brereton's command was not to be renewed. It is difficult to believe that the authors were unaware of the efforts being made by his friends in London to have his command renewed. Indeed, as a result of these efforts, he had his commission extended for forty days after the Self-Denying Ordinance took effect.[1] In this and sub-sequent petitions, the deputy lieutenants consistently called for the appointment of a professional soldier to take charge of purely military affairs. In this and the revised version sent up to Parliament, they asked specifically for Sir John Meldrum, a Scots professional who had served for most of the war in Lancashire. Meldrum had consistently supported their case in his letters to the Committee of Both Kingdoms

[1] *Commons Journal,* vol. 4, p.139.

in 1644. He was unsympathetic to Brereton as a person and had accused him of giving out a false account of the battle of Montgomery which exalted his (Brereton's) importance. He also saw Brereton's high-handed behaviour as being the cause of divisions in the Cheshire leadership.[1] He showed a corresponding interest in and liking for young George Booth.[2] In their later petitions, the deputy lieutenants stopped asking for Meldrum, and simply called for 'an able souldier to command in chiefe'.[3] But they seem to have had Michael Jones in mind (Jones had in fact been appointed commander of Brereton's horse when the latter had eventually gone up to London).[4] It is clear that although he and Brereton were on close terms up to Brereton's departure, Jones was subsequently won over the deputy lieutenants. Colonel Coote, who remained loyal to his old commander, accused Jones of ingratitude towards Brereton, denounced his efforts to further the petitions which sought to prevent Brereton's reappointment at the end of October 1645, and added: 'The Gentlemen of Cheshire who have deserved soe well from you, you may love and honor without dishonouringe him'.[5]

Thus Brereton's absence from the county was itself seen as a prerequisite for the success of the deputy lieutenants' plans for reorganization. A limitation of his power was not sufficient; they were sure that his presence and the position he had established were inseparable.

The third point in the petition[6] reveals that they did not plan to destroy Brereton's outward-looking strategy entirely. They were not purely insular in outlook. They sought a conjunction of forces from Cheshire and neighbouring counties to meet an invasion of Irish Catholics (hardly likely,

---

[1] *C.S.P.D.* 1644—5, pp.5—6.
[2] *C.S.P.D.* 1644, p.543.
[3] Bodl. Lib. Tanner MSS., vol. 60, f. 220.
[4] *Lords Journal,* vol. 7, p.367.
[5] Birmingham Reference Library 595611, p.78 (also p.15).
[6] The second point about the need for naval support does not appear to be significant. Brereton shared their fears on this point.

in fact, to occur at that time), and also to create better opportunities generally for Parliamentarian advances in the area. They hoped that these joint forces would ensure 'the more speedie reduceing of Chester and North Wales & other places in the enemyes possession'. In effect this meant that their strategy was little different from Brereton's. Indeed by mentioning North Wales specifically, they may even have been more sympathetic to Myddleton's demands than Brereton had been.[1] These conclusions are confirmed by the later petition of July 1645, when they called for the creation of a new association, claiming

That for the reducing of these parts, it is of absolute necessitie that there should be an association betwixt this countie & the counties of Salop, Stafford, Darby and North Wales that by the unitinge of the said Forces & mutuall supplies in all accomodacon they maie be the better inabled to goe throughe the workes of soe great concernment wch necessarilie will fall upon these parts.[2]

However, diverging significantly from Brereton's policy, the deputy lieutenants added that 'there may be moneyes and provisions advanced out of other counties and places for their pay and substinance'. This is rather inexact expression of their argument, which emerges in several other sources, that the troops raised in each county should be always supported by that county, and not by the county where the troops were currently serving. Brereton believed in a much more flexible system.[3]

Depriving Brereton of his command might have allowed the deputy lieutenants an opportunity to assert their authority in the county, but it created a further danger: his presence at Westminster could lead to a hampering of their reforms almost as complete as his presence in Cheshire would, and it was to deal with this threat that the sixth and seventh points were inserted into the petition. The call for

[1] On his return Brereton again concentrated all the aid he could spare from the siege on Staffordshire and Shropshire. This was opposed by the deputy lieutenants who claimed in April 1646 that so many troops were commanded away to Lichfield that North Wales was in danger of being overrun (Birmingham Reference Library 595611, p.57).

[2] Bodl. Lib. Tanner MSS., vol. 60, f. 220.

[3] See below, pp.168–71.

fresh elections drew attention to the fact that Brereton was the only member of Parliament from Cheshire still sitting. His fellow member for the county (Peter Venables) and both the members for Chester were Royalists. The wording of Article Six (calling for a 'supply of our defect in Parliamt') is interesting because it was made at the very time when (in Article One) they were assuming that Brereton would be returning to Westminster and taking up his duties as member full-time in accordance with the Self-denying Ordinance.

As a corollary to this, the seventh article stated that Parliament's orders relating to Cheshire were based upon 'private informacons concerneing this countie'. The gentlemen asserted that these were unreliable and suggested that no fresh orders should be sent down until fresh elections had been held. It can only be assumed that their 'private informacons' were Brereton's own correspondence with his friends and allies at Westminster, and that the deputy lieutenants were afraid that his presence in the Commons would simply mean that his old policies would be established directly through Parliament.

In the revised version of this petition, which was actually sent to London, these last two articles were rewritten and compressed into a single request. They now asked that no order relating to Cheshire should be passed until the committee at Nantwich had had an opportunity to comment on it, and that this should hold good until recruiter elections could be held.[1] The revised article was crossed out on the copy of the petition sent to Brereton, but he clearly understood its nature. In his reply to the deputy lieutenants in which he opposed the submission of the petition to Parliament, he wrote: 'I perceive by your last proposition wch you have crossed out that there is suspicion of private informacon to the Parliamt. I am sure there is noe informacon given by mee but such as will abide the open view of all men', and went on to protest that he had never planned to get any ordinance passed without their knowledge or consent.[2] The call for fresh elections remained a constant

[1] B.M. Add. MS. 11331, f. 67.	[2] Ibid., f. 69.

theme of their opposition right up to the petition of April 1646,[1] and the ill will aroused by the issue was intensified by widespread suspicions that either Brereton was using his influence to prevent the issue of writs, or else that he had received a writ and was concealing it from the county. He was accused of bad faith in this matter implicitly by old Sir George Booth and explicitly by young George Booth.[2]

The fifth article, although not personally connected with Brereton, was also concerned with the relations between local and central government. With the desperate shortage of money in the county, the deputy lieutenants were terrified of losing control of any of the sources of revenue; yet towards sequestration their attitude was distinctly ambivalent. On the one hand they favoured a lenient policy towards the more moderate Royalists and opposed the vindictive policies practised by Brereton's hundredal committees against moderates and neuters. This meant that they were prepared to stand some loss of revenue. Yet at the same time this income was being severely threatened by the growing movement amongst the Royalists to admit defeat and to compound at Westminster for their estates. Although this process reached its height only after the surrender of Chester, it had already begun. It was essential, if the deputy lieutenants were to make the most of their resources, that the power to arrange and profit from compositions should lie with them rather than with a Parliamentary Committee in London. On the other hand they, unlike Brereton and his supporters, never opposed the principle of compositions.[3]

But the main proposals for change in county government were contained in Articles Four and Eight. This last article summarized their view of how the military and civilian functions of the war effort were to be co-ordinated; it is clearly intended to complement the first article which called

[1] Birmingham Reference Library 595611, p.58; see also Bodl. Lib. Tanner MSS., vol. 60. f. 428.
[2] B.M. Add. MS. 11332, ff. 70, 119—20. For Brereton's indignant reply to young George Booth's accusations, see ibid., f. 120.
[3] See below p.212 (and particularly, B.M. Add. MS. 11333, f. 3).

for a professional to command the forces in the field and in the revised version this article was placed second, next to the one calling for the appointment of Meldrum. When contrasted with the settlement actually made by Parliament, based on Brereton's own proposals,[1] their failure to profit from Brereton's departure is made clear. The militia committee which they proposed was to consist of 'the chiefe gentlemen of the county'. This is much the same as the arrangements they sought for the management of sequestrations. Their aim was to overthrow the machinery created by Brereton and to reinstate the 'comittee appointed by the first ordinance of Parliamt for Sequestracons': this was a group of substantial gentlemen, mostly drawn from the deputy lieutenancy which had been replaced in the middle of 1644 by Brereton's nominees.[2] Furthermore, even the lesser officials, agents and collectors, were to be purged and replaced by those whom 'they themselves wilbe answerable for upon accompte'.[3] That the sequestrators must 'have responsable estates' suggests that this article was an oblique attack on the standing of those appointed by Brereton, but more significant was their explanation, in the last article, that only the chief gentlemen should be employed, as these were men 'whose interests will make them more vigilant and industrious than others and their counsells more secret'.

To some extent there is a unity of programme behind this petition; to a far greater extent there is a single mentality. It is the mentality of the pre-war oligarchy, and it is finely summed up in the last clause of the petition. Everything Brereton had done, the employment of low-born men with no estates or experience to qualify them, the assumption of personal power, the involvement in a very full way of Cheshire with other counties, the constant interference of Westminster in the affairs of the county, was a denial, not merely of the power and influence of the greater gentry, but

[1] B.M. Add. MS. 11331, f. 97, initially for forty days but confirmed in the *Commons Journal.*
[2] See above pp.86–8.
[3] This is the wording of the revised version sent up to Parliament on 8 May (B.M. Add. MS. 11331, ff. 67–8).

also of their whole philosophy of government and law. Theirs was not a blind reaction to Brereton's pretensions; it was a reassertion of traditional values; power was to rest with those great families accustomed to its use. Parliament was only to intervene after representations from themselves or from those who were elected from amongst themselves; minor officials were to put into practice the policies and decisions made by them, but were not to decide policies. Yet they were not so narrowly local in outlook that they refused to see the problems of area or even national organization. They were prepared to welcome a professional soldier to lead their troops into battle, and to fight outside the county boundaries, but they still clung to the county as the essential unit for recruiting, provisioning, and paying of troops. The county had distinct commitments to support its own men in arms, but that was all. The schemes of Brereton for a genuinely mixed field army, independently paid and supplied by a whole group of counties without direct reference to the number of troops each committed to the field, was alien to their way of thought. They were as determined as Brereton to stamp out Royalist military power, but their conception of the means by which this could best be done rested upon a traditional view of what constituted orderly government.

The other documents and petitions against Brereton add only one other substantial charge to those listed in the petition which we have just considered in detail. The fifth article of the petition of April 1646 stated that 'both cittie and county are very destitute of a godly and learned ministrie through the want of competencie to maintain churches and of power to establish them in the places of delinquents', and asked that there be established a select committee for settling ministers which 'may not be retarded *by the absence of anie one of that committee*'.[1] In the context of that petition, this would seem to be a plea that the settling of ministers should not be delayed until Brereton's return from fighting in other counties. It seems likely that this was not simply in order to save time but also to prevent further clashes over religion.

[1] Birmingham Reference Library 595611, pp.58—9.

There is plenty of evidence to show that Brereton's closest connections amongst the Cheshire clergy were the strict Congregationalists. For example, he received warm and friendly letters from Samuel Eaton, the Congregationalist who had fled from Laud's persecution to the Netherlands and New England, and whom we have encountered as an extremist in the context of the years 1640—3.[1] Another leading Independent who had had to retire from England during the 1630s was George Moxon, at one time Brereton's chaplain. Jerome Zankey, a Shropshire man, was employed by Brereton both as a chaplain and as a captain of horse. He was fiercely Independent in religion.[2]

But the most important of them was Eaton. Now settled in a newly erected chapel at Duckenfield and maintained by voluntary contributions from his large congregation there,[3] his name is frequently linked with Brereton's.[4] In one of his coded letters, for example, Brereton said that Eaton and he had 'bene with 312 at 288 and wee have concluded upon those orders to be published upon the next Lord's day wch I hope wilbe a good encouragmt and direcon unto 318'.[5] But above all there is the evidence of the letters between them. Particularly striking is one from Eaton to Brereton in the early months of 1646 in which he spurred Brereton on in the work which he had undertaken, telling him how God had shown him favour in the constant military successes he had been granted. He also thanked Brereton for having been 'pleased to owne me even to the stirring upp of envy in others', and he called upon him to

adhcarc to God still and his causc, and truth, and honour those that feare the Lord, and lett vile persons bee more and more contemned in your eyes and entrust the Godly for they being faithfull to God will bee soe to you when as others serving you for theire owne ends will prove treacherous unto you and to advantage themselves will turne enemyes

1 See above, pp.37, 50, 53.
2 For Moxon, see Urwick, op. cit., pp.155—7; for Zankey, J.E. Auden, 'Sir Jerome Zanckey of Balderstone', *T. Salop.A.S.* vol. 50, (1940).
3 For Eaton, see Urwick, op. cit., *passim,* particularly pp.288—90.
4 Eaton was one of those who contributed to Brereton's share in the adventure in Irish land (as did John Jones, another minister), K.S. Bottigheimer, *English Money and Irish Land,* Oxford, 1971, pp.153—4.
5 B.M. Add. MS. 11333, ff. 33—4. See below, p.174.

to you, you have experience of it, but they have not, they cannot hurt you because God hath and will uphould you soe long as your wayes please him. [1]

It is clear from this that Eaton looked upon Brereton's supporters as the 'godly'. For him, those entitled to control the administration were not Booth's 'discreet gentlemen', but the elect of God. It was a denial of the deputy lieutenants' political and social philosophy.

The evidence for close contacts between the leading gentry opponents of Brereton and the clergy is much less certain than for Brereton and Eaton. None-the-less it is clear that they enjoyed the support of men like Samuel Torshell of Bunbury, John Ley of Astbury, and Sabboth Clarke of Tarvin: The men had all been allies of the middle group in 1642, they had all signed the neutralist Remonstrance of August 1642 which had been the last attempt of that party which included most of Brereton's opponents to prevent armed conflict within the county. Their religious views will be examined later, but their position can be fairly summarized as one that favoured the reform of abuses in ritual and liturgy and supported a restriction and, if necessary, suppression of the bishops. But they did not favour any interference with the structure of patronage or the removal from traditional hands of the rights of appointments to livings.[2]

The most important of this group, however, was Nathaniel Lancaster of Tarporley. He had supported the moderates in 1641 and 1642, was the most active Presbyterian minister in the Parliamentarian cause, and was official chaplain to the army from 1644 to 1646 (when he was replaced by Samuel

[1] Birmingham Reference Library 595611, p.166. For Brereton's belief in providences, see also ibid., p.138.

[2] For Torshell, see his sermon *The Hypocrite Discovered and Cured...* (London, November 1643); there is a copy in Chester City Library. For Ley, see J.F. Wilson, *Pulpit in Parliament*, Princeton, 1969, *passim*, which deals with several of his sermons. For Sabboth Clarke, see the 'Defence of Church Government in Presbyterian, Classical and Synodical Assemblies', to which he subscribed his name in 1641 (printed in Urwick, op. cit. pp.xi–xii). All three signed the 'Attestation to the Testimony of Our Reverend Brethren of the Province of London to the Truth of Jesus Christ and to Our Solemn League and Covenant', July 1648, which contained an attack on the Independents.

Eaton). He also wrote an official account of the siege of Chester which was generally hostile to Brereton, opposing his retreat before the King's army in 1645, ascribing the taking of Chester to the successful preparations and activity undertaken by the deputy lieutenants during Brereton's absence, and correspondingly playing down the importance of tactical changes made by Brereton after his return.[1] (The most thorough Royalist source, the account by Lord Byron, the Governor, gave all the credit to Brereton.)[2]

Further differences can be seen in relation to the dismissal of delinquent or ungodly ministers and the appointment of new ones. Five ministers sat on the Commission of the Peace during the 1630s; Thomas Mallory, Thomas Dod, George Snell, George Byrom, and William Nicholls. All of them had their livings sequestered for Royalism, yet all of them were moderate in their religious views, all were prepared to conform to a Presbyterian system, and all were defended and fought for by the deputy lieutenants. Since their cases properly belong to a later period than that covered by this chapter, detailed treatment can be temporarily laid aside, but one example might be usefully quoted here. George Byrom had supported the moderate movement in 1641–2 and headed the list of signatures from Thornton (his parish) in the Remonstrance of August 1642.[3] When he was sequestered he was defended by a petition from eighteen leading Cheshire Presbyterian ministers headed by John Ley and Nathaniel Lancaster, and also by a certificate from London clergy including Edmund Calamy and Job Strickland who claimed to have heard him preach and that they did 'conceive his ministry is and will be (through God's blessing) powerful and profitable to the church of Christ'. But he was vindictively pursued by the Edisbury Sequestration Committee, i.e. Brereton's nominees, and eventually lost his

---

[1] For his support of the moderates, see B.M. Add. MS. 36913, f. 60 and B.M. Harleian MS. 2107, f. 10. For his account of the siege, see *Cheshire Sheaf*, 3rd ser., vol. 38, *passim.* For general background see Urwick, op. cit., pp.417–37.
[2] Bodl. Lib. Rawlinson MS. B210, ff. 54–65.
[3] B.M. Harleian MS. 2107, f. 126.

living.[1] In other cases Presbyterian ministers were driven from their livings by local mobs or by the patrons, and Independents substituted. Such was the fate of Gerard Browne in Mottram, who was thrown out of his church by his parishioners. He easily found a parish in another county, but attempts by the deputy lieutenants to reinstate him were thwarted by the intractability of the Macclesfield sequestrators.[2]

The suspension of over half the ministers of Cheshire between 1643 and 1645, and the sequestration of their glebes and tithes, left many parishes unprovided with a preacher. The plight of such parishes was described in a petition from Knutsford in January 1646, where it was stated that the sequestration of the living and the heavy expenses incurred by the inhabitants during the war had left the town unable to maintain a godly preacher, 'the scarcity of godlie men considered'.[3] The petitioners sought an allowance of £30 a year from the sequestered tithes.

The shortage of money and suitable men left the authorities in a quandary. The solution they came up with was to introduce preachers who moved from parish to parish so that all the inhabitants would be served periodically. Few permanent appointments were made until 1646 and 1647. Payment for these peripatetic preachers was authorized either by the deputy lieutenants or by the sequestration committees. Of the nine men known to have been supported by the deputy lieutenants, eight were later to sign the Attestation[4] of the Presbyterian ministers in Cheshire in July 1648.[5] None of the six who enjoyed the patronage of the sequestrators signed it, and four can be shown from other sources to have been Independents.[6]

[1] From the papers of the Committee for Compounding conveniently gathered together and printed in the *Cheshire Sheaf*, 3rd ser., vol. 10, pp.97–100.
[2] For the deputy lieutenants' intervention see P.R.O., SP 23, vol. 149, ff.15–17.
[3] B.M. Harleian MS. 2126, ff. 40–1.
[4] (Ed.) W. Urwick, op. cit., pp.xxv–xxviii. See below, pp.267–8.
[5] The eight were Addams, Hatton, Lancaster, Langley, Marigold, Peartree, Pott, and Sutherland; the ninth was Moyle.
[6] See B.M. Harleian MSS. 2018, 2130, and P.R.O., SP 28/225, *passim.* The four were Eaton, Jones, Roote, and Taylor. See also below, pp.265–6.

Fragmentary evidence of religious divisions is also provided by what we know about the small number of institutions to livings during the years 1643—6. Thus Brereton himself sponsored five ministers, William Swettenham (an army chaplain), Randle Addams (to Wallasey parish), John Brereton (his uncle, described in 1642 as a 'hothead') to Wilmslow, and John Shaw (to Lymm).[1] Of these, only Addams emerges clearly from the extant records as a Presbyterian.

Thus the call of the deputy lieutenants for fresh provision in the county for the settling of the ministry probably reflects sharp conflict over the form of church government envisaged by the two groups. They could do nothing while Brereton controlled the right to eject scandalous ministers and nominate their successors, by dint of the important ordinance of March 1644.[2] This is why they needed a new committee. Without Brereton their powers were extremely restricted.

I have argued that the crucial difference between the deputy lieutenants and Brereton was over the best means of winning the war. The deputy lieutenants were determined to maintain the financial independence and integrity of the county. We saw in the last chapter that the deputy lieutenants, aware of the crippling effect of war taxation on individuals and villages, tended to be lenient and to grant relief wherever possible. This brought them into indirect conflict with Brereton, who was even more impressed by the dangers of an unpaid and mutinous army than of an impoverished countryside.

But the main area of financial conflict was over the payment of troops from other counties who were in service in Cheshire—though even over this the conflict was limited and muffled. Brereton was perfectly aware that Cheshire was

---

[1] Birmingham Reference Library 595611, pp.27, 228; Urwick, op. cit., p.455; (ed.) W.A. Shaw, 'Plundered Ministers' Accounts', *Lancashire and Cheshire Record Society*, vols. 28, 34, vol. 1, p.146.

[2] *Lords Journal*, vol. 6, p.488. See also W.A. Shaw, *A History of the English Church. . .* vol. 2, pp.190—1.

exhausted financially and that she could not maintain her own forces fully, let alone auxiliaries from other counties. On several occasions he joined the deputy lieutenants in letters to the Parliament, to the Committee of Both Kingdoms or to other county committees, begging assistance.[1] However, at times he was prepared to allocate money or provisions raised within Cheshire to troops from outside the county; and above all he took the attitude that money sent down from London was to be divided equitably amongst all the forces participating in the siege (which seems to have excluded those Cheshire troops not serving at the siege, e.g. at the garrison at Nantwich).[2] So much was Brereton in charge of finance that at the siege of Lichfield in Staffordshire, the Shropshire officers wrote to him rather than to the committees of Staffordshire and Shropshire, demanding to know where they could look for regular payment.[3]

As a result of Brereton's policies, 28 per cent of the money paid out by James Croxton during the war was spent on troops from outside Cheshire (£21,023 out of the £74,856). Although 42 per cent (£32,439) was spent on Cheshire troops, much of that was for trained bands and garrisons of the eastern hundreds who never served at Chester.[4] More

[1] e.g. Chester City R.O., CR63/1, Earwaker Transcripts, Box 35, letters from Brereton and Duckenfield to the Speaker (8 Nov. 45), Brereton to the Speaker (20 Nov. 45), and Brereton to the Speaker (undated but next in the series). See also B.M. Add. MS. 11333, f. 116.

[2] This statement is based on the evidence of the Brereton letter books and on an analysis of the warrants in P.R.O., SP 28/224 and 225. These show that in some cases Croxton was ordered to pay troops from other counties from sources of income raised in Cheshire (e.g. sequestration profits), and that only commanders whose troops were at the siege itself (or at the closely co-ordinated sieges at Hawarden and Beeston) were paid out of the money received from London. However, it should be pointed out that the source from which payment was to be made was mentioned in only 28 per cent of the warrants. In the others Croxton was simply authorized to pay on sight.

[3] Birmingham Reference Library 595611, p.95.

[4] These figures are based on Croxton's summary accounts book in P.R.O., SP 28/128, ff. 15–21. They deal with the first three years of Croxton's treasurership, from his appointment in August 1644. Figures covering the months of the final siege alone can be extracted from P.R.O., SP 28/224 and 225, but these must be treated with greater care since they are incomplete. However, in general, they confirm the impressions of the less detailed figures in Croxton's summary.

seems to have been spent on non-Cheshire troops actually at the siege than on Cheshire troops. This does not mean that Brereton favoured non-Cheshire troops; at certain times, particularly at the very end of the siege, there were more troops from outside Cheshire at the siege than there were from the county. But there were so many changes in the composition of the army at Chester, and there is so much uncertainty about the actual dates between which certain forces (e.g. the Shropshire horse) served, that a precise estimate of the extent of their participation cannot be made.

Despite this and despite the fragmentary nature of the evidence, it seems clear that during Brereton's absence in London, the troops from other counties were very ill-paid. In the period up to Brereton's departure, Croxton's payments to non-Cheshire troops accounted for 33 per cent of all his disbursements in pay to soldiers; in the period from his return to the fall of Chester and the period immediately following, 56 per cent went to them; from June to October, while Brereton was away, only 4 per cent out of the surviving records of payments went to them.[1]

At times, the deputy lieutenants gave vent to their concern about the extent of the burden to which Brereton's liberal policies of payment gave rise. In the preamble to their petition of May 1645 requesting widespread changes in the organization of the war-effort, they spoke of 'the constant insupportable charge imposed upon us for the Mainetenance of our owne and other garrisons and forces, of our freinds wch wee are constrained to invite agt the rage and power of the enemy', which together with other charges made them 'scarce able to determin whether the intollerable burden thereof or the Power of the enemy will be more destructive unto our exhausted fortunes and estates.[2]

On one occasion young George Booth wrote to Brereton complaining that Brereton neglected pay for county troops while granting it to 'auxiliaries'. He argued that though not

[1] From the surviving warrants in P.R.O., SP 28/224 and 225.
[2] B.M. Add. MS. 11331, f. 54. See also Bodl. Lib. Tanner MSS., vol. 59, f. 232 where the same point is made.

all the county militia were serving at Chester, they were as fully entitled to pay from London as 'strangers' were.[1] Shortly afterwards Brereton and his leading supporters wrote to the deputy lieutenants saying,

Wee are sensible that there are much arrears of pay to the souldiers of the trayned and freehould bands of the weeklye mize intended by the moddell for the horse and volunteere foote companies uncollected in all the Hundreds wthin this countye, and although the 10,000li ordered by the parlyamt have a greate sound in the countrey, and that many may thinke the same to bee sufficient for the souldiers satisfaccon for all the arrears to them due, yet you cannot but know that it was assigned for the leaguer and forces about Chester where strangers as well as our owne are to have an equall proporcon untill the citye shall bee reduced.

He urged them to gather in arrears of the mise (i.e. monthly assessment) for the payment of county troops not directly involved in the siege.[2]

Although on this point it is difficult to be sure that a clear-cut division of opinion existed, Brereton seems to have felt generally that in the face of such enormous financial problems, money must be allocated strictly according to the immediate needs of the war-effort, with priority being given to maintaining the full strictures of the siege, while the deputy lieutenants sought to ease the particular burden on Cheshire by giving priority of payment to their own troops and thus forcing the other counties to contribute more to their forces. Both sought greater help from neighbouring counties, but Brereton (rightly) believed that a failure on his part to pay troops from other counties would not lead to greater assistance from outside, but simply to widespread mutiny and desertion.[3]

This pattern is complicated further by the concern of the deputy lieutenants to safeguard the countryside from excessive burdens. As we have seen, their attitude to problems of free quarter and their general concern to prevent extreme hardship self-evidently reduced the amount of money available for the pay of the troops. The practical

[1] B.M. Add. MS. 11332, f. 119.
[2] Ibid., f. 128.
[3] The whole question of army discipline will be dealt with below, pp.190–203.

outcome was that during Brereton's absence in the summer of 1645 the troops became far more restive and mutinous than they had been previously; immediately after his return to the county, Brereton was confronted by a string of complaints from military leaders all round Chester that arrears had been mounting and the troops grown more restive. Lowthian, the Tarvin committee, and Commissary Hinde all rushed off requests for immediate relief, and implied that he should take more vigorous action than the committee had done.[1] He rushed off orders to the gentry in each hundred to bring in arrears.[2]

In most cases, his own presence was sufficient to calm down mutinous troops.[3] As he told William Ashurst, 'On Monday the Cheshire foote who were neere two months in arreare for theire pay, were in a high mutinie. But upon my comeing to them the next morneing they were not only well appeased but seemed to bee soe well satisfied as that none demanded any pay.'[4] Brereton put his success down to the fact that the soldiers trusted him to keep his word. During his absences, the soldiers had been fed with empty promises which had then been ignored,[5] with the result that the deputy lieutenants now went in terror of the soldiery and dared not come to the siege in person.[6] Brereton always made less sweeping promises, but he also made a greater effort to fulfil them. Nevertheless, the evidence on balance does not suggest that the deputy lieutenants were startlingly inefficient, just as it is perfectly clear that they were determined, as he was, to destroy all Royalist military power in Cheshire and the whole region around. But they did believe that the destruction of the countryside and the collapse of the rural economy were incompatible with military victory and it is clear that they were less ruthless than Brereton in making additional demands on the county.

[1] B.M. Add. MS. 11332, ff. 14, 15, 23—4.
[2] Ibid., ff. 27, 28.
[3] Ibid., ff. 25, 59.
[4] Ibid., f. 30.
[5] Ibid., ff. 77—8, 103.
[6] B.M. Add. MS. 11333, f. 108.

But it was a question of priorities rather than basic aims. The pattern that has emerged is the same as that shown in the rest of this chapter: the serious disagreements between Brereton and the leading Parliamentarian gentry centred on his readiness to employ methods of local government which bypassed or undermined traditional forms; they sought to employ and to expand their traditional power and influence to meet the requirements of war. For Brereton every means must be employed to ensure the triumph of Parliament over the King. For the deputy lieutenants to have won the war by abandoning the traditional values and forms of the local community would be to have won a victory which was self-defeating.

Four of the petitions drawn up in 1645—6 by Brereton's opponents are signed, and a list of thirty-six gentry can be thus compiled.[1] Analysis of this list provides few surprises. It includes every pre-war Justice of the Peace who had sided with Parliament except for Sir William Brereton and John Crewe of Utkinton.[2] At least twenty-eight can be shown to have had connections with the Booth-Wilbraham faction in 1641—2,[3] the group which I have argued fought desperately to preserve the *status quo* in those years and only went to war with the greatest reluctance.

One last issue requires brief comment. It has been suggested that Brereton was closely associated with the radical leaders in Parliament and was actively promoting their interests in he north-west. Certainly those members of Parliament with whom he regularly corresponded and with whom he was most often associated as a teller—Vane, Haselrig, Prideaux, Lisle, Wentworth, Danvers—were all

---

[1] i.e. B.M. Add. MS. 11331, ff. 54—5, 67—8, 165, Bodl. Lib. Tanner MSS., vol. 60, ff. 220—1.

[2] Based on the lists bound into the Assize Rolls, P.R.O. Chester 24/126, nos. 1—5. One further exception is Henry Mainwaring, but by 1645 he had been dismissed as a traitor.

[3] Based on the signatures to the Cheshire Remonstrance of August 1642, B.M. Harleian MS. 2107, and the petitions of 1641—2 in B.M. Add. MSS. 11333, f. 130, 36913, ff. 60—4.

amongst the leading political Independents in the House.[1] When Brereton's views on national issues are clear, as in his dismayed reaction to Charles's surrender of himself to the Scots, his views are in accord with those of the radicals.[2] The existence of coded letters amongst his correspondence lends support to the view that Brereton was a partisan figure at Westminster; these letters spoke of the attempt of a group of opponents, headed by '133', who were trying to undermine his position both in Cheshire and London. For example, it was this group that in April and May 1645 pressed for Brereton's immediate recall to London, and '133' even appears to have sought to destroy Brereton's credit with the city of London, a manoeuvre countered by a scheme to bring charges before the Commons against this key opponent.[3]

Of Brereton's provincial enemies, only Myddleton was implicated with the London opposition to Brereton. From internal evidence it is clear that he was the opponent covered by the cipher '135', but his involvement, despite Brereton's suspicions seems to have been sporadic.[4] The very fact that Booth and his supporters were so determined to force a by-election to get a voice at Westminster seems to suggest that they did not possess allies there who could act for them. Certainly there is no evidence whatsoever to suggest that Brereton's opponents at Westminster were working on behalf of the deputy lieutenants.

None the less this background does lend support to Professor Underdown's contention that Brereton acted as the agent of the war party in securing the return of their

[1] e.g. see appendix 'a' in D. Underdown, *Pride's Purge*, Oxford, 1971. An exception was William Ashurst, the Lancashire M.P. who acted almost as a personal agent for Brereton and his army while he was in the north-west. Underdown classifies him tentatively as a war-party man in 1643–5, as a middle-party man in 1645–8, and as a religious Presbyterian.

[2] B.M. Add. MS. 11331, ff. 35–6, 46–7, 97.

[3] Ibid., f. 57. There are other letters in a still heavier code where it is impossible to guess even the subject under discussion.

[4] B.M. Add. MS. 11331, ff. 43, 48. The first reveals that Myddleton is not the leading opponent; the second refers to John Jones as related to '135'. Jones was a relative of Myddleton.

candidates at the recruiter elections.[1] But I must differ from him in the interpretation of the evidence that he actually presents, particularly the three letters that Brereton sent to Lisle, Prideaux, and Wentworth. The first and second cannot be said to amount to very much on their own; they comprise accounts of the elections at Stafford and Newcastle-under-Lyme, and presuppose that Brereton's correspondents shared his opinion of the worth of the candidates for whom he had campaigned, but there is no sign that they were 'their' candidates. The letter to Lisle is really about something else: one of the successful candidates was Colonel Edward Leigh who had supported Denbigh against Brereton, but the latter believed that he might be 'gained', since 'I take him to be a religious gent . . . I beseech you use yor intereste in Col Leigh to prevent him from being misengaged.'[2]

Underdown's main argument rests on a letter which Brereton wrote to Peter Wentworth in December 1645. The relevant paragraph runs,

That your list of names is comitted to saffe custody and shall be made use of, if my interest will extend soe farr as to make good what I am already engadged for some of the counties, concerneing wch I should have bin able to give you better satisfacon touchinge some well knowne unto you had there not bin much legerdemeane practised whereof Mr Swinfen who is now with you and will be much serviceable to you can at large informe you. . .[3]

Professor Underdown considers that this list[4] referred to is a list of candidates for the elections in the counties where Brereton had influence which Wentworth had either drawn up or was sending on for someone else. But is this so? The date of Brereton's letter is significant, 15 December 1645. That is seven weeks *after* the elections at Stafford and Newcastle and nearly five months before the next elections in any of the counties where Brereton had any influence, that is Staffordshire, Shropshire, Cheshire, and, to a lesser extent, Lancashire, North Wales, and Derbyshire. There was no

---

[1] D. Underdown, 'Party Management in the Recruiter Elections 1645–8', *E.H.R.* 83(1968), 252–3.

[2] B.M. Add. MS. 11332, f. 46. The Prideaux letter is ibid., f. 45.

[3] Ibid., 11333, f. 22. See Underdown art. cit., p.252.

[4] For my own views on the nature of the list, see below, pp.178–9.

prospect of elections in most of these until after the fall of
Chester, which in the middle of December 1645 looked a
considerable way off. This might have been meant as a way
of being sure candidates were primed and ready when the
time came, yet Brereton goes on to speak about some sleight
of hand being practised against him in these matters, which
surely does not refer to elections. It could hardly be a
reference back to the elections already held, since Brereton
had sent two detailed accounts of these to Lisle and Prideaux
six weeks before; if this close radical group existed,
Wentworth must have heard what had happened, and there
was no need for Brereton to speak so darkly as if of
important new developments.

However, it seems to me that a more damaging refutation
of Underdown's point lies in an analysis of those candidates
we know Brereton supported in various recruiter elections.
At Stafford he supported Sir Richard Sheffington and John
Swinfen,[1] at Newcastle a Mr. Bradshaw who was steward of
the borough,[2] for the county of Stafford Skeffington and
John Bowyer;[3] in Chester city he supported John Bradshaw [4]
and in Shropshire William Steel.[5] Skeffington was Brereton's
brother-in-law, and Bowyer was his nephew. Swinfen was one
of his closest allies in Staffordshire and there are numerous
letters from one to the other in the Brereton Letter Books
dating from long before the election. Assuming that the John
Bradshaw at Newcastle was the regicide and the man
Brereton recommended for Chester, he was one of Brereton's
closest neighbours and friends in Cheshire and had acted for
him as a financial agent in London in 1644–5. So had
William Steele, another Cheshire man whose name is linked

---

[1] For an admirable account of the Stafford election, see Brunton and
Pennington, op. cit., pp.192–4.

[2] e.g. Pennington and Roots, op. cit., p.lxxxii. That this might be the same John
Bradshaw of Marple whom Brereton supported for Chester; see ibid., p.133 and
also B.M. Add. MS. 11332, f. 45 where Mr. Bradshaw the Recorder was said to
have been in London for many weeks; John Bradshaw of Marple certainly had
been there all that time.

[3] Ibid., p.lxxxii.

[4] B.M. Add. MS. 11333, f. 83.

[5] Birmingham Reference Library 595611, p.212.

with Brereton's in the records of the Commonwealth Exchequer. It hardly took a list from Wentworth to recommend these men to Brereton; if the list came and Brereton recommended these men in the place of those contained in the list, the idea of Brereton as the radicals' agent for the election is still unproven.

Furthermore Brereton's direct intervention in elections was very sporadic. Outside Staffordshire he intervened hardly at all, simply asking the Shropshire committee if they would support Steele (who did not get in),[1] and telling Bradshaw how to go about winning votes at Chester.[2] He warned Sir Henry Vane to watch out for trouble at the Derby election, but nothing could stop Gell's interference and success there on his brother's behalf.[3]

We have already seen how suspicious the deputy lieutenants were that Brereton was preventing the issue of a writ for the county of Chester. His room for manoeuvre there was restricted because all the moderates had already decided to support young George Booth[4] and none of Brereton's supporters was sufficiently prominent to stand any chance against him. There is some evidence that he tried to hold back the election,[5] but not for long and to no effect.[6]

So the only determined efforts he made to secure the election of his friends was in Staffordshire. Brunton and Pennington have provided us with an admirable account of his role in the Stafford election, showing how he helped to put across his own nominees, and how his supporters and a handful of troops were involved in trying (with only partial success) to swing the vote on election day.[7] At Newcastle Brereton made an unsuccessful attempt to make the third

[1] Ibid.
[2] B.M. Add. MS. 11333, f. 83.
[3] Ibid., 11332, f. 58. See above, p.145.
[4] B.M. Add. MSS. 11332, ff. 69–70, 119–20.
[5] Birmingham Reference Library 595611, p.42.
[6] The Cheshire writ was issued a fortnight later, on 1 May 1646 (*Commons Journal*, vol. 4, pp.528–9).
[7] Brunton and Pennington, op. cit., pp.192–4.

candidate stand down.[1] The implications of his letters about this election are that he was not present at the vote, which seems to have got out of hand after the spreading of malicious rumours about Mr. Bradshaw.[2]

The clearest evidence of Brereton's intervention in an election in fact comes from material that Professor Underdown does not consider. In April 1646 Brereton was anxiously canvassing support for Skeffington and Bowyer for the county of Stafford. He told Swinfen that he had laboured much, particularly for Skeffington, and had gained promises of help from Sir Charles Egerton and Colonel Bowyer. Later he received a promise of assistance from Lord Paget. He wrote to Swinfen: 'in the meanetyme I desire you will hasten the writts . . . My onely feare is lest it be not whilest I stay and if soe it will occasion a hazard in the eleccon.'[3] It is Brereton who was seeking the co-operation of his friends in London not they, who were using him to further their national strategy. There was a connection, but not so strict or firm a one as Underdown suggests.

The pattern was much closer to that observable from other letters of Brereton. He used his power in the north midlands and his influence in London to get his friends and supporters into key positions. Thus, in December 1645 he was grooming William Edwards to take control of Chester once the city fell,[4] in April 1646 he was campaigning for one of his old military colleagues, Duckenfield, Croxton, Lowthian, or Venables, to be appointed Governor of Chester,[5] and also for John Bruen, another close associate of his against the deputy lieutenants to be appointed Chamberlain of the local Exchequer Court.[6] There were numerous other less important posts he also sought to fill. All the men mentioned above were close colleagues of his, and their reputations and abilities far better known to him than to the radical leaders in

[1] For Brereton's correspondence with Terrick see B.M. Add. MS. 11332, ff. 44, 50.
[2] Ibid., ff. 45, 46.
[3] Birmingham Reference Library 595611, pp.86, 106—7.
[4] B.M. Add. MS. 11333, f. 83.
[5] Birmingham Reference Library 595611, p.36.
[6] Ibid., p.71.

Parliament. Furthermore the supposed list of candidates came not from Prideaux, whom Underdown shows was in the crucial position of patronage, but from Wentworth.

It is extremely unclear what the subject of Wentworth's letter was. One possibility which seems to make greater sense than that proposed by Underdown is that the list was of suggested additions to the subcommittees of accounts in Staffordshire and Warwickshire. Since no members of Parliament sat on the central accounts committee, and since it was rapidly becoming an organ of the political Presbyterian party at Westminster,[1] the fact that Wentworth was not a member of it is less significant than that his local interests were in Warwickshire and Staffordshire (indeed he was a member for a borough seat in the latter). A list of members for these subcommittees would be longer than a list of prospective Parliamentary candidates and, particularly in the case of Warwickshire, Brereton would be unfamiliar with some of the minor figures involved. Above all, we know that there were attempts a few weeks later to nominate fresh subcommittees in these counties, attempts which were resisted by the moderate elements on the county committees.[2]

In any case the evidence seems to support the general argument of this chapter, that Brereton's concern was far wider than that of the deputy lieutenants who, whatever their will to win, were still dominated by local perspectives. Brereton was not tied into some narrow scheme of political plotting with a group in the Commons which saw the outcome of the Civil Wars at something beyond the reassertion of the traditional values of government and society. He was interested to see his friends and colleagues in his local sphere of influence in a position to co-operate in an evolving programme of reform. He hoped he could rely on his friends in London to help him in this where necessary; but this does not mean that his behaviour was underhand or conspiratorial.

[1] D.H. Pennington 'The Accounts of the Kingdom', in (ed.) F.J. Fisher, *Essays ... in Honour of R.H. Tawney*, p.187.
[2] P.R.O., SP 28/256, unfoliated.

## 5

## RECOVERY AND CONFLICT, 1646–1650

### I

Once Chester surrendered in January 1646, the last Royalist resistance was swiftly broken and the county returned to a state of relative peace. Brereton led a force (which included several Cheshire regiments) into Staffordshire, where several garrisons were still held for the King, but the burden of supporting rival forces and the devastating effects of the predatory marches of major field armies ceased. Nevertheless, the full cost of the war had yet to be counted.

To begin with, the soldiers who had won the war had not been fully paid. They had already shown, by desertion and near mutiny, their resentment at insubstantial promises of payment. One of the forces holding them in check had been the definite military objective, with constant skirmishes to keep their minds occupied. Their arrears forced the county to keep them together after the fall of Chester, but their morale and discipline deteriorated as fresh arrears were piled on top of the old ones. Twice, in July 1646 and June 1647, they mutinied and by decisive action secured the money that was not otherwise forthcoming.[1] The reduction in the county's current financial responsibilities was offset by a drastic decline in the source of revenue that had been most steady in 1644 and 1645. In the early months of 1646 the sequestered Royalists flocked to London, paid composition fines to the central government, and were readmitted to their estates. Fresh attempts by the hundredal sequestration committees to uncover those who had previously escaped notice led only to the sequestration of minor gentlemen with incomes too small to make up for that of richer landlords now back in possession of their estates. In any case the leading Parliamentarian gentry were anxious to reconcile old friends who had fought for the losing side. Afraid of alienating them

[1] This subject forms the substance of section III, below.

permanently, they sought to readmit them to a share in the social, if not administrative, leadership of the county. Their success in this can be seen at least partially in the almost complete quiescence of Cheshire during the second Civil War. This in turn helped towards the solution of the problems of finance and the peaceful settlement of the grievances of the army.[1]

Beyond this, there were the less immediate but more insidious legacies of the war. The whole structure of day-to-day county administration, the poor law, the maintenance of roads and bridges, the licensing of carriers and traders in corn, and of ale houses, and the provision for those maimed or widowed in the fighting, had broken down. Problems had been dealt with, if at all, in a piecemeal fashion. The network of patronage and co-operation between village and local J.P. had disappeared, and certainly could not be reconstructed overnight. There were also signs of a determined attack on the gentry's control of church patronage and finances. The great landowners rightly concluded that the traditional values and assumptions of the county community were on the verge of collapse.[2]

## II

In April 1647 a London newspaper recorded the response of the House of Lords to the persistent demands of the moderate gentry throughout the country for a return to 'normality'. In particular,

This day the House of Peers (at a Conference) gave reasons to the Commons, why their Lordships desire their Concurrence for the puttinge downe of Country Committees.

1. Many very great Complaints have been made from all parts of the Kingdome, against them, by those who have ventured their Estates and lives for the publike service.

2. That power which was given to them for the good of the kingdome, they have abused and in an arbitrary manner oppressed the people, to the scandell of the Parliament.

[1] For details, see below, section IV.
[2] For the reconstruction of civil administration 1645–59, see below, chapter 6. For the question of the church, see below pp.263–76.

3. The Continuance of them, is no wayes beneficiall to the kingdome, onely a few particular private men are advanced by it to the prejudice of the people in generall.
4. It wil give a great deale of satisfaction to the kingdome to have the said Committees put downe, and power given to honest magistrates to act as formerly. . . [1]

The struggle for the control of local government was one of the great issues between the factions at Westminster in the years 1645—8. Questions of finance, religion, the treatment of Royalists and neuters, the centralization of government, would be vitally affected by the outcome of the struggle. As the House of Lords saw, the years 1644—6 had seen the overthrow of the moderates who had kept hold of local committees at the onset of war, and Professor Underdown has put it,

In county after county a phenomenon similar to that of Kent and Somerset can be observed. By the end of the war the old leadership is being pushed aside by energetic new men lower down the social scale, lesser gentry and townsmen, often of radical Puritan inclinations, aiming at power as well as Reformation . . . the old gentry were forced out, or withdrew out of resentment at religious radicalism, high taxation and centralization.[2]

He has documented his argument by evidence from many counties, and given a splendid case history from Somerset.[3]

Yet in Cheshire, where the radicals had long enjoyed a large measure of control, the trend was in the opposite direction. The moderates under Sir George Booth enjoyed in the years 1646—8 a greater degree of power than at any other time between 1642 and 1659. The *Scottish Dove,* the weekly London news-sheet which led a prolonged propaganda campaign against county committees,[4] denounced the Cheshire committee for its depredations in the summer of

---

[1] B.M. Thomason Tracts E 384 (8) *Perfect Occurrences,* 9—16 April 1647.
[2] D. Underdown, *Pride's Purge* p.34.
[3] Ibid., pp.29—39, 76—8. For Somerset, the pamphlet by Humphrey Willis *The power of the Committee of the County of Somerset,* B.M. Thomason Tracts E 345 (3), 18 July 1646 is of particular interest. Excellent case studies are also provided by A.M. Everitt, *Kent. . .,* chapter 5, and A.M. Johnson, op. cit., (Buckinghamshire).
[4] e.g. B.M. Thomason Tracts; E 336 (6), 29 Apr.—6 May 1646, E 341 (19), 17—25 June 1646, E 345 (11), 15—22 July 1646, E 350 (5), 5—12 Aug. 1646.

1646. But the following week it published a shamefaced apology, stating that the Cheshire committee was a notable exception to the rule, and that the trouble had been caused by troops who had mutinied without cause.[1]

The explanation for this development lies mainly in the fact that Brereton's control over the county had been a highly personal one. He had never purged the county institutions of his opponents because he could always bypass or ignore them. When he left, his supporters were in a minority on most committees (though they still controlled sequestrations). Furthermore, Brereton did not continue to dominate affairs in Cheshire through his powerful position at Westminster. He was consulted by the House when Cheshire affairs were raised there,[2] and he appears to have furthered the interests of Independent ministers in the county through the Committee of Augmentations, but otherwise he paid little attention to the shire, rarely even visiting it. Throughout the period 1646–53 he was immensely active in the Commons as committee man and teller, and was twice on the Rump's Council of State. But he appears to have reached the peak of his influence during the second Civil War, when he was reportedly one of Cromwell's confidants and one of those responsible for the decision to bring the King to trial. This would certainly help to explain why John Bradshaw, his old friend and neighbour, should be selected from amongst the ranks of second-grade lawyers to preside at the trial of the King.[3] Perhaps his involvement with central government

[1] B.M. Thomason Tracts E 346 (10), 22–30 July 1646; E 349 (7) 29 July–5 Aug. 1646.

[2] e.g. *C.S.P.D.* 1649–50, p.468, where he and the Governor of Chester (Duckenfield) were to be consulted about a new militia committee.

[3] Brereton is mentioned by several contemporaries as having been close to Cromwell at several crucial meetings during the last months of 1648. In each case the reference to Brereton is coincidental to the writer's purpose, which enhances the possibility that these statements are accurate and significant. The most important are: Bodl. Lib. Wood 369, *An Exact and Most Impartial Accompt of the Indictment, Arraignment and Trial . . . of 29 Regicides,* 1660, pp.162, 248; *The Manner of the Arraignment of those Twenty Eight Persons,* 1660, p.162 W.C. Abbott, *The Writings and Speeches of Oliver Cromwell,* 4 vols. Cambridge, Mass., 1937–47, vol. 1, p.734.

kept him too occupied to concern himself with Cheshire affairs, particularly since he was becoming influential on several committees in Surrey, thanks to his new residence there (the archbishop's Palace at Croydon, awarded him by a grateful Parliament for his services in the north-west).[1]

In Cheshire itself Quarter Sessions met again from the end of 1645, and for the next two years was dominated by the old county families—the Booths, Roger Wilbraham, Thomas Stanley, Philip Mainwaring. But there was a change at the end of 1647, possibly the outcome of the shock engendered by the second army mutiny of July 1647, during which some of the Justices had been seized and locked up for three weeks:[2] all these moderate leaders ceased to attend Sessions or carry out their functions as Justices in their hundreds.[3] The most active Justices in the fifteen months up to the death of the King were Thomas Mainwaring, Thomas Marbury, Ralph Arderne, John Crewe, John Wettenhall, and Thomas Croxton. Of these, only Mainwaring and Crewe came from families which had provided representatives to the pre-war Bench, and all were younger men than those who had been the leading moderates in the years 1642—6. All except Croxton and Crewe had opposed Brereton during the war, and three were to refuse to serve during the Commonwealth and Protectorate.[4]

A study of the Commission of the Peace itself[5] suggests a slightly different perspective. Honorary appointments apart, there were twenty-six Cheshire gentlemen on the Commission in 1648, thirteen of whom were former allies of Brereton,

---

[1] For his appointment to committees there, e.g. *Commons Journal*, vol. 5, p.680, vol. 6, p.88; for his activities, his letter book in Chester City Library, *passim*.

[2] See below, pp.200—2.

[3] Philip Mainwaring died at this time, and was succeeded by his son, Thomas.

[4] The above is based on the lists of attendant Justices for each Sessions in C.R.O. Quarter Sessions Order Book 9a, and also on the signatures on documents in the Quarter Sessions Files.

[5] The earliest list is from the Assize Roll of April 1648 (P.R.O. Chester 24/127, no.1); a commission was issued in May 1644 (P.R.O. Index 4213, p.3), but I cannot find an original of this.

twelve former opponents.[1] But most of the thirteen were completely inactive. Duckenfield and Venables were fully occupied with military affairs, as was Croxton until the running down of Nantwich garrison—he was still Governor of the town—at the beginning of 1647. Several of Brereton's minor supporters had been put on the Bench—Gilbert Gerard, Thomas Tuchett, William Steele, Henry Greene—but they also do not appear to have been active. Much stranger was the withdrawal from public life of Henry Brooke and Edward Hyde during this period, not to reappear in local government until 1649. Of all Brereton's close allies, only John Legh of Booths was playing any significant role as a Justice during these years—and he was not involved at all in other spheres of government.

Thus, lists of appointees must be handled with great care, since nomination to a committee cannot be treated as a sign of activity: we cannot take the lists of monthly assessment commissioners, militia commissioners, etc. at face value. During the war these commissions had always contained only ten or eleven names, while there were only thirteen official deputy lieutenants;[2] even allowing for the seven co-opted associates, the total number who ever served on committees for the county was thirty. In the years after the war, the size of each committee rapidly grew. By the beginning of 1648 there were thirty on each committee, a number which remained constant, despite regular purges and recruitment, until 1660.

An analysis of all available lists shows that twenty-four men appeared regularly in commissions in the period up to the death of the King. Ten of the eleven had sat on earlier commissions,[3] and nine of the deputy lieutenants are

---

[1] Three or four of those listed as Brereton's supporters are only tentatively included. This would affect the balance somewhat, but in each case there is some evidence. The twenty-sixth was Peter Warburton, deputy Justice to Bradshaw at Chester whose politics throughout the period are totally inscrutable.

[2] See above, pp.83–4.

[3] The exception is Henry Mainwaring, dismissed by Parliament and suspected of treachery in 1644.

amongst them.[1] The twenty-four was then made up by the leading officers from Brereton's army (Robert Venables, William Massie, James Lowthian, Robert Gregg), who had never previously held important civilian posts, and by a few high-flyers amongst the lesser officials.[2] This group of twenty-four contained twelve of Brereton's former opponents and ten of his former allies, some of whom—John Legh, Jonathan Bruen, Thomas Croxton—were not even named. If the pattern of activity seen in the case of the Commission of the Peace is applicable here, then the moderate gentry would almost certainly have had effective control of assessments, accounts, and the militia. But sequestrations remained in hands of Brereton's hundredal committees.[3]

The accounts of James Croxton reveal the identity of those responsible for the disbursement of money from county funds and it is not at all clear what body was responsible for this task. The eight men who were most involved with it form an odd group. They were Henry Brooke, Roger Wilbraham, Thomas Stanley, John Legh. Philip Mainwaring, Thomas Croxton, Henry Birkenhead, and Edward Hyde. They included more of Brereton's supporters than his opponents, and most of them were otherwise inactive in county administration. Particularly interesting was Henry Birkenhead, who had held no civilian office during the Civil War, though he came from a respectable county family and had held a commission in Brereton's army. He was not included in any commission during the years 1646—9.[4]

Since Cheshire remained solidly behind Parliament during the second Civil War, there were no major changes until after the death of the King, which drove many families into

[1] The exceptions are John Legh, Thomas Croxton, Edward Hyde and John Booth. The last was already suspected of Royalism (he was arrested during the second Civil War), but the omission of the others is inexplicable.
[2] Of the seven associates of the deputy lieutenants in 1643–6, only John Wettenhall was included (he was also an active J.P.). Two former Brereton supporters (William Tuchett and William Davies) were promoted.
[3] See above, pp.86–8.
[4] This is based on an analysis of the warrants in P.R.O., SP 28/224 and 225.

opposition. The first new Commission of the Peace was issued in February 1649 and witnessed the purge of only a few moderates—Henry Vernon and John Wettenhall were the most prominent—and the inclusion of several minor figures. Apart from six honorary appointments, thirty-four gentlemen were named, the majority being former Brereton men.[1] The more radical change came at the end of 1649, when the Commission was pruned down to thirty, including eleven honorary appointments: only nineteen of the county gentry remained. The most significant omissions were young George Booth, Roger Wilbraham, and William Massie, all leading moderates. Also dropped were those whose careers had been entirely military, men like James Lowthian, William Tuchett, and Robert Venables and some minor gentry. The commission was now dominated by Brereton's old supporters and by younger men who had played little part in the Civil War, like Thomas Mainwaring and Thomas Brereton.[2] The commissions for other specific purposes, such as monthly assessments, were reconstituted from the same group of men. The old moderates were excluded except for old Sir George Booth and Thomas Stanley, and the majority were old Brereton supporters.[3]

The same pattern emerges from the activities of the Commission of the Peace. Seven men were outstanding in the years 1649–50 for the frequency of their attendance at Sessions and their activity out of it: Thomas Croxton, Jonathan Bruen, Henry Bradshaw, and Gilbert Gerard were all close associates of Brereton during the Civil War, Thomas Mainwaring, Thomas Brereton, and Thomas Marbury were all young men who had only inherited their estates and become prominent gentlemen since 1646.[4]

[1] I have used the copy in Chester City R.O., CR63/2/696, Aderne MSS., p.61. Seventeen were definitely former Brereton supporters, ten former opponents. The position of the other seven is unclear.

[2] Chester City R.O., Cowper MSS., vol. 2, f. 1.

[3] On this commission, the composition was ten old Brereton supporters, five of his old opponents, and four newcomers. The regular members of other commissions broke down 16, 7, and 5 for the same groups. For these, see e.g. Firth and Rait, op. cit., vol. 2, pp.31, 294, 462.

[4] Cf. above, p.184, n. 4.

The events of the second Civil War in Cheshire can be
summarized briefly.[1] The Royalists, most of whom were just
beginning to settle down on their estates again, were
unprepared to take fresh risks, and in any case they were not
reconciled to the late conversion of the Scots to the King's
cause. John Aston, brother of the prominent Royalist Sir
Thomas Aston, wrote to a friend that 'The Scots have
eternally lost their honor wth us, therefore we heed not
theire invasion'.[2] Hopes that the Presbyterians might join the
Scots were dashed by Sir George Booth's emphatic rejection
of Royalist overtures; he simply forwarded the letter that
they sent him to Parliament.[3] On the other hand, the county
was reluctant to rearm itself to meet the threat. Henry
Bradshaw, trying to recruit a regiment in Macclesfield
hundred, formerly the stronghold of Parliament and
Puritanism, was forced to report that 'there came not Fortie
souldiers in all, and most of those wthout armes, some
Townpps whollie absent'.[4] None the less troops were
eventually raised and, after the battle of Preston, they
succeeded in rounding up 1,500 of the scattered Royalists,
while Lowthian set off into North Wales to help Mytton
defeat an abortive rising there.[5]

There had earlier been persistent rumours that the city of
Chester had wavered in its allegiance to Parliament. William
Daniell, a colonel in the garrison, warned Lenthall on 20 June
that

there was some discovery of the most deep and desperate plot to have
betrayed this garrison . . . into the hands of the malignant party of the
kingdom . . . some of the greatest in this city and county that have
served with and against the Parliament since the begining of the late war
are accused to be prime actors in the business.[6]

---

[1] R.N. Dore, *The Civil Wars in Cheshire*, pp.6̄9–73, for a fuller account.
[2] B.M. Add. MS. 36914, f. 237.
[3] H.M.C. *Portland MSS.*, vol. 1, p.462.
[4] Bodl. Lib. Top. Cheshire e 3 (Letter Book of Henry Bradshaw) ff. 1–4. See
also C.W. Sutton 'Some Cheshire Papers of 1648', *T.L.C.A.S.* 31(1913),
particularly 106–10.
[5] R.N. Dore, op. cit., and *Lords Journal*, vol. 10, pp.455, 459.
[6] H.M.C. *Portland MSS.*, vol. 1, p.463.

Similar accusations against city leaders were made else-where.[1] A week later a commission of Oyer and Terminer was granted to be 'directed unto Peter Warburton one of the Justices of Assize of Chester, Robert Duckenfield, Governor of Chester, [    ] Edwards, Humphrey Mackworth and to such other persons as Sr William Brereton shall present unto them'.[2] With the heightened danger during the Scots march south in July, Duckenfield was granted a commission of martial law in the city to try those implicated in the plot.[3]

Suspicions were probably inflated by the fact that the city, so overwhelmingly Royalist in 1642–6, had found it impossible to replace its whole assembly by men of sufficient stature, and had therefore gained permission to pardon several aldermen who had collaborated with the Royalists. Indeed a majority of the aldermen in 1648 had served in the assembly throughout the Royalist occupation.[4] In the event nothing could be proved against the city authorities, but the lingering suspicion led to an assault on the city's independence. Having lived for centuries in dread of the slightest incursion of its powers by the county, the city now found itself integrated with the county for some administrative purposes. An immediate response to the crisis had been the appointment of several county gentry to the city militia committee.[5] Surviving letters in the mayor's correspondence show that since 1646 the county had been trying, without success, to have joint committees set up for city and county.[6] The rumours gave Brereton in London the opportunity to make a fresh attempt, and on this occasion he was successful.[7] From thenceforth until the Restoration, all militia committees, and some others, were made out jointly, with country squires in a clear majority.[8]

[1] B.M. Harleian MS. 2135, ff. 50–1.
[2] *Commons Journal*, vol. 5, p.616.
[3] *Lords Journal*, vol. 10, p.377.
[4] Cf. the assembly lists in Chester City R.O., AF/26/2,6 and AF/27/5,15, and AF/28/3,4.
[5] *Commons; Journal*, vol. 5, p.623.
[6] Chester City R.O., ML/2/312, 313, 315.
[7] Ibid. ML/2/320.
[8] e.g. Firth and Rait, op. cit., vol. 2, pp.969, 1321.

## III

The development during the first half of the seventeenth century of warfare on a new scale, with large bodies of troops in arms for years on end instead of being disbanded at the end of every campaigning season, led to a new set of dangers for officers and administrators. Mutinies by ill-paid troops and retaliation from an exhausted countryside became endemic to all wars of the period.[1] In England the former is most readily seen in the activities of the New Model Army from the spring to late autumn of 1647, when the rank and file seized the initiative, forced their officers to take up a broad political and constitutional position, and culminated in a direct confrontation with the Parliament. Civilian resistance found its most coherent expression in the Clubman movements of 1645, ostensibly neutralist grass-roots movements but frequently controlled by gentry whose aims may have been less purely apolitical.[2] In fact these are only the tip of an iceberg of disorder which threatened the whole country in the years 1645−7, and which, to contemporaries at least, seemed likely to bring fresh bloodshed and social revolution in its wake.[3]

It is not hard to discover reasons why this situation arose after the end of the fighting. There was no pressing need for the maintenance of a military establishment, but the armies could not be disbanded until their demands for arrears had been met. They were simply placed upon free quarter in garrison towns or in the countryside, which they continued

---

[1] e.g. J.H. Elliott, *The Revolt of the Catalans*, Cambridge, 1963, pp.387−417; R. Mousnier, 'Les Mouvements populaires en France avant les traites de Westphalie', reprinted in his book, *La Plume, la faucille et le marteau*, Paris, 1970; V.J. Polisensky, *The Thirty Years War*, London, 1971, *passim*, for examples from Spain, France, and Germany.

[2] B.S. Manning, 'Neutrals and Neutralism During the English Civil War', Univ. of Oxford D.Phil. thesis, 1957, is the only full account. There are brief accounts in most general books (e.g. Gardiner, op. cit., vol. 2, pp.230−2). For an excellent case study see C.M. Thomas, 'The First Civil War in Glamorganshire', Univ. Coll. of Swansea, M.A. thesis, 1963, chapters 5 and 6.

[3] See my article, 'Mutinies and Discontent in English Provincial Armies', *Past and Present*, 56(1972).

to impoverish. Their very idleness and the absence of any threat from organized Royalist armies increased their discontent. At the same time the central government was increasing its control over the collection of taxes.[1] The local authorities were receiving less money and arrears were actually growing. The result was a series of mutinies in the summer of 1646, followed, after a lull, by a still more serious series in the spring and summer of 1647. Almost every county was affected.[2] Cheshire was no exception.

Available funds had always failed to meet financial commitments to the troops. As a result there had been a constant problem with soldiers who exacted food and other supplies from the countryside by pilfering and plundering. Not that they were simply concerned to seize what would fill empty bellies. One inhabitant of Over township noted having lost to passing troops, 'clothes, a byble and other necessaries' and his record could be multiplied several hundred times from existing sources.[3]

Sometimes these thefts were committed by individual soldiers, but more frequently a whole unit would systematically plunder a village of its provisions, while the officers stood by hopelessly or even joined in, preferring to ensure orderly pillage than face a mutiny from their hungry, ill-clad troops.[4] At times, plundering expeditions from friend and foe alike covered a wide area. One such, when Cheshire troops stationed beyond the Dee went on an extended raid into Wales (April 1645), led to retaliatory action from Brereton, after an official protest from Parliament which had been alerted about the raid by Sir John Trevor, M.P., whose house had been amongst those sacked. Brereton said of the activities of his forces: 'There is nothing accompanieing this service hath more afflicted mee then to see those insolencies

---

[1] e.g. sequestration gave way to composition as the main solution to the Royalist question. Composition produced large sums, but the money so raised came almost entirely to the central treasuries, while sequestrations, largely at the disposal of local treasuries, fell away. See above, pp.105—6.

[2] See my article, loc. cit., pp.53—5.

[3] B.M. Harleian MS. 2126, f. 16.

[4] See above, pp.109—11.

that are sometyme committed by the soldiers and not have power wholy to restraine them . . .' He announced stringent measures to ensure the return of, or compensation for, goods taken from Parliamentarians, and sought out those involved for punishment: for example, all common soldiers sleeping on new sheepskins were immediately suspect.[1] Similarly, there were a few indiscriminate raids by troops within Cheshire, particularly during 1644 and 1645; only occasionally do the officers appear to have been involved, and these were usually junior ones. [2]

After the fall of Chester the Committee of Both Kingdoms was quick to realize the dangers of unrest amongst troops whose task was accomplished, and who were beginning to brood about their arrears. They 'desired the House [of Commons] that Money may be provided for the Payment of the Forces, both in regard of the Poverty of their Country, and that the Soldiers, through want of Pay, may not disaffect the Inhabitants; and thereby hinder their submission to the Parliament'.[3] Nothing was done. At the time of the negotiations for the final surrender of the city, similarly, Brereton had revealingly told Parliament that the large number of negotiators

was proposed by them, and was the rather assented to by us, to the end, better satisfaccon might bee given to the comon Soldyers, when some of their owne officers were intrusted and imployed in Treating & makeing compositions for them, that they might thereby bee alsoe obliged to restrain their soldyers from plunder and vyolation of what is concluded.[4]

On the whole Brereton refused to adopt a repressive stance. He sought to control excesses, but, faced with the impossibility of solving the problem while county finances remained so inadequate, he undoubtedly turned a blind eye to many illegalities. The seizure of food and clothing might be the only answer when men had, as he said, 'not wherwthall to cover their nackedness nor a penny mony in their

[1] B.M. Add. MS. 11331, ff. 20, 25, 26, 30, 63—4, etc.
[2] B.M. Harleian MSS. 1999, f. 70; 2018, f. 69.
[3] *Commons Journal*, vol. 4, p.443.
[4] Bodl. Lib. Tanner MSS., vol. 60, (Lenthall MSS.) f. 393.

pockets; truely I confesse if I had not bin an eye witness I should hardly have believed it. . .'[1]

Organized plunder was the most elementary form of army unrest. More direct were the concerted efforts by whole regiments to exact their arrears. Thus on several occasions troops refused to move to fresh quarters or into action until grievances had been redressed. The most serious mutiny of this kind occurred when Yorkshire troops refused to advance further than Macclesfield hundred (where their military value was neglibible) towards Chester in the spring of 1645.[2] But the Cheshire forces themselves refused to serve on several occasions, notably during Brereton's absence in London following the Self-denying Ordinance.[3] It was this development that led Parliament to grant him a commission of martial law—a right they were most reluctant to grant—after his return to the county. Indeed, during the winter of 1645—6 an informant within the Parliamentarian rank sent a secret message to the city authorities telling them that the whole military operation was likely to collapse because of unrest among the troops.[4]

Distinct from these mutinies were threats by whole regiments to disband themselves. A steady trickle of deserters was inevitable, but the decision of a whole body of troops to desert was a more serious matter. The clearest example is that of Colonel Duckenfield's men, who on several occasions threatened to disband themselves, and on at least one occasion did so. In their case, arrears were only a secondary grievance: as Duckenfield told Sir Thomas Fairfax in 1644,

I have endeavoured (since I knew your pleasure) to get my soldiers into order fit for service, to advance to Nantwich, but they have disbanded themselves, and are following the plough, and from thence they will not be drawn. Yet upon receipt of your letter yesterday, I sent to the captains to join with mee presently, to call their companies together, to march with them and mee to Nantwich; but they refuse to stir yet. They pretend that the dragoons are so uncivil, that they plunder the

[1] B.M. Add. MS. 11332, f. 107.
[2] B.M. Add. MS. 11331, *passim*, particularly ff. 32, 56, 75, 95.
[3] See above pp.172—3 (e.g. B.M. Add. MS 11332, ff. 14, 15, 23—4, 30).
[4] J.Ry.L. Tatton of Wythenshawe MSS., item 94.

country extremely, and they dare not leave their houses for fear of them.[1]

The same fear that their homes and families would be plundered while they were on service at the other side of the county was articulated constantly by this regiment throughout the war years. For example, the Yorkshire forces who refused to move up to the siege were the occasion of a further threat by Duckenfield's men to desert unless they moved themselves from those areas from which his regiment came.[2]

Two petitions from common soldiers have survived from the last months of the war. The first, from Duckenfield's regiment, raised this whole question of the fate of their homes and families as a grievance even stronger than that of their arrears.[3] The other, addressed to Colonel Michael Jones, is marked by bitterness at the trail of broken promises made by the deputy lieutenants.[4] The soldiers called upon Jones to intervene on their behalf, they having 'long waited with patience the performance of the Gents Engagements (which wee see are not to be confided in)'. They warned him, however, that necessity might 'constraine us to dispose otherwayes of ourselves'.[5]

Both the refusal to perform duties and organized desertion lost their effectiveness once the King had been defeated. As a means of exacting arrears, desertion actually became self-defeating. As a result affairs reached a climax in the summer of 1646 when officials were seized by the common soldiers and held to ransom. Even this had been foreshadowed; reluctant to mulct the countryside further, infuriated by the delays and dashed hopes aroused by false promises, the troops had early begun to threaten and extort money from any official reputed to have cash in his possession. In the sequestrators' accounts, there are about thirty reports of the

---

[1] B.M. Add. MS. 18979 (Fairfax MS.), f. 147. Printed in R. Bell, *Memorials of the Civil War,* 2 vols., 1849, vol. 1, pp.79–80.
[2] B.M. Add. MS. 11331, ff. 70, 75.
[3] Ibid., f. 94.
[4] See above, pp.172–3.
[5] B.M. Add. MS. 11332, f. 103.

following kind: 'pd to quiett soldiers when they came tumultuously to the sitting of the committee for sequestr' twise.. .' or 'spent when Colonel Booth souldiers came for the first time for monies to Moberley and toke me with them to bowden and kept mee there two daies a prisoner'.[1] The sums involved were usually very small.

For most of 1646 leading gentlemen in the county were aware that a major crisis was looming.[2] Tensions were heightened by the return of forces from service in Staffordshire and Wales, and by a fresh attempt to settle the Excise in the county—earlier attempts having largely failed. The proceeds were promised to the soldiers, but it was hated by them as much as by the townspeople of Chester and Nantwich; several contemporaries agree that it was a major cause of the ensuing mutinies.[3] In a letter to three of their number then in London, the deputy lieutenants pitched the case very high:

. . . the Souldiery take great dislike at the Excise, the Citty and County almost gennerally distaste it, the gentlemen that are imployed have carryed themselves very well in it and endeavour by all fayre means to effect the same but our feare is that will not perfect the businesse but some constraint must be used, otherwise little will bee made of it to prevent present evill, Wee have tould the souldiers, that they are to bee payd forth of it, and if that take not there is noe way left to satisfye them . . . Wee extreamely feare, if the souldiery joyne not in the tumult yet all or most of them will stand apart and will not assist theire officers and what greater evill will come thereof more then the damage in the excise in this citye which hath cost much blood wee know not, but leave to your serious consideracon. [4]

There was a preliminary crisis at the end of June amongst the newly returned forces at Chester. According to a newsletter of 29 June,

---

[1] B.M. Harleian MSS. 2018, f. 106; 2126, f. 103.

[2] B.M. Thomason Tracts E 511(17) *Perfect Occurrences,* 27 June–3 July 1646; Bodl. Lib. Tanner MSS., vol. 59, ff. 230, 232, 426.

[3] B.M. Thomason Tracts E 511(24) *Perfect Occurrences,* 18–24 July 1646; Bodl. Lib. Tanner MSS., vol. 59, f. 442; H.M.C. *Portland MSS.,* vol. 1, p.390. As far as I can determine, the deputy lieutenants had made this promise without consulting the central government.

[4] Bodl. Lib. Tanner MSS., vol. 59, f. 442.

Sir William Brereton, Coll George Booth, Henry Brooke esq High-shreiffe; and the rest of the Deputy Lieutenants of the County, and other Gentl of quallity, were forsed to ingage themselves for 18,000li at the 1[e]ast (under their handwriting) about the businesse of Chester (besides other ingagements since) which somme was expected out of Delinquents Estates but now fayles by reason of Compositions, so that the souldiery have but a small part of what they expected, and was promised, and being sencible of the fayling therein; they are in a way to fall into the Estates of the Gentry. [1]

Significantly, the Sequestrators and Excise Men were also attacked. [2] But the mutiny was swiftly smothered, the gentlemen raising extensive loans, and making a firm promise of £2,000 from London. [3]

More serious was the mutiny in Nantwich which began on 14 July, when about 500 of the garrison, in open defiance of their officers seized the Nantwich sequestration committee and held them prisoner for two days. The victims later reported that

ffyve Companyes of our Garrison Soldyers of Namptwich being about five hundred unreasonable men without either Captyns or Comanders, in a most outragious maner fell upon us and with great fury (wherefore wee knowe not) did throwe us into the Comon prison amongst prisoners, Cavaliers and Horstealers, neither sufferinge any to relieve us with meate drinke or any necessaryes but what the parsons or some weomen did privatlie convaye unto us where wee (being Ancyent men) did lye upon the boards, not sufferinge our friends to bring us Quyssions nor any Comforde the[y] cold hinder us from for the space of 54 howers, neither would they be perswaded to gyve us better Quarter although the Heughe Sherryff Mr Brooke and most of the Deputie Lieftenants and Justices a peace of the Countie were then in Towne sitting in Quarter Sessions did there best and moved for us and the Governor of the Towne and his man they wounded and abused most cruelly. Soe that the sheriff, Governor and all the Justices went fro the towne not able to suppresse that greate multitude beinge all men and armed, and lefte us in prison to the mercy of those wicked and unreasonable men, wee gyving them noe occasion att all. [4]

---

[1] B.M. Thomason Tracts E 511(17) *Perfect Occurrences*, 27 June–3 July 1646.
[2] Ibid. E 349(7) *Scottish Dove*, 29 July–8 August 1646.
[3] Ibid.; also E 397(1) *Kingdome's Weekly Intelligencer*, 29 June–6 July 1646.
[4] Transcribed from the Composition Papers of Sir Thomas Smyth, *Cheshire Sheaf*, 3rd ser., vol. 1, pp.90–2.

Other contemporary accounts bear out their story,[1] emphasizing that officers were not involved, that Thomas Croxton (the Governor of Nantwich) was attacked and wounded when he tried to intervene, and that the Justices were forced to flee from the town. Again the question of the Excise appears. One report speaks of the collectors being driven from the town.[2] It is in fact surprising that they and the sequestrators should again be singled out; as Malbon said, they knew that the same Committee for Sequestrations never paid theim or noe other soldyers . . . for they receyved their paye alwayes from the Treasurer by warrant of the deputie lieutenants. But as some of theim said, they wolde beate Jacke for Gill.[3]

A more startling feature was that at the height of the mutiny the soldiers, still acting independently of their officers, sent representatives to put their case before the county committee. The report of their meeting shows that their demands were moderate, but they ended in a veiled threat. They hoped to 'bee prevented of takeing any unusuall course to supply our wants, but may bee enabled to behave themselves'.[4]

However, according to one London report, the soldiers were forced to capitulate without achieving their demands, for troops from Lichfield were despatched against them. They had to rest content with a promise from the Governor and committee that they would not be prosecuted, and with the contents of a chest they had discovered—rumoured to contain £500.[5]

The gentry's problems were not yet over. At the end of the month two troops of horse marched to Alderley and Peover and quartered themselves on the homes of two of the leading deputy lieutenants, Philip Mainwaring and Thomas Stanley; when no money was immediately forthcoming, they broke down the doors of the houses and forced each of the

---

[1] Malbon, 'Memorials. . .', loc. cit., pp.208–11, B.M. Thomason Tracts E 511(24) *Perfect Occurrences*, 24 July 1646.
[2] Ibid.
[3] Malbon, p.210.
[4] Bodl. Lib. Tanner MSS., vol. 59, f. 412.
[5] B.M. Thomason Tracts E 511(24) *Perfect Occurrences*, 18–24 July 1646.

gentlemen to pay them £50 to £60.[1] Philip Mainwaring hurriedly sent off warnings to his friends telling them that troops stationed at Congleton and Chester intended

to falle upon theire howses in the like kind & this they profes to act in imitacon of the Nampwchians their brave exployte the last quarter sessions if some speedy course be not taken to prevent theis thinges & from above, by hastning down moneys (the onely way to do it).[2]

Parliament's reaction was slow, but in the short term they were able to ease the situation. On 22 July they set up a Committee of the Commons to 'consider of such expedients to be offered to the House as they shall think fit for the suppression of any mutinies',[3] and on the 24th they empowered the Cheshire Justices to 'examine who were the prime movers of that mutinying there and certify their names to this House; and if they think fit to send up some of the chief of them to receive punishment of the house'.[4] But it was not until the end of September that they got round to discussing disbandment or answered the pleas for hard cash.[5] It was then decided to pay off all the troops except for a residual garrison of 600 at Chester.[6] As a positive gesture towards the settlement of arrears, the Commons decided that £12,000 out of the Compositions fines of Cheshire delinquents should be released by the central treasurers for use in Cheshire.[7]

The question of punishment was avoided by the Justices. Perhaps they felt bound by their pledge to the mutineers. Malbon hinted at something darker: 'They did [nothing]; by reason they were either in some faulte for not beeinge more careful to see the souldyers paid, or els beinge much trobled with the business of the country. But the said Committee [at Westminster] had never any satisfaccon for the same.'[8] A further reason is suggested by a London newspaper:

[1] B.M. Thomason Tracts E 513(3) *Perfect Occurrences*, 8—14 Aug. 1646.
[2] Bodl. Lib. Tanner MSS., vol. 59, f. 448; see also ibid., ff. 426, 436.
[3] *Commons Journal*, vol. 4, p.624.
[4] Ibid., p.627.
[5] Ibid., p.674.
[6] Ibid., vol. 5, p.96.
[7] Ibid., vol. 4, p.674; also P.R.O., SP 28/224 f. 272.
[8] Malbon, p.211.

Those appointed by the Parliament to examine the businesse of the former mutiny at Nantwich, dare not meet about it, desiring rather to know how to keep their own houses from being plundered, and there dare no Committee sit in that County: Some met to sit a few dayes since at Middlewich; but the house where they were was presently surrounded, and they had much adoe to get away. Some course must be taken, or else the flame grow too great to be quenched without much blood. [1]

Certainly tension remained high for some time. For example, a fresh attempt by some horse to seize another sequestrator was only prevented by the fortuitous presence of a large number of local people in his house at the time. [2]

The financial problem was handled with greater skill, particularly since the £12,000 voted in September 1646 had still not arrived in January 1647. Robert Gregg was sent off to Parliament to speed up the delivery, [3] and the Commons issued a renewed order in the following weeks, [4] but it was June before the last of it arrived in Cheshire. In the meantime James Croxton had been diverting all available funds into the settlement of arrears, and directing warrants which he could not honour to hundredal sequestration treasurers for payment. [5] But these expedients were not sufficient. The deputy lieutenants had to borrow large sums of money in anticipation of the money from London. Thus, when the last part arrived in June 1647, the deputy lieutenants ordered it to be repaid to those who had lent money; most of it was owed to them personally (they were presumably at the back of the queue for repayment). [6]

Despite all this, however, there was still not enough to go round. The only men who were paid in full were those who enlisted to cross over to service in Ireland under Michael Jones. [7] Fortunately the deputy lieutenants and soldiers reached a compromise settlement on 2 November 1646 by

---

[1] B.M. Thomason Tracts E 513(3), *Perfect Occurrences,* 14 Aug. 1646.
[2] Ibid. E 513(5) *Perfect Occurrences,* 15—21 Aug. 1646.
[3] P.R.O., SP 28/224 f. 243.
[4] *Commons Journal,* vol. 5, p.82.
[5] P.R.O., SP 28/224 f. 276.
[6] Ibid., f. 261.
[7] Ibid., f. 181.

which the soldiers were to receive a set proportion of their arrears immediately in return for a promise that they would disband quietly. The proportion fixed by this 'New Model' is never specified, but seems to have something over half.[1] Any trooper who refused to accept this agreement was 'from henceforth . . . disbanded and the countrey discharged and hereby required to give them noe longer quarter nor any pay'.[2] As an encouragement to peaceful disbandment, each soldier was promised a 4s. bonus when he handed in his musket or firelock.[3] By February 1647 the process was nearly complete. In that month Nantwich was disgarrisoned and the defences there sleighted.[4]

But the Gentlemen's problems with the soldiers were to reach their height only in June 1647. Unfortunately for the county, the Commons had decided to make themselves personally responsible for the payment of the remaining garrison at Chester. Some pay had arrived on 25 March but nothing came in the following three months, and by the end of June the garrison was four months in arrears.[5] The result was an organized mutiny which began after rumours that there was £3,000 in the city intended for troops in Ireland. But by the time the troops acted, it had already been despatched.[6] On the 30 June, the troops adopted a fresh course, marching out of Chester, one group to Nantwich where they seized a number of deputy lieutenants at a meeting, others taking several gentlemen from their homes around the county, driving them to Chester, 'like rogues and theeves in a base and disgraceful manner'. According to Sir George Booth, those arrested included several deputy lieutenants, 'together with Colonell Massey the Governor of the citty and a captaine with some of the committee and

---

[1] My own deduction from the evidence is that they were promised full arrears for the service up to the time of the surrender of Chester, and half arrears for the remaining period. But the evidence is inconclusive.
[2] e.g. P.R.O., SP 28/224 ff. 178—9, 192—5, 200.
[3] Ibid., f. 193.
[4] Malbon, p.212.
[5] Bodl. Lib. Tanner MSS., vol. 58, f. 323.
[6] B.M. Thomason Tracts E 518(6) *Perfect Diurnall,* 12—19 July 1647.

sequestrators and Comrs of Excise'. The prisoners themselves gave their number as fifteen, but only nine signed their appeal on 3 July (Thomas Stanley, Philip Mainwaring, John Legh, Thomas Croxton, Henry Birkenhead, John Wettenhall, Richard Leicester, William Davies, and James Gartside). We know from other sources that William Massey and Thomas Croxton were also arrested; the identity of the others is uncertain. But it is clear that they were a very representative cross-section of the Parliamentarian movement of the period, including several former officers and close friends of Brereton as well as long-term civilian opponents of his methods and person. If their side of the story is to be accepted, they were vindictively handled. Plague was rife in the city, yet they were herded into a room without food, drink or 'accomodacon for nature but publiquely like beasts amongst ourselves'.

The officers had been powerless to prevent the arrests, and stood by during the mutiny.But they eventually prevailed upon the troops to 'remove us agayne into a house where wee have two or three roomes & necessary accomodacon to preserve our lives'. This time the soldiers were determined not to let their prisoners go until their arrears were paid in full and in their hands. Their demands were simple: £4,000 cash and an engagement from the prisoners 'that the citizens would be satisfied for the quarters of the souldiers'.

With Parliament dithering, the imprisoned gentry managed to raise the money by extensive borrowing. Though the money was said to come from 'our friends and welwishers', everyone exacted 'strikkt bonnds for the repayment of it'. The letter announcing their release was dated 30 July, and in the absence of other evidence it seems possible that their imprisonment had lasted for four weeks.[1] The loans were a millstone which dragged down the county finances for the next two years. In April 1648 Robert Venables reported that his loan of £232 was repayable upon demand, yet despite frequent entreaties he had only just been able to regain the

[1] This account is based on four letters, Bodl. Lib. Tanner MSS., vol. 58, ff. 323, 326 and 429, and P.R.O., SP 28/208 (blue packet marked Chester 208, unnumbered letter dated 25 June 1649).

first £32 of this amount.[1] Some creditors were still unsatisfied in 1650,[2] despite desperate attempts to divert funds
from other sources.[3] This seems to suggest that the relief
voted by Parliament for the county never arrived.[4] None the
less, as in the earlier case, Parliament's reaction is surprisingly
mild. The garrison at Chester was halved to 300 men, and a
committee (which never reported) was set up to

consider of the information given in that some officers and soldiers of
that garrison have formally served against Parliament: they are to
inquire into the occasions and causes of this high mutiny and apply
their interests and best timeliest remedies for the appeasing of it.[5]

   In most respects the Cheshire mutinies fit the same pattern
as those elsewhere in the country. The demands of the
soldiers remained essentially local, their overriding concern
being arrears. There are no signs that any broader political or
constitutional programme was evolved. On the other hand,
the mutinies were highly organized and competently carried
out. In 1646 elected representatives were sent to the
committee to put the soldiers' case (several months before
the election of agitators by the New Model). In 1647 the
troops had to carry out highly co-ordinated marches to
different parts of the county, yet there is evidence that the
officers stood aside—only later intervening to try to make life
more comfortable for the victims. There is no evidence of
any Leveller infiltration of the Cheshire forces. Only in one
respect did the mutinies differ from those in other parts of
the country which I have discussed elsewhere:[6] there is
surprisingly little evidence of a civilian backlash. The Quarter
Sessions Records are full of plaintive appeals about the
excesses of the troops,[7] and villagers skirmished with soldiers
intent on plunder in at least three townships,[8] but there was
no really serious confrontation.

[1] P.R.O., SP 28/225, unfoliated letter to Richard Leigh, 8 Apr. 1648.
[2] P.R.O., SP 28/224, ff. 290–1.
[3] Ibid., f. 286: P.R.O., SP 28/208, as above.
[4] Rushworth, *Historical Collections,* vol. 7, pp.600, 603.
[5] *Commons Journal,* vol. 5, p. 231.
[6] In *Past and Present,* 56(1972).
[7] e.g. C.R.O., Quarter Sessions File 1647, no.4, f. 83.
[8] C.R.O., Quarter Sessions Order 9a, f. 112; Quarter Sessions File 1645, no.1, f.
104; File 1647, no.4, ff. 94–5.

But the effect of the unrest in the army in 1645—7 was to leave a permanent scar on the minds of the majority of the county leaders, which was to have a serious effect upon their politics in the 1650s.

## IV

Fortunately the Parliamentarian gentry faced less of a threat from their former enemies. The Royalists had not only exhausted themselves by the end of the war, but had also, in many cases, become disillusioned with the King. When Parliament offered them the opportunity to regain their estates, they were quick to take advantage of it.

The introduction of compositions was not viewed primarily as a political question of Royalism, but as an assertion of national priorities in finance over local ones.[1] The basic premiss of composition was that a sequestered Royalist, acknowledging his past faults, taking the requisite oaths, and paying a fine based on the capital value of his property, should have his lands restored and his political record indemnified. First introduced in July and August 1644 to raise money for Fairfax by allowing all Royalist prisoners to negotiate the release of themselves and their estates by the payment of fines, the principle was extended in March 1645 to cover all who voluntarily presented themselves to the Committee for Compounding (at Goldsmith's Hall). But it was only in August 1645 that detailed procedures were worked out.[2]

---

[1] For the background to the whole question, see the introduction to vols. 1 and 5 of Mrs. M.A.E. Green's *Calendar of the Proceedings of the Commitee for Compounding*. I am currently engaged upon a general study of the administrative and political problems raised by sequestration and composition at local and central government levels.

[2] Certain named persons, and certain general groups (e.g. Papists in arms) were excluded from the right to compound. There had been earlier localized experiments in compounding (e.g. an ordinance permitting Kentish gentry to compound at rates fixed according to the degree of delinquency was passed in August 1643). For this and much other information about sequestration and composition, I am deeply grateful to Dr. Christopher Hill for lending me his typescript translation of the work of S.I. Archangelsky, 'Agrarian Legislation of the English Revolution', part I.

As an incentive to Royalists to make an early settlement, preferential rates were offered to those who came in by certain specified dates. The earliest and most positive of these was 1 December 1645, and the first group of Cheshire compounders arrived in London just before that date (nine altogether in November 1645). But it was the fall of Chester that persuaded most Cheshire Royalists to make their peace. Sixteen arrived in London during March 1646, twenty-eight more in April, and a total of 107 in the course of the year.[1] By then Parliament had decided that those owning land with a capital value of less than £200 should be exempt from the Sequestration and Composition Ordinances, and a further ninety had had their estates discharged without fine.[2] Only about forty or fifty delinquents still held out, and most of these capitulated in the summer of 1649 after the execution of the King. No Cheshire Royalist with extensive estates held out until 1651—2 to be expropriated by the Acts of Sale by which nearly 800 Royalists across the country had their lands sold to pay some of the Rump's debts. But twenty-five minor Cheshire gentry were included in the third Act.[3]

Compounders had to pay their fines in two stages; when the first half had been paid at Goldsmith's Hall, the local sequestrators were ordered provisionally to release the compounder's lands pending the payment of the second half of the fine within three months. An ordinance clearing the compounder of further liability was then put before Parliament. In practice, far longer than three months was allowed for the payment of the second moiety. Indeed no action was taken against most defaulters until the middle of

[1] Based on the *C.C.C.D.*
[2] P.R.O., SP 23, vol. 259, f. 15[I]. A similar pattern can be observed in Nottinghamshire, where a majority came in to compound shortly after the fall of Newark (A.C. Wood, *Nottinghamshire in the Civil War*, Oxford, 1937, pp.139—40). But cf. Cornwall, where only thirty of the 275 sequestered Royalists had come in by the end of 1648 (M. Coate, *Cornwall in the Great Civil War*, Oxford, 1933, pp.236—7.
[3] For the Acts of Sale, and the high incidence of Royalists buying back their own lands, see I.J. Thirsk, 'The Sale of Royalist Lands during the Interregnum', *Ec.H.R.*, 2nd ser., 5(1952—3), and P.G. Holiday, 'Land Sales and Repurchases in Yorkshire After the Civil War', *Northern History*, 5(1970).

1648. A threat of re-sequestration at that point usually secured prompt payment.

Would-be compounders arrived in London with certificates from their local sequestration committees stating the *pre-war* income from their estates. From this the capital value was calculated at fifteen, eighteen, or twenty years purchase. [1] The fine was fixed as a proportion of this, usually at one-tenth or one-sixth, though it could be appreciably higher in some cases, even up to two-thirds for lawyers and M.P.s. The rate at which a man compounded was also determined by the date at which he entered into composition proceedings and by special clauses in some of the terms negotiated at the surrender of particular towns (notably Oxford), by which those in the garrisons received preferential treatment. The nature and extent of delinquency was not supposed to be a relevant consideration, but in fact both this, and even proof of genuine financial hardship, played a part, particularly when the original fine came up for review after the first half had been paid. For example, Cheshire's two Royalist M.P.s, Sir Thomas Smyth and Peter Venables, should have paid crippling fines at two-thirds, but in each case the rate was cut on review, in Smyth's case to one-third, in Venables's to a sixth. [2]

There was often considerable delay between the initial application to compound and the fixing of the fine. This was usually caused by the lengthy investigations necessary to validate a delinquent's claim that part of his estates (such as dower lands or those tied to annuities made before May 1642) should be exempted for purposes of fine-assessment. There were also complex questions about the delinquents' outstanding pre-war debts. As a result, although most fines were settled within four months, others took years to determine. Ten of the sixty-seven gentry from Cheshire who had appeared at Goldsmith's Hall by April 1646 were still waiting in early 1648 for their fines to be fixed.

[1] See H.J. Habakkuk, 'Landowners and the Civil War', *Ec.H.R.*, 2nd ser., 18(1965).
[2] This question is discussed by Mrs. Green in the introduction to the *C.C.C.D.*, vol. 5, pp.x—xvi, xxii—xxvii.

None the less the central government was soon receiving its first substantial revenue from Cheshire. Altogether, £61,293 was paid by compounders, the bulk of it between April 1646 and July 1648. The total set in fines had been £84,336, but the residue was remitted for various reasons. For example, £10,300 was deducted from the fines of ten gentlemen in return for undertakings that they would alienate tithes worth £830 per annum from impropriate rectories in their hands for the augmentation of ministerial stipends.

Despite the tendency of the committee to set fines at a low rate, some delinquents paid substantial sums. Six paid over £2,000, another seven between £1,000 and £2,000, and four others an equivalent amount in cash and alienated tithes. The largest single fine paid was £7,742 by Lord Cholmondeley, followed by Peter Venables (£6,150), Sir Thomas Smyth (£3,350), and Sir Thomas Wilbraham (£2,500).

Thus, from the middle of 1646 onwards, local revenues from sequestration dropped sharply. Some attempt was made by the local committees to raise fresh revenue by discovering new delinquents and re-sequestering those whom they could accuse of having concealed part of their estates during their previous composition, but neither achieved much success. Almost all the new delinquents were minor gentry who were later discharged as under value.

More significant were the developments that followed the death of Charles I. The Goldsmith's Hall Committee radically reconstituted the sequestration committees in each county, generally placing less influential local figures in control. In part, this was intended to weaken local opposition to their work, but it was also a sign of the decline in the amount and importance of the work left to be done.[1]

In Cheshire the hundredal committees were replaced by a single commission of three men. The chairman was Henry Cockson, who had been one of Brereton's agents in London during the war, at first in handling the money granted there to be sent down to Cheshire and later as Solicitor for

[1] e.g. for Nottinghamshire, see A.C. Wood, op. cit., pp.140–1.

Sequestrations. In 1645 he was said to have shown disregard for the deputy lieutenants before the Committee for Compounding,[1] which confirms his close links with the more radical group in Cheshire. Joined with him for the years 1650—4 were two former sequestrators, William Barret, a Congregationalist preacher who constantly upset the moderates and who had been the most active member of the Macclesfield committee, reputedly the severest, and Thomas Robinson, who had served on the committees of Broxton, Edisbury and Bucklow.[2]

This new committee brought a new vigour to the administration. They pointed out that 'we are every week 2 or 3 days on the service, either in the city or some part of the county, besides other days in the week preparing business. As we cannot act all the business in one place, we are not sparing of our pains and travel to sit for the country's ease'. They usually divided their meetings between Chester, Knutsford, and Northwich.[3]

Behind this activity lay a much more thorough attempt to seek out those delinquents who had escaped earlier discovery. Appeals were made for informers—whose identity they promised to keep secret from the delinquent—who were to be rewarded for discovering new delinquents or uncovering those who had compounded upon false declarations of the extent or value of their estates. Despite their own complaints that their work was hindered because they were not granted the same powers as the earlier committees to call on 'the constables and such other assistance as they thought meet',[4] they quickly increased sequestration revenues in the county. Almost nothing had been raised in 1649, but in 1650 they collected £3,797.[5] Most of their new victims were minor

[1] B.M. Add. MS. 11331, f. 154.
[2] After April 1654 Robinson was appointed sole commissioner (P.R.O., SP 23, vol. 30, f. 96).
[3] C.C.C.D., pp.317—18.
[4] Ibid., p.209.
[5] Ibid., p.429. This lists the income from twenty-eight counties for that year, and Cheshire lies twelfth in total amongst them. But these include the revenues from the estates of Papists as well as delinquents. In revenue from delinquents only, Cheshire came much higher, fifth, behind the much larger counties of Lincolnshire, Dorset, Oxfordshire, and Kent.

gentry,[1] but they also re-sequestered a few substantial landowners. They acted on the flimsiest of evidence. For example, John Ward and Ralph Adderley were accused by single witnesses, Ward producing evidence that his accuser had said openly that 'he did it not out of any affection to the state but because the said Mr. Jo: W: had never done anything for the kinge & moreover, because he would not pay him . . . some monys wch he conceived were due to him'.[2] Ralph Adderley dismissed the charges made against him as simply malicious rumour put about by an aggrieved tenant.[3] Even a great landowner like Sir Richard Grosvenor was not free from suffering re-sequestration on similar evidence; having compounded at £1,250 and alienated tithes worth £130 per annum, and having subsequently constributed freely to the suppression of the Scots invasion, he found himself 'most uniustly prosecuted upon a Review by one Thomas Mercer wch was his tennant, who meerely out of spleene & malice hath informed the Comrs for Compoundinge etc that the said Sir Richard hath compounded att an undervalue for his estate'.[4]

On the other hand much of their work was strictly fair. Many of those who were sequestered had been in Chester during the siege or had committed transitory acts which could be construed as delinquency only on the strictest definitions. This was the line adopted by the new committee, who busily reopened every case in which a suspect appeared to have been treated leniently. Several lawyers who had compounded at a lower rate were now re-sequestered for having misled earlier committees.

In 1651 there was a new rush of business after the Worcester campaign. Few ex-Royalists or Presbyterians declared themselves for Charles Stuart, but there were widespread suspicions and some evidence that the sympathy

[1] See, for example, the groups named in *C.C.C.D.*, p.2499 and *C.C.A.M.*, p.1209.
[2] J.R.L. Bromley Davenport MSS., Papers relating to the sequestration of John Ward of Capesthorne 1650–60, unfoliated examination, taken February 1650.
[3] *C.C.C.D.*, p.2954.
[4] Eaton Hall, Grosvenor MSS., item 33.

for the campaign which covertly existed might have blossomed into action if fed by Royalist victories. The commissioners acted swiftly to sequester all those who were implicated by rumour.[1] But pressures from the local Justices and a generally conciliatory policy in London led to the release of most of the estates after a short time.

The coming of the Protectorate led to a further change. Thomas Robinson was made sole county commissioner and no new business was undertaken; he simply handled the estates of those still under sequestration when he took over, and these rapidly shrank in number as Cromwell's Council of State pursued a policy of favouring those who still proclaimed their innocence. After a seven-year battle, John Bretland was finally cleared of the charges made against him.[2] When a fresh wave of repression did occur, in 1655, responsibility was taken by Major-General Charles Worsley, and his method of exacting double sureties, though widespread, at least stopped short of sequestration.

But the machinery was recreated in September 1659 to deal with the aftermath of Booth's rebellion, and even greater severity practised in the determination of guilt than under earlier committees.[3]

Throughout the period 1643—54, then, there existed sequestration machinery which was distinct from the major agencies of administration and which adopted policies of varying severity towards the delinquents, all of which contrasted with the basically conciliatory views of the deputy lieutenants. Conflict between sequestrators and deputy lieutenants arose specifically at three points. The most important surrounded the extent of the sequestrators' powers to determine what constituted delinquency.[4] The second concerned the distribution and allocation of the money raised from sequestrations, and the third resulted from the reluctance of the hundredal committees to release the estates of those who had compounded.

[1] P.R.O., SP 23, vol. 148, f. 109, or *C.C.A.M.*, p.1451.
[2] See below, pp.216—22.
[3] See below, pp.325—6.
[4] See above, pp.71—3.

We have already seen how the deputy lieutenants tried to play a part in the distribution of sequestration profits at a local level. This led increasingly to tension between them and the sequestrators, particularly after the middle of 1646 when the deputy lieutenants had finally achieved general control over county finance. Their attempts to ensure the fair payment of fifths to the wives and families of delinquents were frequently ignored—in the case of Helen Poole, for example.[1] Similarly, in 1648, when they were trying to pay off the arrears to Colonel William Massie, then Governor of Chester, at a time when James Croxton had no money in the treasury, they asked the Bucklow sequestrators to make the payment. When the latter refused, the deputy lieutenants sent angry but vain demands for compliance.[2]

In the arguments that surrounded the release of the estates of compounders, the sequestrators were faced by the anger not only of their local opponents but also of the Goldsmith's Hall Committee. Thus their refusal to heed an order for the suspension of the sequestration of Ralph Janian led to a rebuke, and a demand that they obey immediately.[3] In all there are about fifteen such cases and the evidence for others may well have not survived.[4] The most severe rebuke arose in the case of Philip Pritchard; the Westminster committee warned the Northwich sequestrators

That hee haveing according to the Ordinance of Parliament submitted to a fyne .. & receyving wthall a letter from the said com[mit]tee to testify the same & to require yw to forbeare further proceedings .. yw not onely refused to conforme thereunto but have lessned the rent formerly agreed on wth the Tenants 11 li 10s and have given them liberty to cutt downe his woods so that eighty trees at least have bin cutt since the fine was satisfyed & severall parcells of his land plowed. And that you do intend to maintaine the tenants in possession till May next. Whereupon the house comanded mee to let you know what acceptance such proceedings finds from them & how ill they resent the same, and likewise that they do expect yw should yeild obedience to

[1] P.R.O., SP 28/224, f. 186.
[2] P.R.O., SP 28/225, unfoliated order of 29 July 1648.
[3] P.R.O., SP 23, vol. 3, p.378.
[4] Because of the inadequacy of the Calendar and notable discrepancies between orders for the release of estates and the records of the local committees in several cases.

their former orders . . . not onely in this but in all othr businesses . . . in default whereof there wilbee further course taken to exact yor conformity. [1]

This example draws attention to one of the most constant features of these cases, the preoccupation of the sequestrators to safeguard the interests of the tenants whom they had installed; it emerges as a more frequent cause of obstruction than the fear of lost revenue. Thus, as soon as they heard that Robert Tatton was prosecuting his composition, they rushed 'to sett the pet[itione]rs husbands demeasnes, rents and millnes to strangers and therby to expell yor peticioner husband, her children'.[2] In these cases their activities and zeal were excessive, even corrupt, but in others they appear to have acted to protect legitimate interests. Thus their reluctance to release the estates of Viscount Kilmorrey sprang from a desire to recompense those of his tenants who had endured his wrath for fighting for Parliament; he sought to end these benefits when he regained his estates.[3]

In a few cases Brereton himself invervened to help or hinder a would-be compounder. Thus he supported Sir Thomas Smyth's assertion that his delinquency consisted only of sins of omission.[4] But in two cases, those of William Burges[5] and Peter Venables,[6] he strongly attacked their record of Royalism and their trustworthiness. Both men provided problems for hundredal committees reluctant to release their estates. In the case of Venables, the fear that he would act vindictively against his tenants recurs; Brereton pointed out that he opposed Venables's composition not only because of his 'verie verulent . . . courses ag[ains]t the Parlt', but also

the importunity of the well affected partie . . The truth is they are afrayd of his restitucon and knowing him an enemy of reformacon and

---

[1] P.R.O., SP 23, vol. 230, f. 65. For an equally tough warning in case of George Watts, see ibid., f. 20.
[2] J.Ry.L. Tatton of Wythenshawe MSS., item 287.
[3] *C.C.C.D.*, pp.1283–4 (petition of James Bullen).
[4] Birmingham..Reference Library 595611, p.22. For his support for Sir Thomas Wilbraham and John Kinsey, see *C.C.C.D.*, pp.978, 1163.
[5] Birmingham Reference Library 595611, p.120.
[6] Ibid., p.132.

a tyrant amongst his tenants who now begin to tremble, being that all his tenants or most of them are either out of lease or want but a peece of a yeare, and many rather desire to pay fines and receive their estates from the Parliamt then to deale wth him.[1]

A petition of 'deputy lieutenants, commanders, officers and soldiers' which called for an end to extensive compositions was sent up from Cheshire to Parliament in November 1645. From its heading, and from internal evidence (including a reference to the ordinance of March 1644 which had given Brereton such extensive powers), it is clear that it represented the views of his supporters. It called for a halt in compositions except with the least active Royalists, and then only to be administered by Brereton and the deputy lieutenants. Their opposition to composition arose from their fears of the effects on county revenues; also the well-affected feared 'the tyrannous yoake or secret practises' of restored malignants.[2] By contrast, Booth and his supporters were not opposed to composition, although they would have preferred that the money raised should be employed within the county.[3]

In general, the deputy lieutenants did not have to intervene when the sequestrators failed to release estates; the London commissioners themselves reacted sharply. But there were times when they did intervene, particularly to secure the release of estates of those certified to be below the minimum value to have to compound; on such occasions their protests were sullenly ignored.[4]

It was in those borderline cases of whether a man's actions could be held to constitute delinquency that the two groups clashed most seriously. As we have seen,[5] many of the men sequestered were only Royalists by the most insensitive definitions. Many can only be properly styled neuters, others had been active for Parliament after early support of the

[1] For his difficulties in getting the sequestrators to release his estates, see *C.C.C.D.*, p.1183, or (in detail) P.R.O., SP 23, vol. 196, f. 460.

[2] B.M. Add. MS. 11333, f. 3.

[3] Ibid., 11331, f. 55.

[4] e.g. the case of Humphrey Forest, *C.C.C.D.*, p.2116.

[5] See above, pp.71—3.

Crown, others had only committed some minor trans-
gressions at the end of 1642; yet this was often enough for
the sequestrators to seize their estates. In such cases the
deputy lieutenants would remonstrate and attempt to
intervene. Whatever the conflict between the hundredal
committees and Goldsmith's Hall over compounders, the
latter almost always supported the sequestrators in these
cases. The clearest statement of their position and of the
tensions in the county is given in this order from London to
the Macclesfield committee in the case of James Renshaw.

this comittee further declares that the proceedings of the gentl' of the
county in the case of the said Renshaw is without warrant and their
order void, they haveinge noe power to discharge seq[uestratio]ns ..
and that the said comittee for Maxfeild Hundred and all other
comittees appointed by Sr Wm Brereton accordinge to Ordinance of
Parlt have equall power for manageinge the busines of Seq[uestratio]n
... It is lastly ordered that notice be given to such as shall hereafter
offer interupcons in the like kinde within the said county by the parties
concerned for the better avoidinge of such obstruccons as are now
complained of and of such sentence as may be occaconed by the same
when this comittee shall come to the knowledge of the offence.[1]

William Davenport of Bramhall was one of those whose
only delinquency had been to attend the Commissioners of
Array in 1642; since then he had submitted peacefully to
Parliament. He has left us a vivid account in his notebook of
the course of his sequestration, of the 'strict and severe'
inventory of his goods by agents backed by a group of
soldiers, of his appearance before a hostile Macclesfield
committee, and of his attempts to get the help of the leading
gentlemen. Between two interrogations by the committee he
'in the meanetime satisfied the Gentlemen and Councell of
Warre, and had a certificate from them to the Sequestrators
to that purpose. They not herewith contented nor with any
reasonable satisfaction I could give them'. The local
committee which had taken this action consisted not only of
Brereton's nominees, but also Colonel Duckenfield, who was
not officially a member but who clearly took a personal
interest in their work.[2] There are several similar cases, though

[1] P.R.O., SP 20, vol. 3, p.347.
[2] Chester City R.O., CR63/2/19, Bramhall MSS., ff. 90–1.

in some the involvement of the gentlemen may well have been intended by the knowledgeable delinquent as a cause of confusion which might afford opportunities of escape.[1]

Even in the complex case of William Leversage the central committee ignored the pleas of the county gentry and upheld the decision of the sequestrators. Leversage, old and infirm, had moved into a Royalist garrison at Kinderton after the second battle of Middlewich to avoid the fury of the scattered soldiery; he emerged after three months once Fairfax had re-established Parliament's hold on the countryside. A certificate to this effect, which stated that his action could not be made to constitute delinquency, was given him by the deputy lieutenants and other leading moderates. Yet his nephew declared him a delinquent and, with the support of the Northwich sequestrators and some troops from Nantwich, seized control of his estates. Leversage senior appealed to London and the committee there ordered that the nephew's occupation was clearly illegal and that the sequestrators must themselves take possession while the delinquency was fully investigated 'and they are to use the trained bands or other forces of the said countie for the purpose'.[2]

Some of the most interesting exchanges concerned ministers. Once again the moderates tried (without success) to protect those whose delinquency they saw as purely technical. In some cases, such as that of George Byrom, the aid of the Presbyterian establishment in both Cheshire and London was enlisted;[3] in others the deputy lieutenants themselves sought to help. Thus George Snell, accused of preaching against Parliament claimed that the charges made against him were either false or misrepresentations, and begged Goldsmith's Hall (without success) to allow his case to be reconsidered by 'Sir George Booth, baronett, & others the present comittee for Chester . . . that they would take a

[1] Robert Brerewood, *C.C.C.D.*, pp.1546—7.
[2] P.R.O., SP 20, vol. 3, ff. 483—4. See also SP 19, vol. 94, f. 64, and *C.C.C.D.*, p.932.
[3] *Cheshire Sheaf*, 3rd ser., vol. 1, pp.97—100.

re-examination of the former deponents & such other witnesses as yor pet[itione]r shall produce for his iustification'.[1]

The most sensational cases are those in which active Parliamentarians were accused of delinquency on the flimsiest evidence. Five leading moderates (two deputy lieutenants—Henry Mainwaring and Henry Vernon, two of their 'assistants'—William Glegg and Henry Greene, and the first county treasurer—George Spurstowe) were all sequestered at some time between 1645 and 1647. Only one, Henry Vernon, had to pay a composition fine; the others recovered their estates and were cleared of the charges made against them. But the process of recovering their estates involved considerable wastage of time, money, and effort. In Henry Vernon's case, he had to endure further harassment when his estates were re-sequestered for the alleged earlier concealment of part of them.[2] No record has survived of the supposed delinquency of Mainwaring and Spurstowe,[3] but the evidence produced in the other cases was extremely feeble and it is not surprising that they were released upon appeal to London.[4]

The fact that they were active supporters of Parliament makes their peremptory sequestration look suspicious, particularly since they were all associated with the party which opposed the policy of the sequestrators. Mainwaring is the most interesting. An active colonel throughout 1643 and the early months of 1644, he was the only senior officer who did not owe his appointment to Brereton, and there is some evidence of mutual dislike and jealousy. He was ordered to be dismissed from all his offices by Parliament in the spring of 1644 (this was during Brereton's period in London). He was in fact sacked as a deputy lieutenant and committee-man, and though his name appears on Commissions of the Peace as

[1] P.R.O., SP 23, vol. 118, f. 501.
[2] e.g. P.R.O., SP 23, vol. 126, f. 475.
[3] For Mainwaring, see P.R.O., SP 20, vol. 3, p.279, 571; vol. 5, p.49; for Spurstowe, *C.C.C.D.*, pp.1728–9.
[4] For Greene, see P.R.O., SP 23, vol. 149, f. 279, *C.C.A.M.*, p.1209, for Glegg, *C.C.A.M.*, p.1118.

late as the end of 1648, there is no evidence that he ever exercised authority as a Justice in the years 1645—8. The evidence surrounding the continuation of his military commission is ambiguous and confusing.[1]

For clear evidence of a conspiracy by Brereton's supporters to harass their opponents within the Parliamentarian movement, however, we must turn to the involved and controversial case of John Bretland of Thorncliff (in the extreme north-east of the county).[2] Bretland, a minor landowner but a prosperous London attorney, had his estates forcibly sequestered by the Macclesfield Sequestration Committee in July 1647. He refused to admit to the charges brought against him and fought for seven years to retrieve his estates, making frequent appearances before the committee at Stockport, appealing to and petitioning committees and Parliament in London, publishing pamphlets, and pouring out a constant stream of abuse.[3] His cause wavered during the political crises of 1647—8, languished under the Rump, revived in 1653, and was crowned with success at the beginning of the Protectorate.

There were twelve specific charges against Bretland, but they can be grouped under four general heads. Firstly he was said to have been closely associated with professed Royalists, being seen armed in their garrisons at Adlington and Wythenshawe in late 1642. Secondly, he was accused of using 'reproachful language' against Sir William Brereton, for example 'that after the defeat at Mydlewych Bretland said amongst other things that Sir Wm Brereton was fitter to lead a flock of geese than a band of soldiers and that Colonel Duckenfield was but a boy and that he the said Bretland admyred that the Parliament would imploy such'. Thirdly, he

---

[1] *Commons Journal,* vol. 3, p.484.

[2] The following is largely based on appendix III of the article by myself and Mr. R.N. Dore, 'The Allegiance of the Cheshire Gentry in the Great Civil War', *T.L.C.A.S.* 77(1967).

[3] The following account is largely based on the following documents: P.R.O., SP 23, vol. 149, ff. 1—170; SP 23, vol. 27, ff. 24, 37; SP 23, vol. 83, ff. 113—42; SP 20, vol. 3, ff. 347, 627—8. The entry in the *C.C.C.D.* is totally inadequate.

had claimed to hold a commission to be captain, 'but whether his commission was for King or Parliament he did not declare'. Finally, he had aided and protected scandalous ministers. [1]

Bretland had a detailed reply to each of these charges.[2] He admitted having been in Adlington and Wythenshawe Halls when they were held for the King, but claimed that:

your pet[itione]r was about Octobr 1642 specially imployed by Sir George Booth knt and baronett since deceased to goe to Thomas Leigh of Adlington esq and Robert Tatton of Wittenshawe esq to diswad them from putting in execucon any commission of Array within the sd county agt the peace thereof.

This fits in well with what we know of Booth's behaviour in the last months of 1642,[3] and a connection between the two men is provided by the answer of several witnesses to an interrogatory that Bretland was 'then and severall yeares after ymployed during the warrs by Sir George Booth and other deputy lieutenants for the County of Chester in matters of public concernment for the said Parl[iamen]t'.

In answer to the charge that the commission he claimed to hold had been a Royalist one, he put forward his war-time record which he asserted showed his loyalty to Parliament. He claimed to have been plundered by Rupert's troops, to have lent money on the Propositions, and to have sent a man to serve under Colonel Duckenfield. This man's evidence has survived, and so has evidence of Bretland's payments for him in the accounts of the township of Hollingworth in which Thorncliff lay.[4]

More specifically, he claimed that in 1644 he was appointed a subcommissioner of accounts—a committee dominated by Brereton's opponents.[5] Bretland's name does not appear in such records of the committee as have survived,

---

[1] The list of charges is in P.R.O., SP 23, vol. 149, ff. 141—2.

[2] These replies are pieced together from the questions and answers in and to Bretland's several interrogatories, P.R.O., SP 23, vol. 149, ff. 11—59, 125—34, 143—82 (summarized in SP 23, vol. 83, ff. 138—9).

[3] See above, pp.57, 65—9.

[4] J.P. Earwaker, *East Cheshire*, 2 vols. 1877, vol. 2, pp.146—52.

[5] See above, pp.90—2.

but his interrogatories include the question 'Was Charles
Whichecote of Tatton gent also after charged with delinquency?'. We know that Charles Whichecote did act on the
accounts subcommittee, that he ceased to do so in 1647, and
then fell into total obscurity. The fact that Whichecote's
name has not yet been found amongst Cheshire sequestration
records is less significant than it might seem, since he would
almost certainly have been discharged as under value. It
seems unlikely that Bretland would have made such specific
allegations and concrete assertions about matters so readily
checked unless they were true.

The allegation that he scorned Brereton's ability as a
commander he answered by putting the remarks in context.
They had followed Brereton's defeat in the second battle of
Middlewich, the extent of which had been greatly exaggerated in the first reports. This explanation was reasonable
enough. The undoubted facts of Brereton's lack of military
experience, his no more than 'competent fortune'
(Clarendon's words), and Duckenfield's youth must have led
many respectable Parliamentarians to have similar thoughts.

Bretland's answer to the fourth charge is the most suggestive of all as to the real nature of his delinquency. According
to him, the 'scandalous minister' whom he was supposed to
have helped was Gerard Browne, who had been pulled from
his pulpit by an armed mob one day in 1643 and driven from
his parish (Mottram-in-Longendale). At the request of Sir
George Booth, Thomas Stanley, Philip Mainwaring, William
Marbury, George Spurstowe, Edward Hyde, and Thomas
Croxton, Bretland had taken action against those involved.
But the Macclesfield Sequestration Committee had upheld
Browne's expulsion, despite the fact that he had no difficulty
finding a new parish in Lancashire. Bretland further drew
attention to the case of John Shallcrosse, parson of the
wealthy living of Stockport, who was sequestered and ejected
in 1644. According to Bretland, Shalcrosse, was not 'sequestered for any delinquency but for not setting the tithes at
Marple at the same rates which the principal of the townsmen
pleased'. He pointedly linked these townsmen with 'Sir

William Brereton who hath the placing and displacing of such persons and ministers as were conceived to be delinquent and scandalous'. Bretland claimed that his efforts to obtain redress for Shallcross were the occasion of Macclesfield sequestrators' 'inveterate hatred' against him.

Throughout, Bretland maintained that he was no Royalist, but a victim of the quarrel within the Parliamentarian movement in Cheshire. He had been the trusted servant of the leading, moderate gentry, headed by Sir George Booth. His enemies were the extremists: at a local level the Macclesfield sequestrators headed by Henry Bradshaw of Marple, major to Colonel Duckenfield; behind them, Bradshaw's brother John, recently promoted to be Chief Justice of Chester, and Sir William Brereton himself. 'Do you know', he demanded of several witnesses, 'that the several committees for sequestrations of these several hundreds within the county of Chester were constituted and authorised by Sir William Brereton, Bart?' He also published a libel in which he attacked the Macclesfield committee and called John Bradshaw, 'a creature to Sir William Brereton'.[1]

Although few of the replies to his interrogatories, and hardly any of the ancillary documents he refers to, have survived, and although Sir George Booth was dead by the time he reopened his case so strongly, there is plenty of evidence, indirect and circumstantial, to support Bretland's claim that 'the principall gentry of that county' were once his employers and remained sympathetic to his cause, while his enemies were the Macclesfield committee, the Bradshaw brothers, and Brereton. It was officially admitted that there had arisen 'a greate disput betwixt the committee for the county and the committee for the Hundred concerning their authority and severall powers to the greate obstruccon and delay in the proceedings of the said Mr Bretland'.[2] When the London Committee for Sequestrations ordered the

---

[1] We only know this libel through John Bradshaw's indignant denunciation of it to Rushworth, J.Ry.L. English MS. 745, f. 28.

[2] P.R.O., SP 23, vol. 149, f. 13; see also ibid., ff. 127, 172.

Macclesfield committee to proceed against Bretland in July 1647, they specified it was to be 'notwithstanding any intimation, order, or declaration from any of the deputy lieutenants or others to the contrary'.[1] John Bradshaw, in his letter to Rushworth, called Bretland 'a notorious malignant attorney, who soliciting many causes, hath found many friends among some of the prime gentry', and said: 'The committee there for sequestrations are looked upon as honest, conscientious men, careful of their oath and trust, *whereof their greater partners are not,* whom this reviler magnifies so much above them.'[2] Bretland also boldly cited witnesses to identify Booth's handwriting on orders appointing him to serve Parliament in January 1645, and asked one to testify that when Sir George received a letter from Bradshaw asking him not to countenance Bretland or make use of him, he had said that 'he was not a little troubled that he could not make use of Mr Bretland, whom he had found constant and faithful in all his undertakings'.

The effects of national changes of power upon the case also fit the pattern that has emerged. The original order to sequester was confirmed by the Committee in London at the moment in July 1647 when the army had forced the eleven Members to withdraw; Brereton was a strong supporter of army intervention, and Bradshaw was now a power at Goldsmith's Hall, probably through Brereton's influence. But there was a check to the army's plans when a London mob reinstated the Eleven and forced sixty-seven Independents to leave Parliament and join the army leaders. When news of this reached Cheshire, Bretland burst into a room where the Macclesfield sequestrators were sitting and 'with much violence and bitter speeches railed' against them. So violent was his language that even his wife begged him to forbear. But Bretland rounded on her and Henry Bradshaw and said: 'Woman, hold thy peace. I have seen his gall. Let me have his guts'.[3]

[1] P.R.O., SP 20, vol. 3, p.347.
[2] J.Ry.L. English MS. 745, f. 28.
[3] C.R.O., Quarter Sessions File 1648, no.2, f. 41.

By September the army were in control again, quartered in the London suburbs, and the Independents, including Brereton, had resumed their seats. It was at that point that Goldsmith's Hall took up Bretland's case again, ordering the Macclesfield committee to use force, if necessary, to seize Bretland's personal estate. In fact, a considerable body of militia was necessary to perfect the job, the collectors first employed being beaten up, and his cattle retrieved from them and driven back home.[1]

For the next six years there was not a great deal Bretland could do. Brereton and Bradshaw remained influential both in the Council of State—of which Bradshaw was president 1649–53—and at Goldsmith's Hall. Guilty of the charges against him or not, Bretland had offended them beyond recall. None the less, he did not resign himself to defeat. He carried out a brilliant and exhausting campaign of harassment of the hundredal, and later of the new county, sequestration committees, employing a wide range of procedural devices to prevent them from declaring his case closed and including his lands in the Acts of Sale.[2] Technically, he was still prosecuting his composition; in fact, he had no intention of paying a fine. He was waiting for a more amenable regime. He found it in the Protectorate.

His personal enemies had been turned out of office, and Cromwell set fair on a policy of healing and settling. Bretland gathered together all his evidence and presented it to the new Council of State, which declared that 'Upon hearing the merits of the said case in pursuance of his Highnes said refference upon the whole proofe before us, wee find noe cause touching ye said Mr Bretland sequestrable within any of the Acts, Orders or Ordinances'.[3] Bretland was almost certainly the victim of a power struggle within Cheshire. Abandoned by his erstwhile patrons because his enemies had powerful friends at Westminster (and because his rank did not warrant great sacrifices on their part?), his victory was

[1] See above, p.112.
[2] P.R.O., SP 23, vol. 149, *passim;* e.g. ff. 91, 99.
[3] P.R.O., SP 23, vol. 27, f. 37. For examination of further evidence about the legal rivalry of Bretland and Bradshaw, see Morrill and Dore, art. cit. appendix III.

the result solely of his own determination and bloody-mindedness. Whithin a few weeks of his vindication he was dead.

The years following the end of the first Civil War thus saw a continuation of the conflict between different sections of the Parliamentarian movement; but these grew less marked as the years passed. The Royalists were quickly seeking to repair their shattered finances; the moderate Parliamentarians, angered and distressed by the death of the King, opted out of, or were dropped from, local government. Many of Brereton's old allies had dropped back into everyday life, or, like Robert Venables (who was later to command the troops sent by Cromwell to the West Indies), had taken up commands with the permanent army;[1] some others sat as Justices or commissioners where they were joined by a group of young men, sometimes of quite substantial estates, who were not preoccupied with old animosities. From the point of view of the Rump, there was nothing to fear from Cheshire. The suspicions and fears generated by the Civil War—of the army, of religious anarchy and political vindictiveness—were not of themselves sufficient to create the unity of purpose necessary to provoke the county to rebellion. It was to take ten more years for the sense of self-identity and trust within the community to re-form after being splintered by the Great Rebellion of 1641—6.

[1] e.g. William Daniell, who served under Cromwell at Dunbar, and was then appointed Governor of Stranraer. Others served in Ireland.

# 6
## THE COMMISSION OF THE PEACE AND THE
## LOCAL COMMUNITY, 1645–1659

'If the Great Rebellion had proved anything, it was the necessity of employing county gentry in county affairs.'[1] Few historians have disagreed with the verdict of Professor Everitt,[2] yet as far as the most significant administrative body, the Commission of the Peace, is concerned, little detailed work on the extensive records has been attempted, and nothing on the scale, or with the excellence, of Professor Barnes's study of pre-war Somerset.[3] I shall be seeking here only to make a few general remarks which suggest that the common view may well be mistaken,[4] particularly with regard to Cheshire. In doing so I want to question both halves of a statement made about the Interregnum by the most recent historian of the Justices of the Peace, to which most other writers would probably subscribe: 'The basic structure of county government might have changed little in form but the system was not working as efficiently as before the Civil War.'[5]

The most obvious change in the Cheshire Bench was in the membership itself. Before the war all the Justices came from a compact group of the gentry, closely interrelated by marriage and dominated by those families who had served the Crown as sheriffs, Justices, or deputy lieutenants for generations. New families were assimilated as and when they

---

[1] Everitt, *Community of Kent. . .*, p.296.
[2] A.L. Beier, 'Poor Relief in Warwickshire, 1630–60', *Past and Present* 35(1966), casts some doubts from its own particular angle.
[3] T.G. Barnes, *Somerset 1625–40: A County's Government During the Personal Rule*, Oxford, 1961.
[4] General considerations of space have forced me drastically to condense this chapter. I hope that the resulting rather impressionistic argument is backed up by adequate citations. It is in fact based on detailed examination of all the magnificent Files and Order Books for the period 1625–60.
[5] E. Moir, *The Justice of the Peace*, London, 1969, p.74.

had become absorbed by marriage and social contact into this network which was expanding at about the same rate as the size of the Commission of the Peace. There were always about twice as many suitable families as places on the Bench. Since there was a constant trickle of men in and out of the Commission,[1] a fair majority of this distinct group of families served during each generation.[2]

This situation was transformed by the Civil War. In all, thirty men were in some fashion active as Justices between 1645 and 1659, but only nine of these belonged to families represented on the Bench between 1603 and 1642, and of these nine only Sir George Booth (who died in 1653) represented those families that Mr. Coward considers to have formed a recognizable elite in the early seventeenth century.[3] The other leading families were excluded by delinquency[4] or for openly opposing the execution of the King,[5] while others refused to serve, even though appointed.[6] Their places were taken by representatives of families with middling estates and less creditable genealogies, men like Henry Brooke, Henry Bradshaw, Thomas Croxton, and Robert Duckenfield. After the death of old Sir George Booth, the active Bench consisted entirely of esquires (before the war there had been sixteen knights, baronets, and peers), but a few of them were of humble origin. Several of Brereton's officers rose from minor gentry birth to the Bench via the Army. Gilbert Gerard and George Manley, for example, both served as head constables—a role far below the calling of a Justice—before the Civil War, while Manley and William Tuchett were both styled yeomen during their fathers' lifetimes. Other men of similar birth, John Wettenhall and Thomas Tanat (both ex-head constables), had risen from minor civilian offices during the war as rewards for their proven efficiency. But these men

---

[1] See P.R.O., Index 4211–2 for the incidental comings and goings 1615–42.
[2] For the effect of this pattern and further detail, see below, pp.233–53.
[3] B. Coward, 'The Lieutenancy of Lancashire and Cheshire in the Sixteenth and Early Seventeenth Centuries', *T.H.S.L.C.* 119(1967), 42.
[4] e.g. Lord Cholmondeley, Earl Rivers, Sir Edward Fytton.
[5] e.g. Sir Thomas Wilbraham, Roger Wilbraham, John Arderne.
[6] e.g. Henry Delves, (young) George Booth, John Crewe.

were the exceptions. The majority of the new Bench came from solid middling county stock. But they were not part of the close web of connection and marriage which had given the pre-war Bench its compactness and unity.[1]

The existence of so many committees for specific purposes after 1642 did not in itself create jurisdictional problems; petitions or other business that strayed to Quarter Sessions and fell within the province of another committee were usually quickly transferred.[2] But their existence did have some effect. Professor Barnes has drawn attention to Charles I's use of special commissioners in the 1630s who were almost completely drawn from the Commission of the Peace, and the pattern for Cheshire resembled that for Somerset.[3] But whereas these committees tended to be appointed for specific short-term purposes, such as gathering a particular grant or making a specific investigation, the post-war committees like the Militia Committee or that for 'Ejecting Scandalous Ministers' were essentially long-term. As a result, an assiduous gentleman like Thomas Mainwaring spent more time in the period 1649–59 on work connected with other committees than he did specifically as a Justice, both in and out of Sessions. No pre-war source has survived that is comparable with his diary for the Interregnum,[4] but it would be surprising if the same had been true of any leading figure in the 1630s.

More important, however, was that some of the other commissions (such as those for monthly assessments and sequestrations) created and controlled their own sets of minor officials. Previously all committees, like the Commission of the Peace itself, transmitted orders through the head constables of each hundred to the parish constables. But the new officials were separate in identity from these

[1] P.R.O., Index 4213, p.3 indicates that a commission was issued in May 1644. But there is no extant list of Justices until that bound into the Assize File for April 1648, P.R.O. Chester 24/ 127, no.1. For the commissions of 1649, see above, pp.186–7.

[2] C.R.O., Quarter Sessions Order Book (henceforth Q.S.O.B.) 9a, ff. 188–9.

[3] Barnes, op. cit., pp.144–7.

[4] J.Ry.L. Mainwaring MS., Book 20a.

traditional agents, were not answerable to the Justices, and in some cases—for instance the collectors and assessors appointed by the sequestrators—were not even concerned with the usual unit of administration, the parish, but with groups of manors which cut across parish boundaries. Most unpopular of all were the Excisemen, usually 'foreigners' to the county and answerable to no local authority whatsoever.[1] Control of these officials was not helped by the divergence in the membership of some of these other committees. Except for the sequestrators, always a different group of men, there was little difference between the Bench and the other committees until after 1649. But then the tendency for a different group to dominate such committees (e.g. those for the militia or for 'ejecting scandalous ministers') became apparent.[2]

This increased density in the fabric of administrative life could not fail to damage the standing and authority of the Bench as the main organ of government in the county. They could easily be seen as just one committee amongst many, and their less exalted social standing than the Bench of the 1630s would reinforce this impression. The increase in the range of their duties was not sufficient to compensate for this. With the disappearance of the church courts, they became responsible for punishing a large and varied number of moral and sexual offenders, and with problems in the economics of the church. For, as the churchwardens of Tarvin pointed out in 1647, 'since the concestory (wch was the court wherein such persones as refused to pay theire church dues where punished) beinge nowe downe, wee humble desire the Honorable Bench . . . to releeve us'.[3] They also took over the non-military tasks assigned to the pre-war lieutenancy.[4] Finally they had to face new problems created by the wars, like finding homes for those Parliamentarian soldiers who had nowhere to live. The most significant of

---

[1] See e.g. Bodl. Lib. Tanner MSS., vol. 59, f. 442, and above, p.99.

[2] See below, pp.256–8.

[3] C.R.O., Quarter Sessions File (henceforth Q.S.F.) 1647, no.4, f. 64.

[4] For their responsiblity for upholding the Crown's religious policy, see B. Coward, art. cit., pp.57–63.

these problems was a massive increase in cases concerning state security. Only two offenders were brought before them on matters related to security in the years before the war, both for mildly uncomplimentary comments about the King; it became a significant problem in the years after 1646.[1]

Connected with this was a general increase in the number of challenges to their own dignity. Between 1625 and 1642 there were only three challenges—two of them clearly occasioned by an over-long visit to an alehouse,[2] the third an indirect snub to Sir William Brereton when he ordered a bear-baiter to be stocked for swearing. This punishment misfired, however, for 'most of the alehouses in the towne sent flagons of ale' to the prisoner, and music and dancing were provided for his entertainment.[3]

After 1645 however, there were cases of disrespect and disobedience at almost every Sessions. Former Royalist soldiers abused them for supposed vindictiveness,[4] radicals abused them for welcoming back compounded Royalists into their social circle.[5] Particular severity was shown to those sectaries and Quakers who challenged the social order. Richard Janney, for example, was punished because 'upon the sight of some deere [he] uttered these words, I hope wee shall in a short tyme bee rydd of gentlemen and bucks or deere also', and went on to make a personal attack on one of the Justices, Thomas Brereton of Ashley.[6] At times, the evidence suggests that the Justices were far too self-conscious and humourless in their attitude; thus Henry Bradshaw dragged Joshua Gerard before Quarter Sessions for saying that 'a strangr would not thinke hee the said Col. Henry Bradshaw were a man of that eminency in the country, hee goeing soe plaine in apparell'.[7] Nevertheless, there were

---

[1] For some comments on the attitude of the Justices to the problems of state security, see below pp.254–6.
[2] Q.S.O.B. 6a, f. 211, Q.S.F. 1629, no.1, ff. 37–8.
[3] Q.S.F. 1629, no.1, f. 37.
[4] Q.S.F. 1648, no.1, f. 41.
[5] Q.S.F. 1654, no.1, ff. 108, 153, 155.
[6] Q.S.F. 1650, no.3, f. 10. See also e.g. Q.S.F. 1656, no.4, f. 86.
[7] Q.S.F. 1651, no.1, f. 78.

disturbing elements, particularly the occasional charges of
corruption made against the Justices, such as Adam Jackson's
claim that Thomas Stanley of Alderley had taken a £10
bribe,[1] or William Sutton of Bradwall's assertion that 'Before
God, itt is gone against mee. I cannot have lawe . . . Mr.
Brereton of Ashley sitts by the Judges, and I cannot have
lawe against Mr. Brereton, meaning Mr. Brereton of
Brereton'.[2]

There were also the problems inherent in the breakdown
of local government during the wars,[3] and in the difficulties
involved in getting the processes working again. In particular,
the Justices were faced by considerable problems in coercing
the constables into gathering the money which they had
ordered to be collected. Before the war they had had to
threaten and fine constables for failure to perform their
duties, but on nothing like the scale that now became
necessary. The permanent extension of taxation during the
Civil Wars to a far wider group of people than ever before[4]
thus occasioned many bitter outcries. With massive arrears
and current commitments to maintain troops remaining a
problem well into the 1650s, it is not surprising that the
Justices had far more difficulty in gathering funds for their
own purposes. They could order the constables to distrain
goods, but gangs of villagers frequently attacked the
constables and seized the goods back.[5] The mutinous state of
the soldiery and a widespread hostility towards them made
their employment impossible;[6] a constable who tried to use
them was condemned by the Justices for 'bringing an odium
uppon the souldiers for executing the civill magistrates
authority'.[7] In many cases the constables were sympathetic

[1] Q.S.F. 1656, no.1, f. 92.
[2] Q.S.F. 1658, no.1, f. 81.
[3] See above, pp.91—4.
[4] e.g. the Cheshire subsidy roll for 1627 in Chester City Library contains only a
little over 1,000 names. For popular resistance to Ship Money which was
extended to a far wider group of the population, see above, pp. 28—30.
[5] e.g. Q.S.F. 1647, no.4, f. 47.
[6] Bodl. Lib. Tanner MSS., vol. 59, f. 442; Q.S.F. 1647, no.4, ff. 94—5, 1650,
no.2, f. 53.
[7] Q.S.F. 1648, no.4, f. 59.

to the state of the villagers and neglected their duty; the traditional threats of imprisonment and fines were not sufficient to coerce them into action,[1] and for the first time the threats had to be followed up by imprisonment of the offenders.[2] This tough attitude and a decrease in the total demands on the county made this less of a problem from the early 1650s.

The attitude of the village communities was not purely negative, however. They were far more self-confident about their own needs and put them forward in petitions with greater forcefulness and regularity. The average number of petitions that the Justices were asked to consider more than doubled, from an average of eighteen in the Sessions between 1625 and 1642 to thirty-eight in the period 1645–60. More significant is the change in their nature and tone. Building, perhaps, on the experience of 1640–3, when so many petitions were being circulated throughout the county, there is a development of petitions that claim to represent the desires of the whole county or (more frequently) of a whole hundred or of a group of parishes, whereas previously petitions had invaribaly come from a single parish. Furthermore they had always been supplicatory in tone and been based on very narrow bases, on statute law, on local traditions, or simply out of humanitarian concern for a particular unfortunate. There was nothing like the following, which claimed to come from signatories throughout the county:

That the captaine of our salvacon is highly dishonord, youth greatly corrupted, mens estates occasioned to bee imbeseld by an excessive number of disorderd and unlicensed alecoates, the nurseries of all ryott, excesse and idlenes, the dens, shops, yea thrones of Satan, the sinkes of sin . . . [3]

Such petitions as this reveal a new state of moral outrage, a sense of right, a burning awareness of the need for reform. From rather vague expressions of the need for the wholesome laws of the realm to be put into effect, petitioners came to

[1] Q.S.F. 1645, no.3, f. 104, 1648, no.3, f. 24; Q.S.O.B. 9a, f. 93.
[2] Q.S.O.B. 9a, f. 100.
[3] Q.S.F. 1646, no.1, f. 76.

demand that the Justices 'do the same wch god requires from you'. [1]

Psychologically this attitude was probably reinforced by a change in the wording of orders from the Chester Judges. Typical was an order from John Bradshaw that his order regarding the suppression of ale-houses was to be implemented 'upon advice had wth the minister and church-wardens or some other of the most religious and discreet inhabitants'.[2] This is in contrast to all similar inquiries before the Civil War which were always referred to 'the most substantiall men' or to the two nearest Justices. The appeal to the minister and the godly rather than to those with substantial lands detracted from the innate respect that the Justices, as the most substantial but not always the most godly, could expect to receive.

All these factors would suggest that efficient admini-stration in the years after the Civil War would be more difficult to maintain and the Justices less well equipped to face the manifold problems that had always made local government inefficient. And on top of all these factors there remains the one that for most commentators has appeared the most crucial of all: for writers like Miss Leonard and Miss James,[3] the effectiveness of local government was largely determined by the amount of pressure exerted upon the Justices by the central government. Thus Miss Leonard claimed that only in the 1630s, when the Privy Council was guiding and directing the Justices, were the more humane and enlightened aspects of the poor law put into practice, and Professor Barnes's study of the response of the Justices to the Book of Orders tends to confirm her findings.[4] This strong guiding hand was removed in the 1640s and 50s.

At first sight, their analysis is correct. Rather feverish and intense activity did occur in Cheshire in the 1630s and the

[1] Q.S.F. 1657, no.4, f. 123.
[2] Q.S.F. 1648, no.3, f. 22.
[3] E.M. Leonard, *The Early History of the English Poor Relief,* Cambridge, 1900; M. James, *Social Problems and Policy During the Puritan Revolution,* London, 1930, pp.242—9.
[4] Barnes, op. cit., pp.196—7.

authority of the Privy Council was invoked in several fresh initiatives and purges, although this impulse was slackening by the mid-1630s. In comparison, the Long Parliament and the Councils of State of the Rump and Protectorate made little effort to intervene directly in the way that Charles I's Privy Council had done, except in matters relating to security or the militia.[1] But apart from general legislation confirming Elizabethan social and economic measures, little administrative pressure was brought to bear, an isolated exception being an order in 1655 for an inquiry into enclosure in Delamere Forest.[2]

But the government did possess one further source of influence which it could employ. This was the Court of Great Sessions at Chester, which acted, amongst other things, as the County Assize Court.[3] In the past, relations between the Judges at Chester and the Justices had been quite frosty, the Justices being very jealous of any attempt by the Judges to interfere in what they considered their tasks.[4]

One important development in the years after 1645 was the appointment of two local men—John Bradshaw and Peter Warburton—as Judges at Chester (previous nominees had always been London lawyers). This may well have helped them in their attempts to intervene and organize those aspects of local government which they felt that the Justices were neglecting. For example, the fresh approach to, and continuing preoccupation with, the problem of unlicensed ale-houses was largely the responsibility of Bradshaw.[5] It was the two Judges who brought together plans for a revised system of financing bridge repairs,[6] and, at a time when the J.P.s were trying to eradicate the Quaker menace, Bradshaw ordered the release of twelve of them following allegations of mistreatment in prison.[7] At times they could be openly

[1] e.g. *Commons Journal*, vol. 6, pp.141—2.
[2] Q.S.F. 1655, no.2, f. 156.
[3] For a summary of the court's powers, see above, pp.1—2.
[4] See above, pp.9—10.
[5] e.g. P.R.O. Chester 21, vol. 4, f. 316 (unfoliated). See below, pp.282—3.
[6] Q.S.F. 1646, no.1, f. 17. See below, pp.242—3.
[7] P.R.O. Chester 21, vol. 4, f. 326.

critical of the J.P.s, as when they spoke of 'the negligence
and connyvance of the officers and ministers of justice', and
ordered their report to be entered by the clerk of the peace
in the Order Book.[1]

Sometimes the impulse behind their concern was a petition
from the county, but more usually it resulted from the
presentments of the Grand Jury or Second Inquest at the
Assizes. Prior to 1642 these representative freeholders had
remained content to draw attention to specific and localized
misdemeanours (particularly unmade roads);[2] after 1646
they became much bolder and more constructive, making
general recommendations and airing general grievances, such
as about the number of ale-houses,[3] the nature of Excise
collections,[4] and they were also sharply critical of the
Justices. Thus in 1648 they presented 'the excessive number
of alehouses throughout the countie, and the Justices neclect
in suppressing the same and suffering the assize of bread &
ale to be broken',[5] and in 1658 they presented the J.P.s of
Nantwich and Macclesfield hundreds for holding monthly
meetings too infrequently.[6] In 1647 and 1652 they suggested
the names of suitable men to be added to the Commission of
the Peace, in the latter year even naming one of themselves.[7]

But there is some evidence that on occasions directives
from London lay behind the initiatives of the Judges. This
was particularly true once Cromwell became Lord Protector,
and we possess one letter from him to Bradshaw demanding
the intervention of the Justices. The main subject of
Cromwell's letter was his fear that the Book of Common
Prayer was still being used in many parishes and 'feeding that
old superstitious spirit.' He ordered the Judges to ensure that
the ban on its use was made effective, and concluded,

[1] Ibid., f. 316.
[2] See above, pp.12–13. I am currently engaged on an article on Grand Juries in
seventeenth-century Cheshire.
[3] P.R.O. Chester 24/127/1, Chester 24/129/1 (1651).
[4] Ibid. 24/129/2, (1651).
[5] Ibid. 24/127/1.
[6] Ibid. 24/132/1, see below, p. 232.
[7] Ibid. 24/127/1; Chester 129/3.

haveing this opportunity, I desire that a more than ordinery care may be had of the suppressing the multitude of alehouses, and a severe punishmt of the abuses therof, for I feare that the dealing of Justices and grand iuries have beene too overly & superficiall in that matter.[1]

Thus, if the old, straightforward relationship between Privy Council and the Commission of the Peace was not paralleled in the 1640s and 1650s, it is clear that the central government did not altogether fail to exert influence on the course of local administration. It must be remembered that, as Professor Roots has recently pointed out, the Major-Generals were not simply a response to the Royalist threat but an attempt 'to impose another age of Thorough'.[2]

None the less, I shall argue below that administration was in many ways more efficient in the 1650s than in the 1630s. Paradoxically the approach that brought the post-war Justices' greatest successes was necessitated by their lack of the most outstanding quality of the pre-war Bench.

Before the Civil War, the Commission of the Peace was heavily drawn from a group of leading families, distinguishable from the bulk of the gentry to some extent by lineage and size of estates, but predominantly by intermarriage. In virtually all the dozens of letters between Justices in the 1630s, the writer calls his correspondent 'cousin', 'uncle', or some such greeting, and, while it is true that 'cousin' in particular was used in a very indistinct fashion, it points to a pattern of familiarity and acquaintance among the Justices which allowed a natural sense of co-operative trust and effort to develop. Administrative decisions were mostly taken out of Sessions by one or two Justices and rubber-stamped by the whole Bench. The country Justice, representative of a social and administrative elite, was very much a dispenser of favour and arbiter of all disputes in the area around his home.

The post-war Bench was very different in complexion. The majority of the Justices came from a common social class, the middling gentry, but they did not possess the same mutual ties as their predecessors. Theirs was an economic

[1] Ibid. 21, vol. 4, f. 316.
[2] I.A. Roots, 'The Central Government and the Local Community', in E.W. Ives (ed.) *The English Revolution 1600—1660*, London, 1968, p.44.

common denominator not, in the broadest sense, a familial one. They were interrelated, but to nothing like the extent of the former Justices. They did not form a self-contained unit; though they had some mutual friends, they did not share one another's friendship in common. This is well illustrated by Thomas Mainwaring's diary;[1] he was one of the few Justices from an old ruling family. The names of fellow Justices frequently appear in the diary, but not as friends: they were colleagues. When he held dinner parties, or visited friends, they were rarely included. On such occasions the names that occur regularly were Sir Thomas Wilbraham, Sir Henry Delves, Lord Cholmondeley, Edward Glegg, John Crewe, and Sir Peter Leicester. Three of these were former Royalists, three disillusioned Parliamentarians who took no part in local government; all were closely related to one another. In 1649 Mainwaring played bowls several times at Halgherton Green with a total of twelve families; only one sat beside him on the Bench. Although he met several Justices at an asparagus feast at Stoake, it was the Wilbrahams and Leicesters he travelled and dined with.[2]

It could be argued that as a member of one of the few pre-war Justice families still on the Bench, Mainwaring was untypical. But on those occasions when he did call in on a fellow Justice, he found him not with other Justices, but with neighbouring, even minor, gentlemen.[3] They were essentially parochial rather than county gentry. And the resultant lack of close, easygoing informality which had marked the pre-war Bench combined with the factors outlined above to produce an entirely new style of administration.

The results of this are most clearly seen in the role of Quarter Sessions as the central agency of administration. Before the wars, Quarter Sessions would consistently lay down the main lines of policy, such as taking the decision to

---

[1] J.Ry.L. Mainwaring MS., Book 20a. For a summary of its contents and value, see Dore, *Civil Wars in Cheshire*, pp.80—8.

[2] J.Ry.L. Mainwaring MS., Book 20a, p.167.

[3] Ibid. p.147 (22 Nov. 1653) and p.167 (9 May 1654).

build a new house of correction,[1] specifying those sections of the Book of Orders which required particular attention,[2] or inaugurating a campaign to stop anyone from shooting at birds and other game (an unpopular move probably intended to boost the profits of Brereton's decoy).[3] The usual categories of criminal offence and all warrants of good behaviour issued by the Justices between Sessions were also tried or reconsidered at Quarter Sessions. But their response to petitions (which in general drew clearer attention to administrative defects than the Grand Jury presentments did) was in a large number of cases to refer the matter to be settled by the local Justices. The number referred in this way after the war dropped to only one-third of the previous figure (25 per cent of all business 1625–42, 8 per cent 1645–60), and many of these were referred to local Justices simply for a report: the Bench was to make a final order at the next Quarter Sessions.

The mentality of the pre-war Justices was nicely revealed when they decided in 1641 that although a case appeared straightforward, 'yet because the partyes delinquent are best knowne to the Justices whoe made the said former order therefore this Bench doth intreate the said Justices to take the matter into theire further consideracon'.[4] After the war, there was a greater awareness of the importance of the corporate decision of the whole Bench; there were even unprecedented occasions when they overruled the recommendations of the local Justices.

As a result the 'monthly meeting' of the Justices of each hundred, which had been evolving in Cheshire since the 1590s and established by the Book of Orders in 1630, was checked in what had previously been an unhindered growth of power and prestige. The term continues to be used in the 1650s,[5] but far less frequently. According to his diary, Thomas Mainwaring—with Henry Bradshaw and Thomas

---

[1] Q.S.O.B. 6a, ff. 286, 294, etc.
[2] Ibid., f. 471.
[3] Ibid., f. 328.
[4] Q.S.O.B. 9a, f. 4.
[5] See e.g. Q.S.F. 1655, no.2, f. 177.

Croxton the most active Justice during the decade[1]—
attended only thirteen monthly meetings in the sixty months
in the years 1650—4; these were usually at three or six
monthly intervals except for the consecutive months June to
August 1652. It seems unlikely that so assiduous a Justice
would miss over three-quarters of the meetings, or that if he
did, the other two Justices in his hundred could have kept
going month after month. The most likely explanation is that
the term was continued, but that in general only one meeting
was held between two successive Quarter Sessions, to gather
information asked for by one and to prepare for the next.

In any case some powers were left to the monthly
meetings; they were responsible for confirming parish
appointments like that of the overseer and for ensuring that a
fair choice was made of churchwardens and constables; they
remained the primary authority for making maintenance
orders in bastardy cases, and supervised the licensing of
ale-houses; they also had to ensure that the poor rate was
fixed in every parish between the minimum and maximum
permitted. They even acquired some new duties, such as the
examination of the wounds of maimed soldiers to ensure that
no one received a war pension once he was healthy again. But
these were essentially supervisory powers; effective power
and decision-making responsibilities were taken over by
Quarter Sessions.

Before the war local Justices were also instructed at
Quarter Sessions to inquire informally into disputes or
petitions and settle them peacefully. Thus at the same
Sessions in 1636 two Justices were instructed to make
Thomas Cowley of Dodleston apologize to a Flintshire
Justice, Roger Grosvenor, for having slandered him, and four
gentlemen were to examine an argument of 'brabbles and
discurtesies', sort it out, and release a carpenter bound over
to Sessions for his part in the affair; in both cases Sessions
only wanted to hear further of the cases if one or both

---

[1] According to calculations as to the regularity of their attendance at Sessions
and the number of documents bearing their signatures drawn up out of Sessions.

parties refused reconciliation.[1] Such informal interventions covered an enormous range of activities; in many cases a petition would arrive at Sessions asking for the local Justices to come and mediate.[2] Yet there are virtually no such references after the war, and in this the evidence of the Quarter Sessions Files is confirmed by the contents of Thomas Mainwaring's diary. It is true that he recorded several expeditions to settle land disputes, but these are a special category, and have little to do with his membership of the Bench. He was frequently joined as arbiter in these disputes by former Royalist landlords.

Another regular feature of the 1630s was the letter which arrived at Sessions from a non-attending Justice asking for a case or a petition due to be heard to be dropped. In some cases this was because he had already intervened successfully;[3] in other cases it was because he was seeking to mitigate an offence, or excuse an administrative fault, as when William Booth (son of Sir George) asked that the men of Etchells be given another chance to repair the highway before the projected action against them was taken,[4] or when William Leversage asked the Bench not to proceed against an honest tenant of his despite his assault on a neighbour.[5] There were also innumerable letters sent by a local Justice to cover and endorse a petition from a village in his neighbourhood.[6] Since the same clerk of the peace was responsible for the collation of documents from 1627 to 1652, it seems unlikely that the almost total absence of this type of material after the war was simply due to a change in the nature of the documents bound up in the File.

A particularly interesting corollary to the decline of the power exercised by the Justices at a local level was the steady improvement in the prestige and role of the head constable. Although this office had always been held by gentlemen, its holders were always very minor figures, frequently in the

[1] Q.S.O.B. 6a, ff. 423–5.  [2] Q.S.F. 1634, no.2, ff. 57, 62.
[3] Q.S.F. 1635, no.1, f. 49.  [4] Q.S.F. 1625, no.4, f. 100.
[5] Q.S.F. 1629, no.1, f. 57.  [6] e.g. Q.S.F. 1633, no.3, f. 29.

twilight land between gentry and yeomanry between which successive generations might alternate. Certainly until the Civil War head constables were treated with scant respect by the Justices, subject to the same peremptory tone as the petty constables.[1] A gentleman of any substance was assured of nothing harsher than a polite reminder of his duties if he erred.[2]

But after the Civil War, they were treated quite distinctly from the petty constables. They were no longer subject to threats of imprisonment or fines, and were given fresh duties and greater freedom of action in dealing with their old tasks. They were involved, for example, in the difficult task of surveying bridges and estimating the likely cost.[3] Furthermore, after 1651 they became paid officials, successfully arguing that, having taken over responsibility for the allocation and collection of the monthly assessment within their own divisions, they should receive the remuneration laid down by Parliament.[4] In the same year they acquired the right to nominate their own successors. Before the war they were kept in office at the Justices' pleasure and replaced at the hundredal meeting by the local Justices' nominee. After 1651 a head constable was allowed to remain or retire at will; when he retired he was expected to draw up a short list (usually of three) of those capable and willing to take office, one of whom was then chosen at Quarter Sessions.[5]

The change in status is clearly demonstrated in the contrast between the following orders. In 1634 the Justices refused to excuse two former head constables from service as petty constables, although they pleaded that their earlier appointment made them too senior to be required to undertake the arduous parish appointment. The Justices

[1] e.g. Q.S.O.B. 6a, ff. 494—5.
[2] e.g. Q.S.O.B. 6a, f. 388. This followed Edmund Jodrell's blatant refusal to pay a perpetual annuity of £10 left by his father for the poor of the parish. The Justices' request for him to obey the law was almost apologetic.
[3] e.g. Q.S.O.B. 9a, f. 257.
[4] Q.S.F. 1651, no.4, f. 135.
[5] For the old system see e.g. Q.S.F. 1625, no.2, f. 88; for the new one, e.g. Q.S.F. 1651, no.4, f. 141.

argued that the office of petty constable 'is of greate necessity and fitt to be supplied by able men and [we are] willing allsoe to doe equall right to all'.[1] In 1648, however, they excused another former head constable from serving as petty constable because 'hee and his ancestors ... had allwayes lived in a ranke farr above the calling of a petty constable'.[2]

As we shall see, the centralization of decision-making in Quarter Sessions was to allow increased scope for planning and implementing new measures, but the decline in the time and effort spent by the Justices in affairs in their own hundreds threatened to lead to a breakdown of communication between village and county authorities. This gap could only partly be filled by increasing the power of the head constables. Fortunately the Justices were also able to harness the new self-awareness of the village communities. The increase in number and the broadening of outlook reflected in petitions in itself helped the Justices to see what problems existed, but they were able to introduce a far-reaching change by arranging for committees of godly and responsible men in each parish to meet regularly to implement Sessions orders and make reports on other matters.

The origins of these committees is obscure. If the research of the Webbs could be relied on, they would be related to the development of select vestries. Unfortunately neither the Quarter Sessions Records nor the parish records for the early seventeenth century make any reference to a body that can be identified with the select vestry taking any part in the administration. Even the churchwardens and overseers, the natural nucleus of such committees, seem to have confined themselves to their statutory duties. The earliest reference to any sort of parish committees can be found in a Quarter Sessions order of 1647 relating to the licensing of ale-houses: the Sessions ordered the local Justices to seek the advice of 'ministers and others of the better sort'.[3] Similarly the same men were ordered shortly afterwards to submit advice about

[1] Q.S.O.B. 6a, f. 345.    [2] Q.S.O.B. 9a, f. 158.    [3] Q.S.O.B. 9a, f. 107.

which maltsters were to be licensed.[1] It was an order from John Bradshaw that first changed the terminology to what afterwards became most frequent, when he ordered the Justices to take counsel 'wth the ministers and churchwardens and some others the most religious and discreet inhabitants'.[2] In only one case are we told how these committees were appointed, when the minister of Rostherne was made responsible for picking suitable men.[3] As time went by, these committees were involved in a wider range of duties; for example, they were asked to co-operate in the Justices' general policy of keeping down the price of grain and in preventing engrossing and forestalling of the market.[4] Whereas before the war the viewing of bridges in need of repair and the assessment of the cost of repairs was invariably the duty—and a very unpopular one—of the Justices, responsibility for this task was handed over to committees of lesser gentlemen nominated by the Bench, or increasingly by the parish committees. Before the war the individual Justice was empowered to order the levy of particular sums for local use; these committees were permitted only to make a recommendation, while Sessions made the order, usually taking their advice. Furthermore the overseer of the repairs had always previously been a neighbouring Justice; now the appointment went to a gentleman on the spot—sometimes a very minor one—or to a head constable.

There was also a real attempt to level out the burden of taxation. The mise assessment roll was increasingly used for all taxes (e.g. monthly assessment).[5] But the roll was frequently out of date, and the commissioners of the monthly assessment were asked to examine grievances that arose from individuals or from whole townships who felt that their share was unequal. These commissioners appear to have met (at least if Thomas Mainwaring's diary is anything to go by) twice a year and heard representations from the parish committees, being empowered to revise the assessments.[6]

---

[1] Q.S.F. 1647, no.1, f. 100.   [2] Q.S.F. 1648, no.3, f. 22.   [3] Q.S.O.B. 9a, f. 138.
[4] See below, pp.249–51. [5] Q.S.F. 1649, no.3, f. 15. [6] e.g. Q.S.F. 1652, no.2, f. 172.

The evidence suggests that these committees continued to flourish throughout the Interregnum. Thus in 1657 a petition with twelve signatures reached Quarter Sessions asserting that

wee whose names are subscribed, inhabitants of the parish of Audelem that doe monethly assemble by way of assistance wth the officers thereof in the discharge of there duties hould it requisite to certifie our dislikes of the byndinge of Richard Eldershaw of Audelem to brew and sell ale it beinge contrary to our returnes upon all ocasions.[1]

Perhaps the most significant point about these committees is the important role assigned to the minister. Although many of the leading gentry were unhappy with the ecclesiastical organization desired by a majority of the clergy,[2] there was no question that generally the new ministers were a more responsible and respectable body of men than their predecessors before the Civil War. As well as being always associated with the parish committees and at least sometimes responsible for appointing them, some ministers were able to use their influence directly with the Justices, by writing privately to Sessions; their letters are the only survival of the pattern we have been describing in the 1630s.[3] Whereas several pre-war ministers had served as Justices, they were invariably those who came from established gentle stock; these new ministers, though excluded by Act of Parliament from serving on the Commission, owed their authority in the community to their pre-eminence as religious leaders. Nathaniel Lancaster and Adam Martindale, both of yeoman stock, were able by their intervention to carry weight with the Justices; others like Burghall of Acton and Cole of Wibunbury were frequent visitors to the table of Thomas Mainwaring; it seems unlikely that their predecessors enjoyed similar privileges in the 1630s.

The formalization of procedures did not, then, produce a breakdown of communication between village community and county leaders. And it had some beneficial effects on the streamlining and improvement of other problems where the

[1] Q.S.F. 1657, no.2, f. 136.
[2] See below, pp.270–6.
[3] e.g. Q.S.F. 1648, no.4, f. 91, 1649, no.1, f. 35.

old system prevented a sufficiently broad approach. This is most clearly seen with respect to bridge repairs. The greatest single hindrance to effective action before the war had been confusion over the responsibility for paying for their maintenance. According to a general order issued in 1616, every hundred was made responsible for all the bridges within its boundaries,[1] and this technically remained the basis of action until 1642. But its effectiveness was diminished by a series of decisions by the Justices in each hundred exempting particular townships from their general obligations; thus Warmincham was freed from payments to the bridges of Edisbury Hundred in return for undertaking to maintain four horse-bridges within the parish unassisted.[2] Even worse were the inconsistencies revealed in cases like that of Wilderspoole Bridge, which the Justices in 1630 declared was henceforth to be repaired solely by Bucklow; in 1638 they ignored this order by instructing the neighbouring hundreds to contribute.[3] In all such cases the effect of lengthy appeals and investigations was to make a major problem of recon- struction out of an initially straightforward repair. The difficult case of Warrington Bridge led to a delay of sixteen years before work could be completed.[4]

The deterioration of bridges in the course of the war made the Justices' problem very acute. But their response was remarkable; initially they sought to make the 1616 order effective by asserting that in future all bridges in each hundred be maintained at the cost of the whole hundred, but in 1648 they made a radical departure from the old policy by ordering an assessment from the whole county for the repair of Winsford Bridge, 'notwithstanding any private agreemt . . . within the county to the contrary'.[5] Later in the year the 1616 order was formally revoked,[6] and henceforth even the oldest exemptions and privileges were swept aside. The

[1] Reissued in Q.S.O.B. 6a, f. 328.
[2] Q.S.F. 1633, no.3, f. 29.
[3] Q.S.O.B. 6a, ff. 262, 478.
[4] Numerous orders in Q.S.O.B. 6a, culminating in Q.S.F. 1642, f. 15.
[5] Q.S.O.B. 9a, f. 174.
[6] Q.S.F. 1648, no.4, f. 46.

Justices refused to grant a petition from Nantwich for exemption from general payments because of the town's obligation to maintain Nantwich Bridge unassisted. When the inhabitants appealed against this ruling to the Judges at Chester, John Bradshaw issued a crucial judgment, asserting that 'the said usage was good and yett but an agreemt . . . wch might be broken at any time'.[1] The Justices then employed this to abolish all similar claims. In future each township had to contribute to the county, but was not required to maintain any bridges without contributions from the whole county.

As an extension to this policy, there was a development towards the idea of a general rate to be expended as and when need arose. This is clear from the way the Justices discussed how to dispose of any money left over when the particular repair for which it had been collected was complete. Thus in 1654 they redirected the surplus from Acton Bridge towards the repair of Byley Bridge.[2] Before the war any overplus was automatically refunded to the villages.

A similar policy was adopted to help those parishes that were seriously overburdened with poor. For example, the crippling cost of maintaining 800 poor in Nantwich was spread out by the granting of contributions from neighbouring parishes both in 1648 and 1651,[3] and other parishes received aid from time to time.[4]

The same kind of greater strategic awareness took other forms, in particular in the Justices' constant battle to keep down the number of ale-houses. Before the war each hundred was responsible for licensing its own, and, apart from on a very few occasions,[5] there is little evidence that the Justices were concerned to limit their number. They were simply concerned to ensure that unlicensed ale-houses and licensed ones which could be shown to have furthered immoral practices (particularly 'unlawful games') were suppressed.

[1] Q.S.F. 1652, no.1, f. 149.
[2] Q.S.F. 1654, no.4, f. 153.
[3] Q.S.O.B. 9a, ff. 166–7; 1651, no.4, f. 82.
[4] Q.S.F. 1649, no.3, f. 18 (Onston).
[5] e.g. Bunbury in 1638 (Q.S.F. 1638, no.2, f. 41).

The only attempt to keep down the number in any given village was half-hearted, no machinery for implementing the order being made, and the records of succeeding Sessions suggesting that little was done.[1]

The post-war Justices were far more attentive to the problem. Their motives offer a good example of their attitude to most problems, an inseparable mixture of the moral and the practical. On the practical side, they were concerned at the effect on food prices (at a time of severe grain shortage) of the production of large quantities of malt from barley (for use in brewing),[2] and they were afraid that ale-house-keepers would take in wanderers and so increase the burden of the poor in the county; on the moral side, they took up the complaints of numerous petitions[3] that alehouses fostered immorality—by the encouragement of idleness and gambling, and by causing men to neglect their families and to absent themselves from church on the Sabbath.[4] Even this had practical consequences: the church was the channel for the transmission of news, information, and orders from the central and local authorities. But increasingly it came to be the place where local taxation was collected. Since all men were supposed to attend church on Sundays, many parish officials took the opportunity to collect the poor rate and other dues immediately before divine service. The churchwardens of Nantwich reported that they collected the poor rate in this manner fortnightly, but complained that many stayed away or arrived late to avoid paying.[5] Many of these lingered in the ale-house.[6]

The Justices tried several ways of tackling the problem but were eventually persuaded to put into effect a scheme laid out by John Bradshaw. According to this plan, each township was permitted two ale-houses, although a limited number in excess of two was allowed to those townships where there

[1] Q.S.F. 1629, no.4, f. 21 (dorse).
[2] Q.S.O.B. 9a, ff. 194–5.
[3] e.g. see above, p.229.
[4] Q.S.F. 1645, no.3, f. 110, 1647, no.4, f. 42.
[5] Q.S.F. 1651, no.4, f. 82.
[6] Q.S.O.B. 9a, f. 219.

was a parish church, those on some major highways, and market towns. All those which were 'infamous or blind', which stood 'forth on the comon road', which could not 'give lodging or entertainment to wayfayring men', or which could not give adequate sureties, were to be automatically suppressed. Of the remainder, the best were to be licensed by the Justices after they had received advice from the parish committees.[1]

The battle to restrict the number of ale-houses was continued throughout the 1650s, and a sudden outburst of petitions from suppressed ale-house-keepers in 1656 suggests that Major-General Worsley's drive was particularly success-ful.[2] The tightness of their restrictions continued right up to the Restoration, and those suppressed 'though no misdemeanour was announced', being simply 'super-numerary', continued to feel aggrieved.[3] Thus Robert Shingler failed to get his licence back after a visit to London, though his was a most superior establishment, one which gave 'entertainment to such as . . . the Right Honourble the Lord Kilmurrey and other worshipful gentlemen who for theire recreation have used & still doe use to resort to Bowles there'.[4]

One of the myths perpetuated by some recent historians is the one that stresses the repressive and harsh Puritan mind which led to unsympathetic and unimaginative local govern-ment. This view was based partly on a misunderstanding of the nature of English Puritanism, and has been exploded completely by the work of Professor Walzer,[5] but it was also based on a lack of detailed research on local records, and two scholars who have recently produced studies of specific problems based on local archives have both challenged the old view.[6] My own findings for Cheshire confirm theirs.

[1] Q.S.F. 1648, no.3, f. 22; Q.S.O.B. 9a, f. 107.
[2] Twenty-two appeals in the Sessions for July 1656 alone.
[3] Q.S.F. 1656, no.2, ff. 259, 261.
[4] Q.S.F. 1659, no.2 (part i), f. 21.
[5] M. Walzer, *The Revolution of the Saints* Cambridge, Mass., 1965.
[6] W.K. Jordan, *Philanthropy in England 1480—1660,* London, 1957; A.S. Beier, art. cit.

One of the few signs of this repressive instinct was displayed by the Rump in its legislation dealing with moral and sexual offences, for many of which it prescribed the death penalty. The Justices showed a total disregard for these sentences and simply imprisoned all offenders for between three and twelve months. On the other hand they were clearly impressed by the need for some penalty, since they rejected a plea from the inhabitants of Rostherne for a remission in the six-month sentence imposed on Thomas Finlow for adultery, although the villagers claimed that his imprisonment had brought husbandry to a standstill; for Finlow owned the only plough and could supply other utensils 'in a better and more readie maner than any other workman.'.[1]

There was also a slightly more punitive attitude towards the parents of bastards. Before the war the Justices had been content to ensure that the child was maintained by the father, mother, or grandparents and not by the parish; further punishment was reserved for mothers who had more than one bastard (unlike other areas where both father and mother were punished; in Lancashire in 1604 a gentleman was whipped for being the father of a bastard, while in Cheshire the only sentence imposed was a spell in the house of correction). After the war all mothers of bastards were sent to the house of correction for three months, but otherwise the only change in policy was to improve the nature of maintenance. Before the war the child was kept by one parent, who was paid an allowance (40s. a year on average) by the other. If the father was ordered to keep the child and the mother pay maintenance, the father usually had to agree with a poor couple to foster out the child and pay them £3 or £4 a year. After the war stricter rules were laid down to prevent a default of payment, and in those cases where the parish officers failed to apprehend and take sureties from a reputed father, the maintenance order was made out against them. More interesting was the provision

[1] Q.S.F. 1655, no.3, f. 140.

that the parents cease to pay maintenance when the child reached twelve, but instead had to find the money to apprentice the child; this was a constructive change.

But the main charge of unimaginative government made by historians against the Interregnum Justices concerned their dealings with the poor. Thus Miss Leonard, in a classic statement of this view, said that 'after the civil war a part only of the system survived ... Never since the days of Charles I have we had. .. so much provision of work for the able-bodied'.[1]

Certainly the 1630s generally, and the early part especially, were marked by considerable activity to deal with the problem of the poor. An attempt was made to put all the provisions of the statutes into effect at the same time. But the only parts that the records suggest were managed successfully were the laws relating to the building of cottages on the waste, the keeping of constant watch and ward in every parish, and an increased provision of relief for the impotent and disabled poor. Other policies were pursued less successfully. In particular, plans first laid out in 1631 to replace the old house of correction—so decrepit that the prisoners could escape at will[2]—took eleven years to put into effect after several false starts and abandoned projects;[3] in some areas the Justices gave up all hopes of acting according to the statutes, ordering four children of Great Budworth to wander abroad in the parish to beg and telling the church-wardens not to levy money for their relief.[4]

But their most surprising failure was in the very field where older commentators found the early Stuart Justices so effective, the provision of work for the able-bodied. From 1629 onwards[5] they expressed their hopes of making the laws governing the provision of work effective, but their attempts were too piecemeal to be successful. As Sir Henry Bunbury pointed out, as soon as the parishes of Wirral levied

[1] Leonard, op. cit., p.132.
[2] Q.S.O.B. 6a, f. 488.
[3] Q.S.O.B. 6a, ff. 286, 294, 488, 9a f. 53; Q.S.F. 1634, no.3, f. 35.
[4] Q.S.O.B. 6a, f. 155.
[5] Ibid., ff. 232−3.

money for a stock to provide work for the poor, men poured
into the hundred from other parts of the county where the
Justices had failed to work with the same speed, and the
scheme    was    swamped    and    ruined.    The    necessary
co-ordination was never achieved; there are occasional
records of a poor man being employed in some such job as
provost marshall to keep watch and ward,[1] but the following
case from 1635 is more typical and sums up the Justices'
failure. Ellyn Heaward was arrested for begging and in his
report Robert Vernon noted that both she and her son were
borne in the parish of Northwich where by lawe they ought to bee
setled & sett to labour; but the old woman confidently affirmeth they
are forced to this kind of liefe by reason the parish of Northwich will
take noe course for them, though they desire it at their handes. It is the
generall fault of most parishes to suffer their poore rather to begge than
sett them to labour, wch the rather induceth mee to give creditt to her
wordes.
The Justices' only response was a negative one; she was to get
financial relief from the parish.[2]
     The Justices were certainly no more able to provide work
after the war. But in general their policies were more liberal.
Faced by a massive increase in the number of poor,[3] inflated
by the effects of the war on agriculture and by the
disbandment of armies, they abandoned the pre-war attitude
of vigilance against wanderers.[4] There were no more attempts
to maintain watch and ward, except in times of plague. This
was partly a response to their own weakness; but their
attitude to the provision of cottages was just as controlled
and far more liberal than that of the pre-war Justices who
had adhered closely to the contents of the 1589 statute. The
new Bench was prepared to find a home for anyone, whether
impotent or able-bodied, if he had the necessary residence
qualification. Whereas the local Justices before the war had
accepted the verdict of courts leet which punished residents
for providing houseroom to a homeless family even if they
had a residence qualification and employment but no roof
over their heads, Quarter Sessions after the war overruled

[1] Q.S.O.B. 6a, f. 389.                    [2] Q.S.F. 1635, no.1, f. 79.
[3] See e.g. Q.S.F. 1651, no.4, f. 81.      [4] e.g. Q.S.O.B. 9a, ff. 166—7.

courts leet who in this way abused the intent of the statute.[1] In cases where men sought to erect cottages on the waste, the Justices made real efforts to get the consent of the legal lord of the waste, and if this was not forthcoming, they themselves approached neighbouring lords for permission to build on their waste land. And whereas earlier Justices implemented the provision in the statute that such cottages be pulled down on the death of the man to whom permission had been initially granted, the post-war Bench was prepared to take a more practical view and consider applications from would-be inhabitants of the empty ramshackle edifices. But, like their predecessors, their greatest success was in providing a steady flow of relief by ensuring that a stiff poor rate was regularly levied, and, as we have seen, they introduced a system whereby areas that were particularly overburdened received assistance from the rest of the county.

But the most startling change after the war was the comprehensive and firm handling by the Justices of the flow and price of grain. It is fairly well established that the years after the first civil war were the worst of the century for many food prices, and Cheshire, as a basically pastoral economy which had to 'import' grain from Ireland and the midlands, was probably worse off than many areas. In the 1620s and 1630s the price of wheat in most years was around 6s. a measure, although this doubled in the poor years at the beginning and end of the 1620s. In 1648 wheat cost 24s. a measure, although the Justices' action swiftly brought the price down to between 12s. and 15s. The price of barley had risen even more steeply,[2] and there was a real necessity for the Justices to implement the statutory powers at their disposal. Their success, however, must be contrasted with the weak response of the pre-war Justices to what were, relative to normal times, serious situations. The attacks on forestallers of the market in 1629 and 1634 were spasmodic and half-hearted.[3] The only evidence we have that malt-

[1] e.g. Q.S.F. 1648, no.1, f. 37.
[2] B.M. Harleian MS. 2125, f. 156.
[3] Q.S.F. 1629, no.2, f. 98, 1634, no.4, f. 69.

making was forbidden is contained in an order for the summer months of 1637 issued by the Justices of the city of Chester, and although this was extended to cover 'maultsters in the County Palatyne of Chester', it is unlikely that they had any power to prevent malt-making outside the city boundaries.[1] Both in 1630 and 1632 the county Justices tried to limit the total amount of barley that might be bought by maltsters, but no proper machinery was created to enforce these orders.[2]

Numerous petitions reached Quarter Sessions in the years 1648–53 complaining about the price of grain. They were unanimous in condemning these monstrous maltmakrs, breadbakrs, alehousekeepers & forestallers of marketts all wch privately pass into the country where they buy whole bayes of barly and other corne', leaving none for the poor.[3] The initial response of the Justices was to follow the same course as their predecessors. Badgers[4] and maltsters were licensed in very restricted numbers and at the height of the crisis altogether banned from the county.[5] Once they were permitted to work again under licence, the Justices were instructed only to license those who had received a recommendation from their own parish committees,[6] and in a later order it is made clear that this policy had proved a success.[7] At the same time further attempts were made to limit the total amount of grain converted into malt, but again this proved impracticable, and when a fresh crisis broke out in 1649[8] the Justices arranged that for the duration of the crisis each maltster should be told from month to month how much he was to be allowed to buy.[9]

These measures show the Justices using traditional measures more successfully than the pre-war Bench. But they

[1] B.M. Harleian MS. 2104, f. 142.
[2] e.g. Q.S.F. 1630, no.3, f. 42; Q.S.O.B. 6a, f. 312.
[3] Q.S.F. 1648, no.1, f. 59.
[4] i.e. common carriers of corn.
[5] Q.S.O.B. 9a, ff. 167–8; Q.S.F. 1648, no.4, f. 45.
[6] Q.S.O.B. 9a, f. 139.
[7] Ibid., f. 240.
[8] See Q.S.F. 1649, no.3, f. 43.
[9] Q.S.O.B. 9a, ff. 227–8.

proved insufficient. As a Nantwich petition pointed out, maltsters, bakers, forestallers, and others

> by buying corne and vittayles by greate quantitye both in the country and in the marketts doe so fill the pockets of the cornemasters that the poore cannot have it in small quantity for their money, but are inforced to buy the same from bakers, badgers and regrators the second, third or fourth hand.

The Justices' reaction was to appoint gentlemen to view proceedings at all market towns to watch out for unlicensed or unprincipled badgers and to stop anyone from buying in bulk until the poor had had a chance to buy their own grain.[1] The problems with this were that these clerks of the market were afraid to act because they 'conceive that diverse the inhabitants of this town are forestallers of the market which rent the richest grounds thereabouts',[2] and that much corn never reached the open market but was 'sould privately at home to breadbakers and none else, and soe the poore are forced to have it uppon their tearmes or else starve'.[3] To deal with this situation the Justices adopted completely new powers which strained the provisions of existing statutes. They ordered that two or three men in every parish and township should have the power to view the barns of all cornmasters and to ensure that the corn was not sold privately but brought to market where the clerks could control its sale. When the cornmasters tried to evade this order by moving corn into their houses and gardens, the right of search was extended to cover all the cornmasters' property; a similar arrangement was made to prevent dairymen from selling in bulk to strangers.[4] Even when this crisis was over, the Justices determined to keep a vigilant watch on the marketing of grain, and after 1652 two men were elected annually in each hundred to keep a watch for forestallers or engrossers and with instructions to report all offenders to Quarter Sessions.[5]

[1] Ibid., ff. 167–8.
[2] Q.S.F. 1648, no.2, f. 25.
[3] Ibid., f. 42.
[4] Q.S.O.B. 9a, f. 179 (this summarizes the earlier order and snags).
[5] Q.S.F. 1652, no.2, f. 145.

This brief examination of the Justices' efforts to control the distribution of grain shows their work at its best: the readiness to use village committees to carry out responsible tasks; a general sense of purpose and planning at a county level; a willingness to alter or extend policies that were failing to produce the desired effects. Not all their work was as effective or as coherent as this, but the same kind of mentality underlay everything they did. In this short chapter there has been no opportunity to discuss many of the problems with which they were faced; the enforcement of apprenticeship, enclosure, security, and church organization are perhaps the main areas not mentioned. In fact, in all these areas there was the same tendency to employ some of the statutory powers granted them in a more efficient manner than their predecessors, sometimes to startling effect.

If we return to the quotation from Miss Moir's book with which we started this chapter,[1] we can now see that, for Cheshire, she was doubly mistaken. Administration was not less effective after the war than before: in some areas it failed to improve on the pre-war record, in others the application of greater foresight and intelligence produced results where muddled effort in the 1630s had got nowhere. More interesting, perhaps, is the fact that these limited successes resulted from very real and substantial changes in the structure of local government, changes which at first sight appear as debilitating weaknesses but which in practice were transformed into a new and positive approach to administration.

The implications of Professor Everitt's remark[2] are that the replacement of the traditional ruling families had led to the collapse of local government and helped to create the groundswell of opposition to the Interregnum. Again, as far as Cheshire is concerned, this is misleading. The moderate and conservative gentry from the old governing families who had taken no part in local administration during the 1650s could not deny the achievements of the existing administration, even if traditional processes had been adapted.

[1] See above, p.233.                    [2] See above, p.233.

Whatever caused a widespread gentry rebellion in Cheshire in the summer of 1659, it was hardly a craving for the firm and responsible local government supposed to have existed twenty years before, which had since been lost.

## 7

# THE GROWTH OF OPPOSITION, 1649—1659

## I

One of the reasons why the rebellion against the restored Rump Parliament in the summer of 1659 succeeded in the north-west and not elsewhere was that no serious trouble from the area was expected. In July 1659 the government countered rumours of a rebellion by issuing orders intended to increase the vigilance of local authorities. In many areas these were detailed and explicit, but to Cheshire only general appeals for attentiveness were thought necessary.[1]

On the face of it, the government's diagnosis of the situation seemed correct. Throughout the decade a handful of malcontents had tried to stir up trouble, but their identity was well known to the authorities and they were arrested whenever their idle plotting seemed likely to lead to any positive action. Thus John Booth, a Parliamentarian colonel who had been disillusioned since 1646, was arrested four times between 1648 and 1656, and John Werden, a former Royalist colonel, was also kept under close surveillance, though he safeguarded himself from serious trouble for his continued indiscretions by turning informer whenever it seemed expedient.[2]

There were realistic opportunities for these men to create trouble on only two occasions, but both times they were unable to muster serious support. During the third civil war, the Scots army passed through Cheshire on its way to defeat at Worcester, but apart from supplies of cheese and other provisions they got little help from the countryside. Despite Derby's appeal to the Presbyterians, both they and the former Royalists stayed at home.[3] A commission from Charles II to four of the leading Justices, all of whom in the

[1] See *C.S.P.D.* 1659—60, pp.15—16.
[2] For Booth and Werden, see D.E. Underdown *Royalist Conspiracy in England, 1649—60,* New Haven, 1960, *passim.*
[3] For a fuller account, see R.N. Dore, *Civil Wars. . .,* pp.74—7.

event appeared openly in defence of the Rump, showed the inadequacy of, and wishful thinking inherent in, Royalist planning.[1] The usually highly suspicious sequestration commissioners reported that

we cannot heare of any in this county who appeared for Charles Stuart. Most of the county declared for Parliament, and 4 regiments of foot and one large troop of horse, raised at the county's charge, marched to Worcester and were at the battle. The old delinquents that had compounded aided the said troops, and kept aloof from Charles Stuart.[2]

In 1655 Werden planned to seize Chester Castle, but the tiny huddle of conspirators who actually turned up on the night stole away when they realized that the guard had been strengthened.[3] Rigorous investigations by Major-General Worsley failed to uncover any plot which involved anyone except those whom the government already with reason treated as the lunatic fringe.

Throughout the period from the end of the war to the Restoration, the Justices had to deal with a stream of cases concerned with security, compared with only three in the period 1625–40. But in almost every case the offence was trivial, usually taking the form of an insult to authority rather than a challenge to it. Thus William Harding was brought before Quarter Sessions for betting John Breave £5 that the Lord Protector would not stand for three years;[4] in such cases, the offender was released if he took the Engagement. There were also those who 'cryed downe the excise'; they were imprisoned.[5] But the extent to which the Justices could afford to take opposition to the government lightly is well demonstrated in the case of Thomas Gilbert, minister of Cheadle. In October 1650 he preached that 'the Scots doe well to stand to their Covenant, and that it was well seene the effect of the Engagmt, and that the invadinge of the kingdome of Scotland nowe was worser than the

---

[1] Chester City R.O., CR63/1, Earwaker Transcripts, Box 30, unfoliated.
[2] *C.C.A.M.*, p.103.
[3] Underdown, op. cit., pp.148–9; A. Woolrych, 'Penruddock's Rising', *H.A.P.* G 29, 1955, p.17.
[4] C.R.O., Q.S.F. 1654, no.2, f. 88.
[5] Q.S.F. 1650, no.4, f. 55.

takeinge of the Engagement'. On another occasion he said that 'if Cromwell loose the day all that have taken the Engagmt wilbee proceeded against as traytors and rebells'.[1] Yet he was released by the Justices once he had fulfilled the one requirement made of him—he was to take the Engagement![2] Even Robert Duckenfield, usually a hard-liner in such matters, called for leniency, since he considered Gilbert's inflammatory speeches unlikely to breed unrest.[3]

The lack of government vigilance towards Cheshire in 1659 is therefore not particularly surprising, and helps to explain why there alone a rebellion did get properly off the ground. But it does not explain why the whole moderate establishment suddenly burst out in open defiance of the government after a decade of almost total quiescence.

None the less a closer examination shows that a certain malaise had afflicted the leading gentry who had supported Parliament during the Civil War. At first sight not much appears to have altered. The commissions issued by successive governments in the 1650s continued to include the names of those families who had served during the period 1643–9, though supplemented as the decade progressed by increasing numbers of militia officers, frequently of minor gentry or yeoman birth. Thus it was literally true that, as Mr. Pinckney points out,[4] appointments to committees in Cheshire show far more continuity than those for, say, Kent. But his assumption that this meant that the same men were active throughout the period is misleading, for many of the leading families named in these commissions refused to serve.

In fact there were thirty-one substantial gentlemen still alive in 1659 who had served Parliament between 1643 and 1649 as Justices or as deputy-lieutenants or on committees serving the whole county.[5] Twenty-four of these were named

[1] Q.S.F. 1650, no.3, ff. 73–4.
[2] Q.S.F. 1650, no.4, f. 64.
[3] Q.S.F. 1650, no.3, ff. 73–4.
[4] P.J. Pinckney, 'The Cheshire Election of 1656', *B.J.Ry.L.* 49(1967), 387–8.
[5] This list is based on active commissioners whose names appear in the records of the Committee for Taking the Accounts of the Kingdom (particularly P.R.O., SP 28, vols. 224 and 225), in the records of the Committee for Compounding with Delinquents, and in the Quarter Sessions Records in the Cheshire Record Office, and additional lists in Firth and Rait, op. cit., *passim.*

in the Commission of the Peace issued in March 1649[1] (four of the others had already appeared as defectors to the Stuarts). But only fourteen of these were ever active as Justices during the Interregnum,[2] and only nine of them were still working in the commission in 1659; two of the nine had been inactive for part of the Protectorate period.[3]

The same happened on other committees. As late as 1655 Thomas Mainwaring attended four meetings of the Committee for Ejecting Scandalous Ministers and there met eight other gentlemen out of the thirty-one. In 1658, however, only Sir William Brereton and Thomas Croxton represented the old group at the three meetings of the same committee attended by Mainwaring. The others were all low-born militia officers.[4]

It seems clear that this non-participation was in most cases either the outcome of horror at the execution of the King or a rejection of the continued political influence and power of the army, but for two men the Protectorate proved too conservative. These were Robert Duckenfield and John Legh, Brereton's closest associates during the war. Duckenfield put their case for them when he rejected Cromwell's invitation to raise a troop of horse during the emergency of March 1655; he did so partly because he believed the county could not support the burden of maintaining such a force, partly because 'my endeavours in this formerly, though verry successfull, have beene taken in ill part', but mostly because

I desire to imitate Caleb and Josua in the wildernes, as neare as may be, and not to seeke a confederacy with those, who limitt God to their passions, and against whom God hath an evident controversy etc. I believe firmly, that the roote and tree of piety is alive in your lordship, though the leaves theirof, through abundance of temptations and flatteries, seeme to mee to be withered much of late.[5]

[1] Chester City R.O. CR63/2/696, Arderne MSS, p.61.
[2] Activity is defined in terms of attendance at at least one Quarter Sessions per annum, or of signing at least one document bound into the Sessions Files.
[3] The seven fully active were: John Bradshaw, his brother Henry of Marple, Thomas Brereton of Ashley, Jonathan Bruen of Stableford, Thomas Croxton of Ravenscroft, Thomas Mainwaring of Baddiley, and Thomas Stanley of Alderley. The two who were mostly active were Edward Hyde of Norbury and Henry Birkenhead of Backford.
[4] J.Ry.L. Mainwaring MS., Book 20a, *passim*.
[5] (Ed.) T. Birch, *Thurloe State Papers*, 7 vols., London, 1742, vol. 3, p.294.

Very few of the remaining gentlemen were old or (as far as we know) unwell or absent from Cheshire during the Commonwealth (ten of them were active Justices after the Restoration), and their absence from the administrative records of the 1650s must be the result of personal, moral, or political renunciation of the regime. To some extent, their inactivity produced little real change: there were nine Justices carrying on the administration who came from solid, traditional gentry stock. It is true that only Brereton of Ashley, Mainwaring of Baddiley, and Stanley of Alderley were from families represented on the pre-war Bench, but all the others were of ancient county descent, if of moderate estates. Joined with these nine, however, were men who had risen from lesser social positions as a result of the war: Gilbert Gerard and George Manley both began public life as head constables but rose through successful military careers to be Justices; others came to the Bench from successful careers as sequestrators. But it was easy enough for most of the gentry to rest contented while the Bench was dominated by the remnant of their respresentatives (Thomas Mainwaring, Thomas Croxton, and Henry Bradshaw were easily the busiest in terms of the number of their signatures contained in the Files).[1]

In 1659, however, this position was threatened. In May 1659 Thomas Hutchins,[2] who had been one of Thurloe's agents in Cheshire, wrote to 'a friend' (unnamed) that as requested he was sending up lists of suitable Justices. Hutchins was obviously writing from an extreme Sectarian position, but the presence of this document among the State Papers suggests that it was intended for someone within the Rump or the army. He gives four lists of gentlemen, one of those 'who have such estates that they are fit for the employment', a second of 'moderate men, free from

[1] Here is a list of the number of documents signed by the ten most active Justices 1646—59: 1. Thomas Mainwaring and Henry Bradshaw (542 each), 3. Thomas Croxton (473), 4. Thomas Stanley (377), 5. Thomas Brereton (354), 6 Jonathan Bruen (349), 7. Thomas Marbury (191), 8. Sir George Booth, d.1652 (159), 9. Edward Hyde (144), 10. Peter Brooke (119).
[2] P.R.O., SP 18, vol. 203, f. 21.

persecuting spirit', a third of 'as cursed persecutors as are in the nation and are in commission', and the fourth of men 'who are in commission and have persecuted friends' but whom he considered less blameworthy. Of the nine gentlemen Justices, four were placed in category three and three in category four. Another, John Bradshaw, is not mentioned in any list, probably because his age and illness made him an infrequent visitor to Cheshire by 1659. Only Henry Birkenhead was placed on one of the first two lists, that is, he alone of all the old county families was to remain on the Bench if these recommendations were accepted. There is no evidence that the existence of Hutchins's list was known in Cheshire or that there was any serious intention to implement these or similar changes. But if rumours of them had leaked out, it must have had a violent effect on many of the gentry who had been happy to show negative disapproval of the regime while men who would broadly follow the same policies in and uphold the traditions of the local administration dominated the Bench. But a Bench headed by men like Gilbert Gerard, George Manley, and Thomas Tanat and supported by obscure militia and army officers,[1] would surely have inclined them towards a more positive course of action.

In May 1651 the Justices of the Peace and Grand Juries of Cheshire petitioned Parliament, asking for recruiter elections and a settled office for the Probate of Wills. But significantly they also wrote that

your petitioners do from their hearts abhor and detest all designs tending to create New Troubles; and do bless God for the happy discovery of them and especially of that lately hatched in these Northern parts; and do make it their earnest Request to your Honours, that all those in these parts who may be proved to have had any hand in such ill Designs whether they be old or new malignants may be brought to condigne punishment.[2]

[1] At least one of those suggested by Hutchins, Edward Alcocke, had been a tenant-at-will before the Civil Wars; he rose slowly to be a captain in Henry Bradshaw's regiment in the Worcester campaign. Several of the others appear to have had somewhat similar careers. The Bench would have been swamped by military personnel under this scheme.

[2] *The Humble Representation and Petition of the Justices and the Grand Jury ... for the County Palatine of Chester, 16th May 1651*, Pamphlet in Chester City Library.

This explicit disassociation of themselves from the plots of Booth and Werden reveals that the preoccupations of the gentry were then, as indeed in 1640 or 1642, above all with the maintenance of stability and established order, and they continued to follow this line through to 1659 and 1660. Whatever their dislike of the religious policy of the Protectorate, for example, they were prepared, on balance, to accept a government which did not challenge the roots of their local power. But one source of ever-increasing disquiet for them was the continued maintenance of a large military establishment. They resented the continued high level of taxation and were horrified that the breeding ground of extreme radicalism should continue undiminished, particularly since they thought its existence no longer necessary. In 1651 they were still afraid of the Royalist bogey of further turmoil throughout the county. But as the 1650s progressed, social life in the county stabilized and the former Royalist and Parliamentarian gentry once more came to share a common social life. The network of blood and marriage ties overcame the animosities created by the war. Just as many leading gentlemen had sought to blunt the zeal of hundredal sequestration committees in the later 1640s, so they fought to protect the lands and fortunes of their cousins and friends against the rigours of Major-General Worsley in the administration of the decimation tax in 1656. As Worsley told Thurloe

I have one thinge to acquaint you with, and that is concerninge the many refferences, that is sent to us by his highnese in behalfe of those that are desimated. I find much redinese amongst the gentlemen of this county to answer the desires of the malignants upon those accounts; soe that if you give much countenance to such certificate as comes from us it will endanger the wholl business [1]

Even Sir William Brereton was prepared to write eloquently on behalf of Edward Warren, certifying this former Royalist's complete reconciliation to Parliament and asking for his release from the Decimation.[2]

---

[1] *Thurloe State Papers*, vol. 5, p.9 (10 May 1656).
[2] Chester City R.O., CR63/2/702, Brereton MS. B 32

But this does not demonstrate the extent of the reconciliation. Thomas Mainwaring's diary reveals that he was socially far closer to former Royalists like Lord Cholmondely and Sir Peter Leycester than to most of his fellow Justices. One example of the easy intercourse of old enemies is provided by looking at guest lists for Mainwaring's dinner parties. Thus in 1658 he entertained round his table Sir William Brereton, conqueror of Chester and opponent of the Protectorate, Lady Gamull, widow of one of the city's stoutest Royalist defenders, and Richard Bradshaw, Cromwell's agent in Hamburg.[1] On other occasions the Royalist Sir Thomas Smith would be playing bowls with the Parliamentarian Sir Thomas Wilbraham while others of each party stood by and chatted.[2] Thomas Mainwaring himself, of course, was one of those who continued to co-operate with successive governments, yet he did not find this incompatible with sharing a common life with Royalists. They were not even completely left out of administration: cases that would normally have been referred to the monthly meetings were sometimes referred to former Royalist Justices for settlement.[3] Of their part in the elections to Interregnum Parliaments I shall also have something to say below.

One important effect of this restoration of normal social relations was that it destroyed the credibility of Cromwell's claim that a permanent army was necessary to keep the Royalists in subjection. The gentry's own way of life told them that this was just not true. They knew that, except for a handful of conspirators, the Royalists had no intention of rebelling, and this would have made them intolerant of the expense of the army, even if they had not had more compelling reasons for fearing its existence. But experience had taught them that the army, even the small garrison at Chester, was itself the greatest threat to the maintenance of order.

[1] J.Ry.L. Mainwaring MS., Book 20a, p.344.
[2] Ibid., p.76.
[3] e.g. to Lord Brereton, C.R.O., Q.S.F. 1656, no.1, f. 128, and to 'the court of Lord Kilmorrey', Q.S.F. 1656, no.4, f. 102.

As far as the gentlemen themselves were concerned, the horrors of the dungeon in Chester, in which fifteen of them had been placed by the army in July 1647, would be no fading memory, particularly since the behaviour of the troops in the subsequent years left little room to doubt that such an outburst could easily be repeated. Both in the Quarter Sessions Files and in the letter book of Henry Bradshaw, there are examples of troops threatening to take events into their own hands to get their pay and freequarter. Thus Henry Bradshaw wrote to the mayor of Macclesfield in November 1650: 'send out yor warrants wth all expedicon. If you be herein negligent, expect that the souldiers who complaine they are much in arreare will visitt you for itt'.[1]

The following year, the Council of State was anxiously trying to persuade the militia commissioners to act cautiously to enforce the disbandment of Captain Griffith's troopers, who had refused to obey former orders to do so, and they went on to ask the commissioners to examine 'the oppression acted upon the country by this troop, and to give satisfaction to be made by the troops, of such of the country as have suffered from them'.[2]

Perhaps most serious of all was the direct interference by the troops in the mayoralty election in Chester in 1650 when 'some companyes [were] drawne to St. Werburgh's church yard to oppose the choyse of this election. . .', and despite the presence of the Governor of Chester some 'drawe to circumround the hall and lane endes & stayres wth light, maches, ther muskets loded in affront & threat to the civill government & ancient privileges of the city in choyse of their maior'.[3]

The fact that these troops appeared to have been acting on orders from the Council of State would probably only have deepened the gloom of the gentry and city leaders. And there is evidence throughout the 1650s that the continuing

[1] Bodl. Lib. Top. Cheshire e 3, f. 9.

[2] *C.S.P.D.* 1651, p.500.

[3] B.M. Harleian MS. 2125, f. 73. The army's explanation of its conduct which confirms the citizens' version is in *Mercurius Politicus* no.19, 10−17 Oct. 1650, pp.318−19.

presence of troops only served to revive anxiety. When the militia committee met in March 1655 to raise fresh troops to meet the threat posed by Penruddock's Rising, Peter Brooke 'very much obstucted it, as farre as in him laye, by declareinge against raisinge any horse or foote at all; and affirminge his thoughts, that his highnesse had some other designe therein then the late insurrections. . .'[1]

In 1657 John Hulme of Broadstone received a severe rebuke from Henry Bradshaw when he petitioned Henry's brother John complaining about the tyranny and plunder of a party of thirty horse.[2] Such was the failure of communication between the city of Chester and the garrison that in 1654 the mayor and aldermen felt impelled to write to Lambert explaining their reasons for repairing two drawbridges, lest 'their actions should be misinterpreted to him by the soldiers in the city'.[3] The political activism of the officers is also demonstrated in the attitudes of Major-General Worsley, whose suspicions of the motives of the civilian leaders contrasted with his opinion of the officers: 'I find in them a spirret extraordinarily bent to the worke, and I plainly discerne the finger of God goeinge along with it, which is indeed noe smale encouragement unto mee'.[4]

One further source of concern to the gentlemen was the religious radicalism of the army: even the moderate preacher Henry Newcome felt the force of their evangelism and was confused by it.[5] This in turn contributed to a growing sense of pessimism with which the Cheshire gentry viewed most religious developments in the 1650s.

Religious opinions were infinitely shaded, and tended to cut across political groupings. None the less four basic groups seem to have existed and to have held distinguishable positions. In full consciousness of the definitional problems

---

[1] *Thurloe State Papers*, vol. 3, p.304.
[2] Bodl. Lib. Top. Cheshire e 3, f. 21.
[3] Chester City R.O., ML/3/377.
[4] *Thurloe State Papers*, vol. 4, p.149. For his attitude to civilians, ibid., vol. 4, p.277 (letter from Worsley wrongly attributed to Whalley).
[5] Newcome's autobiography is in the *Chetham Society*, O. S. vol. 26, pp.26–7.

involved, I have labelled them the Rigid Presbyterians, the moderate Presbyterians, the Erastians, and the Congregational Independents.

Cheshire was one of the few counties that, in the years following the Civil Wars, were reasonably successful in establishing a Presbyterian classical system, and, as a legacy of this movement, Presbyterians remained numerically dominant until the Restoration. But as time went on, there appeared ever-widening divisions within the movement, though the tension had been present from the beginning. On the one hand there were the strict Presbyterians who called for a settlement on the Scottish model, with no toleration but a general acceptance of the proposals of the 'radicals' in the county; on the other there was a moderate party which opposed the 'radical' politicians but favoured an ecclesiastical *rapprochement* with the Independents. The first group's opinions were summarized in a petition of 1646, where they called for a hierarchical Presbyterian organization covering the whole county, self-governing at a national level; for the suppression of all 'separate congregations'; for harsher treatment of the defeated Royalists; for the exclusion from the communion table of those whose religious or political offences had not been publicly acknowledged; and for fair dealing with 'our brethren of Scotland whose honnor it was to begin the worke'. Unfortunately this petition has only survived in an eighteenth-century transcript. At the foot the editor thought fit to write that Henry Bradshaw's name headed the list of subscribers but that otherwise 'the names at the foot of this petition are many of them uninteresting & those of better estates perhaps as well supprest'.[1]

The contents of the petition, and Henry Bradshaw's associations with it, show clearly that the radical political movement in Cheshire was divided on religious lines. While Duckenfield, Birkenhead, and others whose political programme resembled Bradshaw's were seeking to extend Independency, he was endeavouring to destroy the gathered congregations, such as Samuel Eaton's at Duckenfield.

[1] The petition with its silly gloss are in J.Ry.L. English MS. 745, ff. 25—7.

More fragmentary evidence from other sources fits this general pattern. Adam Martindale singled out a group of ministers as 'very zealous (usually called Rigid) presbyterians that were for the setting up of the governance of the church of Scotland amongst us . . . and the utter exterpation of Independencie, root and branch'.[1] More important, it was these Rigid Presbyterians who most strongly advocated the lawfulness of taking the Engagement. Martindale, in common with many of the moderates, was conscience-stricken by this issue and disputed it with 'three great Knockers' of the Rigid brethren at a public meeting held at Warrington.[2] Henry Bradshaw was one of the few Justices to make a determined effort to bring people in to take the Engagement.[3]

In May 1652 the correspondent of a London newspaper bitterly regretted the failure of the ministers in Cheshire to sign the Engagement, praised the army there for its religious work and called for a government settled in the church and for deliverance from popery, prelacy, Scottish presbytery, and the sects.[4] The attack on non-Engagers, the implied intolerance and the call for an established church all suggest that the writer was a Rigid Presbyterian. But it is odd that he called for a deliverance from 'Scottifyed Presbyterians', since earlier this had been a description of the Rigid Presbyterians themselves; however it is possible that there had been a change in terminology. In 1646 the central issue had been one of church government in which the Rigid party had looked to Scotland for a model; by 1652 the connotation had been changed by the political conflict between England and Scotland, the role of the Scots army in 1648—51, and the use made by the moderates of the Covenant as a ground for refusing to take the Engagement.

The Congregational Independents remained a minority throughout the 1640s and 1650s, but were active and vociferous. A letter written by a Lancashire Presbyterian in

[1] Adam Martindale's autobiography is in *Chetham Society*, O.S. vol. 4, p.63.
[2] Ibid., pp.92—4.
[3] Bodl. Lib. Top Cheshire e 3, f. 6.
[4] B.M. Thomason Tracts E 794 (33), *Several Proceedings*, no.136, p.2123.

October 1646 drew attention to a petition drawn up by the 'Sectaries' in Cheshire and forwarded to Parliament: the petition had been drawn up by members of Samuel Eaton's congregation at Duckenfield and circulated secretly around the county. The letter also stated that Independent strength was still very modest, three churches established, three more planned; but there was talk of links with the leading gentry, Master Taylor and Eaton are wonderfully active both in Cheshire and Lancashire. They much improve [. . .] , who is become a great zealot for them, and hath threatened some of the Godly ministers that live near to him to make their places too hot for them for denying their pulpits to Mr Eaton ... [. . .] hath so far encouraged them, discouraged and borne down the orthodox and well affected that they could never to this day get anything done against them.[1]

The two unnamed persons were clearly influential figures; in the context the second one sounds likely to be Sir William Brereton.

The evangelism which characterizes their activity in this letter is more clearly seen in the struggles between the parochial clergy and new autonomous chapelries set up in the following years in such parishes as Bowdon[2] and Rostherne.[3] Their close links with the political radicals is seen in Brereton's wartime patronage of them,[4] the central role of the chapel at Duckenfield set up by Colonel Robert Duckenfield, by the eldership there of William Barret[5] (the hard-line sequestrator who was also a lay preacher), and by their opposition to tithes.[6]

The majority of the Cheshire clergy belonged to neither of these groups: in religious and political terms they were moderates. All the surviving records show that they were appalled at the execution of the King, deeply troubled at having to take the Engagement, scornful of the pretensions of

[1] Edwards, *Gangraena*, p.167. This transcription is from the copy in W. Urwick (ed.) *Historical Sketches of Nonconformity in Cheshire*, Manchester, 1864, pp.xxiv—xxv.
[2] Ibid., pp.373, 383.
[3] Martindale, pp.105—7.
[4] See above. pp.164—5.
[5] For Barret, see Newcome, vol. 1, pp.35—6.
[6] See below, p.274

the army.[1] And, unlike the Rigid Presbyterians, they were also uncertain and ambivalent in their attitude towards the Independents. Thus Martindale spoke of the years 1646–8 as a time when

the Presbyteriall and Congregationall governments were like Jacob and Esau strugling in the womb... I was just come out of Cheshire where Mr Eaton and Taylour (but especially the former) were had in greate esteem, and I inclined to the same opinion concerning their worth, ... yet not so, but that I had the like esteeme of those three worthy men before mentioned of the opposite partie, and would take the boldnesse to tell them freely what I disliked in their churchway. Faine I would have kept communion with all these good and learned men, but it would not be. To be familiar with them of one partie was to render me suspected to the other. [2]

Newcome was equally uncertain.[3] Furthermore it is clear that many others shared their position. Thus in 1651 Ralph Stringer was 'wavering, at least willing at this time to be gracious to that party',[4] Mr. Angier was described as 'a moderate Presbyterian and member of the Manchester classis, but he entertained very kindly feelings towards the Congregationalists'[5] and 'declared himselfe before the ministers of the classis then just setting up so perfect a Latitudinarian that the Episcopall, Presbyterians and Independents might all preache accordinge to their owne judgements yet each by Divine right'. For adopting this position, he was roundly condemned by Peter Harrison, Rigid Presbyterian minister at Cheadle.[6]

Even the 'Attestation to the Testimony of our Reverend Brethren of the Province of London to the Truth of Jesus Christ and to our Solemn League and Covenant' was remarkably tolerant in tone. This was a petition sent up to London with the signatures of two-thirds of the Cheshire clergy in July 1648, calling for the establishment of a national church, yet the section on the Independents is strikingly moderate. It was headed 'divers of the independent way, learned godly

---

[1] e.g. Newcome, vol. 1, p.44; Martindale, pp.89, 110.
[2] Martindale, pp.61–4.
[3] Newcome, vol.1, pp.26–7, 35–7.
[4] Ibid., p.36.
[5] Urwick, op. cit., p.316.
[6] Martindale, pp.62–3.

and charitable to their godly brethren, though Presbyterians. Yet Independency an error, and, as some enlarge the tenet, the nurse if not the mother of many dangerous deviations both from truth and piety'.[1]

On the other hand they were upset by some of the tendencies of the Congregational churches. The attempt to establish independent chapelries in some of the larger parishes, together with the demands of some of the ministers to visit their pulpits, caused some friction, what Martindale called 'the irregularity of such men's thrusting their sickle into my harvest'.[2] Martindale also asserted that the departure of the early Independent leaders led to their replacement by 'many other neighbour ministers, some of them bitter, presumptuous fellowes, to say nothing of the scandalous breaches that shortly afterwards fell amongst them'. He also linked them directly with the villainies practised by the 'Cromwellian army [which] was become rampant' against King and Parliament.[3] Amongst the 'bitter, presumptuous fellows' it was the employment of 'gifted brethren not intending the ministry' which caused both Martindale and Newcome most annoyance. They resented the employment of lay preachers. In fact their growing distrust of the Independents was a compound of their political bias and of their concern with their professional pride and status in preserving the integrity of their parochial responsibility and their peculiar rights to use the pulpit for the moral and spiritual regeneration of their flocks.

None the less, when these moderates formed themselves into a voluntary association in October 1653, the influence of the Congregationalists on the form of their society became clear. Thus Martindale stressed with approval that 'here...we pretended not to any power to convent any before us, or suppresse any minister because dwelling in such a place, within such a verge, and differing from us in practise'.[4] Even more striking as a development away from the Scottish system towards the ideas on church government put forward

---

[1] Urwick, op. cit., p.xxv–xxvi.        [2] Martindale, p.107.
[3] Martindale, p.74.                     [4] Ibid., p.112.

by the Congregationalists was the democratic principle in the affairs of individual churches. Both Martindale and Newcome wrote about the meetings of the whole parish to determine important matters, particularly the choice of a new minister.[1] Thus, when Newcome was about to leave Gawsworth for Manchester in 1657, he was approached by two men seeking his aid in advancing friends of theirs, one offering a £30 bribe, the other a sharp tongue. In fact, however, both here and elsewhere, the retiring minister, the voluntary association, and the gentleman patron were bypassed and the decision reached by a free vote of the whole parish.[2] When a patron actually tried to assert his rights, as John Booth did in 1658, he was liable to be undermined by parish opposition.[3]

The appointment of elders and the powers of excommunication and exclusion of the unworthy from the communion show that the association was essentially Presbyterian.[4] But it is clearly a form of Presbyterianism that took cognizance of existing conditions and the ideas of the Independents. It was not until 1659, in fact, that a genuine *rapprochement* with the Independents was planned (in the light of the growing menace of the Quakers and other extreme radical groups which both deplored). A scheme for union was well advanced when Booth's rising put an end to it.[5] The pattern has much in common with general tendencies in Presbyterianism studied by Professor Abernathy and analysed with great clarity by Baxter, who said that the

institution of Presbytery was such a stranger to England that most of those called Presbyterians were opposed to the *ius divinum* of Lay Elders and for the moderate Primitive Episcopacy and for a narrow Congregational or parochial extent of ordinary churches, and for an accommodation of all Parties in order to accord.[6]

[1] This is an interesting comparison with the developments in local government referred to above, chapter 6, pp.240–1.
[2] Newcome, vol. 1, pp.68–9.
[3] Ibid., pp.91–2.
[4] e.g. Newcome, vol. 1, pp.46, 95; Martindale, pp.112–14.
[5] Martindale, pp.128–31, Newcome, vol. 1, p.108.
[6] Quoted in G.R. Abernathy, 'The English Presbyterians and the Stuart Restoration 1648–63', *Transactions of the American Philosophical Society*, 55, no.2(1965), 2.

In general, the patterns of ecclesiastical organization propounded by all these groups were found uncongenial by the majority of the moderate gentry with whom we have been concerned. Several gentry leaders received such moderate Presbyterian leaders as Samuel Cole, Nathaniel Lancaster, and Edward Burghall regularly at their dinner tables (Thomas Mainwaring is the clearest example of this),[1] while John Arderne of Harden received regular visits both from moderate Presbyterian John Angier and from Samuel Eaton.[2] But we have no evidence positively demonstrating the attitude of those Parliamentarians who opted out of the administration in the 1650s. However, there are signs that their relations with the moderate Presbyterians were fairly remote. Thus Newcome recorded in August 1657 that 'I went to Dunham and preached there the next day . . . and at this time had the first knowledge of and acquaintance with that honourable person Sir George Booth'.[3] Furthermore those clergymen who were supported by Booth and the deputy lieutenants either financially or against the sequestrators were rarely mentioned either by Newcome or Martindale.[4]

Perhaps we ought to look back to the 1630s to study the background to their convictions. Although old Sir George Booth was later called 'of absolute power with the Presbyterians',[5] he was probably not converted until a late stage. In 1638—9 he negotiated a marriage settlement between his grandson and a daughter of the Bishop of Coventry and Lichfield, a match which only fell through because of overtures from the wealthier and better-connected Earl of Lincoln on behalf of his daughter.[6] More substantial was the attitude struck up by the moderates, including Booth, in the petitions of 1640—3, particularly the Attestation.[7] It is clear that Booth and his friends looked for

---

[1] J.Ry.L. Mainwaring MS., Book 20a, *passim.*
[2] Urwick, op. cit., pp.314—15.
[3] Newcome, vol. 1, p.74.
[4] e.g. Randle Addams, Sabboth Clarke, George Byrom, George Snell, Samuel Torshell. The exceptions are Nathaniel Lancaster and John Ley.
[5] Quoted in R.N. Dore, 'The Cheshire Rising of 1659', *T.L.C.A.S.* 69(1959), 45.
[6] J.Ry.L. Tatton of Wythenshawe MSS., items 251—6.
[7] See above, pp.46—54.

a better-educated clergy and an emphasis on godly preaching; their correspondence shows a Calvinist acceptance of divine election. They were good church Puritans. But there is no evidence that before 1643 they sought the overthrow of episcopacy. Their development was probably the same as that of one of the ministers associated with them, Samuel Torshell of Bunbury, who prefaced a sermon in 1643 with the hope that

our great and high court ... [may] remove every burthen which the tyranny of abused episcopacie had layd upon us. I call their courses tyranny and their impositions burthens as having had through the happinesse of these late times, better meanes and opportunity to discerne and weigh them ... I confesse my thoughts were heretofore more favorable, as walking according to those principles I had received in my education. The truth is, though I never thought Episcopacie to be Divine Right, as it was proudly challenged yet I looked upon it as the most antient and prudentiall way of government, and so obeyed it and spoke well of it, though not its mad and furious ways.[1]

All the evidence supports the conjecture that men like Booth would seek reform in the church by strengthening procedures for dealing with godless ministers or men and by adapting liturgy and ceremonial to remove traces of popery and to enhance the importance of the homily and the Word. The self-destructive behaviour of the bishops in 1640–2 forced them to the conclusion that episcopacy had to be severely limited or abolished and some other form of a national church substituted. But at no time did they propound any change in the nature of patronage or finance of the church. Indeed, if their religious beliefs had paralleled their political ones, one of their chief grievances would have been that Bishop Bridgeman had tried to intervene in such sensitive areas as the rights of the gentlemen in the appointment and maintenance of the clergy. Thus they would have been upset by the behaviour of all the groups we have mentioned above, but this general dismay at the failure of post-war governments to produce the sort of religious settlement which they desired can also be demonstrated in relation to some specific problems.

[1] Samuel Torshell, *The Hypocrite Discoverd and Cured,* London, November 1643, Epistle Dedicatorie. From the copy in Chester City Library.

The first of these was the question of patronage. We have already seen that there was a tendency towards the election of ministers by the whole parish. For example in 1648 Newcome was presented to Gawsworth directly at the wishes of the parish.[1] Furthermore, when he left, his successor was appointed by the parish, apparently in the face of opposition from the old patron, since 'I had Colonel Mainwareing to deal with, whose consent I could not in ingenuity act without'.[2] Martindale moved to Rostherne at the call of the people there, and had to fight a long battle against the patron. Peter Venables of Kinderton, before being accepted.[3] Other parishes that tried to put in men of their own choice in defiance of the patron included Bebbington (July 1647),[4] Congleton (October 1646),[5] and Ince (February 1658).[6] Although we have evidence that elsewhere the ordinary rights of patronage were observed,[7] in a majority of cases patronage was taken out of the hands of the local gentry.

Feeling was probably particularly exacerbated during the Protectorate by Cromwell's increasing tendency to nominate ministers directly from London. Immediately after the Civil Wars, some of the deputy lieutenants were appointed trustees with power to safeguard the collection of tithes, to supervise sugmentations and to make presentations to livings where the patron was under sequestration.[8] But Cromwell nominated the ministers to at least ten livings in the 1650s, on at least one occasion in response to a petition from the parish.[9]

A feature which had equally worrying implications for the gentry was the growth of autonomous chapelries with the

[1] Urwick, op. cit., p.206.
[2] Newcome, vol. 1, p.76.
[3] Martindale, pp.77—9, 83—4.
[4] W.A. Shaw (ed.) 'Plundered Ministers Accounts', *Lancashire and Cheshire Record Society*, 28(1893), 183 (in two parts, vols. 28 and 34).
[5] Ibid., vol. 28, p.168.
[6] Ibid., vol. 34, p.218.
[7] For several examples between 1654 and 1659, see ibid., vol. 34, pp.39, 42, 45, 95, 269, 273.
[8] e.g. ibid., vol. 28, pp.146—7, 149, 165, 220.
[9] Ibid., vol. 34, pp.42—3, 49. 52, 53, 57, 89, 116, 136, 233, 243—4.

dangerous tendency of forming themselves into independent parishes, for this struck at the gentlemen's profits from tithes. One of the interesting features of the Interregnum church was the widespread break-up of the larger parishes: sometimes to form entirely new ones, sometimes to enlarge an old small one at the expense of an unmanageably large one. This was essentially a practical matter; in 1656 a scheme was devised to ensure that every man had a thorough grounding in the scriptures, what Martindale called 'the worke of personall catechism'. But as he went on to point out, 'the minister of Great Budworth and I had such vast parishes tó go through, that multitudes of the people would be dead in all probability ere we could goe once over them'.[1]

On a simpler level, the new churches put an end to the inconveniences which had required some families to walk over five miles to church. Where these chapels were set up and the ministers maintained by voluntary subscription, there were few problems. But when attempts were made to turn them into parishes and surrounding areas allocated for the maintenance of ministers through the tithes, a great deal of friction inevitably followed. Thus the creation of a parish at Disley in 1646 led to a reduction of the tithes of Stockport parish amounting to £10 per annum.[2] A similar proposal was made when Harthill chapel was made into a parish by taking five townships from Malpas parish; the incensed patron objected strongly and a high-powered committee of Justices and militia officers was appointed to 'indeavour an accommodation of all differences ... and to consider what maintenance shall be allowed by the said chappelry soe divided out of the viccarage'.[3] Eventually a compromise was struck by which first fruits were to be equitably divided, though the agreement only covered the present incumbents.[4]

Of the ten projected new parishes, seven were planned in 1656 and it is tempting to see the initiative of Major-General

---

1 Martindale, p.122.
2 Plundered Ministers Accounts, vol. 28, p.164.
3 Ibid., vol. 34, pp.137—8.
4 Ibid., vol. 34, pp.155—7.

Worsley behind these schemes; but there is no evidence to support this conjecture.

There are few signs of an attack on tithes themselves, though the complicated history of augmentations[1] afforded myriad opportunities for evasion. But there is one exchange of letters that reveals that it was a touchy subject. Early in 1652 Robert Duckenfield wrote to old Sir George Booth suggesting that Booth should desist from enforcing the payment of tithes for the present, for 'it is better to connive att the endevers of hott spirits sometimes then to reduce things to extremitie'. Booth replied with an indignation worthy of the embattled privileged of any age: 'I entreate yow give me leave to answeare wth as much assurance that my interest in them is as farr above any reason of my friends iealousie as the malice and envie of such as repine att it is belowe my consideracon'.[2]

As a result of all these things, the gentry must have been very disillusioned with the ecclesiastical policies of successive Interregnum governments. To men like Sir George Booth, the financial losses involved in these developments would not have been very serious. But they could be put into a perspective of general decline in their authority and status as county gentry. Patronage and profit had lain in the hands of the same group of men who had controlled the Commission of the Peace in the 1630s.[3] It was one of the symbols of their moral leadership, and it was obscured if not destroyed in the years after 1646.

Furthermore, as the Interregnum wore on, power seemed to pass increasingly from the county to the central government. The Protectorate Committees for Ejecting Scandalous Ministers gave some powers to the county (though, as we have seen, control of the committee soon fell into the hands

[1] Unfortunately there is not space here to embark on this fascinating but subordinate topic.

[2] J.Ry.L. Tatton of Wythenshawe MSS., item 265.

[3] From the tables in Ormerod, op. cit., *passim*, the distribution of patronage in the 1630s was as follows: thirty-three with patrons who were J.P.s; twenty parishes controlled by Crown, bishop, or dean and chapter; twelve with non-Justice gentry patronage; one London company patronage; others uncertain.

of the militia officers). But powers of patronage, of augmentations of livings, and of the redrawing of parish boundaries all passed to committees in London. Dr. Shaw in his calendar of various sets of government papers found more business passing to and fro as the 1650s progressed.[1] This would not endear the Protectorate to men with a consistent record of treating with suspicion any attempt to interrupt the traditional flow of county affairs.

What made this administrative intervention so infuriating was the failure of successive governments to provide a proper legislative framework for religious peace: in particular, the failure of the Rump and Protectorate to prevent the spread of the Sects with their poisonous social and political ideas. What little evidence we possess suggests that the theological ideas of men like Samuel Eaton were not strikingly different from those of moderate Presbyterians, whatever their differences over ecclesiastical organization.[2] So that when Sectarians like the Arian Knowles or the Socinian Harrison were seen in the county, there was a concerted effort by the gentry and parochial clergy to silence them. Of all the Justices, only Gilbert Gerard and possibly Thomas Croxton were prepared to tolerate such men.[3] Their harsh dealing with Quakers,[4] and panic reaction to rumours of Leveller infiltration in 1652,[5] show their determination to stamp out prospective troublemakers.

In fact Cheshire was not unduly threatened by these 'dangerous' groups. But, as one leading gentleman put it, so long as 'every pragmatical illiterate person as the humour served him, stepp'd into the pulpit without any lawful calling thereunto or license of authority',[6] the government stood

---

[1] i.e. 'Plundered Ministers' Accounts', *Lancashire and Cheshire Record Society,* vols. 28 and 34.

[2] For Eaton's theological tenets, see *The Mystery of God Incarnate,* an attack on Arianism, 1650, or *The Quakers Refuted,* 1653. Both are in Chester City Library.

[3] See Newcome, vol. 1, pp.37—40, Bodl. Lib. Top. Cheshire e 3, f. 15.

[4] See F. Sanders, 'The Quakers in Cheshire during the Protectorate', *J.C.A.S.* N.S. 14(1908), particularly 77—82.

[5] *C.S.P.D.* 1654, pp.294—5, 318.

[6] Quoted in W. Urwick, op. cit., p.383.

condemned for its failure to solve one of the most potent problems which had led to the downfall of the monarchy, the cleansing of the church, and the moral regeneration of the people.

## II

The 1650s thus witnessed growing dissatisfaction and alarm amongst many of the gentry at the record of successive regimes. This was not simply concern over constitutional changes and developments, but a wider dismay at the continued influence and power of the army, and alarm at the failure of all attempts to reach a lasting or acceptable settlement of the ecclesiastical problems left over from the confusion of 1646–9. But memories of the Civil Wars and the conservative trends of Cromwell's economic and social policies were powerful restraining factors. Martindale caught the essence of their bemusement when he gave his reason for eventually taking the Engagement: 'They deserve to be try'd for fooles if they beleeved that the Royalists . . . or the Presbyterians which generally were more averse to it, would ever be cordiall friends, so as to suffer with or for them, or to helpe them up againe if once throwne downe . . .' [1]

But further episodes, notably the rule of the Major-Generals and the bitterly contested election campaigns of 1656 and 1658, brought the underlying tensions into clearer focus and added to the impetus of the movement towards greater social solidarity and unity amongst the old ruling families.

Each Major-General was allowed considerable scope within the terms of his instructions to concentrate on whichever of the allotted tasks he pleased. Thus Edward Whalley paid particular attention to social and economic problems (notably enclosure), while he and James Berry were notably less severe in exacting securities from former Royalists than Disbrowe or Worsley. But from almost every point of view, Cheshire, Lancashire, and Staffordshire were placed under

[1] Martindale, p.98.

the severest of all Major-Generals, Charles Worsley.[1] This Lancashire man, the son of a prosperous Manchester merchant who was still trying to establish himself in landed society, found it difficult to gain acceptance from the Cheshire gentry, partly because of his background, but mostly because of his unenviable reputation as a man who had spent the years after 1646 seeking a fortune as an informer against those who had concealed parts of their estates from the sequestrators:[2] he had even accused Sir William Brereton of illegally appropriating the profits from the stewardship of Macclesfield Forest.[3] His appointment, like that of so many other Major-Generals, seems to owe most to his close acquaintance with Cromwell, in whose regiment he had served in Scotland and by whom he was entrusted with the task of supervising the expulsion of the Rump.

He brought exceptional zeal and thoroughness to bear on his tasks, and it was widely reported that his death in 1656 at the age of thirty-four was the result of the ruthlessness with which he drove himself on.

Even before Worsley's arrival, Colonel Lilburne had rounded up a dozen or so leading Royalists whom he suspected of involvement in recent plots. They were kept under guard by Thomas Croxton in Chester Castle, and the intention was to keep them there until the decimation tax had been generally assessed, but 'some few by good friends & some expence procured their enlargement sooner and that by bond with two suretyes'. However, those thought to be particularly dangerous were sent up to London to be examined by the Protector's Council (these were John Booth, Peter Leycester, and George Warburton), but even they were released on sureties of £2,000 after interviews with Worsley. In general the arrests seem to have been speculative and based on little evidence; this seems particularly true of Lord

[1] See P.H. Hardacre, *The Royalists During the Puritan Revolution,* The Hague, 1956, pp.129–30.
[2] P.R.O., SP 23, vol. 149, f. 209.
[3] *C.C.A.M.*, pp.1354–5.

Cholmondeley 'who by reason of his infirmity was not able to remove from his owne house'.[1]

Within a fortnight of his arrival in the county, Worsley had summoned the greatest delinquents before him and questioned them, and had set Croxton the task, completed within ten days, of disarming all former Royalists.[2] He then set to work to assess and levy the decimation tax. Although he claimed that the Royalists submitted 'with readiness',[3] he proceeded on the assumption that they would attempt the same kinds of evasion in the assessment of their income that he had discovered them practising against the sequestrators and he therefore laid down detailed procedures for his agents. He told Thurloe: 'We have taken a course to come to a true account of there severall estates, by comparinge that they bring in with what survay wee have of ther estates in 1640; and if wee find that deficient wee intend to survay anew those estates that wee have a doubt of.[4]

Disillusioned with the results, he complained a few weeks later: 'Wee now find that many in these countryes that have been very active against the parliament, and were looked upon as men of good estates, will hardly be brought within the compasse; for one hundred pounds *per. ann.* is a good estate in these parts'.[5] Thus, he was still confident in December 1655 that there would be enough collected to supply the county troop 'and provide you a considerable some for other uses'.[6] but by April 1656 he had to report that the increased militia, for the pay of which the decimation tax had specifically been introduced, had had to be reduced by twenty men in each troop, in accordance with instructions from the Council. It is even possible that there was unrest amongst the troops, for at the same time Captain Griffiths was sent up to London in person by 'the gentlemen of the country about the souldiers arrears'.[7]

---

[1] These comments are based on a paper in the Leycester MSS. at Tabley House, from a transcript in Chester City R.O., CR63/1/146.

[2] *Thurloe State Papers*, vol. 4, pp.189, 248.

[3] Ibid., p.278.   [5] Ibid., p.248.

[4] Ibid., p.333.   [6] Ibid., p.300.   [7] Ibid., p.748.

We have already seen that the county was suspicious, even hostile, to the presence of armed forces, and that this feeling was manifested at the height of the crisis in 1655 by both Peter Brooke and Robert Duckenfield.[1] The links between the decimation and the militia thus probably increased the dislike of the tax by the moderate gentry. Worsley warned the Council against believing biased certificates sent up by several prominent figures supporting their Royalist neighbours, while Brereton himself was amongst those involved in this resistance to the Major-General's rigorous execution of the policy.[2] Even Thomas Mainwaring and Henry Birkenhead, active supporters of the Protectorate, are known to have 'writte to the Lord Protector on the behalfe of my cozen P. Leicester'.[3] Quite apart from their reluctance to see friends and relatives so treated, and to so undesirable an end, many would probably have agreed with Drake in the ensuing Parliament, when he attacked the decimation as a breach of the Act of Oblivion which 'is against the rule of common safety, it lays a dangerous precedent. It may fall out upon any party'.[4]

Worsley's administration is particularly striking for the severity of its dealings with minor delinquents. Opinions varied amongst the Major-Generals about the likely effects of widespread use of sureties. Goffe was at one end of the scale in his reluctance to act firmly in this direction. He told Thurloe that he was determined to

forbear pressing upon them the bonds mentioned in the additionall orders for the present; and the rather because I doe apprehend, it may be more seasonable after the work of the taxe is over. To put them upon all the hard termes at once it may be would not go down easily'.[5]

Worsley took the opposite view. Not only did he work at getting double sureties 'from all others that were formerly sequestered uppon the assessing of the Decimations, whether

[1] See above, pp.157,263.

[2] See above, p.260.

[3] J.Ry.L. Mainwaring MS. 20a, f. 205. In the week of Worsley's death, fifteen of his commissioners appealed to Cromwell on behalf of a former Royalist, Henry Harpur, *Thurloe State Papers*, vol. 5, p.22.

[4] Burton, *Parliamentary Diary*, vol. 1, p.314.

[5] *Thurloe State Papers*, vol. 4, p.208.

imprisoned or noe',[1] but he also set out to 'find nere 60 gentlemen in this county, many of them younger sonns, that were fit to be sent out of this commonewelth, which done would much tend to the securitie thereof and terrifie others . . .'[2] (a plan which was never put into practice). He was convinced that many leading gentlemen had been involved in a Royalist plot in 1655 and was infuriated by the legal restraints that hindered his investigations. As early as March 1655 Thurloe's agent John Griffiths, complained that

if any person in these parts were authorised to apprehend and examine suspected persons, you might suddenly have a better accompt; but at present I finde, that 30, 40 or 50 cavilleers have lately been very frequent at theire meetings, and given sufficient cause of offence, but no persons here being in power to apprehend them, in order to their further accompt . . .'[3]

Worsley was convinced that Griffiths was right, and after asking the Council to send down their examinations of Booth, Warburton, Leicester, and Werden, added 'I am afraid I shall find some more of that gang'.[4] He prohibited all public meetings and horse races, and boasted that no two or three Royalists could meet together without his hearing of it.[5] This would antagonize loyal racegoers like Thoms Mainwaring as much as anyone,[6] and in any case all the moderates must have been highly sceptical of the very idea of a widespread plot; although Werden and John Booth had made their miserable attempt to take Chester Castle and the evidence against Peter Leicester looks fairly strong, there is no evidence of a wider conspiracy. Certainly there is no sign of one in any of the papers of the exiled Court or in any of the diaries (Martindale, Newcome, Mainwaring) of local figures. Indeed Thomas Mainwaring was still busy dining with the Cholmondeleys and Leicesters at the supposed height of the conspiracy. There had been a large gathering of former

[1] Chester City R.O., CR63/1/146.
[2] *Thurloe State Papers*, vol. 4, p.534.
[3] Ibid., vol. 3, p.226.
[4] Ibid., vol. 4, p.322.
[5] Ibid., p.327.
[6] J.Ry.L. Mainwaring MS. Book 20a (e.g. p.161).

Royalists at Middlewich in early March 1655 which Mainwaring had also attended, but it was intended to settle a longstanding dispute between the two heiresses of the former Royalist commander, Sir Edward Fytton.[1] Perhaps this or a similar event was what prompted the suspicious mind of John Griffith—it might look conspiratorial to a mind conditioned to expect plots everywhere. To men like Mainwaring it was a sign of the restored strength of the social fabric.

The Major-Generals were ordered to send down to London lists of those Royalists from whom they had taken sureties. The returns for many counties, including Cheshire, have survived, and give clear testimony of Worsley's harshness. Mr. Hardacre has quoted the totals for seven counties, showing that whereas Major-Generals Berry and Whalley exacted sureties from fewer than twenty gentlemen in their counties, Worsley exacted them from over 1,000 individuals in Staffordshire—more than three times as many as the next most thorough Major-General.[2] The total for Cheshire was 472,[3] but this figure requires further comment. Since the records of the decimation tax do not appear to have survived, we do not know who was forced to pay it, but from the evidence of the sequestration records and other sources it appears highly unlikely that more than twenty of those who would have been liable to pay the tax were made to provide sureties. It is even possible that Worsley treated sureties as a method of control precisely over those who fell outside the tax net. Indeed only seventy-five of those providing sureties were styled as gentry at all, while over 40 per cent were styled as husbandmen and labourers. Such extensive precautions against the middle and lower social groups is unique to Worsley;[4] most could have caused no security problem as individuals. More puzzling is the geographical distribution of

---

[1] Ibid., pp.220–1.
[2] P.H. Hardacre, op. cit., pp.129–30. The second most numerous county was Gloucestershire with 322 (Major-General Disbrowe).
[3] B.M. Add. MS. 34013, ff. 2–55.
[4] The full figures are: 75 gentlemen, 114 yeomen, 174 husbandmen, 7 labourers. 78 craftsmen, 24 tradesmen.

names. Of the 453 who can be clearly allocated to a home parish, over half came from the hundreds of Broxton and Macclesfield; there were only nine from the hundred of Bucklow and eleven from Wirral.[1] There were also wide differences between parishes within each hundred.[2] Oddly, the areas of highest concentration had contained a predominance of Parliamentarian gentry during the Civil Wars, while in the hundreds of Wirral and Bucklow there were powerful knots of former Royalist gentry.

It is possible but unlikely that this represents an otherwise untraceable pattern of local resistance to the Protectorate amongst the tenant farmers. It might represent varying degrees of activity by the Major-General's commissioners in the different hundreds; but the concentration in particular parishes suggests that it was primarily the result of the zeal of individual constables. Certainly Worsley felt strongly that he could rely on some of the parochial officials only.[3]

Worsley was equally determined to put new life into the civil administration. He restored the Committee for Ejecting Scandalous Ministers; he opposed all manifestations of loose living[4] and strove to provide machinery to reduce sabbath-breaking; he imprisoned those who arranged to get married other than in the manner newly prescribed by Parliament; and he endeavoured to standardize weights and measures.[5] But his overriding concern seems to have been the suppression of ale-houses. The Justices, urged on by John Bradshaw, had worked hard since 1648 to eliminate disreputable ale-houses and to limit them through the reports of committees in each parish to the monthly meetings of the Justices. But Worsley inaugurated a fresh onslaught on the

[1] The full figures are: Broxton—120, Macclesfield—119, Edisbury—89, Northwich—31, Nantwich—29, Wirral—11, Bucklow—9, city of Chester—48.

[2] e.g. heavy concentrations in Prestbury and Macclesfield parishes in Macclesfield hundred, and in Malpas parish in Broxton hundred. In my thesis the pattern is illustrated more clearly by a map (map IV, following p.448).

[3] See below, p.284.

[4] e.g. his opposition to horseracing was probably as much the result of his moral convictions as of his preoccupations with security.

[5] *Thurloe State Papers,*vol. 4, pp.189, 247–8, 278, 315, 485, 522–3, 534.

problem; he reported that 'wee are puttinge downe alehouses, accordinge to the orders, as also such as are not able to entertaine strangers and are of evell fame and name'.[1] and within a month 200 had been closed down.[2] The Quarter Sessions Files for 1656 are full of pitiful appeals from the deprived. For example, Robert Bulkeley petitioned (with the support of an impressive number of his neighbours) that for twenty years he had kept an ale-house without ever being accused of permitting disorder, yet he had been suppressed at a monthly meeting in Northwich 'only as supernumery'.[3] He and twenty-six others who petitioned the July Sessions only had the comfort of having their cases referred back to the next meeting of the hundredal commissioners for reconsideration.

Much of this work can be seen as a continuation and strengthening of the work performed by the Justices in the preceding years. But there are signs of some more radical departures. For example, the inhabitants of Warburton complained to the Justices that

the constables of Lyme [Lymm] have brought to the constables of the said township certaine wandering people & demaunded from the sd constables twelve pence apeece for the same. Who, haveing then not seene the late ordr in that behalfe did refuse to paie the same money. But haveing now come to the sight thereof... [we are] very senceible of the great burthen that may possibly fall on them by payeing 12d to every such person as shall be brought unto them as the ordr is required, & haveing noe wayes to be reimbursed.[4]

From this and similar scraps of information it seems clear that Worsley intended to penalize townships on the borders that were responsible for letting wanderers into the county. This proposal was both new in itself and a complete break with the relaxation of laws against wanderers which had been one of the features of poor law administration during the previous ten years.[5] The importance of the case seems to be further demonstrated by the Justices' decision not to deal

[1] Ibid., p.473.
[2] Ibid., p.523.
[3] C.R.O., Q.S.F. 1656, no.2, f. 261.
[4] Ibid., f. 232.
[5] See above, pp.248—51.

with the case themselves but to refer it directly to the Major-General and his commissioners, an unusual procedure.

Similarly, Worsley seems to have broken new ground in his attitude towards the officials under him. His initial reaction to the Cheshire gentry had been favourable: 'I have this day bene with the commissioners for this county of Chester, and had a very lardg and considerable number of them together and find noe less redinese in them then in those . . . in other countyes.[1] But this support quickly evaporated. The list of commissioners assigned to him in Cheshire contained twelve gentlemen-Justices and ten militia officers and minor gentlemen.[2] Only one letter has survived that contains the signatures of active commissioners, and this was signed by three gentlemen (Thomas Croxton, Jonathan Bruen, Thomas Mainwaring) and seven officers.[3] Thomas Mainwaring himself attended a meeting in the second week of every month from November 1655 until Worsley's death in June 1656, but he never mentioned the names of his fellow commissioners. This is unusual in so far as he normally referred to any of his cousins or close friends whom he met on such occasions (he also usually dined with them), and can be taken as negative evidence that none of his close friends was active for Worsley. Indeed on the one occasion during this period when he does give the names of those at a hundredal meeting in Nantwich, his companions were Captain John Delves, Captain Thomas Hurwar, and Captain Thomas Malbon; at least two gentlemen-commissioners had not turned up.[4]

Furthermore, Worsley was constantly telling his superiors in London that 'I finde a very greate wante of justices of the peace in the countys, both by reason of those that refuse to act as alsoe of the smallnesse of the number'.[5] Likewise he said of the Committee for Ejecting Scandalous Ministers, 'in these countyes we can hardly get a coram, there is soe few named in it, and some that are dead and some that will not

[1] *Thurloe State Papers*, vol. 4, p.189.
[2] Chester City R.O., CR63/1/146.
[3] *Thurloe State Papers*, vol. 4, p.251.
[4] J.Ry.L. Mainwaring MS. Book 20a, f. 242.
[5] *Thurloe State Papers*, vol. 4, p.485.

act'.[1] On his advice both his and the militia committee were enlarged by the addition of several militia officers,[2] but he seems to have failed to have amended the Commission of the Peace. The rise to greater prominence of low-born men was a marked feature of his administration, and must have been viewed gloomily by those who had consistently opposed such developments in the 1640s. To complement these changes, Worsley arranged for minor gentlemen in each hundred to be appointed and 'emploied in the severall parishes ... concerning the Major Generalls & Commissioners articles'.[3] His attitude to them was summed up in a phrase with an ominous ring for the great gentry; he sought to employ 'honest, judicious men'.[4]

Finally he carried out a widespread purge of the petty constables. In January 1656 he reported his intention 'to take some course that honest and sufficient men be put in the plase of constables, for truly the want of that is a great evell to this nation'.[5] Within a month he was able to claim that 'we have further taken care to remove bad constables and put in honest faithfull and judicious men'.[6] To have achieved this he presumably had had to overthrow the traditional procedures by which the office moved by rota from house to house. More significant, however, is evidence of an increased scope and range in the powers granted to the new constables as part of Worsley's drive against immorality: 'There is divers counstables here and there, that are honest, who are doubtfull of what powre they have, and how farr they may proceed of themselves in punishing sin etc. The law is very darke in that; soe that divers have suffred upon that account'. His further comments imply hostility to these changes from the gentry. 'They find it hard to find justises, that will encourage them in that worke. . .'[7]

---

[1] Ibid., p.473.
[2] P.R.O., SP 25, vol. 77, f. 313. For the continuance of this pattern in the period 1656–9, see Firth and Rait, *Acts and Ordinances*, vol. 2, pp.1063 (Assessment), 1162 (Sabbath Observance), 1321 (Militia).
[3] J.Ry.L. Mainwaring MS., Book 20a, p.242.
[4] *Thurloe State Papers*, vol. 4, p.533.
[5] Ibid., p.473.
[6] Ibid., p.522.
[7] Ibid., p.315.

Worsley's reputation as the most oppressive of the Major-Generals thus appears well founded. Indeed it is possible that his energy in some fields was a source of embarrassment to the government. Although they were determined to increase security at the expense of those who threatened the peace, they were anxious to avoid martyrs, and Worsley's determination to uncover and destroy the most tenuous link between Cheshire and Charles Stuart may have proved excessive. Is it merely incompetence in London that though Worsley four or five times asked that the examination of suspects be sent down to him, they were never sent? Equally, why was Worsley's own candidate for the shrievalty ignored and Glynn's nominee, Philip Egerton, son of a Royalist, appointed in his stead, despite two bitter outcries from the Major-General?

I am afraid that hee that's now sheriffe is not a persone that may be justly suspected for his integritie to the present government. I have alreadie found him to be person, whose plesure and delight is onely in those, who I verilie believe are the most dangerous enemyes wee have in these countyes; and I am a little jealouse of him. As to the last design, you neede not feare for all this; for if he but speake or make the least show, I have him.[1]

Cromwell spoke thus to his second Parliament of the Major-Generals: 'Upon such a rising as that was, truly I think if ever anything was justifiable as a necessity, and honest in every respect, that was . . [so] we did find out a little poor invention, which I hear was much regretted'.[2] Cromwell sought to offset the unpopularity of the Major-Generals by stressing in other ways the continuity of social and political life. But Worsley saw conspiracy everywhere; and where there was conspiracy, there could be no conciliation. He had declared his policy: 'Wee shall now fall of snapping some of our old blades, that will not let us be quiet'.[3] Though he never lived to carry out his threat, he left a memory of the power and the intransigence of army rule which hindered the

---

[1] Ibid., p.684.
[2] T. Carlyle, *Letters and Speeches of Oliver Cromwell*, (ed.) C.H. Firth, London, 1904, vol. 2, p.530.
[3] *Thurloe State Papers*, vol. 4, p.300.

gentlemen-ostriches from burying their heads in the sand and pretending that naked military power had gone away.

III

The last important task given to the Major-Generals was the supervision of elections to the second Protectorate Parliament. A few weeks before these took place, Worsley died and was replaced by a stranger to the area, Tobias Bridge, a soldier who had served for several years as captain and major under Okey until the latter had been cashiered, when he took over command of the regiment. He had been a leading spokesman of the movement at the beginning of 1653 to oust the Rump. Since the end of 1655 he had been a deputy Major-General in the south.[1]

Mr. Pinckney's detailed exposition of the course of the campaign need not be re-examined here; but I wish to question some of his conclusions.[2]

Before each Protectorate Parliament a caucus of gentlemen was formed to settle on an agreed group of candidates. In 1654 Thomas Mainwaring records attending a meeting with Sir William Brereton, Thomas Stanley, Thomas Marbury, Peter Brooke, and Jonathan Bruen,[3] which led to the nomination of the four candidates who were subsequently elected. With the exception of Brereton, those at the meeting were the leading civilians active in local government during the first months of the Protectorate. In 1656 the caucus comprised a slightly different group. Stanley, Bruen, and Brooke were again present as were Philip Egerton (the sheriff), Thomas Brereton of Ashley, Roger Wilbraham of Derfold, and John Arderne;[4] these last four were all disillusioned Parliamentarians. Of the others, Bruen and Brooke had ceased to play a full part in local government

[1] See P.J. Pinckney, 'The Cheshire Election of 1656', *B.J.Ry.L.* 49(1967), 395–6.

[2] Ibid., pp.390–426.

[3] J.Ry.L. Mainwaring MS., Book 20a, p.173.

[4] Ibid., p.255. Mainwaring does not state whether he attended this meeting, but he clearly knew of it to record and in the intervening weeks up to the election he is frequently associated with the others.

since the inauguration of the Major-Generals. It seems most reasonable to see this group as concerned above all to select candidates who would oppose military rule in the new Parliament;[1] this is the only reasonable explanation of their choice of Thomas Marbury, Peter Brooke, Richard Legh of Lyme, and John Bradshaw.[2]

This meeting, held on 25 July and followed by several others throughout the county in order to gather support for this slate of candidates, took place before the arrival of Tobias Bridge in Cheshire on 13 August, only a week before the election day. Within forty-eight hours of his arrival Bridge had called a meeting of about twenty of the leading gentry to Middlewich,[3] where he read a letter from Cromwell[4] and asked the gentry to support his own slate of candidates, Thomas Marbury, Thomas Croxton, Thomas Mainwaring, and Edward Hyde. After further discussion, a compromise between the two slates was agreed, Bridge agreeing to the gentlemen's list so long as they undertook to prevent the election of John Bradshaw. He was clearly satisfied that he could rely on the gentry to implement this agreement, for the next day he set off for Lancashire and did not return until after the election.

Soon, however, the Gentlemen Confederates (as the caucus became known) began to have qualms about the possibility of preventing Bradshaw's election. In the remaining days before 20 August they met several times at Richard Legh's home at Lyme. Henry Bradshaw was invited to one of these meetings to discuss his brother's position. His statement that John Bradshaw was determined to stand and to serve if elected clearly caused consternation, particularly because

---

[1] See below, p.290.

[2] See below, p.289.

[3] Reported in a letter from Bridge to Thurloe (Bodl. Lib. Rawlinson MS. A 41, f. 495. The printed version, *Thurloe State Papers*, vol. 5, pp.313–14, is highly inaccurate).

[4] Ludlow later claimed that a letter from Cromwell requiring the county not to elect Republicans was read at Chester during the election. Since there is some evidence that no such letter was read on 20 Aug., it is possible that Ludlow was wrongly ascribing to the 20th this letter from Cromwell read by Bridge on the 15th.

several of the Gentlemen had been spreading rumours that he would refuse to serve if elected, or that Cromwell intended to arrest him rather than let him take his seat. Henry Bradshaw's intervention—he showed them a letter from his brother—only increased their discomfiture, and further meetings were held at Chester on the evening before and the morning of the poll before a decision to adhere to the agreement with Bridge was finally taken.[1] In the meantime Sir George Booth had accepted the nomination as their alternative candidate to Bradshaw.

Clearly the most difficult matter to explain is their initial decision to sponsor Bradshaw. Mr. Pinckney interprets this in terms of the family ties between Bradshaw and several of the Gentlemen Confederates, and argues that the inclusion of Booth—another close relative—was intended to mollify him.[2] This seems to push the importance of genealogical ties too far.

To some extent, the selection of Bradshaw was prudential, in that he had a large personal following, particularly amongst radical groups like the Quakers, but also generally as a widely respected and popular Chief Justice at Chester.[3] If the Gentlemen ignored his candidacy, they could be sure that the task of excluding him at the polls would be a difficult one. But there were other reasons. Bradshaw was a renowned opponent of the Protectorate and both his rebuff to Cromwell at the time of the dissolution of the Rump and his speeches in the 1654 Parliament (which had delighted Ludlow at least) had marked him out as a leading anti-militarist.[4] So was another of the Gentlemen's candidates, Peter Brooke, the outspoken opponent of the new militia in 1655.[5] A third, Richard Legh, was Brooke's nephew by marriage; as the son of a Royalist he too must have been

---

[1] See Pinckney, art. cit., pp.409–11 for references. Also Bodl. Lib. Top. Cheshire e 3, f. 20.
[2] Pinckney, art. cit., pp.404, 413.
[3] Ibid., pp.396, 406–7.
[4] Ludlow, *Memoirs. . .*, vol. 1, p.391.
[5] See above, p.263.

hostile to the Major-Generals. Similarly the nomination of Booth in Bradshaw's place seems to owe less to their family ties than to their temporary political agreement over the threat posed by the Major-Generals. In fact they had been bitterly opposed to one another in local politics for years, and while Bradshaw was an outspoken Republican opponent of the Protectorate, Booth had been expelled from the Commons at Pride's Purge. But he was one of three commissioners who had openly refused to act with Worsley,[1] and had even called the Major-Generals 'Cromwell's hangmen'.[2] This seems to confirm the other indications that the Gentlemen Confederates were planning to make strong representations in Parliament against Cromwell's innovation. The selection of Booth may well have been determined by the need to have an experienced member to lead the county delegation to Westminster; the direction from which he attacked military rule was less important than the determination to oppose it. Finally, if, as Mr. Pinckney has argued, the Gentlemen were negotiating with leading Royalists like the Cholmondeleys and the Egertons to induce their tenants to support their nominees,[3] Booth would have been a happier choice than Bradshaw.[4]

There was one other candidate in the field, the once-formidable Sir William Brereton. His long absence from the county, the reported unrest against his profiteering as seneschal of Macclesfield Forest (where his personal following had been strongest), and his association with the sufferings of the war years, had drained his popularity. As Pinckney says, 'he was the outstanding symbol of old animosities which were better forgotten',[5] but he was still influential. Bridge said of him: 'Sir William Brereton hath bin

---

[1] Chester City R.O., CR63/1/146, Leycester of Tabley MSS., unfoliated.

[2] *Cal. Clarendon St. Pap.*, vol. 3, p.242.

[3] Pinckney, art. cit., pp.410—12. It is rarely pointed out that the disenfranchisement of Royalist gentry under the Instrument of Government did not prevent them from exerting pressure on their newly enfranchised tenants.

[4] Bridge's slate included two active civilians and two militia officers, all of ancient county stock, who would normally have proved acceptable to the Confederates.

[5] Ibid., p.408.

bestirringe what hee can by himselfe and agents to procure voices, but I find his interest among the gent: very litle, only some of the rigid clergy cry him up . . .' [1]

By force of circumstances Brereton and Bradshaw now came to take up a joint stance against the Confederacy; Henry Bradshaw saw it as very unequal: 'It was the indeavour of some of your frends wth more and Sir W. B., when wee come to Flookersbrooke, to drawe Sr W.B. frends (wch were inconsiderable fewe) & yors (wch were a greate number of substantiall men) to ioyne together so to advance him & oppose the 4 noiated gent . . .'[2]

Having secured the Gentlemen's promise to thwart Bradshaw, Bridge departed to Lancashire to handle a tricky election campaign there. His troops do not seem to have intervened despite a letter written a week or so before the election in which he reported that he had 'appointed that troop of the army lying at Nantwich to draw forth near Chester, and be in readiness; as also the county troop and Col. Croxton's Care will not be wanting to secure the castle, in which the election is to be'.[3] But neither Bradshaw nor Brereton mentions the presence of troops in their otherwise unbridled complaints about the handling of the election. It is also unlikely that a letter from Cromwell calling for the rejection of Bradshaw was read out by the sheriff, as Ludlow claimed.[4] It is hardly likely that Henry Bradshaw would fail to report such an incident to his brother. On the other hand, we do know that such a letter was circulating amongst the gentry before the election.[5]

According to Henry Bradshaw's account, his brother was spontaneously nominated by the people both in the shire hall and outside on the Common. This

was much displeaseinge to them in the chaire, and some others, but the maioiritie of the people continued crying upp your name and

[1] Bodl. Lib. Rawlinson MS. A 40, f. 495.
[2] Bodl. Lib. Top Cheshire e 3, f. 20.
[3] *Thurloe State Papers*, vol. 5, p.313.
[4] Ludlow, *Memoirs. . .*, vol. 2, pp.16–17. See above, p.286.
[5] Pinckney, art. cit., p.419.

requireinge the poll which was denied; But the foremencioned indeavor was by me pacified, because I was verie sure it could not possiblie be brought about for Sir W[illiam's] honor att that tyme, and yors was evidentlie promoted'.

But they had not counted on the duplicity of the Gentlemen Confederates, who

heareinge howe unsatisfied and discontented the Generalitie of the free-holders and some Gent were, their Grandees and some others of the Gange smoothed upp the matter, with giveinge seeminge (but un-satisfactorie) plausible reports of and towards you: and some of them said they would by their lettre give you a respective account of their acknowledgements then transactinge, which I dare vouch they never can, and that some of them did never so fully unmask themselves, and if right hadd been done they would further have been laid open. I staied upon the Ground with manie other (good men I hope) until the Grand returned into the City, and since then have neither seen or heard from any of them. [1]

Not surprisingly, for the sheriff had declared the four nominees of the Confederates elected, and Bradshaw excluded.

Brereton also believed that he had been cheated:

Sir William Brereton was duely elected one of the knights to serve in Parliament for the said County by the greater number of freeholders and such as had voyces at the election. Neverthelesse the said sheriff in pursuance of his sd designe wilfully refused and would not graunt the pole, but hath made returne of knights to serve for the same county, omytting the said Sir William Brereton, though hee was duely elected.

He backed up his petition with eye-witness testimony and a Grand Jury Presentment that Philip Egerton had refused a poll. [2] Although the Grand Jury presented this in open court in the presence of John Bradshaw—no doubt to his grim satisfaction—it must be remembered that the panel from which this jury was taken had been nominated by Philip Egerton, who was still sheriff. [3]

As a footnote we might add that ten days after the election, Thomas Mainwaring recorded that 'myselfe & most of the rest of the gentry mette the foure Parliament men for the County at Knottesford'. [4] This might well indicate that

---

[1] Bodl. Lib. Top. Cheshire e 3, ff. 20–1.
[2] Chester City R.O., CR63/2/702, Brereton MSS., pp. B 39–42.
[3] P.R.O. Chester 24/131, no.4, unfoliated.
[4] J.Ry.L. Mainwaring MS., Book 20a, f. 260.

the four were being given a final briefing on the stance they were to adopt at Westminster. Certainly Cromwell showed less enthusiasm for them than Bridge had done, and before Parliament sat, he had excluded three of them.[1] Could this be the result of a late realization that the Gentlemen Confederates were not merely electing four of their number, but were sending them up to London with fixed intentions and orders?

One of the unhappiest documentary losses from Cheshire for this period is the second volume of Thomas Mainwaring's diary. The first ends at the very beginning of 1659, and the third begins in 1670. But the whole Restoration period is not covered, and above all the vital months in the middle of 1659, when so much might be gained from knowing what Mainwaring and his friends' movements were.

As it is, one of the final entries in the first diary tells us that, as in 1654 and 1656, Mainwaring was involved in a meeting of county leaders to settle on their 'official candidates' for Richard Cromwell's Parliament. Unfortunately on this occasion he does not name the other gentlemen involved.[2] Since Richard Cromwell was summoning a Parliament on the old franchise and constituencies, Cheshire was reduced to only two county representatives. The two candidates selected were two of the four members from 1656, Peter Brooke and Richard Legh. Once again the man with whom they had to contend was John Bradshaw. In fact on this occasion there were only three candidates, and since there was general agreement on Richard Legh for first place, the election became a contest between Bradshaw and Brooke. If Mr. Pinckney is right in thinking that in 1656 'much of the support for Bradshaw and Brereton came from a newly enfranchised group which had profited from the revolution',[3] then Bradshaw's hopes in 1659 would have been lower. But he had one immense advantage in 1659 the lack of which in 1656 had been his undoing—he now enjoyed the support of the sheriff.

---

[1] B.M. Harleian MS. 1929, f. 19.
[2] J.Ry.L. Mainwaring MS. Book 20a, p.355.
[3] Pinckney, art. cit., p.419.

In 1656 Philip Egerton had been pricked sheriff, to the dismay of Charles Worsley. The Major-General himself had wanted John Legh of Booths, an old army officer of modest estates who had been one of Sir William Brereton's supporters in the internal dissensions of the 1640s but who had rather dropped out of sight since 1649. But the man Cromwell thus overlooked in 1656 had been pricked in 1658 and was retained for 1659; Legh's bias appeared even more blatantly than Egerton's had done and secured sweet revenge for John Bradshaw.

This is the account of the election given by Randle Holme:

the most part of the aunctient gentry stood for Mr Leigh of Lime & Mr Peter Brookes in opposition of the later other justices stood for the Judge Jo Bradshaw, great Amulation was amongst them, but after three days polleing where Brooks carried it, the court was removed to Congleton where Bradshaw did outnumber him, but it was through the sheriff's friendship, for he haveing take the votes for Bradshaw . . [text worn] adiourney the court, before the contrary parties could come to give their votes.[1]

The sheriff's account of the election dwelt entirely on the abuse to which he was subject from Brooke's supporters. Of the removal of the poll to Congleton he simply said

That the county cort beeing upon adjournmt to Congleton (a towne of good note in the same county) for conveniency sake & for perfecting of the eleccon, Mr Brooke wthout any occasion given in a menacing way stretched forth his hand towards the sheriffe and openly said to him, if you adjourne to any other place I will follow you to the hills.[2]

This glib gloss on the move to Congleton would hardly answer the doubts of anyone who knew that Congleton was Bradshaw's home town, and that he was a popular and long-standing champion of the borough's rights.

Burton recorded the debate of the Committee of Privileges which resulted from the petitions that followed the election, where it was accepted that

if so, it would be in the power of any sheriff to make what knights he pleased; for by the same rule, he might have adjourned to Nantwich, and so from place to place, till he had gathered up a majority of votes

---

[1] B.M. Harleian MS. 1929, f. 20.
[2] J.Ry.L. Legh of Lyme MSS., Filing Box 65, unfoliated.

for which person he had a mind to. Out of the debate, upon the whole the opinion was that the whole election was void, in respect of the adjournment of the poll, whereunto Mr Lee [i.e. Richard Legh] was present,

yet the radical temper of Richard Cromwell's Parliament secured Bradshaw's return and the petition was dismissed by the whole House by a majority of seven.[1]

However, the issues of greatest importance to us are the names of the supporters of each candidate and the platform for which they stood. The first is easier to settle than the second, for we are fortunate to possess a catalogue of the leading supporters of each party in Henry Bradshaw's account of the election to his brother.[2] He listed the supporters of Brooke as Richard Legh, Lord Kilmorrey, Lord Brereton, Roger Grosvenor, Thomas Mainwaring, Philip Egerton, Henry and Peter Brooke, Thomas Cholmondeley, Henry Delves, William Massie, John Arderne, Lord Savage, Lord Bridgwater, Thomas Brereton and Edward Hyde. From other sources we can add to this list Thomas Cotton of Combermere and John Davenport of Woodford.[3] Of these, ten came from Royalist backgrounds, eight from Parliamentarian backgrounds. But of the eight Parliamentarians, only two, Mainwaring and Hyde, were still active in the administration. It was a party of alienated land-owners, all of ancient descent, and all who had themselves or whose fathers had sat on the pre-war Commission of the Peace. Even more significantly, except for Mainwaring and Hyde, it was the group of men who led the Booth Rising. Only Thomas Legh of Adlington (ex-Royalist), Henry Mainwaring of Kermincham (lapsed Parliamentarian), and Sir George Booth himself are absent from the list of what was to be a roll-call of the Rising.

Henry Bradshaw's list of his brother's supporters is equally revealing. As well as himself and the sheriff, he listed Lord

[1] Burton, *Parliamentary Diary*, vol. 4, pp.429–30.
[2] Bodl. Lib. Top. Cheshire e 3, f. 22.
[3] Chester City R.O., CR72, Cotton of Combermere MSS., Box Marked 'letters, 16th and 17th centuries', unfoliated; J.Ry.L. Legh of Lyme MSS., Filing Box 65, unfoliated.

Rivers, Sir Thomas Wilbraham, John Crewe, Robert
Duckenfield, Thomas Stanley, Roger Wilbraham, Henry
Birkenhead, George Manley, Henry Greene and Thomas
Tanat. This is an odd group, with the Papist and ex-Royalist
Lord Rivers and the moderate lapsed Parliamentarian—friend
and relative of Thomas Mainwaring—Sir Thomas Wilbraham,
as most unlikely companions of the leading military men in
Cheshire. The minor gentlemen are there, as are the old
radicals Duckenfield and Birkenhead. But this list comprises
all those who were to lead in the suppression of the Rising
except Gilbert Gerard and Thomas Croxton. And there is
evidence that Croxton was involved since Legh associated the
Governor of Chester with himself in the conduct of the
election. He asserted that

if the sherriffe had not upon good discretion forborne to right himselfe
upon the said publiq affronts there had beene great dangr of confusion
& bloodshed, itt being observed that many of the affronters party were
weaponed & prepared wch by the sheriffes forbearance & care &
prudence of Colonell Thomas Croxton Governor of Chester haveing
men in readines to prevent such inconveniences was happily prevented
both att Chester & Congleton.[1]

Furthermore it is significant that those whose presence on
Henry Bradshaw's list is surprising (Rivers, Thomas, and
Roger Wilbraham),[2] were also inactive during the Rising in
August 1659, and were not appointed to the Commission of
the Peace at the Restoration (of Bradshaw's eighteen known
opponents, fourteen were active as Justices or deputy
lieutenants in the early 1660s; of his twelve supporters, only
John Crewe was appointed to be either).

    The account of the election made by John Legh shows
something of the tension and anger that surrounded it. The
seventeen specific allegations of aggravation that he made
against leading gentlemen like Peter Brooke and Thomas
Mainwaring reveal this far more vividly; the following
examples show the mixture of abuse, heavy threats, and near
violence that resulted from Legh's decision to adjourn the
election to Congleton.

[1] J.Ry.L. Legh of Lyme MSS., Filing Box 65, unfoliated.
[2] Only distantly related to one another.

5. That Rogr Wilbraham of Nantwich esq comeing to give his vote for Serjeant Bradshawe, Mr. Brooke did openly reprove him & in open cort checked one William Gandy beeing a freehouldr & passing his vote for the srjeant, telling him itt had beene more fitt for him to have beene at home & to have paid his fathers debts . . .

8. That Mr. Mainwaring when the sherriffe was takeinge votes at Chester said openly I am sorry you are my kinsman, you are soe farr from beeing a gent. & as hee was comeing from court said to the sheriffe in a threatning way, when you are out of yor sheriffes office I will talk wth you...

14. That att the eleccon att Congleton the said Capn Shepley standing on the staires of the townehall where the polling then was, asked divers persons who they were for & calling up such as were Mr Legh & Mr Brooke lett them pass but kept backe such as were for Mr Serjeant Bradshawe wch was likely to have occasioned much quarrelling and breach of the peace.[1]

Henry Bradshaw testified in his letter to his brother that violence had almost broken out, but that the sheriff had remained calm under extreme provocation.[2]

Far more than in 1640 or 1656, strong passions and bitter partisanship marked this election. Yet it is impossible to discover how far the issues were personal. Randle Holme implied that they were when he said that 'attorney Bradshaw made a speech at Congleton wherein he termed Leigh a child and Brooke a ... [sic]. Therefor it was not for the honor of the county to choose such but look upon abler',[3] Henry Bradshaw unhelpfully says merely that 'wee stood for God & our countreye'.[4] However we do possess one letter that might take us a little further. This was written by John Bradshaw to someone in Cheshire who had complained about Bradshaw's stance at the election; this is how he answered the main complaint,

... I must lett you know (whatever the usuall practise is or hath bin to the contrarie), my course hath bin, and ever shall bee otherwise, for by law elections ought to bee unprovided and free, and the freeholders (which terme comprehends all the degrees of the county what have votes, for you will not saie you have an upper and lower house, Lords

[1] J.Ry.L. Legh of Lyme MSS., Filing Box 65, unfoliated.
[2] Bodl. Lib. Top Cheshire e 3, f. 22.
[3] B.M. Harleian MS. 1929, f. 20.
[4] Bodl. Lib. Top. Cheshire e 3, f. 22.

and Comons there) are to bee lefte upon the place to make their owne choice without beinge sought unto, or imposed upon by anie; and the way of Preingaginge in a divided, combineinge maner... I canot well relishe that expression of your charginge mee wth concealing me desires in this elective busines, inferringe thereby that I should have proclaimed myselfe beforehand or my desire had bin to it, whereas to the former I must tell you, I hold it unlawfull as containinge preiudice in it to the subsequent votes of the county which ought to be most untied and free.[1]

It is unclear how genuine this protestation was. It could be simply a stock defence against a caucus; there is no evidence that Bradshaw supported such a programme as Lord President. Yet as it stands this is still a radical expression of his position, and the rest of the letter suggests a move from the stand he had adopted earlier in his career. In reply to the charge that he had received substantial support from the hated Quakers, he said that 'if they were freeholders and acted as Law prescribes, why should anie be soe arbitrarie as to exclude them or soe simple to be offended at them, this privilidge is a highe parte of their birthright[2] [a dangerous word]. Taken as a whole, this position could be seen as an assault on the whole social and political basis of the gentry. Their right to articulate the county's needs and desires as they saw best would be swept aside. Yet it was this right that was to form the basis of Sir George Booth's propaganda for his Rising.[3] If Bradshaw meant what he wrote, and if his views were widely circulated, then the gentry were fighting to preserve their way of life.

The question of Bradshaw's election thus possibly presented in a very direct way the issue before the gentry all over the country. Richard Cromwell was known to be a man of moderate views, but he was surrounded by army officers, all of comparably extreme views. A Parliament was the one way out for those who hoped to give Richard Comwell an opportunity to pursue policies that otherwise he was too isolated to follow. This would be especially true of religion,

[1] J.Ry.L. Legh of Lyme MSS., Filing Box 65, unfoliated.
[2] Ibid., Filing box 64, unfoliated.
[3] See below, pp.318–24.

where he was known to favour the progress towards a state church which had been made in his father's last years. John Bradshaw now stood as the symbol of all that was opposed to such a course of action. In 1656 he had been in an ambiguous position because of his identification with anti-militarism; but in 1659 Bradshaw was likely to be prepared to co-operate in an unholy alliance between the army and the Republicans.

It is an oversimplification to see the unity of the gentry at the time only in terms of opposition to Bradshaw. For the first time since 1640 the traditional élite families had found common cause. Most of their grievances had existed for years, and were not noticeably more serious in 1659 than in 1651 or 1655. But they now had a self confidence that came with solidarity, and this identification of trust was a great psychological change which might galvanize them into action. A deterioration in the central government and decisive local leadership were all that were required to make them take up arms to reassert those values by which they had always stood.

## 8

## SIR GEORGE BOOTH'S REBELLION
## AND THE RESTORATION

### I

The bizarre alliance of army chieftains and a withered Rump Parliament which took power from the faltering hands of Richard Cromwell in the early summer of 1659 engendered far more widespread distrust and hostility than any of the preceding regimes. Superficially this made the chances of a successful Royalist rising better than at any point since the death of Charles I, yet, as Professor Underdown[1] has clearly demonstrated, all the factors that had bedevilled Royalist plotting throughout the 1650s were still operating as fully as ever. There were irreconcilable differences within the exiled Court, and between the Court and its would-be supporters in England; there was a basic defeatism, even treachery,[2] within the Sealed Knot, central organ of Royalist planning in England; Thomas Scot and other experienced officials kept vigilant watch on all suspected Royalists through spies and a close control of the postal service; above all the army stood as the supreme sanction to the authority of any government to which it gave its support, and no hastily raised insurrectionary force could hope to face it in the field.

The main question to be answered is not why the Rump was threatened by a Rising virtually confined to the counties around Cheshire, but why a Rising gathered such momentum even in one area. The previous chapter has provided part of the answer. Successive governments had never had to face any serious trouble from Cheshire, and saw no reason why they might have to now. Yet imperceptibly the fragmented community had been drawing together again, and individuals who would never have considered acting on their own or in small groups, were prepared, when a firm call came, to join in

---

[1] D. Underdown, *Royalist Conspiracy in England 1649–60*, New Haven, 1960.
[2] D. Underdown, 'Sir Richard Willys and Secretary Thurloe', *E.H.R.* 69 (1954).

a movement which they were confident would be supported by the bulk of their friends and relatives. This confidence in the solidarity of gentry response was decisive. The involvement of Sir George Booth with the Court provided the crucial link that drew the county into a national movement.

Even before the fall of Richard Cromwell, Charles Stuart had initiated a new scheme for a general revolt. Influenced by John Mordaunt, a seasoned insurrectionary,[1] he issued on 1 March 1659 a commission to a small group of men to organize a series of joint Royalist-Presbyterian risings. The Sealed Knot refused to serve on this new group—The Great Trust—and by August, as Professor Underdown has shown[2] actual members of the group came almost equally from Royalist and Presbyterian backgrounds. This in itself was a most significant development for despite wildly exaggerated hopes throughout the decade, the Royalists had never seemed likely to gain the widespread support of disgruntled Presbyterians. Now the Great Trust were empowered to treat with all the Crown's past enemies except the Regicides, and to promise pardons and great rewards to all who appeared for Charles II. As a significant further inducement, Presbyterians were to be allowed to make up their own minds whether they declared openly for the monarchy or whether they took their stand on the rights of the subject and the laws of the land.[3]

Sir George Booth was the contact in Cheshire from the beginning. Inheriting much of the respect and local pre-eminence of his grandfather, old Sir George, who had died in his mid-eighties in 1652, he was the ideal choice in 1659. He had served Parliament loyally throughout the war, despite his poor relations with Brereton, and had then been elected as recruiter member of Parliament for Cheshire. In December 1648 he was a teller in the crucial debate attacking the army which immediately preceded Pride's Purge, and he was one of those who demonstrated most actively against the seclusions. From then on he had retired from public life, never sitting or

[1] In 1658 he narrowly escaped conviction for high treason on the casting vote of the President of the Court.

[2] Underdown, *Royalist Conspiracy. . .*, pp.236–7.

[3] Ibid., pp.237–40.

acting as a Justice or on any committee, although he was still always appointed to them. He was returned to both Oliver's Parliaments where he made trouble by raising objections to the exclusion of some members by the Council of State, and absented himself until they were allowed to sit. In Cheshire he devoted his time to enlarging Dunham Hall in somewhat dubious taste. The predominant thread in his career was anti-militarism, and in 1655 he flared up in the presence of Worsley's deputy, Colonel Howard, and called the Major-Generals 'Cromwell's hangmen'. Despite numerous approaches from the exiled Court, and despite the antics of his uncle, John Booth, however, he refused to flirt with the Royalists. The government were aware of this, which is probably why he was still named at the head of every commission, for he still sought the honour due to his position. One of Thurloe's leading agents in the area in 1655, Captain Griffiths, sumed up the position well:

although some of those, as Sir Thomas Middleton, Sir George Booth etc., in some things possibly were unsatisfied, yet against the cavaleers' interest you may as safely trust them as ever and it will not be convenient to sleight persons of eminency and interest in the country, being assured of their fidelity. [1]

He had obvious advantages as a leader in 1659: his social position, his sincere and consistent record towards the original values of the Parliamentary party of 1642, his campaign for considerate treatment for the defeated Royalists—which suggested a capacity to hold together the broadest based party possible—his wealth, less damaged than that of Royalists who had undergone sequestration, composition, and decimation. His only disadvantages were a lack of real military experience—though Meldrum had praised his defence of Nantwich—and a tendency to impulsiveness, as in his resignation in 1645, his outburst to Howard or earlier his flight from home to France in 1639 after a temporary row with his grandfather. [2]

[1] *Thurloe State Papers,* vol. 3, p.216.

[2] In general, see Booth's biography in *D.N.B.* and R.N. Dore's 'The Cheshire Rising of 1659', *T.L.C.A.S.* 69 (1959), 44—8, 56—8. For his war record, see particularly, *H.M.C. Portland MSS.,* vol. 1, pp.94—6, P.R.O., SP 28, vols. 224 and

When Richard Cromwell resigned and the Rump was recalled, Booth immediately drew attention to himself by joining Prynne and eight others in an attempt to take their seats in the House. The soldiery turned them aside.[1] Whether an intentional act of self-advertisement or not, this once more focused the exiled Court's attention upon him. Initially Mordaunt had not planned a rising in Cheshire for want of a leader (having only looked to the Cavaliers), but his enthusiasm for Booth grew with his acquaintanceship with him. From being 'a stranger to some of us', he became 'questionless excellently disposed' and 'very well fixed and resolved'.[2] Mordaunt's summary of him makes an interesting comparison with Griffiths's, 'a Presbyterian in opinion, yet so moral a man, if ever any of that principle were to be thoroughly depended upon, I think your Majesty may safely on him and his promises, which are considerable and hearty.[3]

Booth remained in London for some weeks and had many meetings with Mordaunt and others. Also in London at the time were Thomas Mainwaring and Thomas Cotton; they had gone to present the Gentlemen's petitions against Bradshaw's election, but according to Cotton 'a good part of the summer was over before we returned'.[4] It would be fascinating to know how much they saw of Sir George or knew of his plans, particularly since Mainwaring's attitude towards the Rising is so uncertain. By the time Booth returned to the county in late May, the general pattern of the projected rising had taken place and he could report it to his friends. By 15 July

---

225, SP 21, vol. 147, f. 467, etc., J.Ry.L. Tatton of Wythenshawe MSS. 251–60. For his rows with Brereton, e.g. B.M. Add. MS. 11331, ff. 66, 67–8, 147; 11332, ff. 70, 119–20. For his career in the Long Parliament, the *Commons Journal* from Jan. 1647 to Dec. 1648, *passim*. For his position at Pride's purge, *Clarke Papers* (ed. C.H. Firth), vol. 2, pp.136–8. His outburst to Howard is reported in *Cal. Clarendon St. Pap.*, vol. 3, p.242. Other incidents referred in the article by Mr. Dore.

[1] *Old Parliamentary History*, vol. 21, p.384.
[2] Cited in R.N. Dore, art. cit., p.60. See *Cal. Clarendon St. Pap.*, vol. 3, pp.472, 482, 490.
[3] Quoted in R.N. Dore, art. cit., p.60 (*Cal. Clarendon St. Pap.*, vol. 3, p.472).
[4] Chester City R.O. CR72, Cotton of Combermere MSS., Box of correspondence, 16th and 17th centuries, unfoliated.

he had been guaranteed general support within the county, and although he was worried by Henry Cromwell's submission to the Rump and resignation of his power to Ludlow (which created a real danger that Cheshire might be invaded from Ireland), he was prepared to promise to go ahead on 1 August.

The general strategy of the rising seems to have been closely connected with that suggested in 1658 by Roger Whitley, a Flintshire gentleman who divided his time between the intrigue at the Court and scheming in England.[1] His plan for a general rebellion, written in his own hand, has survived and has been recently analysed by Dr. J. R. Jones,[2] whose summary can be conveniently quoted here.

... a single rising had no hope of success; concerted action was made difficult by poor communications and a total lack of mutual confidence ... no one could say in advance where the King, or an army from abroad, would be able to land; therefore the plans must be flexible enough to provide for several alternatives ... Whitley advocated decentralisation to solve the problems of coordinating simultaneous risings. England would have to be cantonised, that is divided into associations of counties grouped together for military purposes as in the civil war. Each was to be commanded by a single officer, advised by a small council, and given very wide powers to grant commissions and to treat with those who had formerly fought against the King. He should prepare for action in the minutest detail, issuing commissions to subordinates, enlisting men, procuring supplies, gathering intelligence and keeping the enemy under constant observation. Certain districts could be used for the maintenance of horses without suspicion until the time of the rising. If failure was to be avoided local strategy must not be improvised at the last moment, a great deal could be done in advance to select towns, places and homes to be fortified or used as refuges.

Thus the army, faced by a series of semi-independent revolts, would be unable to act decisively, for by the time it had secured London and the Home Counties and was able to move out, there would have been time for the Royalists to have consolidated themselves, trained their men, and gathered together an overwhelming field army which would

[1] For Whitley's career, see N. Tucker, 'Colonel Roger Whitley', *Journal of the Flintshire Historical Society*, 1966.
[2] The text is in J.Ry.L. Mainwaring MS., Book 24; Dr. Jones's article is in the *B.J.Ry.L.* 39(1957); see particularly pp.422—4.

have more than compensated by its size for its lack of experience.[1] Particularly convincing is the manner in which Whitley rejected the possibility of using 'foreigne force & aydes' (on practical grounds of the unreliability of the promises of foreign rules and because of the hostility which their presence would arouse in England), and decided that success could only be achieved if the impoverished and disarmed ex-Royalists were joined by the Presbyterians.[2] The opening of his proposed 'Heads for a Delaracon'[3] points out how far he was prepared to see Charles bend to gain their support: 'Whereas some corruption and abuses, being crept into the ecclesiasticall & civill Governmt, many honest and Godly-minded Men (endeavoring Reformacon) were engaged in Armes, against the King his Father . . .'. After pointing out the injustices of the governments of men of 'insatiable ambition, avarice, etc, usurping the absolute power' from these moderate men, he advocated a course of action even more favourable to the Presbyterians than that actually promised in 1660:

that those who have bin out of the way, may return to theire duty, we doe hereby assure you, as we shall willingly passe by, and forget, all theire former actings, against us & or Father of Blessed Memory . . . & reward them hereafter wth such Prefermts, offices of Trust, Honors & other Advantages as theire Future deportment & services may deserve; as for the Purchases of Church, Crowne or other lands, they shall either peacibly enjoy theire possessions, or be reimbursed the charge . . . and to remove all Feares & Jealousies, we doe here promise, soe soone as it shall please God to enthrone us; to call a free Parlemt & by theire advise (& that of godly & learned Divines) to settle all differences in Religion soe as shall be nearest to the word of God & having respect to tender consciences, of what persuasion soever & to ease the People of theire grievances, excise, taxes &c, occasioned by the Maintenance of soe many Armyes & Flects . . .

Since Whitley was in close contact with Booth in the weeks before the Rising, he may well have mentioned such explicit promises as a way of substantiating the much vaguer statements of Charles in his Commission to the Great Trust.

[1] J.Ry.L. Mainwaring MS., Book 24, pp.84–5.
[2] Ibid., pp.75–9. He also observed that Presbyterianism was especially strong and amenable in Lancashire and Cheshire.
[3] Ibid., pp.67–9.

In any case the strategic plans laid down in his memorandum clearly foreshadowed the actual organization that evolved. Early hopes of bringing over Major-General Browne in London and of a large-scale rising in Devon and Cornwall foundered, but eventually plans were laid for two principal efforts in the west and in East Anglia, the primary objectives being Bristol and Lynn. There were also to be attempts on Warwick, Worcester, and Shrewsbury. These were to be backed by a whole series of supporting risings, mainly intended to prevent the effective concentration of pro-Rump forces; thus there were firm promises of risings in Staffordshire, Nottinghamshire, Derbyshire, and Lincolnshire. Mordaunt himself was to lead in Surrey, and Royalists and Presbyterians were reported to be ready in Kent.

The Cheshire rising was originally to have been one of the diversionary movements.[1] As in Whitley's plans, a sole organizer was appointed, and he was allowed very considerable freedom to make arrangements in Lancashire and Cheshire.[2] Thus the subsequent fame that Booth achieved by giving his name to the rebellion is somewhat misleading: had everything gone according to plan, his name would have been relegated to an appendix in our general histories. That he momentarily had the chance to take on the importance that fell to Monk in 1660 was not of his choosing. He did not expect so exacting a part as he was forced into playing.

But the same factors that had caused the failure of all rebellions against the Commonwealth were still operating in July 1659. By intercepting letters and by the treachery of leading men, the Council of State came to get wide knowledge of the plots; suspects were arrested; the Sealed Knot, already deeply pessimistic, now successfully sabotaged many of the projected schemes by their letters; many who had committed themselves reluctantly took the first excuse to back down; even those most deeply implicated were

[1] *Clarendon St. Pap.*, vol. 3, pp.472, 477.
[2] *Cal. Clarendon St. Pap.*, vol. 3, pp.460, 477.

prepared to stand aside and await arrest; Charles had at the end failed to give decisive leadership and was still dabbling in auxiliary schemes, trying to involve outside forces; where attempts to start risings were made they were extremely feeble and usually faded away even before they were faced by any military threat. Professor Underdown has given us a depressing picture of the prevailing defeatism and failure,[1] which again contrasts oddly with Cheshire, where the leaders decided to go ahead despite the arrival on 31 July of a dismal letter of foreboding from the Sealed Knot. Probably the leaders had little choice. The 31st being a Sunday, many preachers had called upon their congregations to support the rising and men and arms were on the move. As Mordaunt said, the letter 'changed [Booth's] humour so visibly that from a cheerful temper he was observed to be pensive and sad . . . but certain persons of quality assuring him of their ruin in case he desisted, he frankly determined on the attempt and from that time carried himself very worthily in it'.[2]

The course of the revolt in the north-west can be briefly told.[3] Sir George Booth himself mustered his forces at Warrington on 1 August. Although rumours of the intended rising had reached Colonel Thomas Birch in Lancashire no later than 28 July,[4] the authorities both in Lancashire and Cheshire made no attempt to hinder its inception, and on 1 and 2 August were withdrawing into scattered fortified places. On the 2nd Booth moved up from Warrington to Chester, holding a new rendezvous at Rowton Heath: there he addressed his troops and issued two manifestos, the 'Declaration' and the 'Letter to a Friend'.[5] He was welcomed

[1] Underdown, *Royalist Conspiracy. . .,* pp.258–72.

[2] *Cal. Clarendon. St. Pap.,* vol. 3, p.552.

[3] Four recent accounts of the rising have appeared. Professors Underdown (op. cit., pp.254–86) and Davies (*The Restoration of Charles II,* Oxford, 1955 pp.123–44) and Dr. J.R. Jones 'Booth's Rising of 1659', *B.J.Ry.L.* 39(1957), 416–43, have all placed the movement in its national perspective. Only Mr. R.N. Dore, 'The Cheshire Rising of 1659', *T.L.C.A.S.* 69(1959), 43–69, has attempted to explore the positive reasons for its comparative success in Cheshire. His is probably the best all-round account.

[4] *Clarke Papers,* vol. 4, pp.288–9.

[5] The 'Letter' is printed in 'Civil War Tracts of Cheshire', *Chetham Society,* N.S. 65, 164–5, the 'Declaration' in R. Baker, *Chronicle,* 5th ed. 1665, p.706.

into the city after a majority of the Corporation had implicitly taken steps to associate themselves with him, and the Governor of the city, Colonel Croxton, withdrew with his scanty forces into the Castle.

Short of provisions and men, Croxton might easily have succumbed to a storm ,or a tight blockade, but the blockade was so inadequately pressed that he had no difficulty sending and receiving letters. He thus speedily learnt that the rebellion had collapsed elsewhere and that help was on its way. His resolve strengthened, he held out until after Booth's defeat. But this apart, the immediate success of the Rising in the north-west was remarkable: Colonel Ireland brought over two regiments of the Rump's local forces and seized Liverpool; Sir Thomas Myddleton, raised the standard of revolt at Wrexham and soon gathered together a few hundred men from Denbigh and Flintshire; Parliamentarian forces retreating from the ill-fortified castle at Hawarden to Denbigh were seized by the countrymen and sent under guard to Booth; the gentry of south Lancashire were up in force, and attempts were being made to kindle the revolt anew in Derbyshire. Booth encountered no resistance in Cheshire; those leading gentlemen who did not join him for the most part went to ground. By 6 August Booth had perhaps 4,000 men about him, while there were other small bodies of troops about the county and considerable numbers in the neighbouring counties![1]

On 7 August Booth himself went to Manchester hoping to gain fresh recruits. But already his fate was sealed. On the 4th Lambert had set out from London with over 2,000 men,[2] and news soon arrived that Ludlow had despatched over

[1] All of this can be found in the accounts of the Rising given above, from sources there given. Estimates about the number of troops in service with Booth vary, from that of George Thomson (in a letter to Ambassador Lockhart, *C.S.P.D.* 1659—60, p.88) who estimates 2,000—3,000, through Secretary Nicholas's 6,000 (ibid., p.108), to an anonymous writer's 20,000 (ibid., p.113). Bordeaux, the French ambassador, generally very well informed about the whole revolt, thought Booth had no more than 4,000 (ibid., p.147). Both Dr. Jones and Mr. Dore are satisfied that he had more than 3,000 men with him.

[2] This estimate is given in *'Civil War Tracts. . .'*, loc. cit., p.172. Professor Underdown gives a figure of 4,500, but without citation.

1,000 foot and 500 horse from Dublin to Wales under
Jerome Zankey, the former sectarian major of Brereton's
regiment. From Yorkshire Colonel Lilburne was advancing to
link up with Birch in north Lancashire. The desperate
attempts of Mordaunt and others to start fresh rebellions
elsewhere completely failed.

All this induced Booth to issue a fresh manifesto, the
'Express',[1] a dishonest and dishonourable attempt to appeal
to the oncoming forces in the language of the Agreements of
the People. This desperate cast was of no avail. Booth was
now faced by an unenviable choice. He could gather together
all his forces and attempt to defeat the hardened veterans of
the New Model; he could storm Chester Castle, drive out
Croxton, and sit out a siege in the city hoping that either the
King would invade, or even that Monk, who was rumoured to
be contemplating a declaration similar to his own, would
intervene.[2] Alternatively he could retreat to the Welsh hills
or the Lancashire bogs, for which his gentlemen companions
had no stomach. In fact he was completely indecisive and
adopted none of these courses, simply wandering about in
mid-Cheshire to the dismay of his fellow leaders, who
remained in Chester with other of his troops.[3]

As Lambert approached the county, Booth suggested
negotiations, but was faced by a contemptuous ultimatum
demanding abject surrender. After a few days of manoeuvring
and skirmishing, Booth's army disintegrated after a fierce but
brief battle at Winnington Bridge. The whole movement
promptly collapsed as the gentry leaders fled and then
surrendered themselves. Chester opened its gates to Lambert
and within a week all Lancashire and Cheshire were firmly
under government control. Only Chirk Castle in North Wales
held out, to fall to Zankey (advancing from Beaumaris) at the
end of the month. Most of the gentry leaders gave themselves
up. For Booth himself the end was more ignominious.
Disguised as 'Lady Dorothy', he was driven in a carriage as far

---

[1] B.M. Thomason Tracts 669, f. 21(68).
[2] Baker, *Chronicle*, p.709.
[3] See below, p.311.

as Newport Pagnell, where he was arrested after an innkeeper became alarmed at the presence of a female guest asking for the services of a barber and a razor. By the end of the month he was in the Tower.[1]

## II

There remain three issues about the Rising which have not been adequately discussed by other commentators. In the first place, it has never been clearly shown how Booth recruited his forces; in the second place, there remain doubts about the exact relationship between Booth's aims and those of the exiled Court; and finally it has never been clearly shown how the Rump treated the county in the months following the Rising.

Twenty-eight gentlemen of leading families can be identified as either appearing in arms or as going to the head-quarters in Chester. Of these, eighteen come from Cavalier pasts, ten from Parliamentarian pasts. But such bald figures rather inaccurately suggest a Cavalier rather than Presbyterian bias among the leaders. To begin with, the total is almost certainly incomplete, being gathered from official lists of prisoners and casual references in correspondence. No official documents, either laying out the chain of command or listing the Council of War, have survived. And there is strong evidence that other Presbyterians were involved. John Crewe of Utkinton, Peter Dutton of Hatton, Edward Hyde of Norbury, John Daniell of Over Tabley, Thomas Marbury of Marbury, and Henry Delves of Doddington were all appointed to the Restoration Commission of the Peace; all of them were former Parliamentarians and had been part of the anti-Bradshaw movement during the 1659 election, but none was sufficiently influential to have been placed on the Commission of the Peace automatically. They must have earned their continuation on the Bench from the Commonwealth period by some service to the Crown. In 1660 all but the most hardened Republicans were on the

---

[1] The above is based on the same sources as are the four other recent accounts noted above. My account differs in no important detail from any of the others.

bandwagon. Furthermore, we know that in the investigation following the Rising, Gilbert Gerard was convinced that many were directly involved who had escaped capture: in particular he sought to implicate Thomas Marbury.[1]

It will be remembered that in 1658 Roger Whitley had drawn up a memorandum which had emphasized the need to increase efficiency by decentralization into association, each headed by a single leader with a small council with wide powers to organize and maintain the revolt.[2] Despite Booth's prestige and energy, such unity of command and purpose was lacking. As we shall see, Booth could not even get his subordinates to keep to the terms of his manifesto in their own declarations. Roger Whitley told Mordaunt that Booth's councils were in utter confusion because of the great number of gentry admitted to them.[3] Booth's policy of moving around the country in the last few days before Lambert's arrival was attacked by four of his leading supporters in a letter indicating a terrible lack of communication at the top'

We have received your letter but are much amazed to think of your drawing off so far as Northwich leaving us here. What the real cause maybe we cannot imagine, but in the meantime it still disheartens your friends and hath occasioned already many tears in this city and we have so far considered the business that we cannot imagine your return before you have engaged, neither can there any intelligence pass betwixt you and us nor can you think other than the enemie will immediately clap betwixt you and us and so obstruct all passages and in case you should receive any foil your retreating place is lost and we left to stand by ourselves . . . We could wish we had been made known to your intentions sooner, but this sudden result and motion relisheth not well and looks with a very bad face to all and to [Lord] Brereton, J. Booth, H. Brooke, Peter Brooke.[4]

The military organization may have been rather better, with a colonel appointed to recruit troops in each hundred. For example, Booth himself was responsible for Bucklow, Thomas Leigh of Adington for Macclesfield, Henry Mainwaring of Kermincham for Northwich. As we shall see, recruitment was well organized.

[1] C.R.O., Q.S.F. 1660, no.3, f. 149.
[2] J.Ry.L. Mainwaring MS., Book 24, pp.81—3.
[3] *Clarendon St. Pap.*, vol. 3, p.552.
[4] Bodl. Lib. Tanner MSS., vol. 51, f. 138. Quoted in Dore, art. cit., p.66.

The most important reason for Booth's complete success
in mobilizing Cheshire was that many of the gentry who did
not support him remained neutral. The sheriff, John Legh,
and Thomas Stanley both went into hiding,[1] and others, like
Thomas Mainwaring, may well have done the same. Why did
they do so? The most obvious explanation is that they were
afraid of arrest. But there is no evidence that Booth made
any move against them; there is no record of anyone being
locked up, although this could have been achieved at the
outset if he had so wished. It is much more likely that they
were so pessimistic of the Rump's chances against what they,
with Booth, expected to be a national movement, that they
abandoned hope and retired until they saw which way the
conflict was going. Even so staunch a Parliamentarian as
Henry Bradshaw remained inactive. On 4 August the Rump
gave him a commission 'on consideration of his past fidelity
and good services to raise and enlist a company of volunteer
foot for the perservation of the state in the present danger of
which he is to be colonel and to appoint officers'.[2] Yet he
never acted on this commission and his letter book records
two interesting communications with Booth. In the first he
told Sir George that

I hadd not nor have in the least measure advised, acted or consented
unto anythinge against you or any in yor armie or that hath relation to
you, neither was nor am privie to any plott, contrivemt or raisinge of
men either directlie or indirectlie against you ... and being so minded
therefore hadd & yet have hope of yor contynued respect & protecon.

This follows an account of the searching of his house for
arms by troops under Colonel Holland, a search which he
claimed would not have happened 'hadd you been acquainted
with any [such] design of any under yor command'. His
confidence was clearly well founded, since he quickly
received by reply 'yor curteous letter & the order there
inclosed'. But in a second letter he warned Booth that

I also received certayne intelligence of a considerable armie cominge
from Parliamt towards or county: I beseech you be pleased to give me
leave to intreate you that you would seriouslie consider of the cause
thereof & yor publike intencons & accons & the consequence thereof &

[1] Martindale, p.139.                    [2] C.S.P.D., 1659—60, p.74.

in time decist & submitt to the all seeinge decree & providence of or merciful God.[1.]

Bradshaw had been an obvious candidate for arrest, but he showed no signs of defiance, and he was left unmolested by the rebels; if Henry Bradshaw was unwilling to support the Parliament against the Restoration, it is unlikely that many others would act differently. As a result, the only gentlemen who made any attempt to stem the tide which was flowing so strongly for Booth were Thomas Croxton, the Governor of Chester, Robert Duckenfield the Sectarian who had refused to serve the Protectorate, and Gilbert Gerard, in religion the most extreme of all the gentry and the only Justice who had voted against the imprisonment of a Socinian preacher in 1652,[2] who was to prove the most vehement agent of the Rump after the Rising had been suppressed.

One interesting feature common to all the commissions sent down from Parliament to the county was that they authorized the enlistment of volunteers only. This was true not only of the orders to Bradshaw[3] and Croxton[4] but even of the one sent to the leaders of Chester after the extent of the revolt was realized.[5] In the context this could only mean that they were afraid that conscription would further alienate the population or that they might go over with their arms to Booth, an interesting contrast with their confidence in calling out the militia during the Worcester campaign. In fact by the time that this order reached the city, the Council had already ordered three companies of foot to be raised and armed for Booth and the monthly assessment diverted to the defence of the city.[6.]

It is particularly difficult to assess the importance of the ministers in fanning the flames of the Rising. That many of them were involved is undoubted. Thus Colonel West wrote to Colonel Birch on 3 August 'I forbeare to tell what horrible

[1] These letters are in Bodl. Lib. Top. Cheshire e 3, f. 23.
[2] Newcome, pp.37–40.
[3] Bodl. Lib. Top. Cheshire e 3, f. 23.
[4] C.S.P.D. 1659–60, p.67.
[5] Ibid., p.73.
[6] Chester City R.O., Assembly File Calendar 1624–85, p.47.

things have been spoken in pulpitts last Lord's day',[1] and a
newsletter of the 6th claimed that 'The gentry and ministry
of Cheshire and Lancashire appeare much in this insurrection
which makes their number much encreased'.[2] We also know
of several individuals who preached for the rebellion. For
example, Peter Harrison of Cheadle had been privy to the
design for some time,[3] and on 31 July he preached in
Cheadle on the text 'Pray for the Peace of Jerusalem'.
According to Reginald Taylor, he had preached to this effect,

where is that lyon-like spiritt of the man of this nation to speake of this
Tyranicall Government, comparinge itt to the Egyptians bondage, for it
is noe tyme now for David to stand nibling with his harpe when Saul
was redie with a Javelyn to pin him to the wall, and now when the
Gentry and the Church were in daunger, hee likewise excited persons to
lay out themselves, and not Naball like keepe their heapes whole and
suffer David and his men to perish in the wilderness.

Besides this, Harrison's claim to the sequestrators that

he did in his preachinge say though somewhat unseasonably and with
less discretion than good meaninge, that men must not only pray for
the peace of Jerusalem, but pay and fight also when the need of the
church shall require, but saith that he did not apply that sayinge ... to
the persons then in armes,[4]

is hardly convincing. Equally, we have evidence of sermons in
Warrington and Chester for the Rising. But we also know that
both Newcome and Martindale, though aware, through leaks,
of the intended Rising, were not approached in advance and
asked to support it. Both were sympathetic, but neither was
prepared to speak out openly. Martindale in retrospect gave
several reasons for his non-co-operation: personal pique at
not being forewarned played its part ('tis a bad dog that is
not worth whistling'); more substantial were his judgement
that 'it was easie, without a spirit of prophecie, to see they
were not like to stand', and his feeling that there was
dishonesty in Booth's declaration and assertions about an
imminent Quaker revolt. In fact the documentation with
which he backed up these claims shows that they were based

[1] *Clarke Papers,* vol. 4, p.33.
[2] Ibid., p.38.
[3] Newcome, p.109.
[4] Printed in J.P. Earwaker, *East Cheshire,* London, 1877, vol. 1, pp.226—8.

on evidence of which he could only subsequently have become aware. It all sounds like special pleading to excuse cold feet.[1]

Altogether more important was the relationship between the leaders of the revolt and the village communities. A study of this reveals an unsuspected depth to the support of the movement. Most of the commentators on the Rising have accepted the government propaganda version that the troops led by Booth were largely pressed into service; indeed no one has attempted to say how Booth raised his troops, the vague implications being that they were tenants of the gentlemen leaders and a few volunteers who flocked to the colours after being roused by the ministers.[2] In fact Booth had effectively captured the traditional machinery of government and had raised troops on a systematic basis in the townships.

John Ward of Capesthorne claimed freedon from complicity in the Rising on the following grounds. The traditional military liability of Capesthorne was two trained soldiers, one to be found by himself and one by the township. During the early days of August the constable had received a warrant from Thomas Leigh of Adlington requiring two men to attend a muster at Macclesfield and these two had been sent; he claimed that no 'men, horse armes or any military provision whatsoever had been sent out of towne of Copeston to the sayd Sr G.B. or his confederates in the sd insurrection but in obedience to the sayd warrant'.[3]

In the Quarter Sessions Files for 1660 there are a number of petitions from members of the trained bands complaining that they had never been paid for their service to Sir George Booth by the townships for which they served. Many recorded that their service followed the receipt of warrants issued by Booth or his commanders;[4] in some cases these had even been directed through the head constables.[5] Traditional

[1] Martindale, pp.135–9.

[2] e.g. Jones, art. cit., p.437, Davies, op. cit., p.140.

[3] J.Ry.L. Bromley Davenport MSS., Papers relating to the sequestration of John Ward of Capesthorne, unfoliated.

[4] C.R.O., Q.S.F. 1660, no.3, ff. 34, 48, 53.

[5] Ibid., f. 28.

machinery had been adopted and was widely successful. Many of the men who served claimed to be the trained soldiers for the township concerned,[1] one petition even speaking of 'the raisinge of the Militia in the late ingadgmt of Sir George Boothe'.[2] Other townships just speak of sending 'hired soldiers'.[3] But one petition from Lymm says that the constable was ordered to set forth 'two souldrs for every trayned souldier the towne stands charged wth'.[4]

Such a system of recruitment had many advantages, the most important being that it would help to produce men who had had some military training. But it also laid the burden of maintaining the troops on the townships. Experience had shown that any attempt to levy general taxation or to live on free quarter would be a slow and unpopular business; but townships would much more readily support men whom they knew. Thus the three Mottram soldiers were given £3.10s.0d. advance money and promised 12d. a day.[5] Other towns promised their men six months' pay, or a lump sum such as £4.4s.0d. or £5.[6] The use of warrants also had a valuable psychological effect. The natural instinct would be one of paralysis and indecision. A general demand would have reinforced this. But the arrival of a warrant making specific demands, addressed personally to the constables, and with an immediate threat of punishment for disobedience meant that refusal constituted the more positive reaction. As John Ward implied, acquiescence to a normal administrative instrument was less of a political act than its denial.

In fact, if we map those areas that we know responded to the warrants, an interesting pattern emerges.[7] Support came from the north and east of the county in a broad arc. That arc has the appearance of being cut from a circle centred on

[1] Ibid., ff. 40, 43.
[2] Ibid., f. 56.
[3] Ibid., ff. 32, 39, 71.
[4] Ibid., f. 45.
[5] C.R.O., Q.S.F. 1600, no.4, f. 60.
[6] Ibid., no.3, ff. 34, 40, 46.
[7] In my thesis, a map was in fact provided to illustrate this point (map V, following p.448).

Manchester. This fits in with our knowledge that Manchester Collegiate Church was one of the powerhouses of propaganda for Booth, and with the fact that Booth raised his own standard not at Chester but on the Lancashire border at Warrington. The so-called 'Cheshire' rising is thus probably a misnomer. The area where Booth's supporters were strong was the old Parliamentarian stronghold during the first Civil War, but the church at Manchester had been very badly treated by the Rump in 1651–3: several of their ministers had been imprisoned, their collegiate status had been cancelled, their church invaded by the soldiery, and the 'gathered congregation' of Major Wigan had been allowed to exist right under their noses.

In fact the nature of the evidence makes it impossible to determine just how many troops came from this source. Certainly the tenants of the leaders provided another section of the army. Nor were they all necessarily pressed. Thus John Ranger of Styall recorded that he, 'beinge tenant to the Right Worshipfull Sr George Booth in August 1659 . . . sent forth his eldest sonne and a horse to waite on Sr George Booth to be ready for what service hee should be comanded',[1] and in Pownall Fee, of which Booth was lord, some of the inhabitants claimed they were ready 'to have laid their hands under the feete of him the said Sr George Booth at that tyme',[2] and we know that in at least eight towns—Norbury, Kettleshulme, Matley, Rainow, Peover, Wilmslow, Cheadle, and Capesthorne—there was a meeting of the whole township to discuss the Rising. In each case they decided to obey the warrant and send forth troops.

Booth's greatest headache appears to have been the gathering of arms. Lambert claimed that many of his opponents were poorly equipped,[3] and Booth, who seems to have been determined not to act arbitrarily against neutrals, did authorize the seizure of horses and arms.[4] Sir Thomas

[1] C.R.O., Q.S.F. 1660, no.3, f. 26.
[2] Ibid., f. 71.
[3] 'Civil War Tracts of Cheshire', *Chetham Society*, N.S. vol. 65, p.169.
[4] Earwaker, op. cit., pp.227–8; J.Ry.L. Bromley Davenport MSS., Sequestration Papers of John Ward of Capesthorne, 1650–60, unfoliated.

Myddleton's accounts book reveals that on the day of the uprising he paid 5s.6d. for 'a newe locke to the ould spannishe peece of 1558 make'.[1]

All in all, then, Booth had a more impressive hold on the county than has usually been thought. But he was still in no condition to face a commander of Lambert's experience with nearly as many soldiers as he himself had, and they the seasoned campaigners of the Cromwellian wars.

### III

There remains the problem of what Booth himself stood for. Dr. Jones and Professors Davies and Underdown all state Booth's objectives as laid down in his 'Declaration' and 'Letter to a Friend', but do not seek to explain how he reconciled these with his commission from Charles II, Mr. Dore claims that to Booth a Free Parliament would be one that included King and House of Lords and that he was fighting for a Presbyterian—Royalist settlement,[2] and although he is broadly correct in this, it will probably be as well to examine the subject rather more fully than he does.

The central difficulty is, of course, that Booth himself never declared for Charles II. In his two major propaganda handouts—the 'Declaration' which he issued at the rendez-vous on 2 August, but which appears to have been read in many pulpits on the previous Sunday, and his 'Letter to a Friend' which was intended primarily for the gentry[3]—there were no references to the monarchy at all.

The 'Declaration' stated that Englishmen were without any 'settled foundation in religion, liberty or property'. The army had exceeded its role as preserver of the Parliament and become the instrument of ambitious men; there was no one

[1] W.M. Myddleton, *Chirc Castle Accounts,* vol. 1, p.53.
[2] R.N. Dore, *Civil Wars in Cheshire,* p.90.
[3] There is a summary of all the printed statements in Davies, op. cit., pp.135—8. The 'Declaration' is printed in Sir Richard Baker's *A Chronicle of the Kings of England,* 5th ed. London, 1665, p.706, and reprinted in *Cheshire Sheaf,* 1st. set., vol. 2, p.39 (where it is wrongly ascribed to 1648). The 'Letter to a Friend' is printed in the 'Civil War Tracts of Cheshire', *Chetham Society,* N.S. vol. 65, pp.135—7.

to whom grievances could be addressed. The aim of the rising was to vindicate known laws, liberties, and properties. Booth promised arrears to the soldiers and security for all men's consciences. The keynote was that they desired 'the Vindication and Maintenance of the Freedom of Parliaments against all violence whatsoever'.

The 'Letter to a Friend' is altogether more interesting. It was essentially an appeal to all those who had fought for Parliament in the 1640s but had seen their conservative aims destroyed by 'a mean and schismaticall Party': in it Booth stressed the importance of the traditional gentry leadership. Events 'put an obligation upon us, as we are considerable members of our countrey, to have more sober and couragious thoughts in the time of extremity than other men have'. He discussed the events of the past ten years; and stressed the impossible constitutional position of the Rump

what a slavery it is to our understanding that these men that now call themselves a Parliament should declare it an act of illegality and violence in the late aspiring General Cromwell to dissolve their body in [16]53 and not to make it the like in the garbling the whole body of the Parliament from 400 to 40 in 1648.

Again he turned to attack the New Model which had become a mere mercenary tool of army leaders who 'under another shape act the condemned acts of Usurpation and Tyranny in their old Generall'. The result of this situation, based 'upon presumption of the unity of their army' was that they 'depresse the Nobility and understanding Commons', and threaten 'our religion'.

The final paragraph is crucial, but has been ignored by all commentators;

We are faithfull and peaceful in the land, and if they in authority will decline hostility, and agree of a means *to admit the old members of both Houses,* or to call a new free Parliament, let him bee, and he is onely a Traitor that resolves not his judgement and obedience unto their determinations. [My italics].

Confirmation that Booth was thinking predominantly of the restoration of proper Parliamentary authority before the question of kingship was raised, comes in a pamphlet written by Prynne in January 1660, where he entered a plea for

leniency to Booth and the Cheshire gentlemen who had 'but
endeavoured and affected to fill up your House with its own
(supposed most legal) Members . . .'.[1]

Booth was not simply reasserting traditional values; he was
positively advocating a return to the constitutional position
reached in 1648; it was perfectly acceptable to him that the
old Long Parliament be restored in full. This is in accordance
with his political behaviour throughout the 1650s; it was a
thoroughly argued case and not, as some have suggested, a
ploy to secure a base of support broader than he would have
gained by proclaiming Charles II. To have done this latter
would have been to imply a return to 1641, not 1648. His
dealings with the Court, his general political awareness, and
his own preferences were for a restoration of the monarchy,
but as the result of a negotiated settlement. He had not
forgotten that he had fought against the Crown and he
accepted the legality of actions taken between 1642 and
1648. Peace could only be secured by a settlement between
the elected representatives of those with an interest in the
kingdom and the Crown. Initially he must have known that
elsewhere in the country the King would be proclaimed
unconditionally, but he had avoided pragmatic positions in
the past, and he did so again now. Once he was aware that he
alone had risen, this became even more important. If he
could now succeed, even though the odds were so much
against him, he really could impose the sort of settlement he
genuinely desired. The argument that he would gain more
supporters by declaring for a Free Parliament only was itself
dubious. For, as Martindale said, the fact that he took up
arms on 'noe authority but We, Lords, Gentlemen, Citizens,
Freeholders etc . . . (as Sir Peter Leycester said) proclaimed
them an illegal Rout'.[2] His determination only to fight for
the old cause is further demonstrated by the fact that
although he took the Royalists into his councils, he refused
to allow Catholics to join him.

Although he was willing to work with former Royalists, he
was obviously horrified when some of them started openly

[1] B.M. Thomason Tracts 669, f. 23 (1).        [2] Martindale, p.138.

proclaiming Charles II. When this was done at Warrington Bridge on 3 August 'Sir George Booth hearing of it, said it would bee theire ruine',[1] and he appears to have tried to counteract the move by getting the Chester Common Hall to petition for a Free Parliament.[2] But by this time Myddleton had declared for Charles II at Wrexham,[3] and on 7 August at least two ministers in Chester had prayed for Charles II, 'to the no little joy of the people wch drawe teares fro the eyes of many'.[4]

The central issue was not that Charles II should be King, but how this was to be brought about. Thus Booth and his followers were particularly anxious that there should be a negotiated settlement, particularly in matters of religion. This is how Martindale described the divisions within the party:

This armie . . . was like Mahomet's angellicall cockes, made up of fire and snow; for many, both of the commanders and souldiers, were not onely different, but contrarient in their principles . . some were zealous for the restoring of the king in pursuance of their covenant, which excluded the prelates; and some were resolved that they would have both or neither. Mr. Henry Bridgeman told another minister and me at Dunham that he forsooke them at Manchester because he perceived that some of the grandees were cordiall for the king but not for the church.[5]

One interesting point is that the government itself either misunderstood or deliberately chose to misrepresent Booth's intention. Whitlocke's letters to the Rump's supporters always claimed that Booth had proclaimed Charles Stuart,[6] he made the same assertion in a major speech to the common council in London on 9 August and in the official proclamation that Booth and the other named supporters of his were traitors.[7] That this was a deliberate misrepresentation is suggested by the evidence that many other people were aware of Booth's real position. Royalist agents were quite clear as

[1] *Clarke Papers*, vol. 4, p.38.
[2] Ibid., p.40.
[3] *Clarendon St. Pap.*, vol. 3, p.552.
[4] B.M. Harleian MS. 1929, f. 21; N. Tucker, 'Richard Wynne and the Booth Rebellion', *Transactions of the Carnarvonshire Historical Society*, 1959, p.48.
[5] Martindale, pp.136–7.
[6] e.g. *C.S.P.D.* 1659–60, pp.77, 104.
[7] Chester City Library, collection of pamphlets, items 95 and 100 from handlist prepared by Mr. W. Brown.

to the situation: Nicholas was told that apart from Myddleton 'the others [are] declaretory for the freedome of Parliaments as to the settlement of sacrett and civill rights and are zealously consecrated to the quarell by the Presbyterians Pulpiteers in those parts which caused them to be stiled here Bellum Presbiterale'.[1] The French ambassador was able to report that 'His speeches show that there was a misunderstanding between him and the other chiefs, because he refused to proclaim the King'.[2] Dr. William Denton in the midlands heard a report which quite contradicted the official one:

the only thing that looks like countenancing Sir George is the intended petition of the city for a free Parliament as they say . . . I do not hear of any one cavalier in all this affair but that it lies wholly on the presbitery and those that fought and engaged for that they call the good old cause.[3]

It is very difficult to determine what the common soldiers thought he stood for. There is a great lack of contemporary evidence, and evidence from after the Restoration (in the Quarter Sessions Files for example) is open to suspicion. Thus Roger Wilbraham of Nantwich later recorded that '1659, Aug.11 Sr Geo Booth [afterwards Lord Delamere] being then in arms to restore King Charles 2nd, tooke up his Quarters at my H[ouse] for one night'.[4] Most of the Restoration petitions talk of 'the service of His Majesty' or 'his Majesties speedy service',[5] though some just speak of being 'affected to Sr George Booth'.[6] Only one mentions 'service for a Free Parliament'.[7] But none of the original warrants have survived, and the terminology of these petitions in 1660 may well reflect nothing more than a retrospective forgetfulness induced by the fact of the Restoration.

However there is also evidence that many of the supporters of the movement were misled by false propaganda about an

[1] (Ed.) G.F. Warner, *Nicholas Papers,* London, 1920, vol. 4, p.177.
[2] *C.S.P.D.* 1659—60, p.163.
[3] H.M.C. *7th Report,* pp.482—3.
[4] N. Tucker, 'Richard Wynne. . .', p.52.
[5] C.R.O. Q.S.F. 1660, no.3, ff. 53, 68; no.4, f. 47.
[6] Ibid., no.3, ff. 28, 71.
[7] Ibid., f. 46.

impending Quaker uprising.[1] We know for certain that men were called upon to join Booth in suppressing this rebellion in Manchester,[2] Cheadle,[3] Warrington,[4] and Chester.[5] The extent of this scare might suggest that it was part of a general scheme of deception; in fact it probably ran parallel to the Catholic Fear which gripped much of England in 1641. It is clear that this Quaker Fear caused widespread alarm, and it may well have been the product of a single lie unconnected with Booth or his supporters. In any event, Martindale, who was very open in his condemnation of what he considered underhand in Booth's declarations, seems to acquit him of complicity in this matter.[6]

We have observed above that the Sealed Knot's letter rattled Booth. The news which reached him in the following days added to his depression and helps to explain his rather purposeless movements. Ludlow recounts how Colonel Temple arrived in Chester to find Booth's men in possession. Booth let him carry on to Ireland (a striking example of his leniency towards his opponents), but not before he had questioned him. Temple told Ludlow that 'being asked by Sir George Booth if he had not heard of any rising in other parts, and having informed him that he found all quiet on the road from London, Sir George seemed much surprised and discouraged, saying, that other promises had been made to him'.[7] On 7, August after the sermon, Booth was with Newcome, and 'with much sorrow told us how basely he was deserted. Five hundred lords and gentlemen, of the best of England, were engaged, and were all either prevented or had failed their trust'.[8] He was advised by the ministers of the classis and by Henry Bradshaw to throw himself on the mercy of Parliament, but he knew that the opponent marching against him was the merciless Lambert who had

[1] Underdown, op. cit., pp.255−7.
[2] Newcome, p.109.
[3] Earwaker, op. cit., vol. 1, p.228.
[4] Underdown, op. cit., p.273.
[5] B.M. Harleian MS. 1929, f. 20.
[6] Martindale, p.137.
[7] Ludlow, *Memoirs. . .,* vol. 2, p.108.
[8] Newcome, p.110.

sworn 'that hee will perishe or not allowe life to any gentle-men engaged, or above 200li per annum to any of that perswasion surviving'.[1] Indeed the Royalist agent who reported Lambert's statements 'wished they were as publique and [sic for as] the Diurnalls; they would be more serviceable than a Declaration'.

As Lambert drew close, Booth's nerve broke and he issued an 'Express'[2] which is a strange and dishonest document. In part he still used the moderate language of the earlier documents, particularly in calling for a 'free Parliament', but for the rest he employed every kind of argument that might gain him support. He promised the soldiers their arrears, but also called for a reduction in taxes; he promised an attack in patents and monopolies, encouragement to trade, a guarantee to uphold the rights of the poor against enclosure of the commons, and the restoration of all land formerly belonging to the people. A promise of complete toleration and a denunciation of coercive power in religion was the most shameful pledge made in the face of lifelong beliefs. His call for a 'common and equal bond of freedom and unity' and claim that the Rump denied the people laws and customs 'general equal and impartial to all without respect of persons, rank, quality or degree', was the complete reverse of the traditional view of society put forward by him a fortnight earlier.

This desperate manoeuvre failed, and he made an appeal to Lambert for a negotiated settlement. When Lambert replied that his terms were inflexible—the immediate laying down of all arms and the personal surrender of the leaders to await the mercy of Parliament—Booth had no choice but to take the long-odds gamble of attempting to defeat Lambert's veterans.

The craven appearance of the last days of the campaign,

---

[1] *Nicholas Papers. . .*, vol. 4, pp.177—8. The Rump was also formulating an act that any tenants of gentlemen engaged in the rising who opposed their landlords should enjoy their leases in fee, paying chief rent to the state, 'a precedent dangerous to all estated gentlemen', (see newsletter of 9 August, *Clarke Papers*, vol. 4, p.40).

[2] B.M. Thomason Tracts 669, f. 21 (68), summarized by G. Davies, op. cit., pp.136—7.

reaching their nadir with the unshaven Lady Dorothy taken by a village constable, must not be allowed to change our view of Booth's initial integrity. He did not simply angle at all times for the broadest possible support. For ten days he fought for a programme whose pedigree was recognizable to all those who had gone to war in 1642 to uphold the traditional values of government and society. The last attempt to put the clock back to 1648 had failed.

## IV

For several hectic months after the battle of Winnington Bridge, the county was in turmoil. The early expectations of severe reprisals were prevented by the disagreements that sprang up between Parliament and army, leading ultimately to Lambert's expulsion of the Rump. The local sequestration committee, revived at the end of September, continued haltingly at its task, and Booth and his fellow leaders languished in the Tower until their release in February 1660, but the only real sufferers were the city leaders. Chester had its Charter destroyed and was made for all administrative purposes part of the county. After five months of agony, the city was restored to its old position by the Long Parliament in March 1660.[1] In the meantime the city endured army rule, with regular searches and full quarter.[2]

The county got off more lightly, not least because both Brereton and Bradshaw—who wrote to the Rump from his deathbed pleading for leniency—sought to mitigate the Parliament's fury.[3] The sequestration committee[4] was hampered by inadequate and unclear instructions,[5] but they were driven on by Gilbert Gerard, 'the anabaptist fanatick' against whom complaints poured in to the Justices after the Restoration.[6] Gerard was convinced that many leading

---

[1] B.M. Harleian MS. 1929, ff. 10–11, 26–7; *Cheshire Sheaf,* 2nd ser., vol. 1, p.106.
[2] B.M. Harleian MS. 2125, f. 162.
[3] Martindale, pp.140–1.
[4] B.M. Harleian MS. 1929, f. 22; P.R.O., SP 23, vol. 264, f. 52.
[5] *C.C.C.D.,* pp.746–52, 767, 770–2.
[6] e.g. Q.S.F. 1660, no.3, f. 149; no.4, f. 65.

gentlemen had been involved in the rising but had managed to escape capture or direct implication; he was particularly keen to get evidence against Thomas Marbury.[1] Two witnesses, who were to give evidence on behalf of Lord Kilmorey and John Brooke, were not called upon to do so but ordered to tell Gerard who they had seen in Chester during the rising, Gerard naming 'most of all of the Gentry and yeomanry' to them to refresh their memories.

Once Monk reached London, conditions in the county quickly eased, with the release of all the leaders who had been imprisoned in the Tower. When the Convention Parliament was to be elected, Lord Chomondeley wrote to his wife: 'I have received your last . . . where I was by earnest invitation and obligation wth my tennants to contribute my assistance for the election of those persons who the gentlemen of this shire had cast theire eyes on.[2] These persons were Sir George Booth and Thomas Mainwaring, two moderate Parliamentarians of the 1640s whose careers had diverged in the 1650s. Also in March 1660 a fresh militia commission was issued for the county.[3] All but one of the fifteen named in it had appeared with Sir George Booth in August 1659;[4] eight were from former Parliamentarian, seven from former Royalist families.

When the Restoration itself came, Peter Venables and William Lord Brereton (an Irish peerage) were returned as members for the county. Both were former Royalists, both were strong Anglicans (Venables was one of Adam Martindale's persecutors).[5] In the 1670s, they were to appear as Tories, while both Booth and Mainwaring were Exclusionist Whigs; there had thus been a further swing to the

[1] Ibid., no.3, f. 149.

[2] C.R.O., Cholmondeley MSS., DCH/X, bundle 10, unfoliated. For Richard Legh and the Lancashire election, J.Ry.L. Legh of Lyme MSS., Box 65 (T. Howarth–R. Legh, 13 Mar. 1660).

[3] Chester City R.O. CR63/2/696, Arderne MSS., p.149.

[4] The exception is Roger Wilbraham, whose actions in August 1659 are unknown. A supporter of the moderate party in the 1640s, he had taken no part in Commonwealth administration, and was one of the more unexpected supporters of Bradshaw in the 1659 election.

[5] Martindale, pp.146, 155.

'Right' since the elections to the Convention Parliament. But the Commission of the Peace was still a reflection of the alliance which we have seen at work in the last years of the Commonwealth—it was almost a complete reissue of the men who had fought with Booth, with the addition of a few moderates (Mainwaring, Marbury, and Hyde being the main ones). Of twenty-seven men who sat on the Bench at Quarter Sessions in the early years of the Restoration, fifteen came from Parliamentarian and twelve from Royalist families; on the other hand only nine had acted at some time between 1649 and 1660. Of the twelve Cheshire gentlemen Charles II intended to institute into the order of the Royal Oak, six were from Parliamentarian and six from Royalist families. Oddly, only three appear to have been concerned in Booth's rising. Among those nominated were Thomas Mainwaring and Sir Thomas Wilbraham.[1]

Both Newcome and Martindale record the heartbreak and disillusion of the Presbyterians at the Restoration; Martindale in particular had to face considerable hostility from the restored Royalist gentry. But the defeat of their religious hopes does not seem to have driven the Presbyterian leaders back into opposition or into inactivity. The most active Justices in the 1660s were the continuity esquires, Mainwaring and Marbury, who had remained active since 1646 except for the blackest years 1658—9. Although an informer called Evan Price claimed to have uncovered, in 1663, a plot against the King led by Sir George Booth, Robert Duckenfield, and Thomas Croxton, it does not appear to have been treated very seriously.[2]

On the other hand there were frequent scares of fresh uprisings and it was probably this that kept the Presbyterians in line for the time being (many of Booth's supporters were later to support him as a leading Whig during the Exclusion crisis; Cheshire was one of the leading Whig centres in the country). In 1661 Parliament issued commissions in each county for the collection of money as a present for Charles

[1] *Cheshire Sheaf,* 1st ser. vol. 1, p.18.
[2] 'Eye Salve for England', London, 1663, reprinted in *Local Gleanings,* vol.10.

II. Sixty-two were named in Cheshire.[1] The only prominent figures not named were Robert Duckenfield, Thomas Croxton, Henry Bradshaw, Thomas Stanley, John Legh, and Henry Birkenhead. These were also (Bradshaw excepting) the collaborators with the Rump in 1659, and at the Restoration they seem to have had a rough time. The first four were all questioned in London about their past, and the county seems to have had highly ambivalent feelings about helping them. Thus, although Peter Venables led a petition to save Stanley from trouble, others including Thomas Cholmondeley and Philip Egerton were prepared to testify against him.[2] Whenever there was a scare, some of these were rounded up and locked up for a while. As late as August 1665 Croxton and Gilbert Gerard were amongst a group arrested for suspected treason,[3] though no evidence of their actual complicity in plots has survived.

## V

The Restoration thus failed to lead immediately into a period of equilibrium and stability. Charles II's government had everything in its favour in the overwhelming desire of the majority of the population for permanent and firm rule. But the events of the previous twenty years had established a climate of suspicion and fear that would not be dispelled overnight. The policies adopted in 1660 towards the localities were designed to ease tension. There was a return to consensus government by the old county élite. There was close continuity not only with the 1630s but also with the 1650s. Only two families not represented on the pre-war Bench came to sit there permanently after 1660, the Leycesters of Tabley and the Shakerleys of Holmes Chapel. Equally, though there had been a lively land market in the 1640s and 1650s, no family had seriously compromised their

[1] C.R.O. Arderne MSS., DAR/D f. 119.
[2] J.Ry.L. Legh of Lyme MSS., Box 65 (letters of 25 Aug. 1660 and 29 Sept. 1660). For arrest of H. Bradshaw, see J.Ry.L. English MS. 745, f. 37.
[3] *Cheshire Sheaf*, 1st ser. vol. 1, p.176.

economic position in the county except the Earls of Derby, who were non-resident anyway.[1]

The Restoration also witnessed a partial continuation of the administrative methods of the 1650s. There was no return to the pre-war emphasis on the Justices' action in their own hundreds; Quarter Sessions retained their central administrative importance. Yet despite the existence of select vestries in some parishes, the close formal contact between village community and Bench ceased. The J.P. now had to take on additional responsibilities to search out and investigate matters on his own initiative, though he also had to refer back to his colleagues at Quarter Sessions for confirmation of his actions and decisions.

But several of the more advanced policies of the 1650s were continued. In particular, the more flexible arrangements made for bridge repairs and for a more equitable sharing of the burden of poor relief were retained. Thus in 1662 the Bench ordered the collection of two mises throughout the county to be distributed to parishes overburdened with the poor.[2] Although the Act of Settlement of 1662 transformed much of their work in this field, the more humane Interregnum policies were continued: in particular, they continued to support those seeking to erect cottages on the waste, they set out to ensure that illegitimate children were adequately supported and apprenticed, and they adopted a highly flexible and pragmatic approach to the statutes governing apprenticeships.[3]

Restoration government was consensus government; it was also an implicit acceptance of the principles for which the gentry had fought since 1642—the maintenance of their social and political predominance within the county and against the encroachments of the central government. It was not until the late 1670s that Charles II openly challenged this basic premiss of the Restoration. Once again the county was

---

[1] B.M. Harleian MS. 2010, *passim.*

[2] C.R.O., Q.S.O.B. 10a, f. 80.

[3] These statements are based on a close study only of the records for the years 1660—9.

riven into factions, but in 1689 both Whigs and Tories were united in their opposition to James II's divisive centralizing policies, which threatened the integrity of local government and the cohesion of the county community. James was situated in 1688 as Charles I had been in 1640. But he failed to survive the initial onslaught to reach his 1642.

## VI

I do not intend to summarize this book or to lay down firm conclusions. My aim has been to convey an impression of a whole community under stress, and the diverse strands cannot be neatly brought together or unified. All I can hope to do here is to reiterate those themes that have been developed to a greater extent here than in similar local studies, and to make a few observations of their value to historians working in allied fields.

In Cheshire, as elsewhere, local tensions and preoccupations proved more important than national issues or abstruse constitutional principles. The overriding political unit was the county community, and the particular situation in Cheshire diffracted the conflicts between King and Parliament into an individual and specific pattern. As a result, all rigid, generalized explanations, particularly of the socio-economic kind, are unhelpful if not downright misleading. In this respect I have followed the lead given by Professor Everitt in several pioneering works. None the less in several respects I have gone further than he has done. In particular I have argued that one of the principal motivations of the political action of the leaders of the county establishment during this period was a very real fear of social revolution; and that this was as true of their actions in 1640–2 as in 1646–9 or 1659–60. As a corollary, I have tried to show that in this period the whole of society experienced a much more profound crisis than Professor Everitt has allowed, when he claims that the Civil Wars passed most people by and were only one of a series of economic and social crises during a century in which plague and other arbitrary devestations were endemic and occasional. To demonstrate this, I have attempted to describe the impact of the Civil Wars on the village communities in financial and administrative terms.

I also argued that in the 1640s and 1650s the village communities developed a new self-conciousness which found expression in various forms: through the petitions in which they articulated their demands; through the development of new forms of local government which allowed the village to play an active instead of a purely passive part in their own affairs; and through their demands to play a more vital role in controlling the church (e.g. in the appointment of ministers). The role of the church, after all, was not simply liturgical and pastoral, but also served as a focus of the community's economic, recreational, and (broad) educational needs. The meetings in many parishes in 1659, where corporate decisions on whether or not to support Sir George Booth were made, serve to symbolize this development; such meetings could not have taken place in 1642.

In the course of the Great Rebellion, many found themselves making a range of decisions affecting the nature and quality of their lives that they would not have dreamt of making before the precipitation of the crisis; as can be seen from the committees which met to decide issues such as who was to run the local ale-houses, or whether (and how) to repair or replace an old bridge. Such meetings took over from, and were a radical extension of, the old manorial courts controlled and dominated by the lord. It is here that the 'democratic' element in these years must be sought, not in the quest for an extension of the franchise. For a century at least before 1640, Parliament was a body meeting infrequently to vote taxes which the majority were not obliged to pay and to pass laws which the local Justices could ignore or adapt to local needs. Only occasionally did Parliament have a tangible bearing on their lives. The call for a radical change in the franchise in the late 1640s was a brief response to the more positive intervention by Parliament in their everyday life.

The events of these years posed a dual threat to the power and continuity of the essentially conservative élite; one was of social revolution in their midst; the other was of creeping centralization, the imposition of national priorities over local ones. This latter threat had loomed large in the 1630s, and was greatly increased by the exigencies of war; yet despite the more deliberate efforts of successive governments after 1646, it had never triumphed. We have seen how the ruling families, who had allowed largely personal animosities to divide them in 1642, came together again in the face of this threat. The alien and dangerous activities of a man like Charles Worsley, who amply justified his reputation as the most radical of the Major-Generals, was just one of the pointers to the leading gentry of the dangerous forces released during this prolonged period of crisis.

Yet the administrative, ecclesiastical, and social innovations of this period (which by the 1650s made the rebellion worthy to be called a Revolution), largely vanished at the Restoration. A historian writing about the 1660s, after studying the period up to 1640, but ignorant of the events of the intervening decades, could hardly be expected to give an adequate account of what had happened between these two dates: the Revolution left few permanent traces on the institutions of church and state. The disappearance of parochial committees and the associated self-consciousness was of a piece with other reversions to pre-revolutionary conditions. Obviously, our curiously ill-informed historian could gauge something of the events of these years from the number of licences for nonconformist meeting-places taken out in 1672,[1] from the institution of new taxes, from the abolition of feudal tenures, from the dismantling of conciliar government with the ensuing imbalance between executive and legislature, and, arguably, from a new spirit of economic liberation.[2] But most of the story would be left untold.

Across the country the old ways predominated; not only the personnel but also the methods of local government were largely restored. But a crucial question remains unanswered; had the county community learnt its lesson? Would the same

[1] e.g. F. Bate, *The Declaration of Indulgence,* London, 1908, pp.xix, lxi.
[2] e.g. C. Hill, *Reformation to Industrial Revolution,* London, 1967, pp.115–52.

*naivete,* which had led the gentry to misunderstand and misinterpret the crisis of 1640–2 and to allow largely local preoccupations to dominate their actions, determine their future political conduct?[1] Professor Everitt has dispelled once and for all the fallacy that the politics of the early and mid-seventeenth century can be understood from the vantage point of Westminster and the Court. But did provincialism die in 1660? Historians of the Exclusion Crisis and the Glorious Revolution still treat Parliamentary and Court factions as paradigms of political action throughout England. Clearly they were important; but historians have yet to consider whether the particular configurations of each local community were again important in determining attitudes in the provinces. When the community of Cheshire divided into 'Whig' and 'Tory' factions in 1678–81, or when it stood united against James II's assault on the church and drive towards absolutism in the state, it seems a large assumption that the model that Professor Everitt devised, which I have here adapted, is not applicable.

[1] See above, particularly pp.38–56.

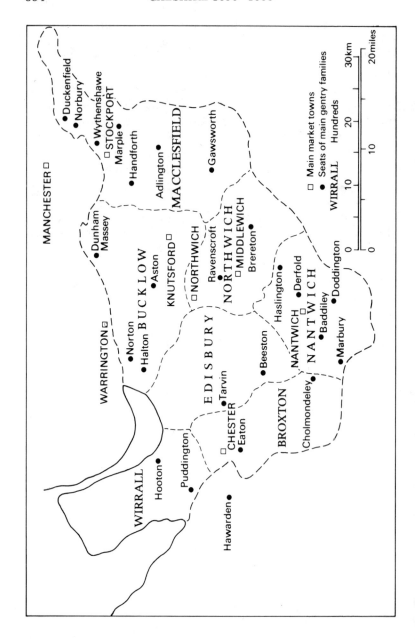

# BIBLIOGRAPHY

The following bibliography contains only the sources cited specifically in this book.

## I. MANUSCRIPT SOURCES

### a. Public Record Office

| | |
|---|---|
| SP 16, SP 18, SP 21, SP 25 | State Papers, Domestic Series, 1625–60. |
| SP 19 | Proceedings of the Committee for the Advance of Money. |
| SP 20 | Proceedings of the Committee for Sequestrations. |
| SP 22 | Proceedings of the Committee for Plundered Ministers. |
| SP 23 | Proceedings of the Committee for Compounding. |
| SP 28 | Commonwealth Exchequer Papers. |

In each of these series, references have come from a large number of volumes. But in the case of the SP 23 series, particularly substantial use has been made of vols. 147–9; in the SP 28 series vols. 128, 152, 196, 208, 224–5 are of fundamental importance for an understanding of war finance in Cheshire.

| | |
|---|---|
| Chester 3, 4, 21, 24 | Papers of the Palatine Courts at Chester. |
| Index 4211–13 | Crown Office Docquet Books (for changes in the Commission of the Peace, 1625–60). |

### b. British Museum

| | | |
|---|---|---|
| Harleian MS: | 1943, 1999, 2018 2126, 2128, 2130, 2136, 2137, 2144, 2166, 2173, 2174 | Financial accounts of the Civil War period. |
| | 2135 | Civil War letters and documents. |
| | 1929 | Chronicle of Chester 1649–60. |
| | 2107 | Returns to the Cheshire Remonstrance, August 1642. |

|  | 1944, 1970, 2002, 2004, 2043, 2054, 2071, 2081, 2093, 2095, 2102, 2104, 2125, 2155 | Historical Collections. |
|  | 1920 | A mise book. |
| Additional MSS.: | 5478 | Accounts book of Samuel Avery. |
|  | 5494 | Sequestration Correspondence. |
|  | 6032 | Woodnoth of Shavington MS. |
|  | 11331—3 | Letter Books of Sir William Brereton 1642, 1645—6. |
|  | 18979 | Fairfax Correspondence. |
|  | 18980—2 | Rupert MSS. |
|  | 33498 | Miscellaneous Papers, 16th—19th century. |
|  | 33936—7 | Moreton of Moreton MSS. |
|  | 34253 | Civil War Letters. |
|  | 36913—5 | Aston of Aston Papers. |
|  | 34011—7 | Major-Generals' Returns 1655—6. |

| Sloane MS. 1519 | Fairfax Correspondence. |
| Stowe MS. 577 | Commission of the Peace, 1651—2. |

*c. Bodleian Library*

| Ashmole MSS.: | 36 | Miscellaneous Collection. |
|  | 830 | Seventeenth-century Tracts. |
| Rawlinson MSS.: | A 40—1 | Thurloe State Papers 1655—6. |
|  | B 210 | Lord Byron's Memoir of the Siege of Chester. |
| Tanner MSS.: | 66—51 | Lenthall Papers. |
| Top. Cheshire e 3 |  | Letter Book of Henry Bradshaw, 1648—59. |
| Wood MS. 369 |  | Pamphlets of 1660. |

*d. Cheshire Record Office, Chester Castle*

Quarter Sessions Files, 1625—69.
Quarter Sessions Order Books, 1618—50, 1660—9.
Quarter Sessions Presentment Books, 1618—62.
Cholmondeley of Cholmondeley MSS.
Cowper of Chester MSS.
Arderne of Crewe MSS.
Accession 1729, Militia Correspondence 1595—1600.

*The Rights and Jurisdictions of the County Palatine of Chester,* (DDX/2).
Various Parish Records, particularly churchwardens' accounts books.

## e. Chester City Record Office, Town Hall, Chester
Mayors' Letters 1625—60.
Mayors' Books 1625—60.
Assembly Files 1625—60.
Assembly Books 1625—60.
Quarter Sessions Rolls (some surviving fragments, 1625—60).
Cowper MSS.
Earwaker Collection (CR63/1), forty boxes of transcripts.[1]
Earwaker Collection (CR63/2) Original Collections[2]
  Arderne MSS. (private correspondence).
  Bramhall MSS. (Commonplace book of John Davenport of Bramhall, 1609—50).
  Brereton MSS. (correspondence and private papers 1631—57).
  Crewe of Utkinton correspondence.
  Crewe of Utkinton commonplace book, 1640—50.
  Jodrell of Yeardsley MSS. (correspondence).
  Legh of Adlington MSS. (book of militia correspondence 1625—40).
Cotton of Combermere MSS. (CR/72).

## f. John Rylands Library, Manchester
Bromley Davenport MSS. (particularly sequestration papers of John Ward of Capesthorne).
Legh of Lyme MSS. (private correspondence).
Mainwaring of Baddiley MS., Book 20a (Diary of Thomas Mainwaring, 1649—59).
Mainwaring of Baddiley MS., Book 24 (Papers of Col. Roger Whitley).
Tatton of Wythenshawe MSS. (items 197—310, correspondence and official papers 1635—56).

| English MSS.: | 726—7 | (Lancashire Catholics in 1639). |
| | 745 | (Memoirs of the Bradshaw family). |
| | 957 | (Wirral Sequestration Papers). |
| | 1091 | (Letter Book of Thomas Cholmondeley, 1637—41). |

## g. Birmingham City Library
Reference Library 595611 (Letter Book of Sir William Brereton, 1646).

[1]These are currently being sorted and listed under places, families, and subjects. The new numbers are not yet available.

[2]Recently transferred from Chester City Library.

*h. Eaton Hall, Chester*
Grosvenor of Eaton MSS.

*i. Tabley House, Cheshire*
Leycester of Tabley MSS.


II. PRINTED WORKS

*IIa Sources and Calendars*
*Acts and Ordinances of the Interregnum,* eds. C.H. Firth and R.S. Rait,
    3 vols., London, 1911.
Aston, J., the Journal of . . ., 1639; in 'North Country Diaries', *Surtees
    Society,* vol. 118, 1910.
Aston, Sir T., *A Remonstrance Against Presbytery,* London, 1641.
Burton, Thomas, *The Diary of Thomas Burton esq., 1656–9,* ed. J.T.
    Rutt, 4 vols., London, 1828.
Calamy, Edmund, *An Account of Ministers and Others Ejected and
    Silenced,* ed. and revised, A.G. Matthews, London, 1934.
*Calendar of Clarendon State Papers.*
*Calendar of the Proceedings of the Committee for the Advance of
    Money.*
*Calendar of the Proceedings of the Committee for Compounding with
    Delinquents.*
*Calendar of State Papers Domestic.*
Carte, T., *A Collection of Original Letters and Papers Concerning the
    Affairs of England from the year 1641 to 1660,* 2 vols., London,
    1739.
*Cheshire Sheaf,* 1st, 2nd, and 3rd series, 1883–1968.
*Chester and North Wales Archaeological Society, Journal of the,* vol.6,
    1899, ed. R.H. Morris, 'Sidelights on the Civil War in Cheshire,
    1643–5'.
*Chetham Society*
O.S., vol. 1, 1844, Journal of Sir William Brereton.
    vol. 2, 1844, Civil War Tracts of Lancashire.
    vol. 4, 1845, Autobiography of Adam Martindale.
    vol. 26, 1852, Autobiography of Henry Newcome, vol. 1.
    vol. 39, 1856, Farington Papers.
    vol. 49–50, 1859, Lancashire Lieutenancy Papers.
N S., vol. 65, 1909, Civil War Tracts of Cheshire.
*Clarke Papers, The,* ed. C.H. Firth, 4 vols., London, reprinted 1965.
*Commons Debates of 1629,* eds. W. Notestein and F.H. Relf,
    Minneapolis, 1921.
*Commons Journals,* vols. 2–7.
Cromwell, O., *The Writings and Speeches of. . .,* ed. W.C. Abbott, 4
    vols., Cambridge, Mass., 1937–47.

Historical Manuscript Commission
  *Reports* 2, 3, 4, 5, 6, 7, 13.
  *Cowper MSS.*, vols. 1 and 2.
  *Portland MSS.*, vols. 1 and 3.
  *Letter Book of Sir Samuel Luke* (vol. JP 4).
Hyde, E., Earl of Clarendon, *History of the Great Rebellion,* 6 vols., ed.
  W.D. Macray, Oxford, 1887.
—— *State Papers, Collected by. . .,* 3 vols., Oxford, 1767—86.
*Lancashire and Cheshire Antiquarian Society, Transactions of the,* vol.
  31, 1913, ed. C.W. Sutton, 'Some Cheshire Papers of 1648'.
*Lancashire and Cheshire Record Society.*
  vol. 1, 1878, Commonwealth Church Survey.
  vol. 11, 1885, Chester Exchequer Depositions, 1558—1642.
  vol. 12, 1885, Distraint of Knighthood Proceedings (in a
  miscellany volume, pp.191—223).
  vol. 19, 1889, T. Malbon, Memorials of the Civil War in Cheshire,
  and, E. Burghall, Providence Improved.
  vols. 24, 26, 29, 36, 72, 95, 96, 1891—1942, Lancashire
  Royalists' Composition Papers.
  vols. 28, 34, 1893, 1897, Plundered Ministers' Accounts.
  vol. 67, 1913, Moore Papers
  vol. 94, 1940, Cheshire Quarter Sessions Papers, extracts
  1559—1760.
  vol. 106, 1956, Chester Council Minutes, 1603—42.
*Lords Journals,* vols. 4—10.
Ludlow, E., *The Memoirs of Edmund Ludlow 1625—72,* ed. C.H. Firth,
  2 vols., Oxford, 1894.
Nicholas, Sir Edward, *The Correspondence of. . .,* ed. G.F. Warner, 4
  vols., London, 1886—1920.
Rushworth, J., *Historical Collections,* 8 vols., London, 1659—1701.
*Statutes at Large; Public Acts of Parliament,* vol. 2, London, 1735.
Thomason Tracts.
Thurloe, John, *The State Papers of. . .,* ed. T. Birch, 7 vols., London,
  1742.
Torshell, Samuel, *The Hypocrite Discovered and Cured,* London 1643.
Walker, John, *The Sufferings of the Clergy,* ed. and revised A.G.
  Matthews, London, 1948.

As well as the pamphlets and newspapers in the Thomason Collection in
the British Museum, I have used several pamphlets and sermons from
Chester City Library which I did not find in the Thomason catalogue.
Most of these are listed by Mr. E. Brown in a typescript handout
produced by the Library. A further series of sermons, forming part of
The Earwaker Collection, are currently still in the Library, but may be
transferred to the City Record Office in 1973.

## IIb Secondary Sources

Abernathy, G.R., 'The English Presbyterians and the Stuart Restoration', *Trans. of the American Philosophical Society*, vol. 55, 1965.

Andriette, E.A., *Devon and Exeter during the Civil War*. Exeter, 1972.

Auden, J.E., 'Sir Jerome Zanckey of Balderstone', *T.Salop. A.S.*, vol. 50, 1940.

—— 'My Case with the Committee of Salop', *T.Salop. A.S.* vol. 48, 1936.

Aylmer, G.E., *The King's Servants: The Civil Service of Charles I, 1625—1642*, London, 1961.

Barnes, T.G., *Somerset 1625—1640: A County's Government During the 'Personal Rule*, Oxford, 1961.

Beaumont, H., 'Events in Shropshire at the Outbreak of the Civil War', *T.Salop. A.S.*, vol. 51, 1941.

Beck, J., *Tudor Cheshire*, Chester, 1969.

Beier, A.L., 'Poor Relief in Warwickshire, 1630—1660', *Past and Present*, vol. 35, 1966.

Blackwood, B.G., 'Lancashire Cavaliers and Their Tenants' ,*T.H.S.L.C.*, vol. 117, 1965.

—— 'The Cavalier and Roundhead Gentry of Lancashire', *T.L.C.A.S.*, vol. 77, 1967.

Bottigheimer, K.S., *English Money and Irish Land*, Oxford, 1971.

Brunton, D., and Pennington, D.H., *Members of the Long Parliament*, London, 1954.

Clark, P., and Slack P., (eds.) *Crisis and Order in English Towns, 1500—1700*, London, 1972.

Cliffe, J.T., *The Yorkshire Gentry from the Reformation to the Eve of the Civil War*, London, 1969.

Coate, M., *Cornwall during the Great Civil War*, 2nd edn., London, 1963.

Cooper, J.P., 'The Counting of Manors', *Ec.H.R.*, 2nd ser., vol. 8, 1954.

—— 'The Social Distribution of Lands and Men in England 1436—1700', *Ec.H.R.*, 2nd ser., vol. 20, 1967.

Coward, B., 'The Lieutenancies of Lancashire and Cheshire in the Sixteenth and Early Seventeenth Centuries', *T.H.S.L.C.*, vol. 119, 1967.

Craig-Gibson, A., 'Everyday Life of a Country Gentleman in Cheshire during the Seventeenth Century', *T.H.S.L.C.*, vol. 3, 1863.

Davies, G., *The Restoration of Charles II*, Oxford, 1955.

Dodd, A.H., *Studies in Stuart Wales*, London, 1953.

Dore, R.N., *The Civil Wars in Cheshire*, Chester, 1966.

—— *The Civil War in the Manchester Area*, Manchester, 1971.

—— 'The Early Life of Sir William Brereton', *T.L.C.A.S.*, vol. 63, 1953.

—— 'Sir William Brereton's Siege of Chester and the Campaign of Naseby', *T.L.C.A.S.*, vol. 67, 1957.

—— 'The Cheshire Rising of 1659', *T.L.C.A.S.*, vol. 69, 1959.

—— 'Sir Thomas Myddleton's Attempted Conquest of Powys', *Montgomeryshire Collections*, vol. 57, 1962.

—— and **Lowe, J.**, 'The Battle of Nantwich', *T.H.S.L.C.*, vol. 113, 1961.

—— and **Morrill, J.S.**, 'The Allegiance of the Cheshire Gentry in the Great Civil War', *T.L.C.A.S.*, vol. 77, 1967.

**Earwaker, J.P.**, *East Cheshire*, 2 vols., London, 1877.

**Everitt, A.M.**, *The Community of Kent and the Great Rebellion*, Leicester, 1966.

—— 'Suffolk and the Great Rebellion', *Suffolk Record Society*, 1960.

—— *Change in the Provinces 1603–60*, Leicester, 1969.

—— 'The Local Community and the Great Rebellion', *H.A.P.* G 70, 1969.

**Ferris, J.P.**, 'The Gentry of Dorset on the Eve of the Civil War', *Genealogists' Magazine*, vol. 15, 1965.

**Firth, C.H.**, and **Davies, G.**, *A Regimental History of Cromwell's Army*, 2 vols., London, 1940.

**Fisher, F.J.**, *(ed.) Essays in the Economic and Social History of Tudor and Stuart Englarᵈ in Honour of R.H. Tawney*, Cambridge, 1961.

**Fussell, G.E.**, 'Four Centuries of Cheshire Farming Systems', *T.H.S.L.C.*, vol. 106, 1954.

**Habakkuk, H.J.**, 'Landowners and the Civil War', *Ec.H.R.* 2nd ser., vol. 18, 1965.

**Hall, J.**, *A History of Nantwich*, Nantwich, 1883.

**Hardacre, P.H.**, *The Royalists during the Puritan Revolution*, The Hague, 1956.

**Harrod, H.D.**, 'A Defence of the Liberties of Chester, 1450', *Archaeologia*, vol. 57, 1900.

**Hassell-Smith, A.**, 'Justices at Work in Elizabethan Norfolk', *Norfolk Archaeology* vol. 34, 1967.

**Hill, J.E.C.**, *The Economic Problems of the Church*, Oxford, 1956.

—— 'Puritans and the "Dark Corners of the Land" ', *T.R.H.S.*, 5th ser.. vol. 13, 1963.

**Holiday, P.G.**, 'Land Sales and Repurchases in Yorkshire after the Civil War', *Northern History*, vol. 5, 1970.

**Howell, R.**, *Newcastle-upon-Tyne in the Puritan Revolution*, Oxford, 1967.

**Ives, E.W.**, (ed.) *The English Revolution 1600–1660*, London, 1968.

**James, M.**, *Social Problems and Policy during the Puritan Revolution*, London, 1930.

**Jones, J.R.**, 'Booth's Rising of 1659', *B.J.Ry.L.*, vol. 39, 1957.

Jordan, W.K., *Philanthropy in England 1480–1660*, London, 1959.
—— 'Social Institutions in Lancashire 1480–1660', *Chetham Society*, 3rd ser., vol. 11, 1962.
Ketton-Kremer, R.W., *Norfolk in the Civil War*, London, 1969.
King, D., (ed.) *The Vale Royal of England*, London, 1656.
Lamont, W., *Godly Rule*, London, 1969.
Leonard, E.M., *The Early History of English Poor Relief*, Cambridge, 1900.
Leslie, F.J., 'James, 7th Earl of Derby', *T.L.C.A.S.*, vol. 5, 1889.
Lowe, J., 'The Campaign of the Irish Royalists in the northwest 1643–1644', *T.H.S.L.C.*, vol. 111, 1959.
Moir, E., *The Justice of the Peace*, London, 1969.
Morrill, J.S., 'Mutinies and Discontent in English Provincial Armies', *Past and Present*, 1972.
Morris, R., *The Siege of Chester*, Chester, 1923.
—— 'Sidelights on the Civil War in Cheshire', *J.C.A.S.*, vol. 6, 1892.
Ormerod, G., *History of Cheshire*, (revised G. Helsby), 3 vols., London, 1882.
Pearl, V., *London and the Outbreak of the Civil War*, Oxford, 1961.
Pennington, D.H., 'County and Country: Staffordshire in Civil War Politics', *North Staffordshire Journal of Field Studies*, no.6, 1966.
—— and Roots, I.A., *The Committee at Stafford, 1643–5*, Manchester, 1957.
Petty, R., 'The Rising of Sir George Booth', *J.C.A.S.*, vol. 33, 1939.
Philipps, J.R., *Memorials of the Civil Wars in Wales and the Marches*, 2 vols., London, 1874.
Phillips, C.B., 'County Communities and Local Government in Cumberland and Westmorland 1642–1660', *Northern History*, vol. 5, 1970.
Pinckney, P.J., 'The Cheshire Election of 1656', *B.J.Ry.L.*, vol. 49, 1967.
Richardson, R.C., *Puritanism in North West England*, Manchester, 1972.
Sanders, F., 'The Quakers in Cheshire under the Protectorate', *J.C.A.S.*, N.S. vol. 14, 1908.
Shaw, W.A., *A History of the English Church during the Civil Wars and Under the Commonwealth*, 2 vols., London, 1900.
Stephens, W.B., 'The Overseas Trade of Chester in the Early Seventeenth Century', *T.H.S.L.C.*, vol. 120, 1968.
Stoye, J.W., *English Travellers Abroad 1604–67*, London, 1952.
Styles, P., 'The Evolution of the Law of Settlement', *Birmingham Historical Journal*, vol. 9, 1953.
Sylvester, D., 'Rural Settlement in Cheshire', *T.H.S.L.C.* vol. 101, 1949.
—— 'The Manor and the Cheshire Landscape', *T.L.C.A.S.*, vol. 70, 1960.

'Parish and Township in Cheshire and North East Wales', *J.C.A.S.*, vol. 54, 1967.

and Nulty, G., *A Historical Atlas of Cheshire*, Chester, 1958.

Tatham, B., 'The Sale of Episcopal Land during the Civil Wars and Commonwealth', *E.H.R.*, vol. 23, 1908.

Thirsk, J., (ed.) *Agrarian History of England and Wales*, vol. iv, Oxford, 1967.

—— 'The Sales of Royalist Lands during the Interregnum', *Ec.H.R.* 2nd ser., vol. 5, 1952–3.

Tollitt, S., 'The First House of Correction for the County of Lancashire', *T.H.S.L.C.*, vol. 105, 1953.

Trevor-Roper, H.R., *Archbishop Laud*, 2nd edn., London, 1962.

Tucker, N., 'Colonel Roger Whitley', *J. Flintshire Historical Society*, 1966.

—— 'Richard Wynne and the Booth Rebellion', *Trans. Caernavonshire Historical Soc.*, 1959.

Underdown, D.E., *Royalist Conspiracy in England 1649–60*, New Haven, 1960.

—— 'Sir Richard Willys and Secretary Thurloe', *E.H.R.*, vol. 69, 1954.

—— 'Party Management in the Recruiter Elections, 1645–8', *E.H.R.*, vol. 83, 1968.

—— *'Pride's Purge*, Oxford, 1971.

Urwick, W., (ed.) *Historical Sketches of Nonconformity in Cheshire*, Manchester, 1864.

Wark, K.R., 'Elizabethan Recusancy in Cheshire', *Chetham Society*, 3rd ser., vol. 19, 1971.

Webb, S. and B., *English Local Government*, 8 vols., London 1906–29.

Wilson, J.F., *Pulpit in Parliament*, Princeton, 1969.

Wood, A.C., *Nottinghamshire in the Civil War*, Oxford, 1937.

Woolrych, A.H., 'Penruddock's Rising', *H.A.P.* G 29, 1955.

Young, P., *Edgehill*, Kineton, 1967.

Zagorin, P., *The Court and the Country*, London, 1969.

## IIc Unpublished Theses

Archangelsky, S.I., 'Agrarian Legislation of the English Revolution', (typescript translation from the Russian kindly lent me by Dr. C. Hill).

Blackwood, B.G., 'Social and Religious Aspects of the History of Lancashire 1635–1655', Univ. of Oxford B.Litt. thesis, 1955.

Gentles, I.J., 'The Debentures Market and Military Purchases of Crown Land 1649–1660', Univ. of London Ph.D. thesis, 1969.

Holmes, C., 'The Eastern Association 1643–6', Univ. of Cambridge Ph.D. thesis, 1969.

Johnson, A.M., 'Buckinghamshire 1640—1660', Univ. Coll. of Swansea M.A. thesis, 1963.

—— 'Some Aspects of the Political, Constitutional, Social and Economic History of the City of Chester 1550—1662', Univ. of Oxford D.Phil. thesis, 1970.

Manning, B.S., 'Neutrals and Neutralism in the English Civil War', Univ. of Oxford D.Phil. thesis, 1957.

Thirsk, I.J., 'The Sales of Delinquent Estates during the Interregnum and the Land Settlement at the Restoration', Univ. of London Ph.D. thesis, 1950.

Thomas, C.M., 'The First Civil War in Glamorganshire', Univ. Coll. of Swansea M.A. thesis, 1963.

Thomas, G.R., 'Sir Thomas Myddleton 1588—1666', Univ. Coll. of Bangor M.A. thesis, 1966.

# INDEX

**NOTE:** In arranging the sub-headings of this index, I decided that a chronological system would be of greater service than an alphabetical one. I also decided to list first all administrative, judicial and military appointments, and then to give the details of a subject's political career. More general references are given at the end of each entry. In two cases (*see* Brereton of Handforth, Sir William, and Committees), I have adopted a separate, but, I hope, self-explanatory, procedure.

28; as leading "Baronet", 59; raises volunteers for Parliament, 80; leading opponent of Brereton, 83; and the 1646 mutiny, 197–8; and the 1647 mutiny, 201; and the Bretland case, 218
— Sir Randle, and the 1628 election, 31–2
— Thomas, 241, 303; as a J.P., 184, 187, 225, 235, 257–8, 257n, 258n; as sub-commissioner of accounts, 91; his private and public life, 234, 261; relations with Major General Worsley, 279, 281, 284; and the 1654 election, 287; and the 1656 election, 288, 292–3; and the 1659 election, 293–8; and the Booth Rebellion, 312; and the Restoration, 326
Mainwaring of Kermincham, Henry, 53, 185n, 272, 295; as a J.P., 9, 16; as a collector of Proposition Money, 102n; as an Assessments Commissioner, 86; raises a troop of horse for Parliament, 80; and the Treaty of Bunbury, 66; changes sides (1644), 71; sequestration of, 215; and the Booth Rebellion, 311
Major Generals, the, 276–87
Malbon, Thomas, 57, 75n; and the 1646 mutiny, 197; and Major General Worsley, 284
Mallory, Thomas, 166
Malpas, 6n, 18, 282n
Manley, George, 224, 259, 296
Manchester, 19, 308, 317
Marbury of Marbury, Thomas, as a J.P., 184, 187, 258n; and the 1654 election, 287; and the 1656 election, 288; and the Booth Rebellion, 311, 326
— William, as a deputy lieutenant, 83; as an assessments commissioner, 86; as a leading "Baronet", 59; raises volunteers for Parliament, 80; and the treaty of Bunbury, 66; and the Bretland case, 218
Marigold, John, 167n
Marriage and the Cheshire gentry, 16

Marston Moor, Battle of, 77, 148n
Martial Law, Brereton's Commission of, 193
Martindale, Adam, leading moderate Presbyterian, 241, 265, 267–9, 272, 273; and the Engagement, 276; and county government, 241; and the Booth Rebellion, 314, 320, 321; and the Restoration, 326, 327
Massey of Puddington, leading recusant family, 18, 52n
Massie of Andlem, William, as active committeeman (1646–9), 186; dropped as a J.P. (1649), 187; Governor of Chester and the 1647 mutiny, 200–1; and the goods of delinquents, 120; and the 1659 election, 295
Matley, and the Booth Rebellion, 317
Meldrum, Sir John, 143, 146, 152, 156, 302
Mercer, Thomas, sequestration informer, 208
Merchant, Richard, 122
Middlewich, 9, 75, 281; battle of, 73, 216
Militia, Charles I's reforms of, 26; and the Bishop's Wars, 30, 38; the Militia Ordinance, 43–4, 56; payment of, 98, 105, 168–171; and the Booth Rebellion 315–17
Millington, William, 116
Mobberley, 14
Montgomery, Battle of, 149, 158
Monthly Meetings, 8, 9, 11, 232, 235–6
Moore, John, 146
Mordaunt, John, and Royalist plotting, 301, 303, 307, 311
Moreton of Moreton, William, 22, 42
Moreton, William, Bishop of Chester, 18–19
Mottram, and the Booth Rebellion, 316
Moxon, George, 19n, 164
Murcot, Job, solicitor for sequestrations, 105
Mutinies in Cheshire, 154, 172, 190–203